Tommy Sheridan:
From Hero to Zero?

A Political Biography

Tommy Sheridan:
From Hero to Zero?

A Political Biography

Gregor Gall

Welsh Academic Press

Published in Wales by Welsh Academic Press, an imprint of

Ashley Drake Publishing Ltd
PO Box 733
Cardiff
CF14 7ZY

www.welsh-academic-press.com

First Impression – 2012

ISBN
978-1-86057-119-0

British Library Cataloguing-in-Publication Data.
A CIP catalogue for this book is available from the British Library.

Typeset by White Lotus Infotech Pvt. Ltd., Puducherry, India.
Printed by MPG Book Group Ltd, Bodmin, Cornwall.

Contents

*To my partner Fiona – this one really did
take over both our lives*

Preface

Writing this biography should have been an unadulterated joy but it was not as the progress of Tommy Sheridan's career as the leading socialist politician of the post-war period in Scotland was cut short and put into sharp reverse by his conviction for perjury on 23 December 2010. Ploughing through the voluminous press coverage of his success in connecting socialist politics with popular appeal all the while kept prodding my mind with 'what if?' questions. What if he'd been the same popular socialist figure in the post-2007 period of the third and fourth Scottish Parliaments that he had been in the first two? What if he'd been this figure as the financial meltdown turned into an economic depression and that then brought us the age of austerity? What if he'd taken the advice not to sue in 2006? What if he'd been more like Joe Higgins, Tony Mulhearn, Terry Fields and Dave Nellist rather than Derek Hatton, George Galloway or Arthur Scargill? What if he'd been more like his abstemious political hero, Tony Benn?

Acronyms and Notes

APTU	Anti-poll tax union
ATTR	*A Time to Rage* (Polygon, 1994) written with Joan McAlpine
Evening News	Edinburgh-based *Evening News*
Evening Times	Glasgow-based *Evening Times*
CWI	Committee for a Workers' International, the international tendency of which the former Militant in Britain and now Socialist Party of England and Wales is the main affiliate. The affiliate in Scotland is the Socialist Party Scotland (previously the International Socialists and CWI Scotland), which emanated from the minority faction within SML.
DGS	*Democratic Green Socialist*, online magazine and network of non-CWI/SWP members within Solidarity
DTTSS	*Downfall – the Tommy Sheridan story* (Birlinn, 2011) by Alan McCombes
ILP	Independent Labour Party
ISM	International Socialist Movement, the internal platform within the SSA/SSP which emanated from the majority faction of SML.
LPYS	Labour Party Young Socialists
Mirror	*Scottish Mirror*
NoW	*News of the World*
SLP	Socialist Labour Party
SML	Scottish Militant Labour
SPEW	Socialist Party of England and Wales
SSA	Scottish Socialist Alliance
SSP	Scottish Socialist Party
SSP EC	Scottish Socialist Party Executive Committee
SSP NC	Scottish Socialist Party National Council
SSY	Scottish Socialist Youth, an autonomous body but *de facto* part of the SSP
STUC	Scottish Trades Union Congress
SWP	Socialist Workers' Party (between May 2001 and August 2006 *Socialist Worker* Platform within the SSP)
TST	*The Sheridan Trial* blog, written and compiled primarily by James Doleman on each day of the 2010 trial (see http://sheridantrial.blogspot.com/)
WRP	Workers' Revolutionary Party

Acknowledgements

I would like to thank Ashley Drake of Welsh Academic Press for all his help, support and assistance in seeing this biography through to publication. I also gratefully acknowledge the support of my University, the University of Hertfordshire, in doing so too. My thanks are also to John Kelly, Peter Lynch and James Mitchell for providing helpful comments on the manuscript.

List of Photographs

Photograph 1: Tommy campaigning against the poll tax outside the Scottish Labour Party recall conference in Govan, 1988.

Photograph 2: Addressing a protest to stop a pounding in Lasswade, Midlothian.

Photograph 3: Tommy addressing the first Scottish Anti-Poll Tax Federation conference.

Photograph 4: Tommy and Gail.

Photograph 5: Tommy with SSP candidates for the 1999 Scottish Parliament election.

Photograph 6: With actor Peter Mullan on a demonstration in Glasgow.

Photograph 7: Tommy with Colin Fox during the 2003-2003 firefighters' strike.

Photograph 8: Addressing the Calton Hill 'Independent Scottish Republic Declaration', 9 October 2004.

Photograph 9: Tommy celebrating the election of Colin Fox as SSP national convener, Perth City Halls, 13 February 2005.

Photograph 10: Tommy outside the old Scottish Parliament building in October 2002.

Cover – Front: Tommy Sheridan, 2003

Cover – Back: Tommy Sheridan and Rosie Kane launching the Calton Hill 'Independent Scottish Republic Declaration', 9 October 2004

Photographs courtesy of Craig Maclean (1,2,3,4,5,6,7,10 & Cover Front) and Alister Black (8,9, & Cover Back)

Foreword

The Last Revolutionary? After the Left and the Coming Gathering Storm

Gerry Hassan—political analyst, commentator and writer

This is an important story that needs to be told, retold and understood. It reflects not just on the central actors and the wider array of participants, but all of us. And it should give us cause to pause and reflect to fully consider its lessons. This is a morality tale of modern Scotland, of the power and limits of personality politics; the role of charisma, belief and hubris; the inherent weakness in hyper-left politics, and the role of a certain kind of Scottish man. The rise and fall of Tommy Sheridan and the Scottish Socialist Party (SSP) is a gripping tale, worthy of fiction, and one which touches on many aspects of Scottish life.

The rise of Sheridan and the SSP has to be seen in the context of Scottish politics and culture. The SSP emerged as Militant in the 1980s with a very public role in the struggle against the poll tax. However, it made a bigger national impact when a New Labour Government under Blair and Brown bestrode the centre ground. The establishment of the Scottish Parliament saw in its first eight years a Lab-Lib administration which was unsure of its place and political antenna, nervous about the shadow of New Labour or breaking free from its influence. This provided a platform for hard left politics, an opening and vacuum, with the uber-cautious nature of Labour, along with the struggling SNP opposition in those early years, offering a prefect storm for Sheridan's appeal. This was thefertile environment which saw Sheridan first elected in 1999 and then provide the groundwork for the breakthrough 2003 election and the short-lived 'rainbow Parliament'.

'The Long Revolution' of Post-war Scotland

A longer, deeper set of trends contributed to this, namely the intertwining of class and nation in Scottish politics and around the Scottish dimension.[1] Increasingly over the last thirty years, the influences of class and nation have shaped Scottish politics, identities and culture, aided by popular experience and perceptions towards Thatcherism and then New Labour. Scotland has in the last thirty years become less working class 'objectively' and how we understand employment, jobs and status, but conversely people see themselves as more working class. One survey showed that 66 per cent of Scots identified as working class, while a majority of the middle class identified as working class, something that was not the case in 1979.[2] The Scottish Election Survey found a similar pattern in 2007 with those who identified as working class seeing themselves as more Scottish than the middle class did, reinforcing the politics of class and nation.[3]

In England, the pattern is very different with the 'death of class' first celebrated by New Labour, then lamented by writers such as Lynsey Hanley and Owen Jones.[4] A recent survey by *Britain Thinks* found 72 per cent of English and Welsh respondents identified themselves as middle class, whereas a mere 23 per cent saw themselves as working class.[5] Other surveys point in a different direction with a majority of English people still choosing a working class identity, but there is little doubt that the importance and interpretation of class has developed increasingly different connotations north and south of the border.[6]

Class changes over time in socio-economic realities and how people interpret and use it, but there is something very significant in these differences beyond statistical interpretation. Scotland and England are two societies which are not that different in many terms, in 'objective' class terms, in occupational structure, and in how people think of key policy choices. Scotland, despite the ubiquitous narrative of difference, is not really that different from England. But such a statement ignores how people 'feel' and the importance of lived experience.

Scotland has been defined for generations by a left politics, but increasingly in modern times it has done so without an active left: instead, only having the memory and folklore of a left. This has contributed to the deep mythologising and romanticising of Scottish society, culture and politics. One of the most powerful expressions of this has been the power over the last forty years or so of the 'myth' of 'Labour Scotland'. This became the normative set of assumptions through which two generations of Labour politicians from Willie Ross to Gordon Brown saw Scotland - as collective, semi-socialist and all-pervasively Labour.

What's Left of the Scottish Left?

All of this raises big questions about what kind of left Scotland has produced and may do so in the near-future. In trying to answer these questions, we have to take account of three decades of left retreat, defeat and widespread disillusion in what is left of the left. A Scottish public culture shaped in significant part by the left but without an active left as well as a public realm with both a paucity of a left and pretensions to a left was a climate which was hospitable and receptive to the charms of Tommy Sheridan and the SSP.

There have been in the years of left decline many personality cults: Jimmy Reid, Tommy Sheridan, George Galloway, and all of them have had talents and skills as well as flaws and weaknesses. I would argue that all of these political figures have been given an over-importance, a 'Big Man' status because of the state of the left and its decline, rather than coming from and contributing to a vibrant left.

Tommy Sheridan and the SSP did at points have influence and worried mainstream politicians, at the time of the poll tax struggle, and even more, in the early days of the Scottish Parliament. Yet, at the same time their influence was always episodic and analysis too simplistic and filled with caricature and contradictions. There was the one dimensional Marxism of the Militant influence, persuasively analysed by former member Alex Wood as 'elitism, moral vacuity and the infantile factionalism of his [Sheridan's] politics which led him to sue the News of the World'.[7] In the latter stages of the SSP, this became a fantastical, prophetic, almost millennial style politics, of the triumph of will, 'anger' and 'rage' which did not mature in its analysis of class and politics.

Never did the Sheridan left set out to develop a politics which told a complex story of modern Scotland, and hold those in power to account, including the establishment voices and institutions which pay passing lip service to social democracy. A vibrant, bold, challenging Scottish left would have taken institutional Scotland to task for the grotesque state of much of Scottish life, for the scale of poverty, inequality and exclusion in one of the richest lands in the world. Instead, Sheridan and the SSP took the line of least resistance, of playing to the Scots narrative of difference and believing in the 'myth' of a collectivist, solidaristic nation. In this, it could be argued that despite the SSP's origins, it became for all its rhetoric, an insufficient challenge, and even part of 'the Scottish consensus', afraid to ask difficult questions.

The Future of the Left and The Future of the Future

This leads us to the present terrain - one post-left with a neo-liberal vandalism standing at the gates. What kind of politics of resistance is possible? What different kind of world is possible and desirable? How can we imagine and create it? What kind of agency can we develop, and what notion of transformational change can we develop? What Scottish contribution can we make which develops self-government and statehood beyond the SNP's vision? After the vanguardist revolution, after the retreat of social democracy in the face of the neo-liberal revolution, can we imagine a different, democratising vision of revolution?

Finally, to understand what happened and shape the future, we have to ask how was Tommy Sheridan possible? The Sheridan story tells us something about the politics of gender and Scottish masculinity. At points in his rise Sheridan seemed to represent an emotional intelligence and insight rare in Scottish political life. Instead, he went down a predictable road of self-aggrandisement and self-destruction, a pattern familiar to many in the tradition of the West of Scotland working class local hero.

Sheridan, the man, the politician and phenomenon springs from our political and public culture, its myths and folklores, its hollowness and shallowness, and our want to believe too much of its conceits. Scotland sees itself as a compassionate, caring, inclusive society, one which is egalitarian, welcoming and anti-hierarchical. In the maintenance of this, we choose to tell ourselves comforting, cosy stories which don't challenge our own assumptions or acknowledge the complexities of power and inequality in modern Scotland.

Scotland in this sense is a mixture of post-democracy, the term coined by Colin Crouch to define the increasing concentrations of corporate power which have distorted public life and democracy across the West, and a rather insipid, compromised social democracy.[8] This is the environment Tommy Sheridan swam and sank in. We gave him power, potency and status. It is a tale of personal tragedy, for the many activists, campaigners and people who gained voice and hope through the rise of the SSP. But most of all it is a tale and warning about us.

Gregor Gall has told this byzantine, fascinating story in great detail and with a forensic ability to treat it as fairly as possible, given the many agendas and sense of hurt and betrayal that so many people feel. It can be read as a story of a narrow part of the left who some will think was always going to self-destruct. It can also be read as an indictment of the depth and health of the Scottish body politic.

Yet it is also a book asking questions about us and the future. Hard left posturing does not get us very far, but then neither does social democracy or the post-social democracy of New Labour. The challenges we face in Scotland, the UK, in the eurozone and globally, are of an out-of-control hunter-gather capitalism which seems to be entering a hyper-destructive phase of its development, attempting to undermine the economic and social rights many used to view as the hallmark of a 'civilised society'.

After Tommy Sheridan, the traditional left and the promise of the 'near-left' of Blair and Clinton, we have to develop a politics which goes beyond mere resistance to market vandalism. Even more, we have to create spaces and capacity which challenge 'the official future', the remorseless logic of the world as it is, and take back and create the idea of a different future. That was once the promise of the left, and we desperately need to learn a new politics of change, imagination and democratising the future.

Notes

1. Hassan, G. and Shaw, E. *The Strange Death of Labour Scotland*, Edinburgh University Press, 2012.
2. The latest available data is from 2005. Personal communication from *Scottish Social Attitudes Survey*. See also Paterson, L., Bechhofer, F. and McCrone, D. *Living in Scotland: Social and Economic Change since 1980*, Edinburgh University Press, 2004, p. 99.
3. Johns, R., Denver, D., Mitchell, J. and Pattie, C. *Voting for a Scottish Government: The Scottish Parliament Election of 2007*, Manchester University Press, 2010, pp. 81–82.
4. Hanley, L. *Estates: An Intimate History*, Granta 2008; Jones, O. *Chavs: The Demonization of the Working Class*, Verso, 2011.
5. *What about the Workers? A New Study of the Working Class*, Britain Thinks 2011. Private information from authors. The UK publicised figures were 71 per cent 'middle class' and 24 per cent 'working class'.
6. See for example Heath, A., Martin, J. and Elgenius, G. 'Who do we think we are? The decline of traditional social identities' in Park, A., Curtice, J., Thomson, K., Phillips, M. and Johnston, M. (eds.) *British Social Attitudes: The 23rd Report*, Sage, 2007.
7. Wood, A. 'An ethical emptiness' *Scottish Review*, 20 January 2011, http://www.scottish-review.net/AlexWood72.shtml
8. Crouch, C. *Post-Democracy*, Polity Press 2004.

1

Making Trouble, Making Waves

Introduction

Type the words 'Tommy Sheridan' into any internet search engine, await the results and you get a sense of the scale of his public recognition. This was equally true before the 2006 court case as it was before the 2010 perjury trial. For those that have even just a minimal awareness of where Tommy came from, what he stood for and what he did before these two court cases, this public recognition – and influence – was as the leading socialist *fighter* of his generation in Scotland. Tommy was not only a socialist *par excellence* but one with the 'X' factor and star quality, and he used these to put socialism back on the political agenda in Scotland and further afield. More than this, Tommy was just about the only socialist of any genuine national prominence and certainly the only one with mass appeal. Much of this was to do with him as an individual – his talents, skills, personality and character. But as this biography will document and explain, properly locating the individual in time and place is equally important to understanding what Tommy became and what he was able to do. This requires focussing upon the interdependency of the individual and their social context and social surroundings, where one can influence the other and vice-versa. In other words, this biography will focus upon the relationship between the individual and the different forms of social agency, whether these be social movements or political parties.

Any biographer must have some measure of innate sympathy for the subject being written about – there seems little point in constructing a hatchet job solely to run down the individual concerned. This is undoubtedly so in this case. But that does not mean this biography will turn into a hagiography either, where the subject is, in effect, beatified.[1] Rather, the approach will be to be sympathetic without being uncritical so the analysis proffered is both robust and rigorous. In being a *political* biography, this book represents a study of Tommy's thought and attitudes, his actions and behaviours, and his policy and practice. It necessarily means examining the influence of Trotskyism, and of Militant and the SSP in particular, without becoming a study of those as such. This book is, therefore, a study of the politics and socio-psychology of Tommy and, in so doing, the biography is also a study of activism and leadership through the prism of one of its finest operators and exponents, namely, Tommy Sheridan. It, therefore, presents a study of the person, the personality and his politics and the dialectics between them.

Much is now known in the public domain about Tommy from his penchant for fake tans, to his love of football and to his various sexual proclivities. There has been wall-to-wall coverage of the latter as a result of his resignation as national convener of the SSP in 2004, the ensuing internal faction fight, and the two court cases of 2006 and 2010. This biography will not ignore these different facets just because they are already widely known of. Yet it will not recount them in any detail, and it will not recount them simply to show there is a personal side to the public face of the politician, Tommy Sheridan. Instead, it will examine them to ascertain how they fit in with – or contradict – his politics, political activity and wider reputation. This would be the so even if the court cases of 2006 and 2010 had not taken place. For example, Joan McAlpine, lead co-author with Tommy of *A Time to Rage* (see later) believed that his relationship with Gail Sheridan (nee Healy) helped transform, to paraphrase, 'Tommy – the intense political activist' into 'Tommy – the socialist politician who was also a normal bloke', and in so doing gave him and his politics a wider and more homely appeal. But far more significantly for a biography, this study will highlight a number of previously undiscovered, unidentified, unexplored and unexplained threads and traits in his character which have had immense political significance for him and for the radical and socialist left in Scotland and further afield. In particular, these threads and traits arise from fresh material casting new light upon our existing knowledge and understanding. The obvious threads concern Tommy's personal relations with a number of collaborators and how Tommy has acted and responded under unprecedented levels of public scrutiny and political pressure. In doing so, the biography will neither de-legitimise nor downplay Tommy's achievements of prior to 2004 simply because of what happened after 2004. But at the same time, it will not shrink from highlighting a number of threads in his attitudes and behaviour that crossed the boundary between the pre-2004 and post-2004 periods.

For some, there will be a question as to why this biography should be written at all. Their reasons may range from not wanting to rake over the disheartening coals of another disaster for the radical and socialist left to those of giving any sort of considered treatment to somebody they believe to be a charlatan and traitor to the socialist cause. Some may want to see him not just jailed but politically buried. Others may have reasons of not liking an in-depth examination of Tommy because it asks and answers some uncomfortable questions which they would rather not have asked and answered.[2] Beyond the simplistic platitude that the left needs to learn from its past if it is to better influence the present and future, there are some evident reasons for writing such a biography. There is what Tommy achieved and what the political project that he was part of achieved when both were at their heights. For example, Colin Fox, SSP leader and, thus, no uncritical observer, had no problem recognising Tommy as a 'giant of the socialism movement' prior to 2004. And the *Scottish Socialist Voice* also recognised Tommy as 'one of the most monumental figures in Scottish socialism ... [and] one of the most outstanding campaigners for socialism in Scotland'.[3] So despite what happened after 2004, there is a need for the study of the period up to 2004. But there is then also the issue of how such a promising development could end up going so badly wrong, so is it the case that the radical and socialist left should not have such leaders or leaders *per se* as some have argued? And, there is the gap that is left wanting for a serious study no matter how much wall-to-wall media treatment an individual or organisation is given. In one regard here, the biography is a source book albeit with an accompanying political analysis. Finally, in terms of the rationale for researching and writing this biography, there is also the issue that the left as an agent wishing social change, and which is historically weaker than its opponents, must come to grips with this patent weakness especially at a time of continuing ideological and political crisis for its opponents.

Bouquets and Brickbats

The figure of Tommy Sheridan has always excited strong comment one way or another. There is a sense that he has been either loved or loathed, with little existing in between. Indeed, the colour and flamboyance that he brought to politics in Scotland, and socialist politics in particular, stirred strong feelings amongst the press pack. The appellations of 'folk hero', 'firebrand', 'working class hero', 'man of the people' were mixed and prefixed with 'local', 'socialist', 'militant' and so on to provide floral bouquets by which to describe Tommy. Outside of the rightwing press of the tabloids (*Express*, *Mail*, *Star*, and *Sun*) and broadsheets (*Scotsman*, *Telegraph*, and *Times*), these were used by the centre and centre-left press not so much as terms of abuse but as terms of achievement, righteous significance and, sometimes, endearment. So the *Independent* variously talked of Tommy as a 'local folk hero',

'Glasgow firebrand' and 'Scotland's foremost working class hero'.[4] Meantime, the *Herald* reported him as the 'Militant icon and mass demonstration specialist', 'local firebrand', 'socialist firebrand', 'leftwing firebrand', 'man of people' and 'people's tribune'[5] while its sister paper, the *Sunday Herald* called Tommy 'Scotland's favourite socialist' with 'an embodiment of heartfelt Marxist ideology'.[6] In echoes of Scottish revolutionary, John Maclean, Tommy was 'Scotland's Lenin'.[7] Amongst the mass circulation of the centre left tabloids, the *Daily Record* saw him as a 'folk hero'[8], the *Sunday Mail* as a 'man of the people'[9] and the *Mirror* as a 'working class hero'.[10] But even amongst the rightwing press, there was also some similar acknowledgement. So to the *Mail on Sunday*, he was the 'real conscience of Scotland'[11] and to the *Scotsman*, he was 'friend to the masses'.[12] Its sister paper, *Scotland on Sunday*, on one occasion went even further, describing Tommy as a 'man of principle' and the 'most ... ideologically pure MSP'.[13] Although part of the same stable as the *Scotsman* and *Scotland on Sunday*, and even though reporting on a son of Glasgow, the *Evening News* had no problem categorising Tommy in non-dismissive terms as a 'firebrand socialist' and 'socialist firebrand'.[14] The plaudits were no mere couple of words here and couple of words there. Some are worth quoting in full. Early on the *Herald* proclaimed:

> To his constituents in the Pollok housing scheme on Glasgow's South Side, Sheridan is a local hero; a working-class David defying an army of political and corporate Goliaths. To his foes, he is a reckless rabble-rouser fanning the flames of popular discontent for destructive political ends.[15]

It followed this up with calling Tommy 'Glasgow's foremost organic intellectual at work, rest and play. In other words, talking politics' and 'the last repository of our long discarded idealism'[16] when covering his appearance on Channel 4 television's 'If I was PM'. In a two page spread, the *Sunday Mail* wrote:

> Arguably, he is the most charismatic politician of his generation. He has the looks, the charm and the youthful integrity to make voters swoon and spin doctors go weak at the knees. But you won't find Tommy Sheridan's name within a million miles of the list of Labour approved candidates for a seat at Holyrood. In yet another week of sleaze claims, Tommy is the spectre at the New Labour feast – the socialist who refused to sell out. Just 34, he's already a legend in his lifetime, an urban guerrilla for the sick, the poor and the unemployed. To some, he's a joke – a Citizen Smith rather

than a Che Guevara. To others, he is a brilliant maverick with a fatal flaw – his refusal to compromise his beliefs. But for many Scots in poverty, he's a folk hero. ... His past reads like a war zone of radical causes – poverty, poll tax, warrant sales, unemployment, low incomes, state oppression. Tedious, knee-jerk, leftie issues – to well-off people, perhaps. But issues that mean lifelong imprisonment for the poor. And that's precisely why Tommy's so widely respected – because he's never stopped fighting to release people from the poverty trap. ... Over the years, he's become an expert in the art of demos, sit-ins and direct action. ... He became the original poll tax warrior.[17]

In this piece, the *Sunday Mail* – as with many other features on him prior to 2003 – made Tommy's messages on his answering machine the most well-known in Scotland: 'Hi, this is Tommy ... sorry I can't come to the phone just now. I'm probably out campaigning for New Labour to start tackling rich fat cats and stop attacking lone parents and ordinary workers'. Other versions before and after were: 'Sorry, I'm not in now, I'm probably out fighting the Tories' and 'Sorry, I'm not in now, I'm probably out fighting Blair's new Tories'.

But ironically, and in a way that would have no doubt pleased his mother given her comments encouraging Tommy to 'walk in the light' (see later), the most feted comment came from Richard Holloway, former Episcopalian Bishop of Edinburgh and leader of the Scottish Episcopal Church. Covering the furore surrounding his comments, the *Express* reported that Holloway 'hailed Tommy Sheridan as a modern-day Jesus Christ because [as a courageous and selfless fighter for the poor] he was 'The closest thing we have to one of these uncompromising Christ figures' [according to Holloway]'.[18] So too would comments from Christian socialist, Tony Benn, who respected Tommy and held him in 'very high regard' and 'dearly love[d him]'.[19] More recently, former Labour and Respect MP, George Galloway, has been a vocal cheerleader for Tommy. In well reported public meetings for the 2007 Scottish Parliament elections, he declared: 'Tommy Sheridan is the most popular, most charismatic, most capable leader on the left', 'I think that you personally are the most outstanding leader of Scottish progressive opinion' and 'Tommy is without doubt the most recognised, the most popular, the most charismatic and the most capable progressive leader in Scotland today'.[20]

Whilst there are hundreds more tributes (as well as condemnations[21]) that could be mentioned from the press, this small selection gives a good indication of not only how much the figure of Tommy Sheridan had impinged upon the public psyche by 1999 – before he was elected an MSP – but also the manner in which this had been done. From 2000 to 2003, the appellations for him of 'working class hero', 'people's hero', 'folk hero', 'firebrand socialist', 'Citizen Tommy', 'Citizen Sheridan', 'man of the people', 'Robin Hood of politics', 'Caledonian Robin Hood', 'Scotland's only professional class warrior', 'self styled Cuban of Cardonald', 'Che Guevara of Pollok', 'Glasgow's Che' and 'Scotland's Che Guevara' were used countless times in newspapers. That he was voted twentieth in a poll of 'Great Scots'[22] and then number two in the *Sunday Herald*'s[23] ten greatest living Scots are short, sharp indications of the impact he was able to make. For more serious commentators, Tommy was 'a throwback to a Red Clydeside tradition of articulate, passionate working class radicals'.[24]

Political Stature

To get a better historical measure of the heights that Tommy scaled, comparison with others, mostly Scots and or those active in Scottish politics, is instructive. This is important because those on the left in Scotland who remain within the Communist and Labour parties tend to have a rather begrudging attitude towards Tommy in as much as he has made headway doing what they neither favoured not thought was possible, namely, building an independent socialist project outside Labour.

Within post-war Scotland, Jimmy Reid, the main leader of the successful Upper Clyde Shipbuilders work-in of 1971–1972 is one obvious comparator.[25] But Reid was unable to cement his profile and influence as a subsequently elected national politician for either Communist or Labour parties, and ended up joining the Scottish National Party (SNP). Thereafter, he was more known as a journalist and commentator rather than a political activist. So while remaining a trenchant critic of neo-liberalism, he did soften his politics considerably so he is probably better remembered as a social democrat than socialist. Jim Sillars, one time creator of the Scottish Labour Party[26] and victor over Labour for the SNP in the 1988 Govan by-election, is another comparator but he lacks the persistent and high-profile presence of Tommy to be truly comparable, much less the radical socialist politics. Bill Speirs, former STUC general secretary, was a widely regarded socialist, anti-imperialist and supporter of Scottish devolution. In many regards, he was similar to Tommy, especially in trenchant criticism of 'new' Labour. However, despite having a wide profile as a radical union leader, Speirs was less able to speak exactly as he saw things compared to Tommy. In other words, his position also constrained him somewhat and this marred his ability to scale the heights that Tommy did. George Galloway is an obvious comparator for high-profile excoriation of 'new Labour', neo-liberalism and US imperialism and leading a political party, Respect, which was to the left of Labour. But his anti-imperialism and quasi-fetish with the rights of Palestinians left little room for him to become a domestic politician concerned with the rights of workers and the poor in Scotland (or Britain). Not being elected to the Scottish Parliament in 2011 cemented this tendency. Others like Mick McGahey, vice-president of the National Union of Mineworkers (1974–1987) and Lawrence Daly, general secretary of the National Union of Mineworkers (1968–1994) were not only less well known but were probably seen more as focussing upon a narrower terrain of issues. Earlier figures like acclaimed revolutionaries, James Connolly, John Maclean and Harry McShane, and Willie Gallacher, Communist MP for West Fife between 1935 and 1950, or a number of the 'Red Clydesider' Independent Labour Party MPs (like James Maxton) elected in 1922, may have equally good claims to share the same mantle with Tommy of giving socialism a mass appeal but the quite different political and social contexts make difficult any productive historical comparisons.[27]

Outside Scotland and Scottish politics, there are the obvious figures of former Militant MPs, Terry Fields and Dave Nellist, former Militant Liverpool councillors like Tony Mulhearn and Derek Hatton as well as Arthur Scargill and a small band of socialist current and former Labour MPs like John McDonnell, Jeremy Corbyn and Alan Simpson. But for similar reasons of lack of breadth and depth of sustained profile and influence as *individuals* to those above in the Scottish orbit, none quite come up to scratch in comparison with Tommy. For example, Derek Hatton did not lead a mass movement, was not a party leader and did not have the same longevity of career. The figure of Tony Benn,[28] former Labour MP, is quite different though. With a now grandfatherly halo as an elder statesman of socialism, his reputation has benefitted from many years of being a critical backbench MP who then left Parliament in 2001 to, in his own words, 'spend more time involved in politics'. But there are two obvious reasons why Benn is no better a comparison with Tommy. First, there is his time in government in the 1960s and 1970s which, despite his move to the left in the 1980s, marks him out as a social democrat or democratic socialist rather than a revolutionary socialist (notwithstanding the similarity of the Bennite 'alternative economy strategy' to Militant's transitional programme). Second, there is Benn's reputation for honesty and integrity. This would have been a good basis for comparison but for the events of 2004 onwards in Tommy's life. Ken Livingstone, former Labour leader of the Greater London Council, Labour MP and both independent and Labour Mayor of London may be thought of as another comparator given his longevity, outspokenness and radicalism. But his younger days at the GLC, his association with the Labour left (the Campaign group and Socialist Action) and his anti-Blairism *et alia* still do not put him in on a par with Tommy in terms of Tommy having been a leader of a mass movement, a leader of resistance and a radical, campaigning anti-capitalist socialist throughout. Finally, there are the figures of Bob Crow and Mark Serwotka, RMT and PCS union general secretaries respectively. While both known as campaigners and socialists, again being union leaders has – compared to Tommy – limited their freedom to be active as socialists and narrowed their focus. Where they have played a wider political role for socialism, it has been in a supportive and not a leading way. [29]

Outside Britain, for example, Arlette Laguiller of the (Trotskyist) Workers' Fight and Olivier Besancenot of the (Trotskyist) Revolutionary Communist League (and now the New Anti-Capitalist Party) in France are figures who broke through into the political mainstream with the amount of electoral support they secured in their presidential bids albeit without attaining elected office. The figure of Joe Higgins, leader of the Socialist Party and the United Left Alliance in Eire, is a better parallel because of the Militant heritage, leading a popular revolt and being singularly elected to Parliament between 1997 and 2007. Starting off as a Dublin councillor and involved in Eire's equivalent of the poll tax revolt (over the bin tax), Higgins then became an MP and MEP. As the Socialist Party's only national politician, he has played a pivotal role as the public face of socialism in Eire (albeit he is considerably more straitlaced and less flamboyant than Tommy). Higgins was re-elected to the Irish Parliament in 2011 along with four other members of the United Left Alliance.

This brief overview makes a strong case that Tommy has made a greater contribution to the cause of socialism as a political salesperson and achieved a greater standing as a radical socialist leader than pretty much all of the aforementioned other relevant figures with the exception of Joe Higgins. Like Joe Higgins, Tommy has not only led a successful revolt that humbled a government but was then able to go on to lead a growing socialist party and gain an elected national political position (albeit with proportional representation). For these reasons, the assessment of Steve Arnott, supporter and witness for Tommy in both the 2006 and 2010 court cases, was not far wrong: Tommy was 'probably the most significant socialist icon of the post-war period'.[30] Certainly, until 2010, Tommy had the characteristic of not falling by the wayside through his own volition like many others, with the *Herald* calling him 'indefatigable'.[31] Of course, Tommy's crucible has been the relatively small society of Scotland with the effect that he has had limited wider portent and presence.[32]

Structure and Sources

This chapter has established the political significance of Tommy for radical and socialist politics in Scotland and further afield. In other words, he is more than worthy of study and biography. The second chapter provides an account of his childhood and early years of political activity as a means of establishing the social and political background from which he came. The third chapter examines the period from his election as a councillor in Glasgow in 1992 to his election to the Scottish Parliament in 1999 as part of the development of a new popular socialist force in Scotland. Chapter four covers the period of his first term as a Member of the Scottish Parliament (MSP) in conjunction with the further building of a new socialist political force. Chapter five considers the years of his re-election in 2003 to that of losing his seat in 2007. Chapters six and seven cover the period 2004 to 2011 with regard to his defamation and perjury court cases. The chapters after this consider his personality and his political worldview. The conclusion provides an overall assessment of Tommy, as well as a consideration of his future. Throughout the mainly chronological narrative, the biography assesses the meaning and significance of actions and events in order to go beyond merely providing a descriptive account of Tommy's life and activity to date. Thus, many chapters are peppered with overviews, assessments and consideration of political themes. The point at which some political themes are dealt in this way arises because at certain times in the chronology of Tommy's life certain issues taken on a greater prominence than at other times or because understanding Tommy's actions requires explaining the political situation and perspective of the time.

The materials for this biography are derived from interviews with Tommy and his close political collaborators and associates as well as members of his family (see Appendix 2) and close and distant personal observation of Tommy from the late 1980s onwards. These are then supplemented by media coverage, primarily through the Lexis-Nexis database of newspaper articles but also including newspapers of the political parties which Tommy was a member. Further details on these materials and methods, and the issues contained therein, can be found in Appendix 1.[33] When quotes are used, the source of the quote will be stated in an endnote unless the quote is from an interview carried out for this biography. Thus, all quotes[34] which are not attributed to a specific source are from the fieldwork interviews. It is worth noting at this point the provenance of many of the interviews in terms of their personal and political relationships with Tommy. In particular, Keith Baldassara, Alan McCombes and George McNeilage were extremely close to Tommy from early on and had an intense and on-going relationship with Tommy until 2004. Although they knew him before, their close relationships with him began in 1988, 1984 and 1986 respectively.

Conclusion

Lord Bracadale, in sentencing Tommy on the 26 January 2011, gave a concise overview of Tommy's achievements:

> On any view, you were a highly effective and hard working politician. You supported individuals in the community; both in the parliament and in the street, you were able to use your undoubted powers of oratory to press home your cause; you led the Scottish Socialist Party to considerable electoral success; and your contributions to the anti-poll tax campaign and the abolition of warrant sales will become part of the fabric of Scottish social and political history.

Tommy scaled immense heights in making socialism popular again in Scottish politics and society. Mark Steel recognised Tommy as 'one of the most popular and best known political figures'.[35] Unlike, for example, George Galloway, Tommy was the 'real deal' of a working class youth from 'the scheme'[36] who 'made good' through cutting his political teeth by not just participating in but leading popular struggle and revolt. Being the 'real deal' meant not only speaking in an articulate manner but doing it in his own Glaswegian working class tongue and without seeming to be a political anorak. He was – he became – for many a 'working class hero'. As John Lennon, one of Tommy's favourite lyricists wrote in his 1970 song, *Working Class Hero*, it was not just that 'A working class hero is something to be' but also that 'If you want to be a hero well just follow me'. Tommy Sheridan became not only a socialist politician who was a working class hero – something today uncommon outside the ranks of the odd footballer – but he also had many who would follow him. He became a force to be reckoned with in the battle for social justice and socialism. But as a result of a spectacular political misjudgement, he carelessly and crassly sacrificed this achievement. Found guilty of perjury, after earlier winning a libel case concerning his sex life, for many he became the 'working class zero' to take the *Daily Record's* term.[37] This was because of his willingness and ability to tear apart not just his own stature and influence but also that of the most successful socialist party in Scotland in the post-war period, and to do so over telling lies in order to cover up his sexual peccadilloes. It has been said by some that the tearing apart of the most successful socialist party in Scotland in the post-war period is the one 'crime' Tommy will never stand trial for in a court of law.[38] It used to be the case that the 'love' or 'loathe' Tommy Sheridan phenomenon was a clean and clear left/right split. From 2004, the greatest intensity of this was within the socialist left. It is for these reasons that this biography is entitled 'From hero to zero?' Ultimately, it is up to readers to decide whether the question mark is justified or needed.

Notes

1. Tommy believed the biography would be a 'hatchet job' (*Scotland on Sunday* 20 March 2011), with his lawyer, Aamer Anwar saying: 'We will use every legal avenue to stop it from being published' (*Scotland on Sunday* 20 March 2011). I had already made it clear that it would be 'neither a hagiography nor a hatchet job' (*SSAHRI Showcase 2007*, University of Hertfordshire, p. 27). In this regard, Manning Marable (*Malcolm X: a life of reinvention*, Penguin, 2011, p. 13) wisely commented: 'The great temptation for a biographer of an iconic figure is to portray him or her as a virtual saint, without the normal contradictions and blemishes all human beings have'. Some of the same methodological issues in studying a political figure for which the biographer has a political affinity (see Appendix 1) are also briefly discussed by Ian Birchall (*Tony Cliff – a Marxist for His Time*, Bookmarks, 2011).
2. Indeed, for those that uncritically support Tommy, it should be borne in mind some criticism levelled at him can also be levelled at other socialist politicians but because this is a biography of him, criticism of these others is left aside.
3. 25 August 2006.
4. 10 September 1997, 13 May 1999, 24 April 1999.
5. 16 April 1997, 6 September 1997, 2 October 1999, 8 October 1999, 20 November 1999, 15 December 1999.
6. 4 April 1999, 26 December 1999.
7. *Evening News* 28 November 1998, *Herald* 20 December 2006.
8. 12 May 1999.
9. 20 June 1999.
10. 30 December 1999
11. 30 May 1999.
12. 19 November 1999.
13. 10 October 1999.
14. 13 May 1999, 10 September 1999.
15. 13 March 1995.
16. *Herald* 17 August 1996.
17. 12 July 1998.
18. 16 April 2001. Richard Holloway hoped that Tommy was 'likely to be a thorn in the side of the Scottish establishment for many a long happy year' (*Sunday Herald* 15 April 2001). Other figures Holloway cited in this regard were Peter Tatchell and Ralph Nader.
19. See *Guardian* (12 July 1992) and Benn, T. *Free at Last: Diaries 1991–2001* (Hutchinson, 2002), p. 612 and p. 207 respectively.

20. Respectively *Guardian* 26 April 2007, *Scotsman* 26 April 2007, *Herald* 26 April 2007. But interestingly in his book *I'm Not the Only One* (Penguin, 2004), which takes its cue from Lennon's 'Imagine', Galloway does not mention Tommy even though doing so would lend credence to the book's title. Before that, Galloway often slurred Tommy with the phrase 'Trotsky Tommy Sheridan' (for example, *Mail on Sunday* 30 April 2000, 18 June 2000) in the way that Labour referred to the SSP as 'Trots'. Suggesting some of their recent personal and political closeness may be due to both being down on their luck, Galloway was not present at Tommy's wedding in 2000 because he was not invited.

21. Like the 'working class zero' of the *Daily Record* (23 March 2001) and the standard attacks on his character as arrogant, vane, egotistical and narcissistic and his politics as 'loony left'. One good example of the latter was Andrew Neil, writing in the *Scotsman* (14 March 1997), where he commented Tommy's 'idea of a socialist utopia looks like Albania on a bad day'. Former Labour spin doctor, Tim Luckhurst (*Mail on Sunday* 6 August 2006), believed an independent socialist republic in Scotland led by Tommy Sheridan would be like 'Cuba with midges and drizzle'. Later, the *Sunday Times* (6 August 2006) ventured Tommy was a 'Supertrot of proletarian legend'.

22. *Herald* 3 December 2001.

23. 25 January 2004.

24. Hassan, G and Fraser, D. *The Political Guide to Modern Scot*land (Politicos, 2004), p. 398.

25. When Reid was a columnist for the *Herald* in 1999, he wrote many warm words on Tommy. For example, he believed Tommy had 'c[o]me out with credit' (*Herald* 1 May 2000) with his bill to abolish warrant sales.

26. See Drucker, H. *Breakaway: the Scottish Labour Party* (EUSPB, 1978).

27. See also Mills, V. 'Trouble ahead for SSP' *Morning Star* 19 November 2004.

28. Benn records in his *More Time for Politics: Diaries 2001–2007* (Hutchinson, 2007, p. 207) that he 'dearly love[s]' Tommy.

29. Other possible candidates for comparison may be found in Routledge, P. *The Bumper Book of British Lefties* (Politicos, 2003).

30. *Herald* 27 July 2006.

31. 19 February 1997.

32. This is all the more the case with Joe Higgins.

33. These details are put in an appendix at the end of the biography so as not to break the flow of the chapter.

34. When these quotes are used, they are necessarily used partially and selectively. Thus, where an interviewee gives a view which is praiseworthy (or not) of Tommy, this should not be seen as implying they have other views which are necessarily praiseworthy (or not) of Tommy. Consequently, the wider views or opinions of an interviewee about Tommy should not be inferred from just the quotes that are used. Nonetheless, the use of quotes from the interviewees will show the fullest possible range of their views to ameliorate the aforementioned danger. Finally, that some interviewees have not been quoted at length as others does not mean their views have not been taken into account for often their views have been aggregated together to inform analysis.

35. Steel, M. *What's Going On? The meanderings of a comic mind in confusion* (Simon and Schuster, 2008), p. 115.

36. A Scottish term for a council housing estate.

37. Of 23 March 2001.

38. For example, Frances Curran, when being cross-examined by Tommy in his perjury trial, told him: 'The crime that you are in the dock for is not your worst. Your biggest is the sell out of the party and those who voted for you' (*Herald* 28 October 2010).

2

Early Life and
Formative Influences

Introduction

Human beings are social creatures whose personalities and traits are socially constructed as a result of interactions with their families, peers and friends in their communities and social circles as well as the wider economic and political environments they exist in. In being so constructed, these personalities and traits are heavily influenced, although not determined, by these social forces, networks and contexts. Consequently, it is important to understand where Tommy came from socially and politically to gain some understanding of what he became, what he was and what he achieved.[1] To do otherwise would be to wrongly wrench Tommy out of his social, lived context.

Family and Community

Thomas Sheridan was born on 7 March 1964 to Alice and Tommy Sheridan (senior) and lived in a two-room and scullery home in McKechnie Street in Govan along with his older sisters, Lynn and Carol,[2] until 1966 when the family moved to Linthaugh Road in Pollok, part of a newly created council estate or 'scheme' built on part of a then country estate. The family had an Irish Catholic background on his father's side although there was also some Italian ancestry on his mother's side. Life for the family was not poverty stricken but it was not one of plenty either. There was a fairly hand-to-mouth existence despite two adult wage earners in the household.

Alice was undoubtedly the foremost influence upon Tommy socially and politically.[3] She agreed that she was something of a 'role model' for Tommy. Variously, Tommy said of her: 'She's not only someone I love very deeply, she's a political soul mate'[4]; she's been a 'source of strength ... support ... and inspiration to me'[5]; 'She is a constant source of strength, hope and inspiration to me'[6]; and 'She taught me to stand up for myself, to believe in myself and to fight for my beliefs'.[7] A strong and passionate character, Alice was more driven personally and politically than his dad as Tommy freely admitted,[8] being both his moral compass and political educator. She is also a self-confident and outspoken character who is pre-occupied by fighting social injustice in its many guises. Some of this came from her family background which overlaid the experience of working class deprivation with a history of agitation (like her grandfather being branded a troublemaker for campaigning for toilets for workers in a shipyard) as well as the Irish Catholic community's experience of injustice. Alice was a union activist in the pub trade for the Transport and General Workers' Union in the early 1970s, becoming an official with it for four years. But she was also an activist in the 'battered wives' movement as it was then known (or campaign against domestic violence as it is now called) and the local Labour Party, and more latterly a mature student who then became a social worker and counsellor.

According to *Scotland on Sunday*, 'His mother Alice says he was always intense, even as a little boy. Even his play was very focused. He would spend hours lining up his toy soldiers into battle formations. He would leave them that way for days, coming back and forward to change a soldier here, a detail there'.[9] Ironically, when he was very young, Alice recalled that Tommy told her he hated unions because 'she was always out and about because of them'. In *Scotland on Sunday*, Alice recounted it was because: 'They took her away from him'.[10] She recalled she read the young Tommy Keir Hardie's biography at bedtime when he was four years old and taught him about the miners' strikes of the early 1970s and why there were consequent power cuts.[11] All this 'made quite an impression on him' although Keith Baldassara believed the story about reading Keir Hardie to Tommy was 'ludicrous [but] she's been this way with Tommy for a long time'. According to *Scotland on Sunday*, 'Alice taught her children that everything, even waiting for a bus, was political'[12] – because waiting revolved around the politics of the state of public transport. Through these and other issues, she believes she instilled in Tommy as a young boy – Thomas as she has always called him – a considerable burning sense of injustice. Alice said of him: 'I brought him up to have fire in his belly ... [to have] passion with a brain... [to be] intolerant of injustice but tolerant of people'. She went further by saying: 'I've always brought my children up to challenge injustice, regardless of the cost to themselves, because you have to live with yourself'[13] and 'I brought up my children ...

to believe that if you see injustice, you must challenge it, whatever the cost to yourself. If you don't, you pay an even greater price ... not being able to live with yourself'.[14] A level of political discussion at home meant that the rule of 'never talk about politics or religion' was not adhered to. However, reflecting on this, Tommy said:

> I'm not sure I had this sense of injustice ... I look back and there were moments when I think I felt anger – if that's possible for someone so young – and one of those moments concerned my uncle Jimmy who was blind but happy and the epitome of life. He was moved to a block of flats on the fourteenth floor in Cardonald from his flat in Govan due to renovation. These [new] flats were isolated and isolating ... that was one of those moments ... I better understand what I was feeling then later on when I could articulate it because at the time I just felt it was 'bad'.

As important as the political education his mother dispensed was the sense of self-confidence and self-belief that she helped instil in him.[15] According to her, he is 'probably the most balanced person I've ever met ... kind, thoughtful, he listens to people, doesn't talk about people in the negative sense ... [there's] not a jealous bone in his body ... he is very honest ... about [his own] performance ... [and] was able to evaluate [situations with his] analytical mind ... early on'. But there is more to her estimation of him than this: 'he's a bit special ... I knew the minute he was born there was something about him ... I just knew he was different'.[16] A Militant activist who got to know Alice well during the anti-poll tax revolt and Tommy's incarceration recounted that Alice told her she considered aborting the foetus that would become Tommy but received a divine message not to because he was destined to lead the working class – giving a further basis to the sense that Alice saw Tommy as 'special'. Keith Baldassara, a former close friend of Alice as well, confirmed this: 'She has always felt Tommy was put on this earth for a reason' while Joan McAlpine believed 'his mother thinks he's Jesus Christ' with Rosie Kane recounting that Alice told her that Tommy had a glow of light or halo around him on one occasion.[17] And when discussing Tommy's strengths and virtues, Alice could offer no faults or weaknesses.[18] Alan McCombes recalled that Alice had an 'incredible, almost spooky, obsession with Tommy ... she put him on a pedestal ... by contrast, she never spoke about Lynn like that'.[19]

Regardless of whether or not Tommy was 'special', this forceful message from a forceful character is likely to have given him a powerful sense of self-belief and self-assurance even though on the way to interview Alice, Tommy cautioned to take what his mum would say about him with 'a pinch of salt', saying: 'Her views of me are very coloured by the fact she is my mum'.[20] Keith Baldassara believed, however, that Tommy's 'supreme confidence in himself and his own abilities has only in small part come from Alice' with Rosie Kane believing the impact of Alice's devotion to Tommy was to be a 'cheer-leader' and 'shield' for Tommy inside SML/SSA/SSP. While Tommy highlighted that his childhood was 'warm, happy, very positive ... I always had confidence as a kid and was secure ... the emotional security afforded to us stood us in good stead ... and I was the baby of the family',[21] he also believed:

> I've probably had a thick skin all my live ... from my self-confidence as a result of growing up in a loving family ... to the football at school ... to be a Jack-the-lad pursuing the opposite sex and so on ... I've always been a character ... when it came to an occupa-tion, someone had to go in first, when it came to a packed meeting in a university canteen someone had to stand on a table first ... I thought 'Fuck it—you've got to do it' and consciously and unconsciously I've built up the experience, the courage and the determination.[22]

Yet, nonetheless, it seems that his early sense of moral compass and of being highly self-reliant and resilient were also etched into his psyche by his mother who told him to 'stand up' for himself and 'take responsibility for [his] own life and actions'. Indeed, Tommy told the *Evening Times* that Alice: 'instilled in me this sense of injustice that burns me up'.[23] Thus, from Alice, some of Tommy's drive, determi-nation and self-discipline are likely to have been derived. And from these can be identified personal courage and an inner strength. Later in life, friends and adversaries would admit he had 'balls of steel'. To use terms Tommy uses of himself, this helps explain why he is 'fearless' and 'unflinching'. But it was the direction that Tommy decided to apply these that is explained by other factors other than just the influence of his mother.

One thing that Tommy did not take from his mother was her spiri-tualism and religious belief. At his 2006 and 2010 court cases, she blessed both with holy water and of the 2006 court verdict said: 'Our prayers have been answered'.[24] For Alice, there is a close affinity between her socialism, Christianity and spiritual sustenance[25] in terms of the way to treat people and the struggle for social justice. Tommy was brought up as Catholic, although more by school than by his parents. Of this he said: 'I don't think I've ever [genuinely] believed ... I have never consciously believed'. He went to prayers once when fifteen or sixteen years old when he thought he 'had got a girl pregnant. That was the height of my beliefs'.[26] Alice recounted that when he was about nineteen, Tommy told her he no longer believed in God to which she replied: 'That's all right son, because he believes in you'.[27] Tommy became a militant atheist albeit one that was capable of showing respect for the heartfelt beliefs of those that are religious for reasons of human compassion. Indeed, he said he had more respect for the Church of Scotland than the Catholic church as the former was less pro-establishment. Another thing that Tommy did not get from Alice was his attitude to sex (see later). Keith Baldassara recalled: 'Alice is appalled at the amount of explicit sex on TV, appalled at pornography – she's the opposite of Tommy here so his desire for sex comes [entirely] from himself'. One other salient facet here is Tommy's attitude towards social workers. The *Sunday Herald* reported: 'When Alice Sheridan became a social worker, young Tommy argued she was helping to hide the mess created by an unequal social system. He thought she should have no part in covering up the consequences. But his mother argued that socialism is based on humanitarian principles and that alleviation of suffering should be their first concern'.[28] His views on this moderated after his sister, Lynn, also became a social worker.

School and University

Tommy attended St Monica's primary school in Pollok and Lourdes secondary school on the south side of Glasgow in Cardonald. As he told many interviewers when asked as an MSP, he enjoyed school for the camaraderie, the sport (especially football) and some of the lessons.[29] He seldom got in trouble with the teachers for 'bad behaviour'. During his school days, he played football in local teams and, according to Alice, Rangers looked at Tommy a few times but took this interest no further as he was being brought up a Catholic. At school, Tommy obtained five 'O' grades (in economics, modern studies, English, chemistry, and maths, with four A grades and one B grade) and four 'Highers' (B grades in modern studies, English and economics with a C in chemistry).

Alice pushed Tommy to go to university and not settle for the (socially constructed) lower expectations of working class kids 'getting a trade'. He recounted: 'My mum saved me from the deference factor that comes with social inequality'.[30] So it was Alice that insisted that after doing well at his 'O' grades, he returned to do his Highers rather than stay on working at clothes retailer, Burtons.[31] This encouragement and guidance came not so much from the desire of a parent to see their child do well and gain a career or well paid job but more from the political standpoint that he was told by her never to forget that he was working-class, and that as such he had a duty to be educated, a duty to educate himself and use this to the benefit of the working class. She also told him that educationally 'he could do anything he wanted'. Yet there was always a political dimension lurking in the background, so the urging to get a higher education was also premised on the belief that: 'If you want to beat the system, you need to know the system'.

This encouragement chimed with something of an epiphany of being taught modern studies in fourth year.[32] Two teachers in this subject, according to Tommy, 'gave lessons in truth [so that t]hings on television [like apartheid] began to make sense'[33] and this stimulated his interest in politics.[34] He told *Scotland on Sunday*: 'Modern studies seemed more to do with reality than geometry'[35]; the *Scotsman*: 'Modern studies was my favourite subject. It was the awakening of inert passions because, when I began to read, I discovered apartheid in South Africa. That just wakened up a sense of justice in me'[36]; and the *Herald*: 'Modern studies was my favourite subject because it discussed subjects which I could relate to as they appeared regularly in the evening news ... it encourage[d] young people to ask the essential question which is simply: 'Why?''.[37] Growing self-confidence and his willingness to speak his mind came from the encouragement of his modern studies teachers and doing karate. According to Tommy: 'If you acted like an adult they treated you like an adult and they gave you some confidence that what you had to say was worth something'.[38] Of karate, he said it 'disciplined[ed my] mind and body. It gave me a lot of confidence'.[39]

Teachers such as these told Alice at a parents' evening that Tommy could achieve more than he thought and wanted: 'At the end of third year, I wanted to be a car mechanic. My teachers said I was setting my sights too low. I didn't know what they meant. I thought being a car mechanic was the bees' knees'.[40] Around this time, he was offered an apprenticeship with St Johnston FC and was quite taken by the prospect of the buzz and thrill (rather than the money) of becoming a professional footballer. However, although he was accepted at Glasgow and Strathclyde universities to study social sciences, under the influence of Alice, he went to the University of Stirling to study politics and economics between 1981 and 1985.[41] Her reasoning was that it was not an ancient university, it had the highest percentage of working class students in Scotland and had been a centre of political radicalism in the early 1970s.[42] For Tommy:

'it allowed me to move away from home, which was a big issue for me. I predict I'd have failed because of all the distractions of friends and so on in Glasgow. I was a bit intimidated and I had this constant feeling that I shouldn't be there. I was terrified of failing because I was the first in my family and the first in my street to go to university. I just read and read'.[43] He added that he felt a weight of expectation that he would fail and, determined not to, he worked hard. Alice gave him a biography of John Maclean to take to university.[44]

Despite the influence of Alice and his modern studies teachers on his political development at an early age, Tommy was far from being the political animal that he would become by the time he went to university. Football, hanging out with pals and the opposite sex were still his abiding passions (see later). In the summers between taking 'O' grades and Highers and getting the results, he worked in Burtons, and at Pickfords, a removal firm.[45] He again liked the camaraderie and the craic, indicating that despite what Alice and his two favourite teachers thought of him, he was pretty much a 'young laddie' with 'young laddie's' concerns.[46] He joined the Labour Party, according to his own recollection, in either late 1980 or early 1981 as a result of a membership drive in Pollok. Luckily for what was to come, Pollok had been a leftwing constituency since the 1960s and Militant's stronghold in Glasgow.[47] It was also the largest Constituency Labour Party in the city. But it took an extended process to set Tommy on the course that he would become known for. He explained this in part by recalling that people joined Labour through family connections rather than explicit political reasons. However, upon arriving at Stirling, he was immediately attracted to the Labour Club and fairly quickly – via it – to Militant.[48]

Growing Politicisation and Militant[49]

Showing signs of further conscious politicisation, Tommy recalled that his first essays were too 'polemical', by which he meant they took conscious positions when his lecturers advised him to be 'more objective'. Early on he read Ralph Miliband's two seminal books, *The State in Capitalist Society* and *Parliamentary Socialism: a study of the politics of Labour*, as well as Trotsky's *History of Russian Revolution*. What this reading alerted him to was that 'history' was either that of the victor or the vanquished. According to Tommy, studying what he termed 'labour history' allowed him to add an extra dimension to his knowledge and understanding of the world which modern studies had not given him: 'We learned about Martin Luther but not Malcolm X, Waterloo [but] not Peterloo'[50] as well as coming across the ideas of Karl Marx and Marxism. So '[h]ere was a new theory, a view of the world which related to my own experiences. Everything came together [and] I began to enjoy the idea of education in and of itself ... totally convinced of Marxism as an outlook on life'.[51] For Tommy, this education 'was a politically-transforming experience',[52] especially because he 'learned that [Marxism] was not fairy-tale idealism'. Put simply, he believed that his degree helped him to understand as a Marxist 'how things work'. Later on he recalled: 'The more I read of Marx on the course and the more I discussed the practical application of Marxism, the more convinced I became that it was a philosophy which was an excellent guide to life and offered an explanation of society which had been lacking'.[53]

The other side to this process of education was the one that took place outwith the classroom and university degree reading list. It was coming across Militant within the Labour Party. According to his mother,[54] the turning point happened 'when he came home from Stirling university [after his first semester] ... he [had] decided to join the Militant Tendency ... we were all in the Labour Party ... we all thought what Labour and the unions were about – should have been about – was changing society'. Being inside and part of Labour made Militant more appealing because it seemed far more to be part of the wider labour movement, rather than standing awkwardly outside it like many other of the Trotskyist groups like the WRP or SWP as well as the Communist Party (even though it orientated upon Labour and worked with the Labour left). This added to a sense that Militant was 'real' Labour, being about what Labour should have been about. But there was also the aspect to Militant that appealed in a different way to Tommy, whereby it was practically engaged in communities and used direct action in a way that other far left groups were not and did not.

Feeling a bit of a fish out water at university and even in the Labour Club itself, Tommy found he had more in common with the student and non-student members of Militant (than other left groups) because of a common social background and lifestyle. Suffice it to say, its membership was less influenced by the hothouse effect of student politics, which at a campus university like Stirling can become all the more accentuated. Student politics can be very introverted on student issues at the same time as being disconnected from the outside world even when non-student issues are addressed. With its student section more orientated on Labour and the labour movement than many other far left groups, and the Militant branch for the university being part of the town branch (that met in the town), Tommy found the politics as well as social background and dress sense of Militant more comfortable, more appealing and less challenging.[55] For example, he commented: 'Militant was more working class' and 'the class issues of wages and so on were more to the fore and this made the Militant an easier organisation for working class people to drift into'. But there were also other helpful aspects. Tommy warmed to Militant's overly economistic, mechanistic approach to politics as well as to revolution being created through Militant conquering Labour and parliament rather than the 'big bang' of the October 1917 Russian revolution. Militant gave Tommy a sense of certainty for its politics were clear, unambiguous and predictive (as Trotskyism tended to be).

During holidays from university, Tommy got some temporary jobs like being a health instructor one summer. But he kept up his involvement with Militant, in 1982 going to hear Terry Fields – soon to be an MP – in Pollok. Militant was relatively strong in the wider Pollok constituency[56] before it became synonymous with Tommy so his connection to it was less of 'a flash in the pan' bound up with the new found freedom of being at university and away from home. What seemed to really make an impact upon Tommy above all else was the connection of Scotland, Glasgow, Militant and Marxism: '[W]hen you read about Marx, or learn about revolutions elsewhere, it seems very far away'.[57] So 'Red Clydeside' of the Clyde Workers Committee, the rent strikes, the Independent Labour Party, the apprentice strikes and the UCS work-in was a revelation to Tommy. Above all else, the figure of John Maclean made a huge impact. For Tommy, it was 'vital to have this sense of history and pride – something to relate to'.[58] More significantly for Tommy, it told him that revolt and resistance had been done before in his own backyard, and critically could be done again.

His politicisation was an extended process. But the event that put 'theory' and 'ideas' into practice was the 1984–1985 miners' strike. As Tommy recalled later on in this regard: 'It's one thing talking on the sidelines, but it's another proving what you can do on the pitch'.[59] Even while a member of the Militant at university, football remained his first love (along with karate and running). He would put it before reading the latest Militant pamphlet, and commented he was 'not really politically committed even after joining Militant'.[60] So while he attended many Militant meetings and did some of the suggested reading, he said he was 'not an activist' at this point. However, returning to Pollok for his later summer holidays from university, the deindustrialisation and accompanying impoverishment of his neighbourhood became apparent to him.[61] It was this, the 1983 Stockport Messenger dispute between Eddie Shah and the NGA print union and then the miners' strike that brought home to Tommy the need not only to be active but to see the possibility of how a different social order could be created from workers' struggles. Attending the mass picketing at the Stockport

Messenger where its workers were confronted by mass ranks of police, he saw what he believed was clear evidence of the class war and the beginnings of a paramilitary era.[62] Thus: 'I remember[ed] comparing it with the steel strike a couple of years before, when there was just a bit of pushing and shoving between bobbies and the picket line. Now all of a sudden you had a paramilitary force of riot police on the streets. Here, in front of your eyes, was the class struggle'.[63] This view was further reinforced by the miners' strike. To him, the miners' strike was not only a 'civil war without guns' as Militant described it but also 'the harbinger of a new society'.[64] This was because the year long struggle waged by the miners was against profit and for social need and because the response of the Tories and the state took the metaphorical blinkers off many people's eyes about what was happening in Britain, with thousands upon thousands of these becoming active to support the miners.

Before returning to university for his last year in September 1984, Tommy had started visiting the picketline at the Killoch colliery in Ayrshire along with the likes of future actor, Gary Lewis. Upon returning to university, Tommy – along with others – started visiting their nearest pit that needed support on the picketline, this being Castlehill in Fife. Visits to the picketline – where he was arrested three times[65] – furnished the miners with physical solidarity to help shut down working pits while bucket collections raised money as the Thatcher government attempted to force the miners back to work through destitution. 'Becom[ing] embroiled in the miners' strike ... [meant] much less time on [my] studies' as a result of being an organiser for students visiting the picketline. The grateful response of the miners to this solidified his commitment. Tommy called this: 'a baptism of fire ... a coming of age politically' by putting ideas put into practice as up until then: 'I was probably just playing with politics'. Alan McCombes remembers Tommy's seriousness, drive and potential of that time.

But there was another reason why Tommy thought that the miners' strike was a harbinger of a new society – this was because the experience of fighting and mobilisation, in his view, prepared working class communities for the battle over the poll tax.[66] But before that, when he returned home from university after graduating in 1985, fully politicised by the experience of the miners' strike, he became very active in Labour in Pollok, recruiting members to it and to Militant. In the course of this activity, he met again a former school mate, George McNeilage. Helped by Tommy, George found a purpose in, and understanding of, life, turning himself from a drug-using, substance-abusing petty criminal to student, footballer and active socialist.[67] George went so far as to say: 'Tommy saved my life'.[68] Of their time together, Tommy recounted: '[t]here's been a bond between us ever since'[69] and that being in Militant gave George self-confidence and self-respect. Come the run-up, in 1987, to the introduction of the poll tax, George and a host of others alongside Tommy were in a position to start discussing what it represented – a transferral of wealth from poor to rich – and how to resist it. They developed their understanding of the poll tax as a means by which the Tories sought to undermine 'municipal socialism', a local form of the welfare state based on collectivism and progressive taxation. For the poll tax revolt, the resisters had a key advantage compared to other opposition movements to the Tories because the implementation of the poll tax depended upon citizens' cooperation and because it affected the mass of people in the same way at the same time.

Graduating with joint honours in economics and politics,[70] Tommy was not interested in the milk rounds of employers signing students up to their graduate entrance programmes although he had some fleeting interest in investigative journalism, being impressed by John Pilger, and also in joining the fire service. Instead, he said: 'I wanted to be full-time revolutionary' and had already been approached to be a Militant full-timer for youth work. Alan McCombes backed him for this post as what was required here was motivating people rather than being an organiser of people.[71] Yet Tommy also wanted to work for a year to get some work experience and not move straight to being a full-timer. To this end, he worked for Strathclyde Regional Council for a year on a hypothermia programme where he joined the National Union of Public Employees (NUPE) and became a shop steward. After this he took up the post of west of Scotland full-time youth organiser, signing on the dole to do this.[72] By 1987, he was nominated for Militant's Central Committee as part of an enlarged Scottish section of a single national slate created by the national leadership around Peter Taaffe. This was ahead of many other longstanding members including some of the sixteen-odd full-time Militant organisers in Scotland.[73] The leadership's reasoning for his accelerated rise was that Tommy had shown tremendous potential leadership for such a young comrade through his skills of oratory in the anti-Youth Training Scheme *Youth Trade Union Rights Campaign*, the anti-Benetton campaign and the March for Jobs activities.[74] Tommy's subsequent election that year to the Central Committee was primarily the outcome of the actions of Bob Wylie, the leader of Militant in Scotland and a future BBC journalist and media relations officer. Tommy recalled: 'Bob was a big inspiration to me and a big guide to me politically ... I was groomed by Bob for a higher leadership role'.

Much of Tommy's growing political stature by this time resulted from his power of oratory. Although many might be able to deliver the same content and message, the intensity of delivery gave him an almost unrivalled edge. He reflected:

By ages of 19 or 20, I realised I had a talent for speaking ... I was encouraged by the Militant to learn about something and then speak about it ... I realised I had a talent for projecting my voice [and] my emotions but I also learnt things ... I would write things out ... Militant encouraged the format of attack capitalism, then the Tories, then Labour, then the soft left then put our position which became a shell for any speech ... I had a strong voice, and probably an authoritative voice ... I never had any formal training even in Militant ... it just developed ... [and] took off with the poll tax.

Some of this ability Tommy put down to 'always [having] been quite confident, a good talker, a good socialiser because these things were encouraged in our household ... always had loads of people around me', and which rings true of some of his mother's comments. It is from these days that a number of close-at-hand observers recall that Tommy honed his speaking style of 'keeping the message simple' and making the same basic two or three points in different ways but over and over again.

The Poll Tax

But before the battle proper to axe the poll tax began, Tommy were involved in another series of actions that further honed some of the tactics and skills he would later use to good effect, whether these be supporting the Caterpillar workers' occupation of their plant to stop its closure or the direct action of a sit-in of Benetton's Glasgow shop in protest against their policy on apartheid.[75]

Tommy was not at the forefront of the policy-making process by which Militant adopted the 'Don't pay, don't collect, don't comply' strategy as he made clear in *A Time to Rage*[76] – he was still too young and too junior in Militant at that stage of late 1987/early 1988 to play such a role. Indeed, when Militant in Scotland was deciding its policy, Tommy was for non-registration.[77] Rather, this policy decision was made by older cadre like Chic (Charles) Stevenson (who was to become a councillor) in late 1987, and the Scottish and British full-time Militant leadership (and ratified at its April 1988 special Scottish conference). For example, in the spring of 1988, Militant full-timer, Alan McCombes, wrote a pamphlet called *How to Fight the Poll Tax*. In practice, Militant centred its strategy upon a community-based campaign of non-payment (as opposed to non-registration by citizens and non-collection by local authority finance workers) and this was crucial to the revolt's success. This along, with the size of Militant and its leadership of the anti-poll tax struggle – even though in Glasgow as elsewhere other APTUs had been started either before the one in Pollok or alongside it and by other political forces on the left – helped explain why the revolt from below was successful. In so doing, the revolt outflanked and brushed aside the respectable, mainstream offerings from Labour and its political allies in the STUC (called variously 'Stop It' and 'Return to Sender' with its eleven minute 'at the eleventh hour' strike). Donald Dewar, then Labour leader but not yet 'father of the nation', told campaigners and Labour members that they could not pick and choose which laws to obey and which laws to break. As leader of Labour in Scotland, with some 50 MPs and still chasing the prospect of power in Westminster, Dewar stated that no matter how immoral, unfair and unjust the law here was, it had to be obeyed until Labour could rescind it when it entered office. To him, breaking the law merely postponed the day of winning office no matter the cost and hardship along the way. The old slogan of the London Poplar councillors of 'better to break the law than break the poor'[78] came back into vogue. In so doing, the revolt from below also packed more of a punch than the Scottish Labour Left's Committee of One Hundred and the SNP's non-payment campaign which were both based on the strategy of 'can [afford to] pay, won't pay'. Such a strategy, while maybe well intentioned, did not seek to mobilise the mass of people into what could be a powerful force. Instead, the politicians and the great and the good offered to try to fight their fight for them. Along the way, Tommy in particular stood accused by his opponents of hurting the poor. In a contortion of moral logic, those encouraging non-payment were accused by Labour, Liberal and Tory politicians of being responsible for cuts in local government services and raising the level of the poll tax.

Militant made community resistance the centre point of its strategy for a number of reasons. Although it did attempt to win unions and organised workers to the non-payment campaign, it recognised unions were in a weaker position as collective fighting organisations than before and most national union leaderships supported Labour's stance. Furthermore, Militant did not believe that Labour councils could be relied upon not to collect the tax, nor National and Local Government Officers (NALGO) members not to process payments. Where attention was given to union and Labour members, it was at the grassroots level which was compatible with mobilising the mass of ordinary citizens.

Along with George McNeilage and others, Tommy founded the Pollok APTU in April 1988 following the holding of a 400-strong meeting called by the Pollok Unemployed Workers' Group – the 'front' that Militant used to call the meeting in the face of hostility from the local Labour MP – on fighting the poll tax. Tommy became its secretary.

The success of the meeting gave Tommy and his Militant comrades the platform to go elsewhere in city to found APTUs. A sense of community cohesion and developing resistance as well as intense activity springs from pages of *A Time to Rage* as the original APTU in Pollok became subdivided into one for each area which were then organised into a Pollok federation. The Strathclyde APT Federation was established on 10 July 1988 with 330 delegates from 96 community groups, union branches and APTUs.[79] Tommy was elected its secretary and a non-Militant Labour member the chair. Around this time, Keith Baldassara came on the scene in Glasgow, having been sent up to Scotland by Militant's leadership from London. Together with Tommy, George and Keith in particular formed a close working relationship in all their anti-poll tax activities. George recounted he became known as 'Tommy's right hand man'. The Scottish Federation of Anti-Poll Tax Unions was established a little later with Tommy as its chair.

By late 1988 and with the deadline of 1 April 1989 approaching when the poll tax would come into force, only the Federation and Militant were now advocating mass non-payment. The battle to keep the Federation to non-payment was a long, hard battle as some forces on the left like the SWP wrongly dismissed community-based resistance as unable to sustain itself. The first key staging post in the revolt in Glasgow and Scotland was the Federation's first demonstration, attracting some 15,000 marchers on 18 March 1989. Tommy declared afterwards that the revolt had lit the touch paper and now the flame had to be fanned into a bigger fire. Guessing the mood correctly, helping cohere it into a fighting force as well as providing its leadership meant that strategy, tactics and mobilisation were vital. Mass mobilisation through phone trees, flying pickets and occupations became the order of the day. Through a long, hard slog of meetings and activities non-payment was built up until it reached epic proportions of between 500,000 to a million in late 1989/early 1990 in Scotland. Indeed, such was the demand for Tommy to speak at meetings far and wide in Scotland and south of border, he was often double booked so that the chair of the Strathclyde APT Federation would speak in his place.[80] The first poinding (for non-registration) was successfully stopped in summer of 1989.[81] By November 1990, some one and a quarter million citizens in Scotland had stopped paying, and on 25 November 1989 in Manchester the All-Britain APT Federation was formed with Tommy as its chair.

Alongside non-payment, the other highpoint of the revolt were the mass demonstrations on 31 March 1990.[82] In Glasgow, some 40,000 marched with around 200,000 in London.[83] Tommy spoke at both post-demonstration rallies. It was the London demonstration that became notorious because of the violence between protestors and police. Tommy condemned the violence of some protestors and of the police but not those that fought back against the police brutality.[84] This became contentious as anarchists and some on the left called him a 'grass'.[85] Nonetheless, the riot as an embodiment of mass revolt, along with divisions on Europe within the Tories,[86] helped seal the fate of Prime Minister and Tory leader, Margaret Thatcher, when she resigned on 22 November 1990 as well as that of the poll tax itself.[87] Indeed, Tommy predicted earlier in March 1990 that the poll tax and Thatcher would be brought down by 'people power'. Ironically, looking ahead before the poll tax riot, Tommy commented: 'My long-term future is perhaps a bit more of a grey matter'.[88] The irony was that Tommy spent the next few years still fighting the poll tax in terms of poindings and warrant sales as various councils carried on collecting debt from defaulters and non-payers. In the course of campaigning against the poll tax, Tommy established relations with the SNP, especially then left wingers, Jim Sillars, and future MSP, Kenny MacAskill, because he was excluded from Labour and Labour had set its face against non-payment. This indicated an ability to work with others of different political persuasions on the left. However, the more important close personal and political relationships he established in this period were with Alan McCombes, the emerging theoretician and strategist, and Keith Baldassara and George McNeilage.

So neither Tommy nor Militant 'jumped' on the poll tax bandwagon as many detractors alleged. Rather, they were the main horses pulling the wagon and giving it direction. Tommy and his fellow travellers within and without Militant saw nothing odd in this accusation from political opponents nor in the reality of the revolt, for often the highpoints of history have been explicitly created and driven by the massed ranks of the grassroots below. Indeed, Tommy and Militant saw their role with the poll tax as being similar to the Communist Party-led National Unemployed Workers' Movement in the 1920s and 1930s (which led the Hunger Marches).[89] This also makes the point, despite accusations to the contrary, that the Strathclyde and Scottish Anti-Poll Tax Federations were not Militant 'fronts' for the scale of the effort involved and the size of the organised, collective civil disobedience meant no group as relatively small as Militant could substitute itself for these organisations nor operate as they did as mass democratic and participative bodies.

Expulsion from Labour

Being an increasingly high profile and influential Militant activist, especially on the poll tax, had marked Tommy's card. His expulsion from the

Labour Party was initiated by a request in 1988 from the sitting Labour MP, Jimmy Dunnachie, for the party's national executive committee to investigate the activities of Tommy as the secretary of the North Pollok branch of the constituency Labour Party in Pollok. This began a process of an investigation on 31 August 1988 led by Joyce Gould, Labour Party Director of National Organisation. Based in London, Gould travelled to Glasgow to interview a number of Labour members (including Tommy on 2 February 1989). The charge was essentially of being a member of an entryist organisation – that is, being part of a party within a party with Militant having its own parallel structures, staff, policies, newspaper and finance. Militant spokesperson, Bob Wylie, branded Gould as a McCarthyite 'witchfinder general' and pointed to the existence of other internal groupings across the political spectrum within Labour. Tommy called Gould a 'witchhunter general' and vowed to tell her: 'the Labour Party should be spending its time and resources fighting the Tories instead of investigating people building a campaign against the poll tax'.[90] Following the investigation into Tommy and others including Lynn Sheridan, Gould's report found that party rules had been breached and recommended that Labour's national constitutional committee consider the case for expulsion. Action was taken against Tommy before the others, leading him to comment in a characteristically bullish way: 'It's nothing more than a web of gossip, hearsay, and lies. I'm disgusted that I am suspended before the constitutional committee meeting. It's like saying: 'Here's the verdict, now we'll have the trial''.[91]

Since returning from university, Tommy had helped revitalise and grow the almost moribund branch by recruiting in excess of 100 new members as well as gaining support for policies to the left of the current leadership, which included poll tax non-payment. He would also become something of an unofficial councillor in the course of these activities as he and Militant were developing a reputation for resolving local grievances. According to Alice Sheridan, it was a case of: 'Get the Militant as they'll do things, sort it out, bring it attention'. By 1988, the North Pollok branch had become the biggest in the constituency. The likelihood of the investigation leading to expulsion – as it had done for the leadership of Militant in 1983 despite Labour always having been a 'broad church' – was met with what would become a typically robust response from Tommy. He and his comrades in the branch and constituency decided to challenge Dunnachie at the forthcoming re-selection, and to make the whole process as public as possible. So the question he led on was why the Labour leadership was willing to so ferociously attack socialists and not the Tories. In order to make sure they could win the reselection, Tommy and his allies like George McNeilage recruited more to the party but many were refused when their applications were submitted. This response and the forthcoming expulsion were the beginnings of the end of Labour as the 'people's party' imbued with a social democratic ideology and a mass membership of working class citizens. Social democracy was not socialism but it did believe that the process of market and its outcomes had to be moderated and ameliorated. Under Neil Kinnock, the party began its journey to become a party of social liberalism of the 'Third Way' (a variant of neo-liberalism).[92] Or, as Tommy, put it:

> Thatcherism exposed the savage nature of capitalism. This is what Labour wanted to emulate under Kinnock and still want to emulate under Smith. This is what they want to manage better. Managing capitalism is like managing a slaughterhouse. No matter how efficient you are, no matter how humane, blood is spilled in the end. Slaughterhouses could not exist without death. Capitalism would not exist without exploitation.[93]

The result of the investigation in the summer of 1989 was that Tommy along with all the other activists in Pollok were banned from holding party positions, that all members of the North Pollok branch be suspended and that Tommy be charged with bringing Labour into disrepute. He was expelled in October 1989 for five years just as he secured a branch nomination to stand against Dunnachie. Given the closeness of the previous selection contest, it seems credible to suggest that some of Dunnachie's motivation here was to prevent a challenge for the nomination from Tommy. Tommy then pledged to reapply for membership when the ban had elapsed and as late as July 1991 commented that he still supported Labour[94] but events later that year, namely, the creation of SML, intervened.

Looking back upon his expulsion many years later in 2004, Tommy reasoned that the expulsions of the Militant leadership (in the form of its editorial board) in 1983, those in Liverpool around Derek Hatton and Tony Mulhearn's effective leadership of the council and over the poll tax led him to question Militant's entryist strategy. Thus: 'I think on reflection it was a loosening of my political perspective of the whole Militant outlook ... while I accepted the need for subterfuge to secretly organise ... I found it difficult to lie ... if you are going to be honest with the class it seemed a bit odd ... [and especially] when we engaged in much more public work ... it became stupid'. This attitude would form a crucial part of the rationale for Militant in Scotland striking out on its own as an independent political party.

Balance Sheet of the Early Years

By all accounts, Tommy had developed into quite a remarkable individual by his mid-twenties. His notoriety of being a remarkable young man was that he was also a leading socialist and working class fighter and one that was making an impact for these causes. In other words, he applied his considerable skills and talents to these causes. In charting and explaining his development, it is worth taking stock and pausing for reflection on where he stood by this young age.

Politics

His family background, his mother and Militant gave Tommy a basic (working) class instinct through which to interpret the world. In particular, he owes a great debt to the politics of Militant for his basic political worldview of class exploitation and class antagonism (although as he would show later he was not trapped by Militant's version of this but could develop onwards from it). As he saw Labour, dominated by the right, 'selling out' whatever socialist soul it had, Tommy also saw Militant as a worthy successor to the ILP which gave Labour its soul.[95] There was a definite sense that the politics Tommy developed in the 1980s focussed concretely upon the basic concerns of many working class people, even if the approach to them was grounded in the transitional method (see below). It was this combination of politics and associated practice that made him seem more authentically working class than leading activists from other far left organisations. Their politics did not spring organically from the concerns of the council estate and as a consequence their activities had not only less of a focus upon this arena but less purchase overall. To such working class people, these other organisations' politics seemed distant, remote and not connected to them. Ideas of revolutionary socialism, workers councils, state capitalism and permanent revolution seemed somewhat impractical and far-fetched when faced with rising damp and increasing rents. By contrast, the outward politics of Militant and Tommy eschewed the 'high' political theory associated with these other organisations and concentrated upon economistic concerns. Coming from a working class background in Pollok, the importance of decent housing and employment, and their inter-relationship, had all the more been keenly impressed upon him. Rather than simply parrot that drug use would be reduced with higher levels of employment, the politics of Militant led its members to work to maintain and extend community facilities as an alternative to dependence upon drugs (and the crime to fund them) for young people.[96] As a result, a 300-strong 'Just say no' rally against drugs, house break-ins and gang fighting was organised by Tommy, George and Keith and others in February 1990 in Pollok.[97]

All this tapped into the heart of municipal and state socialism – or 'old' Labour as it would become known in time – and emphasised both that at this point most working class people still looked to Labour as the 'people's party' *and* that Militant positioned itself within Labour as the radical heir to this mantle. Better than any other example, this was expressed most successfully through the poll tax organised revolt, a revolt of pounds and pence and anti-Thatcherism. The transitional method, referred to above and originated by Trotsky, comprises a strategy to use the fighting for certain demands to raise workers' consciousness to a more advanced level and, thus, more ambitious demands. Ultimately, rising demands become such that they cannot be met within the confines of capitalism and so the mass of workers understand the need, and are prepared to fight, for socialism. Of this method, Tommy said:

My whole political perspective is based on the transitional method ... because we are not going to take the whole of the working class from A to Z without having to go through the whole of the alphabet ... raise demands to show that they are not realisable under capitalism ... but the best ones are those that can be realised and build confidence and opens people's eyes to the possibility.

Applied to housing in Glasgow in the late 1980s/early 1990s, Tommy opined: 'Our 'Cancel the Debt – Don't Pay the Interest' campaign will radicalise those who get involved. They will ask, How do we cancel the debt? We break the law. Then they will ask: Who is the debt paid to? The banks. Fine, let's nationalise the banks. So you move from a local concrete demand for dry warm housing to challenge capitalism's economic foundations'.[98]

That said, Tommy's politics had a fantastical side to them, and this led him to consistently over-estimate[99] the extent and depth of politicisation of working class people from the poll tax, given that relatively few of the hundreds of thousands of resisters either joined Militant or became activists – or stayed the course in either.[100] *The Guardian* reported him as: 'Now he believes he is leading a campaign which will end in the triumph of socialism'.[101] This was not Tommy's fault alone for at the time, Peter Taaffe, Militant leader, prophesised that Britain was entering the 'red nineties'.[102] Again this was not borne out by subsequent events in either Labour or society as a whole.[103] At the heart of this misdiagnosis lay two phenomena. The first was that the impact of the defeats of workers and the left in the 1980s upon collective consciousness and confidence was not wiped out by the anti-poll tax victory. The second was that some limited social reform was possible even within neo-liberalism and as the economy grew. The two came together in the birth and rule of 'new' Labour.

Militant's political culture (as with other far left organisations) along with Tommy's ebullient and confident personality led him also to a tendency to use bombast and hyperbole. For example, he claimed in 1991 in relation to the Labour-controlled Glasgow City Council: 'Make no mistake, this move to ban us [the Scottish Anti-Poll Tax Federation] from hiring schools is the political practice of fascism'.[104] Another, amongst others, was his claim that the defeat of the poll tax was 'the defeat of Thatcher and the state' for this ignored the impact of Tory divisions on Europe and the continuation of Thatcherism and the (capitalist) state. Whilst providing colour to his voice and sound bites for the media (see below) as well as inspiring some activists and potential activists, this style also repelled some because of its exaggeration and embellishment. For example, David Archibald recounted: 'He was somebody who always tended to make outlandish claims about what would get done ... there was always a certain element of bravado attached to [him] ... it was quite important to Tommy to be seen the best and strongest'. Taking what Tommy said with a pinch of salt also meant for some taking Tommy with a pinch of salt.

Drive and Energy

With the poll tax as with many other activities in this early period, Tommy threw himself into activity and campaigning, whether inside or outside Militant, with vigour and drive. This meant amongst other things speaking at countless meetings in Scotland and then in England. At the height of the poll tax revolt, he was speaking five or six nights a week, often with much travelling to get to these and on his tod. Colin Fox recalled that Tommy was 'in demand [to do] meetings constantly' where:

> What was incredible about Tommy was that he doing the same meetings, the same speeches day in day out, night in and night out ... what strikes you is the stamina, the energy, the performance and putting his own life secondary when there was massive repetition ... [and] when sometimes you don't get the size of the audience you've been promised.

Generally, Tommy worked seven days a week as a political activist, with many of these being long days. The gaps, few and far in between, were for football, family and socialising. His commitment to intense activism was facilitated by being as often as not single at the time. With the energy and vigour of youth and newly found intense political commitment, Tommy recalled that he neither felt any sense of fatigue nor noticed the repetition of giving the same speeches over and over again: 'I didn't notice it because it was what needed to be done and I was proud to be doing it'. Some of this energy no doubt came from being physically fit (through playing football and running) as well as being a 'conviction' politician with a big political vision and a disciplined mind. Moreover, Militant tended to encourage a respect for physical fitness as a sign of working class people having respect and pride for themselves – as working class people – as well as to be able to prosecute their class interests.

Character and Presence

Later in his life, some observed that Tommy had become a good actor – almost like a method actor – who could play the part of 'Tommy Sheridan'. The characters of 'Tommy – the man of the people' with the 'common touch' and socialist tribune began to be developed, perhaps unconsciously, at this early age. Able to articulate and project passion, empathy and charisma, along with reason and intellect, he found a winning combination. Militant and Alice Sheridan helped give him an outlook of certainty and knowing on the world. In many social situations, Tommy developed the Clintonesque-like charismatic ability when speaking to people of making them feel that he was only and intensely concerned with them – that he was only speaking to them. This trait is one that very few have.[105] No less real for the creation of this public personae – compared to the 'wee daft boy' that Gail sees (see later) – this character was an authentic and powerful one. His mother defined the humility that she saw Tommy having 'as the surrendering of his ego ... for something bigger than himself ... he does not know it but he has'. Yet no matter how politically driven left-wing activists are, and especially given the likely material and financial deprivations involved over a long period of time as a result of their activities, they need to personally gain something from their political activity such as affirmation of the self or their chosen purpose in life. For Tommy, the reward and incentive of being a socialist leader was: 'I'm doing what I want to do ... and I get paid for it ... it's like a vocation'. But there is more to it than this. Thus, the sense of making more of a difference than others because of leadership roles, being a mover and a shaker, being in the limelight and at the centre of action need to be added. Even at this stage, Tommy was no mere ordinary activist. Indeed, it is the sense of ego that spurs on the sense of purpose, propelling it to a higher level, and making it realisable (subject to wider social forces). None of this is necessarily untoward because sense of the self is a key component of being able to lead a social agency for change. So, personal satisfaction and gratification as well as the buzz of being at the centre of things and in demand are important components here. Compared to what he was to become later, Tommy reflected: 'Back then I thought of myself as small cog in the machine that would be a catalyst for change ... I didn't see myself as the person that would lead the change or be part of the leadership'. Although it may seem overly self-deprecating, the small cog in the machine at this stage was at the level of not ordinary (Militant) membership or activism but actually one of junior leadership.

Public Speaking

In line with her view of Tommy as 'special' and somewhat God-given, Alice Sheridan saw his oratorical ability as a 'gift' albeit one 'which he developed ... [with] passion and reason ... [because it] isn't just shouting and bawling but about light and shade, humour, using examples, being good with one-liners'. Although Tommy was not unwilling to admit to his prodigious talent here, it was in a rather self-deprecating manner: 'If I have any talent I think it's for public speaking'[106] and 'That's my forte, speaking to the crowd'.[107] Tommy's style, honed in the battle against the poll tax, was to exhort, inspire and motivate. According to his comrades of the time, Tommy was an outstanding speaker – by being straight talking and hard hitting – but he was not the best. That 'honour' went to Bob Wylie.[108] Tommy's analysis of how he developed his skill was rather more prosaic than his mother's explanation: '[During the poll tax revolt,] my style became finely honed ... because I was saying the same thing over and over ... I didn't need notes as it was in my heart and in my head'. So his public speaking skills, along with his ability to avoid nervousness,[109] were refined through addressing thousands of public meetings, mass meetings, street meetings and demonstrations, especially in the cut and thrust of the anti-poll tax unions. Comrades of the time like Jim McVicar recalled how his delivery became more polished as time went on without the basic message changing. Hallmarks of his delivery were passion and volume – and for some almost shouting – but also repeatedly making a small number of points in different ways.[110] In terms of content, Tommy's skills related to both members of the public with lower levels of consciousness as well as activists (campaigns, Labour and Militant) with higher levels of consciousness where different arguments and levels of arguments, and different mixtures of the heart and head, were appropriate. Whatever his audience, the intention was to inspire active resistance.

Tommy's style and nature of speaking was learnt from Militant and this included a keen nose for using as many available facts, figures and research from mainstream sources – whether government, newspapers or academics – in the belief not that knowledge is power but rather that it is a power resource when it helps to lead to collective action.[111] One of the themes Tommy developed for himself was to use facts and figures to both create and justify righteous anger. Another was he would always try to use local examples and everyday experience to convey a tangible sense of what the facts and figures meant for his audience. When speaking in public, particularly to an audience that has consciously chosen to come to hear him and him only (such as a public meeting), Tommy concurred that he got a 'buzz' from being able to do what he did and in doing so hold them in an intense rapture for the duration of his speech. However, David Archibald remembered that Tommy's style was 'not about posing questions or challenging the intellectual arguments [of opponents]. You won't leave the meeting with questions in your head – that's not what Tommy's trying to do, he's trying to generate an emotional response which he is very good at.'

Media Relations and Reception

In the initial stages of the poll tax revolt, Tommy as the leading voice was shut out from media or when he or the anti-poll tax opposition were mentioned, it was with disdain and criticism.[112] For example, he lamented the fact that he held weekly press conferences on anti-poll tax activities but these were not always well attended by journalists. To get the message across to working class people, leaflets, placards and painted walls were used, requiring a constant round of raising money to pay for these and then producing and distributing them. While these methods of communication for propaganda, agitation and action were not to be forsaken, Tommy pioneered the development of productive relations with what most socialists had taken to be an inherently hostile capitalist media. This testified to an ability not only take a more nuanced view but also to be capable of implementing it too, and speaks to Tommy's creative deployment of his powerful and persuasive personality. In other words, early on he understood the need to go beyond the formal means of mere press releases and press conferences. Reflecting on this, Tommy recalled particularly with regard to the *Evening Times* (with Ron McKenna working there):

My attitude was we needed them ... this was different to the usual
disdain of other comrades [which] was counter-productive ...
What I found was that if we gave them stories, we got a good
bite at the cherry [next time] ... [Coverage] gave us profile ... it
allowed us an avenue to talk to the class as a whole even if it was
one that wasn't entirely clean or forthright. The relationship with
the Evening Times meant they didn't give us an easy ride but
they were less antagonistic than you would have expected from a
mainstream paper ... [You have to remember the Evening Times]
was the working class paper [of Glasgow] ... what they liked
about me was that the story was a working class boy from Pollok,
from the scheme, taking on the Labour establishment.

In other words, through his own direct experience and interaction, Tommy
started working out which journalists to build relationships with and how,
and what interested them. Media interest in the poll tax rebellion south
of the border took off after the poll tax riot and many smaller skirmishes
outside town halls in England at meetings which set the rates. This led to
the British media at large finding Tommy and allowing him the platform
to shine in this recognised role as anti-poll tax figurehead and spokesperson. For example, the *Guardian* reported on Tommy as an individual,
recognising him as being 'bright and articulate' with 'good looks and
charm' as well as dedicated with a somewhat monastic life.[113] However,
it also reported on his opponents like Jimmy Dunnachie MP of accusing him of being 'enormously egocentric' and others of him being head-
strong, uncontrollable, too quick to denounce and unable to debate.[114]

So Tommy became an adept media performer. As outlined elsewhere, being photogenic and very personable were key assets in making Tommy and what he had to say sufficiently colourful and interesting
to the media that they chose to cover it. Playing to the Robin Hood or
folk hero image, he often referred to himself as the 'wee boy fae [from]
Pollok'. Early on he developed an ability to deploy what are now called
'sound bites', namely, short punchy statements and phrases that use
alliteration, not only to get a message across but make it quotable for
the media. So of those who defeated the poll tax: 'It was the punters not
the pin-stripe politicians'[115] or Alex Salmond was a 'nationalist Neil
Kinnock'[116] or when on German TV in this period, he said: 'Mrs Thatcher
is Britain's Iron Lady but we will melt down the Iron Lady' through the
poll tax revolt.[117] Later, he would say of her: 'Remember, she had stood
on the steps of Downing Street when elected for her third term and
announced the poll tax legislation was to be her new Government's flag-
ship policy. In the end, it turned out to be her Titanic'.[118] Critics often
take cheap shots against socialists when socialists put key demands

that arise from more complex arguments into edible components called slogans. The cheap shot is the accusation of sloganeering. Understanding this, Tommy considered their use, nonetheless, appropriate when they are 'poignant, poetic and powerful all at once [as long as they are not e]mpty slogans [which] just demoralise'.[119]

Reception and Relations Inside Militant

Tommy's skills were widely recognised within Militant but he also created something of a stir by being prepared to challenge the leadership on tactics – rather than strategy – over youth work and the poll tax, and being seen by some as rather brash and cocky, bordering on arrogant. Tommy often had a sharper nose and could see how things could be better done, like not shoehorning all campaigns under Militant's banner or those of its front organisations. As Militant's strength in Scotland grew and as SML developed, Tommy clashed with the likes of Frances Curran and Ronnie Stevenson on issues of priorities and resources. Consequently, Peter Taaffe, who was responsible for Scotland within Militant, remembers Tommy was 'always a controversial figure right from the first time he entered our ranks'. Some of this was, according to Taaffe, also down to his 'exaggeration of his own personal ability in terms of being able to relate to a certain situation and how his own personality could grate on others'. Nonetheless, Tommy was fortunate that the dropping out of Bob Wylie from his leadership role – after returning from South Africa on Militant work and where his life was threatened – not only created a space for Tommy but a need within Militant for someone with his speaking talents to be able to be a 'front man'. Alan McCombes recalled that the leadership decided to set Tommy to work on the poll tax as its 'figurehead' and 'front man'.[120] When Tommy was put to work on the poll tax, he worked out of the Federation's office which served to emphasise what would become his semi-autonomous style of working (especially from his fellow Militant full-timers). Because of his concentration on the poll tax, Colin Fox recalled: 'He knew the poll tax inside out and could make contributions on that but on other issues he was shallow and rah-rah because he was a rah-rah man ... he was put up to inspire the troops'.

Leadership

Within Militant, Tommy at this stage was not an architect of policy because he was so young in an organisation of many older experienced cadres. The same was true to a large degree in the anti-poll tax movement because Tommy took his cue at this stage from the Militant leadership. It was it which decided to engage in 'open' work, i.e., not working exclusively through Labour by establishing APTUs, and to recruit 'rough' 'untrained' elements from the APTUs into Militant.[121] However, Tommy did become a leader – or as Alan McCombes put it 'his role was as the frontman, the populariser, the spokesperson' – in the field and this then allowed him to begin to influence policy and how it was to be implemented and achieved. As part of this, his early years saw the beginnings of him developing a 'transformational' style of leadership where force of argument and ideology is combined with force of personality to create positive changes in 'followers'.[122] They are transformed into states of being inspired and willing to take actions and do so in certain ways that they would not have otherwise done. Thus, transformational leadership enhances the motivation, morale and performance of followers. The reason why followers are prepared to follow is not because of what they expect to gain personally (in material or status terms) but because of the cause that they believe in. In doing so, the only gains they received are self-affirmation and advancement of their chosen political cause. Therefore, transformational leadership creates significant change in people by reconfiguring and redesigning their perceptions and values. By contrast, the transactional style of leadership is based on notions of material or status exchange where loyalty and action are bought and sold (although not necessarily in monetary terms). Patronage is the obvious practice here. Followers of these leaders only do what they think will benefit them and the leaders know this and work on that basis. The transactional style of leadership is a more nakedly and more necessarily instrumental, rather than ideological, way of operating. Transactional leadership compels a narrower, more sectional view of the world compared to a transformational one. Moreover, transformational leadership creates trust, admiration, loyalty and respect so that followers are prepared to do more than they expected at the outset. In a nutshell, transformational leadership inspires and is often equated with the deployment of charisma in the prosecution of a cause. In far left organisations like Militant amongst others, transformational leaders are not uncommon. Other than Tommy, Bob Wylie and Derek Hatton are examples. Indeed, early on the *Guardian* compared Tommy to Hatton for this type of reason.[123]

As sure as night follows day, it is also self-evident that leaders need followers. Tommy certainly began to have many followers in this period but without them as diligent and consciousness foot soldiers the work and campaigning that he aspired to lead could not have been achieved. These were the people that delivered the leaflets and got others to come to the meetings that Tommy spoke at. But more than this, the relationship was not as unambiguous or as cleanly and clearly delineated as 'leader' and 'followers' would simply suggest for common ideologies adopted by 'leader' and 'followers' as well as some culture of egalitarianism had a levelling impact. In other words, both parties had signed up to a common purpose and there was some evidence at this point of a two-way street of direction and account-ability with the effect that teamwork and mutual dependence became a hallmark of their joint-operation. This made Tommy akin to *primus inter pares* – first amongst equals – at this time.

Conclusion

Putting these traits and strengths together in one person made them greater than the sum of the parts because of the way that one trait height-ened the purchase of another. Putting them together in the context of Militant, Pollok, Glasgow and the poll tax rebellion[124] created a tipping point where Tommy was able to make his mark and become a significant figure. In doing so, he was able to move from becoming a campaigner to a politician as the next chapter shows and, as George McNeilage believed at the time, become a 'new modern John Maclean'. As leader of the poll tax revolt, Tommy led a successful social movement based in commu-nities and based on community action. This was a once in a lifetime accomplishment he would not repeat even though he added others to it.

Notes

1. Many of the political events from 1984 to 1994 are recounted and analysed from the perspective of Militant in Taaffe, P. *The Rise of Militant: Militant's Thirty Years, 1964–1994* (Militant Publications, 1995).
2. Lynn Sheridan became an important activist in Unison at a local level and was active in the Militant and its successors (SML, SSA and SSP) but again at a more local level and not to the extent that Tommy was. Carol Sheridan, according to Alice 'only lat-terly became more political [in attitude rather than activity] in the 2000s'.
3. Some of this is attributable not to his parents separating but rather his mother being the 'disciplinarian in the house because my dad was very easy going' (*ATTR* p. 9). But it was also because, compared to Alice, his dad was, according to Tommy, 'a very passive, easy going guy ... not a particularly political animal ... more a get-on-with-life person' (*ATTR* p. 6) although a member of the Labour Party and, for a short time a shop steward, at his work, Rolls Royce in Hillingdon. Tommy Sheridan's (senior) commitment to community was through managing a local football team, Pollok United. This chimed with Tommy seeing a kind of proto-socialism in community activities (*ATTR* chapter 1, *Scotsman* 25 November 2000).
4. *Scotland on Sunday* 16 January 2000.

5. *Evening Times* 11 October 2002.
6. *Scotland on Sunday* 18 March 2007.
7. *Sunday Express* 5 August 2007.
8. *ATTR* p. 9.
9. 16 January 2000.
10. 16 January 2000. See also *Scotsman* 25 November 2000.
11. An extensive feature on Tommy in the *Herald* (13 March 1995) helped cement the popular perception of him as a folk hero by telling the story of his childhood and youth as a form of political education from his mother (and teachers).
12. 16 January 2000.
13. *Herald* 13 March 1995.
14. *Herald* 27 January 2011.
15. As the matriarch of the family, it seems Alice also instilled into other family members a directly and indirectly supportive environment for Tommy – direct in that Tommy seems to have been supported and encouraged more than his sisters (or at least differently) and indirect in that his sisters were brought up to be mutually supportive of their other siblings.
16. In the *Herald* (13 March 1995), Alice had long maintained there was 'something special' about Tommy. Later she told the *Sunday Mail* (12 July 1998): 'He's a very special human being'.
17. Richie Venton also reported: 'In his childhood, he was regarded by Alice as the chosen one, just about literally in a messianic, religious sense'.
18. All she could proffer was that he did not keep enough time for himself because he was so keen to help others and engage with them (see Chapter 8). Indeed, the sense of specialness felt by Alice can be conveyed in that she appeared to believe Tommy has Jesus-like traits although she never used that term. This should not sound such a bizarre comment to make given the one Richard Holloway made. Alice accepted that Tommy was not a 'thinker like Alan McCombes' but that he was still a 'deep thinker'.
19. Later, Alan McCombes wrote: 'Alice made no bones about her conviction that he [Tommy] was destined to become some kind of political messiah' (*DTTSS* p. 20).
20. Even if Tommy did think he was special, he had the political nous not to say so publically. Keith Baldassara believed that while he has 'quite a comradely relationship' with Alice, he disagrees with her and can be 'quite firm in these disagreements'. Meantime, George McNeilage observed that Tommy would cut over Alice at meetings and be sarcastic and disrespectful towards her.
21. Often Tommy commented that despite his parents separating when he was seventeen, there was no lack of love and emotional warmth in later years: 'My mum was a wonderful mum and my dad was a wonderful dad. They just didn't make much of a couple' (*Scotland on Sunday* 16 January 2000) and that he was probably emotionally spoiled by them (*Scotsman* 25 November 2000), with this resulting from being not just the youngest but also the only boy.
22. Whilst working at the University of Stirling, Tommy came to speak to students about fighting spending cuts in higher education in 1994. In the meeting, I suggested to Tommy that he lead an occupation of the Principal's office by those fifty or so students present in protest at these cuts. He declined to take up the suggestion, highlighting that his boldness was not boundless.
23. *Evening Times* 17 May 2001.
24. *Daily Record* 5 August 2006, *Sunday Mail* 6 August 2006, *Herald* 27 January 2011.
25. Of his mother, Tommy said she was 'quite a spiritual person' (*ATTR* p. 3). Alice used self-healing and alternative forms of therapy (*Evening Times* 11 October 2002) which fits with her particular form of spiritualism.

26. See also *ATTR* p. 9.
27. *Herald* 27 January 2011.
28. 11 April 1999.
29. For example, *Scotsman* 11 August 1999, *Scotland on Sunday* 2 April 2000.
30. *ATTR* p. 11.
31. *Scotsman* 11 August 1999. Later, Tommy would have a job as a car park attendant in the late 1980s (*Mail on Sunday* 6 August 2006).
32. Alice recounted these teachers said Tommy had an 'instinctive sense of understanding'.
33. *ATTR* p. 11.
34. *Holyrood* 22 November 1999.
35. 2 April 2000.
36. 11 August 1999.
37. 12 June 2001.
38. *Scotsman* 11 August 1999. See also *Holyrood* 22 November 1999, *Scotland on Sunday* 2 April 2000.
39. *ATTR* p. 7.
40. *Scotland on Sunday* 2 April 2000, see also *Scotsman* 11 August 1999.
41. *Scotsman* 11 August 1999.
42. *Scotsman* 11 August 1999, *ATTR* p. 12. This included a protest against the visit of the Queen in 1972.
43. *Scotsman* 11 August 1999, see also *ATTR* p. 12.
44. *Scotsman* 5 August 2006. Separately, Tommy reported that his mother gave him a copy of Nan Milton's biography of her father, John Maclean.
45. At Burtons, according to Alice, Tommy was offered a managerial job there as he was so good, with the gift of the gab. Tommy (*ATTR* p. 11) admitted that he had a penchant for selling ties there.
46. *ATTR* p. 11.
47. See McLean, B. 'Labour in Scotland: myth and reality' in Hassan, G. (ed.) *The Scottish Labour Party: history, institutions and ideas* (Edinburgh University Press, 2004), pp. 43–44.
48. It may, thus, be a bit of a stretch to claim in September 1989: 'I have been associated with *Militant* [the newspaper] from the beginning of my political activity' (Sheridan, T. 'Foreword' to Sewell, R. *Battle against the poll tax*, Militant, 1989).
49. Militant was a Trotskyist entrist group within the Labour Party based around the *Militant* newspaper that was first published in 1964. It came to increasing prominence in the late 1970s and early 1980s, leading to the expulsion of its national leadership in 1983, but without breaking its influence in Glasgow, Liverpool and London or defenestrating its three (Labour) MPs. Arguably, the peak of its influence within Labour was reached in the mid- to late 1980s. In 1991, Militant began its break with Labour by becoming Militant Labour and then the Socialist Party of England and Wales in 1997. This signified that no longer did it believe that Labour was the mass party of the working class. While active within Labour, its central political platform was the demand for the nationalisation of the 'commanding heights of the economy' by a Labour government as the major means of achieving a socialist transformation of society. In its view, the Soviet Union had become a 'degenerated' workers' state (see *ATTR* p. 197), requiring a political revolution to restore workers' power.
50. *ATTR* p. 12.
51. *ATTR* p. 12.
52. *ATTR* p. 12.

53. *Herald* 13 March 1995.
54. Alice herself joined Militant after Labour leader, Neil Kinnock, made his speech attacking the Militant leadership of Liverpool City Council at the 1985 Labour conference with the 'grotesque chaos' of a Labour council 'hiring taxis to scuttle round a city handing out redundancy notices to its own workers'.
55. *ATTR* p. 14.
56. For example, in the first round of the reselection battle in Pollok in the run up to the 1987 general election, Bob Gillespie (print union official and father of Bob Gillespie of Primal Scream) secured 30 votes, Davie Churchley, Militant member, 42, and Jimmy Dunnachie 30. In the runoff, the right voted with the soft-left to select Dunnachie by 50 votes to 41. See also Venton, R. 'The Battle for Pollok' in *Our Stand for Socialism* (Militant, 1992), p. 31.
57. *ATTR* p. 14.
58. *ATTR* p. 15.
59. *Herald* 13 March 1995.
60. *ATTR* p. 25. See also *ATTR* p. 14.
61. *ATTR* pp. 15–17.
62. He also helped organise student support for the printers by way of collecting money and organising transport to the picketline.
63. *Herald* 13 March 1995.
64. *ATTR* p. 25.
65. *Daily Record* 20 September 2000.
66. *ATTR* p. 28.
67. In Chapter 2 of *ATTR*, Tommy writes of George in affectionate and empathetic terms. His recounting of George's life changing transition is completely at odds with bringing up his criminal past some twenty five years later in court to mount a character assassination of him. In *ATTR*'s Chapter 7, Tommy recounted how George protected him physically and became a model leader of his community. Later, Tommy somewhat proudly recalled: 'he [George] always says I save his life' by helping him get off heroin.
68. From a conversation on 13 October 2004 at Cuba Norte (Glasgow) press conference for Gordon Gentle, a soldier from Pollok who was unlawfully killed in a roadside bombing in Iraq on 28 June 2004 as a result of a failure to fit electronic countermeasures to the Land Rover he was travelling in.
69. *ATTR* p. 33.
70. Dennis Canavan MSP (*Herald* 13 December 1999) observed that of the three most famous politicians to have emerged from University of Stirling – the others being future Labour cabinet member, John Reid, and future Scottish First Minister, Jack McConnell – Tommy was the only one to have 'stood by his revolutionary principles'.
71. See also *DTTSS* p. 2.
72. Until he became a councillor in 1992, he drew unemployment benefit and other benefits to fund himself as an unpaid but full-time party worker and campaigning activist. The deal was dole plus £10 top-up from Militant. According to George McNeilage: 'money wasn't something that interested him ... as long as he had enough to put petrol in the car to go to a meeting and to eat [he was happy]'. Clothes were supplied either by hand-me-downs from friends or from birthday and Christmas presents. He also attended Cardonald College so that he was registered as a student, ironically for typing, for his Militant youth work amongst further education students (*Scotsman* 5 August 2006, Surhone, L., Tennoe, M. and Henssonow, S. (eds.) *Tommy Sheridan – socialist, politician, solidarity*, Betascript Publishing, 2010, p. 2).
73. This included Colin Fox. Of losing out to Tommy for a seat on the Central Committee, Colin Fox told the perjury trial in 2010 in response to an accusation from Tommy about

some notion of longstanding rivalry between them, 'I got over it'. However, the under-lying issue was about the process by which only one slate – from the leadership – was put to conference. Of portent for later, the Women's Caucus within Militant opposed Tommy's candidature on the grounds of inappropriate sexual behaviour (see also *Herald* 2 February 2011).

74. The painstaking behind-the-scenes building of Militant's youth base in the west of Scotland, in terms of contacts, recruitment, integration and development, was carried out by Colin Fox, Gerry McGuire, Jackie Galbraith, Frances Curran, Willie Griffin and Frank White.

75. The Benetton action was an idea put into Tommy's head by Bob Wylie, and saw Tommy being arrested.

76. *ATTR* p. 38.

77. *ATTR* p. 46. Although Militant supported those that wished not to register, it believed politically and tactically the non-payment battle was the best ground to fight upon (especially as this, unlike non-registration, did not bar the ability to vote in elections).

78. See Booth, J. *Guilty and Proud of it: Poplar's Rebel Councillors and Guardians, 1919–25* (Merlin, 2009).

79. *ATTR* p. 63.

80. *ATTR* p. 114.

81. A poinding is the valuation of eligible household goods by sheriff officers in prepara-tion for a warrant sale of these goods. Sheriff officers are bailiffs, that is, officers of private companies licensed by courts to recover debts.

82. Tommy recalled that being approached by Ricky Ross and Lorraine McIntosh of Deacon Blue and other musicians to play to the marchers was a sign that the anti-poll tax movement had become a significant phenomenon for wider layers.

83. Around this time, Tommy first defended himself in court after being denied legal aid following the charge of breach of the peace for throwing egg at Thatcher in Irvine when she visited the Volvo plant. He was fined £100 which he did pay (*ATTR* p. 119). Alan McCombes suggested there may have been the element of a stunt in throwing the egg (see *DTTSS* p. 6), this contrasting markedly with Tommy's version of events (*ATTR* p. 119).

84. *ATTR* pp. 121–128.

85. See *ATTR* p. 133, *Financial Times* 2 April 1990.

86. Tommy declared with what would become characteristic flourish and exaggeration: 'Thatcher is now politically buried and we have been her buriers. What we have done is stopped the bailiffs, clogged up the courts and made the poll tax unworkable and uncollectable' (*Guardian* 26 November 1990).

87. Unfortunately, defeating the poll tax was only half the battle as its successor, the council tax, was introduced in 1993 and, because of its iniquities, was subject to a further battle led by Tommy to replace it – in Scotland – with a Scottish Service Tax when the Scottish Parliament came into existence from 1999 (see later).

88. *Guardian* 8 March 1990.

89. *ATTR* pp. 73–77.

90. *Herald* 1 February 1989.

91. *Herald* 23 March 1989.

92. See Giddens, A. *The Third Way: The Renewal of Social Democracy* (Polity, 1998).

93. *ATTR* p. 100.

94. *Sunday Times* 21 July 1991.

95. *ATTR* pp. 102–107.

96. This logic, Tommy believed, even extended to road safety as working class kids with nowhere to play often played in the streets but were then the victims of road

accidents or decided to look for their fun elsewhere in the form of drugs and other anti-social behaviour (see *ATTR* p. 240).

97. Comments by Tommy at this rally, George recounted: 'put my life in jeopardy'. Tommy encouraged people to report a family in the area to the police. Fearing being shopped and losing territory, George had a gun put to his head and was hung upside down by his ankles from the top of a tower block by associates of this family. This led to a gun with silencer being acquired by Tommy via his contact with (now reformed) Glasgow gangster, Paul Ferris. To add to the drama, the car in which Tommy was carrying the gun (in the boot) was stopped by police in a routine check as it made its way across Glasgow. Tommy's comments at the rally caused divisions as he did not consult or notify comrades of these. This information emerged at the 9 November 2004 SSP EC meeting where Tommy used it as an example of why socialists should not always be entirely forthcoming about the 'truth' and why socialists had on occasion the need to lie. This event, and others like George covering for Tommy when stopped by police over having stones in his jacket – and while still on bail conditions from Timex – at the anti-BNP march (which became a riot) in Welling, London on 16 October 1993 or George attempting to stop Tommy getting arrested by police at Timex on 22 March 1993, himself getting arrested for this instead, indicated the debt that Tommy had rung up with George.

98. *ATTR* pp. 246–247.

99. It is, thus, somewhat ironic that Tommy wrote that SML can stand accused of underestimating the extent and depth of radicalisation (*ATTR* pp. 230–231).

100. See *ATTR* pp. 230–231, *Daily Record* 11 December 1998.

101. 8 March 1990.

102. *Militant* January 19 1990.

103. Of course, Militant was not alone on the Trotskyist far left in letting its hopes and desires run far ahead of attested reality. Tony Cliff, leader of the SWP, made an equally stupendous and wrong-headed prediction that the 1990s would be like the '1930s in slow motion'.

104. *Independent* 8 December 1991. See also *ATTR* p. 215.

105. Later developments in his life from 2004 would suggest that the foundation of this trait was his political authority. As this waned, then his Clintonesque ability also declined.

106. *ATTR* p. 222.

107. *Sunday Times* 22 March 1992. Later on, as a thundering speaker who seldom needed a microphone, he would get coaching to use his diaphragm more in order to put less strain on his throat (*Sunday Herald* 16 May 2004).

108. There were also others at the time, like Militant organisers Douglas Blackstock and Jackie Gabraith, who were talented speakers.

109. *ATTR* p. 222.

110. The author recalls Tommy's talk at a National Union of Students (NUS) conference at Blackpool in the late 1980s where he topped the ballot for guest speakers and delivered an extremely confident, determined, passionate and rousing speech on fighting the poll tax. He was by far and away the best speaker of that conference and other NUS conferences the author attended before and after it.

111. This is a key part of the process of moving people from anger to action, whereby *anger* leads to *hope* that the wrong can be righted and this then leads to people into *action*. Put more simply, the saying is 'don't just get angry, get even'.

112. See *ATTR* chapters 2 and 3.

113. 8 March 1990.

114. *Guardian* 8 March 1990. The point on debating does not seem to hold water given his subsequent experience as councillor and MSP, especially as he won 'Debater of the Year' at the 2001 *Scottish Politician of the Year* awards.

115. *ATTR* p. 174.

116. *ATTR* p. 175. Like Neil Kinnock, Salmond was on the left of his party, with his membership of the republican socialist '79 Group' leading to expulsion in 1982 (see Torrance, D. *Salmond – Against the odds*, Birlinn, 2010).

117. See also *ATTR* p. 117.

118. *Herald* 20 April 1999.

119. *ATTR* p. 77.

120. *Scotland on Sunday* 29 March 2009, *DTTSS* p. 11 respectively.

121. These decisions would further create a more conducive environment for Tommy to operate in.

122. 'Followers' refers to those both within and without organisations that Tommy was a member and leader of because leaders have both internal and external followers. However, as Tommy's later career would show, his 'external' leadership was by far the most important, that is, his pitch to, and orientation towards, those members of the public outside the SML/SSA/SSP/Solidarity. Here, he was a salesperson to those who had not yet 'purchased' socialism (by dint of paying membership of these organisations or giving donations of money and time to them) but were considering doing so.

123. 23 August 1988.

124. One aspect of the receptiveness of the rebellion to the likes of Militant and, thus, Tommy, was the former's maintenance of many traits of 'old social movements' such as 'bread and butter' issues (see Bagguley, P. 'Protest, poverty and power: a case study of the anti-poll tax movement', *Sociological Review*, 1995, Vol. 43, No. 4, pp. 693–719). -

3

The Road to
Glasgow City Council

Introduction

There are many characters on the radical left that proverbially 'rise like a rocket and fall like a stick'. Almost as soon as they gain some wider, even national, stature, giving them an ability to extend the reach of their ideas, they lose that stature. They are one hit wonders, whether the loss of stature was their fault or not. The course of events that led from the poll tax revolt in 1988–1990 would further cement Tommy in the public mind as 'the man' who fought the Tories' hated poll tax and from this basis propel him into mainstream consciousness as an elected politician. Using the mantle of the respectability and credibility that this stature gave to him, he became no mere flash in the pan. Ironically, the basis of this rise to influence was the common misconception of friend and foe that Tommy was jailed for not paying his poll tax and on this basis a sense of martyrdom was created. Rather, he was jailed for opposing a warrant sale. In his own estimation, Tommy became a public figure from 1991/1992. Not for the first time, Tommy was able to turn an attack on him into an advantage.

Towards Turnbull Street

The next stage in the battle against the poll tax – even after it had been holed below the waterline – was to defend those who had broken it from the retribution of a system that was still being implemented. Tommy, along with others, organised and led these activities in and around Glasgow. A guerrilla war fought over poindings and warrant sales. Through barricades of people barring physical access to premises over 4,000 poindings were prevented. Through occupations of many sheriff offices many poindings were rescinded.[1] And through use of the law as a backup to these direct actions, delay and halting of many benefit and wages deductions were achieved. After a run of successes in cancelling many poindings, Tommy was able to declare of an area of Glasgow: 'This is now a sheriff officer and poll tax free zone'.[2] But it was the success in stopping the first and only warrant sale in Scotland over non-payment that created the right kind of notoriety for his political liftoff.

The Strathclyde Anti-Poll Tax Federation got a tip off a from journalist on the *Greenock Telegraph* that a warrant sale was due to take place on 1 October 1991 at Turnbull Street in Glasgow concerning the poll tax debt of a Port Glasgow woman whose furniture had been valued at £360. Turnbull Street, a former police station, was chosen as the site after auctioneers refused to hold it on their premises for fear of protest and disruption. With less than a week to go, the Federation mobilised its supporters to bar the sale from taking place. Less than a day before it, Tommy was served with an interdict (or writ) barring him from being within 100 yards of the sale in order to prevent him from attending, disrupting, impeding or interfering with the sheriff officers when carrying out the warrant sale. The firm of sheriff officers had recognised the importance of Tommy to the likely protest and so applied for, and gained, the interdict. Between 200 and 300 protestors besieged Turnbull Street. In the subsequent court case, the two Abernethy McIntyre sheriff officers feared there would be a 'total riot'[3] if the warrant sale went ahead so it was called off. Indeed, they said that they did not leave their van for fearing of precipitating a riot. Again, in the subsequent court case, the police said although nobody was going to be killed, they could not guarantee that no one would not get injured, and so on the grounds of public safety, the police cancelled the sale. Another way of reading the situation was to say that the demonstrators far outnumbered the police and sheriff officers. Tommy tore up the interdict when giving a speech at the protest, recounting:

> The interdict banned me from taking part in a legitimate protest. I would ignore it. ... I tore it up publicly during the protest ... because I had contempt for what it said and the way it was served [not in person and through his letter box in Linthaugh Road and without sufficient time to challenge it]. But I would have been jailed whether or not I did that, because they wanted to make an example of me.[4]

His compulsion to attend was not just because this was the first warrant sale for poll tax non-payment but because 'Everybody was talking [saying they were against warrant sales] but nobody was acting'.[5] Of the victory at Turnbull Street, Tommy argued: 'Now every working class person in Scotland knows that they don't have to surrender to these heavy tactics and we appeal to the [Labour] council not to do the Tories' dirty work for them'[6] and 'This warrant sale is cancelled and so is every other warrant sale'.[7] Later, he said it felt like: 'we were the anti-poll tax team and we had just won the cup'[8] because no other warrant sale for poll tax debts was then attempted by late 1993. In response, the *Sunday Times* went as far to call for Tommy's arrest and jailing as it claimed the police and courts were shirking from their duty to uphold law and order.[9]

Not long afterwards, Tommy was arrested on 10 December 1991 for 'deforcement' which was then changed to breach of the peace and breaking the terms of the interdict.[10] His trial in Edinburgh[11] began on 23 January 1992, where he denied leading the crowd to stop the sale and stated warrant sales were barbaric, constituting a war against the poor. Seeing a similarity between himself and John Maclean when he was charged with sedition for his anti-war activities, Tommy pled not guilty because 'to admit guilt to these people would be to submit to their laws'.[12] It became clear that the judiciary wanted to make an example of him for proceedings against another targeted anti-poll tax activist, Davy Landels, for attending the Turnbull Street protest were dropped. Tommy was sentenced to six months on 28 January 1992 for 'flagrant, calculated and deliberate' breach of the interdict by tearing it up in front of the crowd (thereby saying that crowd should also ignore the law), for contempt of court, and for encouraging others to stop the sale with inflammatory speeches. This, again, suggested the court wanted to make an example of him because he was being jailed for a civil offence. When he was sentenced, he recounted: 'I couldn't show I was upset'[13] as this would make it worse for Alice as well as show his political enemies that they had triumphed. Instead, as on other similar and subsequent occasions, he remained steadfastly defiant and unbowed. He claimed he was a political prisoner given a savage sentence. Upon being taken down, Alice shouted: 'God go with you. I am proud to be your mother'.[14] He later recalled upon getting to prison:

Yes [being a single councillor] ... can be nerve racking and it can be embarrassing doing it on your own but it's nothing compared to being delivered to Saughton ... and then having to be stripped naked in front of nine males in uniform [who] you've never met before, [being] asked to bend over to be [anally] searched and then getting into a cell ... and for a guy from Glasgow ... all the telly and speaking in the chamber means fuck all compared to that ... and I've got that [experience] in the bank ... it was the most humiliating experience in my life and if you can come through that [intact] you can come through anything.

After being processed, he was first taken to Cell 28 in B Hall at HMP Saughton in Edinburgh (or 'Hotel Saughton'[15] as he called it) where, along with the naked strip search and public shower, he felt 'vulnerable' and 'daunt[ed]'.[16] Subsequently, he was moved to D Hall. However, Tommy was freed three days later through interim liberation (after undertaking not to attend any warrant sales) and pending an appeal by the Crown. Despite his lawyer arguing that the punishment of imprisonment was excessive on the grounds of there being no physical intervention by Tommy to stop the warrant sale, the appeal was won so Tommy was sent back to Saughton to Cell 23 in D Hall on 6 March 1992, with him proclaiming: 'For the crime of defending the poor [I] have been imprisoned'.[17] Then after a week, he was moved to the prison's Training for Freedom unit as he was a civil prisoner (although he did not take his full entitlements as civil prisoner out of compassion for and solidarity with the criminal prisoners). In the time of his initial incarceration,[18] he was visited by SNP MPs Jim Sillars and Dick Douglas who paid tribute to his role in defeating the poll tax. In the vigils that were held outside Saughton in protest at his jailing, his mother held aloft a giant photo of him, leading some Militant activists to suggest that Alice saw Tommy in a Jesus-like way. According to Joan McAlpine, Tommy became a national figure at this time as result of his jailing.

The Scottish Turn

In the time that Tommy was fighting to stay out of jail, moves towards founding Scottish Militant Labour (SML) as an independent political party were being taken. After much internal discussion, these moves began in late 1991 and climaxed with the public launch of SML on 30 January 1992 (when Tommy was first jailed over breaking the interdict) and its founding conference on 29 February 1992. There were a number of specific reasons for its founding. Amongst these were that the Communist Party and Labour left were declining in force so providing the perceived need and space for a new far left organisation while the poll tax revolt had, it was believed, made many more receptive to the kind of politics SML would pursue. At the same time, Militant saw the need to prevent any radicalisation towards the left as a result of the poll tax revolt and anti-Thatcherism being colonised by or diverted towards Scottish nationalism in the form of the SNP.

Prior to late 1991, the issue of standing independent Militant or anti-poll tax candidates was discussed within Militant in Scotland and more widely. In remarking: 'A significant minority [in Militant in 1990] at time of poll tax argued to stand candidates against Labour ... I was against this because the Labour Party was still a party of working class and it could be taken back ... but by end of 1991 it was clear we had to think of something new and in 1992 we launched Scottish Militant Labour', Tommy highlighted the changing view of Labour's worth which above all else was the key driver. But there were others. Tommy recounted that the problem for Militant as an organisation at this stage was that in addition to some of its members being inside Labour, many having been expelled and new Militant members not wanting to join Labour, Militant 'didn't get as much out of the poll tax as it wasn't openly organising [by for example, recruiting to itself] ... Scottish Militant Labour ... should have been launched earlier to benefit from it ... because it wasn't that easy to get people to join the Labour Party'.[19] Thus, Militant's core, reliable membership peaked at and stuck around 6,000 of which 600 were in Scotland.

Putting the 'Scottish' in front of Militant Labour – the name Militant adopted when it left Labour in 1993 – recognised and reflected Scottish national identity, while 'Militant' was a statement of aspiration and 'Labour' constituted being part of the labour movement. To Tommy, it indicated Militant in Scotland was 'no longer a single issue [i.e. anti-poll tax] organisation'.[20] The debate inside Militant over the 'Scottish turn' and the 'Open turn' in England and Wales precipitated a split with a minority around Ted Grant and Alan Woods staying in Labour and establishing Socialist Appeal. This had a historical later parallel when a minority of SML members stayed with the successor to Militant, the Socialist Party (SPEW), while the majority of SML members (including Tommy) left, forming the International Socialist Movement (ISM) group in 1998 (which left the CWI in 2001 and dissolved itself in 2006). The differences and debates centred round how socialism would come about with the CWI groups favouring Marxist vanguard parties and others favouring broad, pluralist socialist parties. It is a measure of Tommy's skills and profile in the context of the poll tax that he escaped the impact of SML being set up quite late in the day. This meant SML was probably smaller than it might have otherwise been. Nonetheless, with the fillip of being jailed, Tommy's appeal become far wider than that of SML's even if his position as the public face of SML could have been stronger with a larger organisation behind him.

'Slammed Up but not Shut Up'

In this context, the SML leadership decided in late 1991 that Tommy should fight the Pollok seat in the April 1992 general election (with other SML candidates standing in Cathcart and Garscadden). The

Sunday Times predicted this would not raise an electoral 'breeze in a teacup'.[21] Before being able to do this, however, it seemed the Crown's appeal to end his interim liberation was heard quickly so Tommy could be returned to jail and scupper his chances of standing in the election – albeit not before he addressed a rally of 1,000 people in Glasgow. Yet, SML decided to turn the tables here by using his incarceration to good effect by making it – and why he was there – a centre point of his campaign and candidature. Indeed, his jailing sealed the intention to stand. He claimed he would win the seat initially and again after canvass returns.[22] In the event and standing against the sitting Labour MP on 9 April 1992, Tommy helped reduce his majority down from 23,239 votes at the 1987 general election to 14,170, gaining 6,287 votes himself (19% of votes cast) and coming second. He believed that as a result: 'We now had a mandate to speak for the schemes'[23] and that 'You ain't seen nothing yet ... the lesson [for Labour] is you cannot win by out-Torying the Tories'.[24] In the campaign, Keith Baldassara was Tommy's election agent, and spoke on his behalf outside Saughton while Richie Venton, with previous experience of electoral campaigning, was drafted up from Liverpool by Militant to help organise the campaign. He believed Tommy's 'impassioned, rousing speeches ha[d] a powerful impact [upon voters]'.[25] Again with parallels with John Maclean when he stood for election from his cell, Tommy was able to stand – as he was a civil prisoner and one who had been jailed for no more than a year – and had the legitimate ability to communicate with his electorate, hold press conferences and launch his manifesto on 23 March 1992 from Saughton. At these press conferences, Tommy had to exert some considerable patience with the press as they seemed more interested in what he missed by being inside than in his politics,[26] trying some humour to focus attention back on his campaign: 'You can't kiss babies from behind bars'.[27] In an innovation far ahead of its time, he addressed supporters in Pollok via a mobile phone, giving new meaning to the then term 'cell phone'. The phone was paid for by various Rangers, St Johnstone and Dunfermline football players. Describing himself as a 'modern day Robin Hood',[28] his election platform focused upon a minimum wage, increased NHS and welfare spending, increased benefits, nationalisation, higher taxes on the rich, better housing and education, a reduced working week, and the creation of a Scottish Parliament. In putting forward this, Tommy proclaimed that he campaigned on 'what Labour used to campaign on [before] its heart and soul were ripped out'[29] and claimed the mantle of 'old' Labour and Red Clydeside. Thus, he stated he stood for organisation and action and not 'bluster and blether'.[30]

The general election saw the return of the Tories but with a smaller number of MPs in Scotland, precipitating the launch of Scotland United, a cross-party campaign of the left, involving figures like MPs Dennis Canavan and George Galloway and Bill Speirs of the STUC. Scotland United sought to hasten the return of a Scottish Parliament. Tommy was particularly critical of the STUC's involvement in Scotland United[31] and the unwillingness of the STUC and Scotland United to promote mass civil disobedience (as opposed to the elite lobbying of the great and the good) to make Scotland both ungovernable and free from Thatcherism.

Winning 6,287 votes provided a sound base for standing in the elections for Glasgow City Council, where Tommy made the first of his many breakthroughs, again ably assisted by many others back in Pollok. Again he was able to hold a press conference to launch his manifesto in prison. He started picking up well-known support from the likes of actress and comedienne, Elaine C. Smith, and Deacon Blue frontman, Ricky Ross. Still inside Saughton as civil prisoner number 292, Tommy was elected on 6 May as a councillor, becoming the first person to be successfully elected to a council from prison in Scotland. He won 52% of the votes cast with a majority of 447 votes over Labour whose majority had been 1,799.[32] Along with three other successful candidates (Nicky Bennett, Jim McVicar and Chic Stevenson), SML now had four councillors in Glasgow and just lost out on a fifth seat in the city as well. Two including Tommy were elected as SML councillors and two were elected as independent Labour councillors who had been expelled from Labour for not paying their poll tax and then joined SML.[33] Given that SML had only contested seven seats in Glasgow, and in these seats had accrued 6,659 votes (40.2% of votes polled there), this was such a significant breakthrough that Tommy talked of SML 'coming of age' and 'arriving', and in doing so, putting genuine, radical socialism back on the agenda. He was quick to point this out as a victory for the underdog, and highlighted that if this much could be achieved in less than a year, how much more SML would achieve in the next few? More widely, he argued: 'The [working] class was hugely disappointed that Labour lost in 1992 so they were willing to give us a chance in the local elections of 1992 so that's why we had some success'.[34]

Upon being released on 1 July 1992, some two months early for good behaviour, he was greeted outside the prison by Alice Sheridan and Keith Baldassara and when his train reached Glasgow Queen Street station, he was met by 200–300 supporters with George McNeilage[35] being one of the two supporters to carry Tommy aloft from the station across George Square and over to the chambers of Glasgow City Council for Tommy to claim his seat for the first time in person. Sitting

in the Lord Provost's seat, Tommy exuberantly claimed that SML
would hold this position in two years' time. He told reporters: 'I have
absolutely no regrets. I certainly don't wish to go to prison again, but
if I'm faced with the exact same circumstances that's what will happen
because I'm not going to be frightened nor cowed by four months in
jail. Warrant sales are barbaric and should be banned. If it means people
going to jail to stop them then so be it'.[36]

Devolution to Independence

In the background to the 'Scottish turn' was Militant's developing attitude to devolution. In the referendum in 1979, Militant in Scotland,
like the Communist Party, supported devolution.[37] Tommy recounted:
'Militant in Scotland had always backed devolution – even though some
of its leadership in Scotland in the 1970s were against it'. However, as
devolution became more a focus of attention, the attitude of Militant in
Scotland – and then SML – developed because the more closely that
devolution was examined, it became clear to Militant that, according to
Tommy, 'a devolved parliament was limited in power ... [so] we needed
independence and self-determination' and the struggle to achieve these
could unite the movements for political and economic control to reside
in Scotland. This sparked conflict with the leadership of Militant in
London, Tommy recalled, for while:

> The idea of greater autonomy was never an issue ... what did
> become an issue was the political understanding of Scotland as
> a nation and the application of devolution to changing people's
> lives ... because devolution in and of itself doesn't change lives ...
> SML called for the devolved government to take over manufactur-
> ing concerns, to expel nuclear weapons [and] so it became clear
> to us that we were really talking about an independent Scotland
> so we engaged in a year long discussion on whether indepen-
> dence should become part of our core demands or to just con-
> tinue with devolution ... it was a lack of courage that led us to say
> that we're in favour of Scottish independence if that's what the
> Scottish people want but we shouldn't support it ourselves ... so
> we were saying 'if the train was full let's get on it and if it wasn't
> then let's not'.

But it was also the way in which the struggle for socialism would
come about that inclined the majority in Militant in Scotland to support
independence as Tommy outlined:

Because we realised that the revolution is a process – not an event – which develops through ebbs and flows [we understood] the idea of a socialist Britain by the early to mid-1990s was far less likely with the decline of the Bennite left and the Labour left ... so we in Scotland began to reassess our world, British and Scottish perspectives and wanted to play our role in developing revolutionary change in the country of our birth.

However, this was not a straightforward or quick process for in 1994, Tommy made clear he favoured a Scottish Parliament (albeit a socialist one) within a union with England and Wales rather than independence[38] and it was not until 1998 that SML clearly and openly supported independence.[39] On this basis, nonetheless, in 1993 Tommy and SML were invited to be involved in the campaign for a Scottish Parliament.

Councillor Sheridan

Given his wider public standing prior to being elected, Tommy assumed leadership of the SML council group and vied with the Tories for SML to become the official opposition to Labour (which had 54 of the 66 seats).[40] He, and his fellow SML councillors, pursued an agenda of trying to secure decent housing, eradicate poverty and stop council corruption and junketeering. This agenda was both highly political and practical in the light of the problems for Glaswegians in Pollok and other working class areas of the city. On housing, he lambasted the 'people's party' for their inaction and advocated suspending the council's interest payments on its housing debt as 73% of rent revenues were spent on this. In tandem, he proposed alternative housing budgets comprising more repairs, smaller rent rises, and spending council surpluses, along with promising to build and renovate many houses if SML controlled council, which in so doing defied Tory spending limits.[41] But he also worked on a plan to create better tribunals for tenants so that the work was not just about raising demands but also about acting in a practical and immediate manner. This meant his stance could not be easily dismissed as reactive and negative.

Related to this focus upon housing, Tommy was highly critical of the council's inward investment strategy to regenerate Glasgow on the basis of giving incentives to business to create low paid jobs in the service sector and increase the private housing stock. For Tommy, this continued the major themes he had established for himself before 1992. For example, in 1990 he was involved with the Workers' City project against gentrification during Glasgow's year as 'European City of Culture'. But the one issue he made his own more than any other was his relentless and tenacious pursuit of councillors, especially those of the 'people's party', for moral corruption and dubious financial practices. For example, in 1993, this concerned which company was awarded the tender to deal with the council's travel budget. On this, he defeated Labour by appealing directly to Labour councillors. On two occasions in 1993, he was expelled from the council chamber for his attempts to expose councillors over their expenses. As often as he could, he used humour and alliteration to disparage Labour on this issue. So on overseas housing trips by Labour councillors: 'Maybe we should have log cabins in Drumchapel or wigwams in Easterhouse'.[42] Of the cover-up by Labour of 'votes for junkets' despite its own internal investigation, he declared: 'I'm surprised Billy Smart hasn't been appointed as the whole fiasco has turned into a circus'.[43] On other occasions, he accused Labour councillors of riding the 'Glasgow gravy train'.

In using the platform of being a councillor, his activities were not confined to the council chamber. Rather, council and extra-council activities on the same issue were mutually supportive. For example, Tommy and others in 1993 disrupted a meeting of the Strathclyde Regional Council's finance committee meeting.[44] The extra-council activities were critical to building political leverage as SML was more often than not forced by dint of numbers on the council, and through its political perspective, to call upon Labour to act. But each of Tommy's moves and initiatives in the council were intimately choreographed with his public profile in the press. His maiden speech was fully reported in the *Herald* on 28 August 1992 and he gained substantial coverage for his actions by engaging in strategically timed and attention seeking activities. These were supported by releasing the text of his letters to councillors to the press, with the backstop measure of writing letters – which were invariably published – to the press and especially the *Herald*.[45]

More generally, Tommy used being a councillor to attack the Tories as the government and then Labour's *de facto* adherence to Tory policies by lambasting their fecklessness in fighting the Tories. To many, he must have sounded like a stuck record in always calling for defiance and pointing out the lack of lead in Labour's pencil: '[W]e don't want to see Labour councillors running away from battle before the first shot is fired'.[46] Thus, in the context of Glasgow, this meant more specifically airing issues and exposing Labour, and getting press for this. His role was to present SML as the genuine people's party, taking politics back to the people. Here, SML was still a vanguard party but no longer quite of the narrow revolutionary Trotskyist sort for the potential to have a more widely supported radical left party was being recognised.

Even though Jean McFadden, Labour leader of Glasgow City Council, admitted Tommy was a 'charming young man',[47] Labour continued its long and personalised vendetta against Tommy and the SML, both inside and outside the council chamber. Janey Buchan, Labour MEP, took pots shots in the *Herald* letters page – to which Tommy responded that she was part of a left that was too rarefied to get its hands dirty – and Labour tried to stop SML having access to schools for holding meetings in Glasgow. Inside the chamber, the Labour group initially voted to urge Tommy to resign his seat as he was in prison and called him an 'enemy of people' by depriving the council of revenue and getting citizens into debt through the non-payment of the poll tax campaign. Meantime, the Tories branded him a 'self-appointed martyr'. Labour also changed the council's standing orders to limit questions from SML councillors while leading Labour councillors, like Jean McFadden, kept up the barrage that Tommy suffered from an ego problem, was a thug, a fake, an extremist, a parasite on the labour movement and was also loutish and ignorant.[48] Tommy responded robustly in word but never by way of libel action.

While a councillor, his poll tax arrears were deducted from his councillor's allowance – he refused to agree to this voluntarily so they were deducted by court order which ironically stopped him from being declared bankrupt and, thus, ineligible to be a councillor. Nonetheless, Tommy and his fellow SML councillors defied the law by voting in council while in arrears with their poll tax. They also successfully applied the tactics they had adopted fighting the poll tax to the council when in 1992 they occupied the chamber in a dispute over office accommodation when SML had been deprived of its own office.

Behind the scenes, there were some issues of controversy. In leading from the front, Tommy was often in danger of rubbing his fellow SML councillors up the wrong way. Jim McVicar recalled that even though the constant battles with Labour forced them together:

One of the things Tommy was bad for doing was coming in in the morning and saying 'Listen, I didn't have time to talk to anyone about it and I've done this or submitted this motion'. We ended up having to back him up even if we disagreed with it because [SML] was under fire from all sides so you've to be seen to be united. Ronnie Stevenson had to try to arbitrate. If Tommy had to withdraw a motion or back down, it wasn't just Tommy that would look bad. We had to grin and bear it for the group. … We had no option but to support him as it would make all of us look stupid. … Tommy was always very, very forceful in arguing his position in the council group but he wasn't always right [even] if he won the day. [There were even times] before we entered the Council Chamber when the comrades said: 'This is a mistake and we shouldn't be doing this' but this was a collective decision we'd come to. ... His aura and presence were powerful in making his arguments convincing. The other thing is he is an absolute charmer.

Richie Venton, Ronnie Stevenson and Peter Taaffe confirmed this tendency. For example, Ronnie Stevenson believed: 'There's an impatience with Tommy ... a fundamental lack of understanding on his part of the benefits of taking more people with you, of persuading them before you act rather than after the event. Sometimes things didn't need to happen yesterday; they could have waited to take more people on board'. Nonetheless, Peter Taaffe suggested Tommy was not the only one do to so and that such tendencies were partly inevitable in heat of battle. However, he did allude to an issue of ultra-leftism that he had to deal with when he was responsible for Militant in Scotland: 'When he [Tommy] was a councillor, there would be headlines in the *Herald* about revolution and some would go along with him [but I had to say] 'Look, this is not the best way to pose things to reach the best of the working class at this stage ... you have to present things in a more transitional fashion. It was a bit like the SWP then but not today saying 'One solution revolution' as a mantra. You have to start from where the masses are'. There were also differences of opinion over how much casework Tommy did. While George McNeilage claimed he did a considerable amount of casework, getting issues over anti-social behaviour resolved, thus, freeing Tommy up for other work, Keith Baldassara thought Tommy did his own case work until 1999 unless on holiday or away. Tommy claimed he did his own case work.[49] And third, Tommy was cute enough to claim credit for progress that was already in the pipeline in his councillor bulletins or for concerns that were already expressed by others. This indicated that Tommy, in George's words, viewed the work of a councillor as 'a front for public consumption'. Intriguingly for subsequent years, Keith commented that 'what [he and George] are guilty of is doing [things] in Tommy's name'.

SML: Onward and Upward?[50]

Using its City Council bridgehead, SML won two seats on Strathclyde Regional Council in late 1992 with the election of Christine McVicar and Willie Griffin. Greeting this news, Tommy declared: 'The Labour party must get off its knees and fight back instead of kneeling at the feet of the Tories'[51] and 'We have a message for Labour. There must be no more bending of the knee, no more tugging of the forelock. It is time to stand up and fight the Tories. That is what the working class of Scotland wants them to do, and if they continue to refuse, we will continue to embarrass Labour in their heartlands'.[52] This electoral advance gave further credence to SML's claim that it was not a 'one-man band', with recognition from Labour that it was now a force in Scottish politics[53] – even if Tommy's statements like no Labour seat in Scotland was now safe with the rise of SML were patently untrue.[54] The stalling of the initial momentum of Scotland United helped the cause of SML as the party of action and agitation where it became clear that SML's twin strategy was to take votes from Labour at the same time as show SNP members and supporters SML was the best and most robust opposition to Labour.

Comparison with Derek Hatton as 'Glasgow's Derek Hatton'[55] and of SML in Glasgow with Militant in Liverpool[56] neither hampered Tommy nor Militant in this period of continuing anger with the Tories and the inability of Labour to sidestep responsibility for what should have been its victory in 1992. Becoming 'a local hero who went to prison for the people'[57] allowed Tommy and the SML to launch a campaign against water privatisation in 1992 called 'Hands of Our Water' (HoW). Tommy recollected:

> The HoW campaign was not just about water, but about public ownership and privatisation and about the difference about what was happening in England and Wales compared to Scotland ... [it was an] ideological campaign [as well] ... With HoW, we managed to build a broader campaign even though we did it with SML.

Although Tommy predicted and promised a massive campaign of civil disobedience and non-payment on the scale on the poll tax,[58] this was not to be. Despite advocating it, Tommy and SML could not turn water into another poll tax revolt. Yet, broader political opposition, including HoW, did have the effect of stopping privatisation but not the handing over of water to unelected quangos, thus, piquing popular anger at privatisation. Tommy characterised this as a victory, recalling that 'it was a bloodless defeat unlike the poll tax which was a bloody defeat'.[59] However, this was not before various actions were taken such as occupying the offices of the bank in Edinburgh which was charged with preparing the privatisation, invading the Glasgow Stock Exchange and turning off the water to the Scottish Secretary's official residence.

Yet after 1992, the going seemed to get a bit tougher for SML, although not necessarily quite so much for Tommy. Feeling like SML was riding the crest of a ever-rising wave, after winning 35% of the vote in a council by-election in Dundee in January 1993, Tommy declared: 'The myth that we are a Glasgow Party has been laid to rest and we are the main opposition to Labour ... We've now established ourselves outside Glasgow as the main opposition ... We've written off the SNP'.[60] However, the copy greeting this and many of SML's subsequent electoral forays were of failing to gain this and that seat after making such bold statements in press releases and public pronouncements. The irony was that SML continued to poll well in most instances but because it talked up its chances of winning, it had further to fall when it did not live up to its own predictions. Thus, in September 1993 in a by-election in Springburn it polled 700 votes, coming second to Labour, and in December of that year in Alexandra Park, SML only lost out to Labour by 300 votes. With five councillors, SML would have become the official opposition to Labour on Glasgow City Council by displacing the Tories from that position – who had five councillors then and were then reduced to three through death and defection. In the process, SML would have obtained a seat on every committee and gained more resources with which to campaign and promote itself. In two other by-elections in Dundee, SML also did well. Given his 'star quality', Tommy was always used to promote SML election candidates – such as the five occasions in last three months of 1993 alone. It was always, therefore, his voice in which the bold statements were made. Yet for reasons of his positive relations with journalists, he appeared pretty Teflon-like in that the journalists still came back for more despite asserting that, for example, no Labour seat in Scotland was safe with the rise of SML.[61]

Looking back on this time, Tommy remembered: 'The spadework we did between 1992 to 1994 showed us that there was the room for a political force on the left other than Labour ... we showed there was electoral room to the left of Labour ... We became better known politically, we began to have a bit more influence, have a bigger and broader audience than we'd ever had ... being the SML gave us a cutting edge we didn't have because we could challenge Labour electorally'.[62] This he put down to two components in particular: '[We] could unite and marry socialist principles with the right to self-determination as a progressive right' and, playing to Militant's tradition of concentrating on bread-and-butter issues: '[W]e did well as SML in representing people ... developing housing policy ... I realised that unless we could do the nuts and bolts of getting wee Mrs Smith's repair done and getting Mr Smith's garden sorted out then people would conclude 'why have you?' ... we worked at that and we built up a good reputation ... we had to look after our base'.

But in spite of Tommy claiming that SML had 1,000 members,[63] by early March 1993 it had 500 members and sought to double this by the end of 1993.[64] Five hundred members was not an inconsiderable number for a far left organisation in Scotland at this time but it was well short of the size of membership SML needed to spread out beyond its Glasgow citadel. In its Alexandra Park campaign, SML increased its membership in the ward from 1 to 27. However, this did not seem to be representative of how well SML faired in recruitment stakes in other electoral campaigns,[65] and such numbers did not necessarily lead to an overall rise in membership as, with many far-left organisations, other members also leave or drop out. Asked why Glasgow was SML's only citadel, Tommy reflected it was not 'any more complex than we didn't have anything like the community base that we had in parts of Glasgow ... [where] we were a recognised player ... We attempted to put roots down elsewhere but we didn't make any breakthroughs else other than a few pinpricks'. This merely described that situation but did not explain it, especially with regard to why Glasgow as a city was different politically and culturally from Aberdeen, Dundee and Edinburgh.

Nineteen ninety four was a topsy-turvy year for SML. It lost both its Strathclyde Regional Council members even though it gained 9,277 votes across city in the six (out of 104) seats it stood in. It also stood in another six seats outside Glasgow in these regional elections but without any great effect. Attempting to come out of this fighting, Tommy proclaimed: 'Those who write us off only wish to do so because of the fear they have for our future development. Rumours of our death have been greatly exaggerated'.[66] However, this did represent a loss of momentum that was not undone by Tommy winning 12,113 (7.6%) in Glasgow in the European election in June (and in the process beating the Tories into fourth place). Some of this was because he had promised to pip the SNP in his election campaign against 'bosses, bureaucrats and billionaires'. At the end of June, SML came second (to Labour) in a by-election in the Keppochhill ward in Glasgow with 519 votes (44%). Although Tommy was able to claim: 'This confirms yet again that we are the only real opposition to the Labour establishment in this city', Labour MP Michael Martin, whose constituency contained the ward, was also able to claim: 'They keep claiming they are going to win but there are no second prizes'.[67]

Trouble at Timex

Tommy's panache for making well-intentioned but often outlandish statements continued unabated. In January 1993, Timex proposed lay-offs at its Dundee factory. The workers balloted for strike action, with 92% in favour. Meantime, requests for negotiation and arbitration were ignored by the company. On 29 January, the workers came out on strike and, upon offering to return to work on 17 February, Timex told them they would come back to a 10% pay cut. When the strikers refused to accept this, they were locked out and strikebreakers brought in as replacements. On 28 August 1993, Timex shut the factory. Of the Timex dispute, Tommy claimed: 'It will be the biggest picket Scotland has ever seen, surpassing everything we have seen since the Second World War'.[68] Taken literally, this would mean the picketline would be bigger than those of the miners' strike of 1984–1985, amongst others. What Tommy was, in effect, trying to do was use his stature to put out a call to persuade others to try to make it the biggest picket possible. In tandem with this, he and SML were heavily involved in the Timex dispute, with him urging the strikers to occupy the factory, supporting the idea of a workers' buy-out as well as calling upon the STUC and TUC to call a 24-hour strike in the strikers' support. He was fined for breaching the peace on the picketline and given a court order to stay away. Although the leading stewards at Timex were critical of Tommy and SML's stance on the dispute,[69] Tommy was able to use his political stature to publicise Timex as an example of (capitalist) globalisation and the 'race to bottom', and in so doing expose the strikers' union for its unwillingness to take more robust action.[70] Nonetheless, SML's activity in the dispute as a 'party of solidarity' did help it sink some deeper roots in Dundee.

A Time to Rage

A Time to Rage was published as a combination of autobiography, political manifesto and social history. It was serialised in the *Scotsman* on 12 and 13 May 1994 and published the following week as being written by 'Tommy Sheridan with Joan McAlpine'. Following hours of taped interviews conducted by Joan with Tommy and many anti-poll tax resisters, it was nonetheless written by Joan in the first person voice or hand of Tommy. Through this means, she put his voice and word onto the written page. The book became something of a minor hit and easily sold out of its print run. Joan's motivation for engaging in the project whilst also working full-time as a professional journalist was partly explained in her acknowledgement to the book. In it, she gave a radical interpretation to the role of journalists, being 'to give a voice to the unheard' and in an unsanitised manner, especially where the unheard are the creators of turning points in history. To her, the story of the poll tax revolt was one such instance. She continued that Tommy gave the unheard here a voice and that as such he was the vehicle through which their story and action could be told. But apart from this, there was a certain political allure to Tommy himself. She saw him in terms of being a historical figure at the centre of a social protest movement which was innovative in its grounding in the community and in many of its tactics. In addition to this, she saw him as a very young but very serious figure who was authentically from 'the scheme', was 'articulate in Glaswegian [i.e. working people's own tongue]' and 'did not come across as a young political apparatchik [even though] he was a politics graduate'. Moreover, he 'exuded energy', was able to 'motivate and organise people who were not political ... [in the guise of a] pied piper'. Coming herself from a radical background within the SNP, the political allure of Tommy also seemed for her to be not only about the combination of national identity and radicalism but doing this in a way that posed a threat to Labour in its heartlands. For Tommy:

> Joan was a right good gutsy journalist working for the Scotsman, covering stories on the poll tax that no one else was ... like the occupations of sheriff officers' offices ... we were determined to avoid the story of the poll tax being written up by the bourgeois ... so either we asked her or she asked us ... she was independent and had stature ... it was an excellent book ... it was going to be great launch for it with TV and press at the People's Palace but then John Smith died that day and we were torpedoed ... but it went on to sell over 5,000 copies and is out of print ...

In the last chapter, Tommy provided a simple but searing critique of capitalism: capitalism cannot provide decent living standards for workers, Labour does not want to challenge and change the system, business always comes first and advocates trickledown economics to justify this, marketisation and privatisation are the tools of the capitalist class and so on. He was able do to so, that is draw such general political conclusions, because of the grounded approach he took to his experiences of working class communities. Journalist, Ian Bell, gave it a warm review in the *Herald*, pointing out that Tommy and Militant were able to play the prominent role they did against the poll tax because others – Labour and SNP – chose not to.[71]

Looking for Other Campaigning Issues

Although the campaign against poindings and warrant sales necessarily carried on, with Tommy being arrested alongside Alice at one such action in Greenock in late 1994,[72] the search for issues to convey the broader socialist message after the poll tax – but in the manner of the poll tax – continued. One attempt was the Defiance Alliance against the *Criminal Justice and Public Order Act 1994* and another was VAT

Busters against VAT on fuel and energy bills. Again, the attempt was made with VAT to create an audience for renationalisation of utilities. However, political will could not overcome the reality that these issues were unlike the poll tax in many ways so that when Tommy promised that the *Criminal Justice Act* would be broken just like the poll tax[73] or that on this issue: 'Laws are just bits of paper. We have ripped up laws before and we will rip up laws again',[74] he was wildly wide of the mark. Nonetheless, Tommy always took the opportunity when given – like being invited to debate at university unions – to highlight the class contrasts and injustices of capitalist society, whether it be that crime springs from deprivation of benefits, hope, jobs and a future or presenting his arguments as a new 'common sense' against the free market.

'There's Only One Tommy Sheridan'

The continuation of toughening conditions for SML saw Tommy returned as its only Glasgow City councillor in April 1995.[75] Tommy had begun the campaign saying SML was confident of replacing Tories as the opposition to Labour, with wins predicted in Drumchapel and possibly in Govan, as part of intending to stand in 19 seats in Glasgow (and another eleven outside). His line was one of 'Labour, Liberals and SNP have become like soap powder sellers, all promoting the same brand of free market capitalism wrapped in different packages'[76] so that SML easily stood out as a socialist alternative, which for example, opposed the 'Great Rain Robbery'[77] of attempts to privatise water. Although he polled 1,019 votes (48%) in Pollok (compared to Labour's 769), the SML vote went down significantly in areas like Easterhouse. At the election night count, Labour supporters sang to the SML activists, with echoes of dredging up the one-man band tag: 'There's only one Tommy Sheridan'. Tommy explained and justified this retreat by saying:

> There was always a question of the 1995 election ... by 1994 under Smith Labour began to recover ... this continued under Blair making it difficult for us to retain our seats ... some of us got increase votes but still lost out ... I was voted in again in 1995 for another four years because I had a bigger, wider profile. Without that I would have got beaten as well. I benefitted from everybody's hard work although it wasn't that there was more work done in Pollok because we stood in 25 seats ... [there was a debate within SML about] whether we should just concentrate on just Glasgow or go broader ... the reason I rejected the 'just defend what you had' argument is that some votes increased even though we lost the

seats ... it was more to do with the objective situation that anything
to do with what we did ... we were trying to be a new party and
you can't just do that in Glasgow ... we had to try to spread our
wings ... we emerged with just one seat but more members and
if we'd gone for the retrenchment strategy we'd have still only
emerged with one seat and less members ...

Behind the scenes, SML's decision to stand in 25 seats indicated the
growing confidence of a newer and younger section of the leadership which included Tommy (as SML convener). For example, Chic
Stevenson, one of the 'old guard' had argued that SML should just stand
in seats to defend what it had and no longer were the likes of Tommy
prepared to be quite so deferential to this type of political authority.[78]

However, some help was at hand in the form of a number of campaigns in 1995 and 1996, the most prominent of which were the protest
against the building of the M77 motorway through Pollok Park and the
establishment of the Pollok Free State, and the campaign against school
and service closures in Glasgow. These were not campaigns that SML
could piggy-back off in a parasitic way or take over once they were up
and running – more that SML could help them grow and develop, and
in the process encourage wider resistance and augment its standing with
others. In Pollok, the issue was not just the destruction of the natural
environment but the destruction of people's environment with all the
ensuing forms of pollution that a motorway brings. The Free State was
initiated by local resident, Colin Macleod, who began a treetop protest
against the M77 motorway in the early 1990s. Over several years, this
grew into a series of camps across Pollok which tried to save one of
Europe's largest inner city public commons – land that had been gifted
to the people of Glasgow. In so doing, the campaign raised issues over
the rights of local people to determine the use and development of public
space. Not only was the Pollok Free State way ahead of its time given
that the European and world social forums did not arise until the 2000s
but at this time the environment was not a big issue for the radical left.
Tommy recollected:

I don't think there was an intellectual blueprint for this [envi-
ronmental campaign] but rather there was a genuine involvement
in local communities which demanded a response to localised
issues ... a lot of the left was campaigning on a Westminster or
London agenda that didn't resonate ... we never set the agenda but
we were prepared to get involved ... articulating their frustrations
and were able to respond because we were not parachuted in but
part of those communities.

Whilst the Free State was unable to stop the motorway, it did succeed in giving the people of Glasgow a sense of their own collective power. But before that, Tommy was accused of being 'Pied Piper of Pollok' by a Glasgow councillor when he led school pupils to one of the M77 protests where there were clashes with the police. Batting back the criticism of being this political Svengali, he said 'I can't even play the flute'.[79] In court in November 1995, Tommy conducted his own case, winning his appeal against a £750 fine as excessive – so that it was reduced to £150 – for his part in an M77 protest in 1994. He was convicted of a breach of the peace for pushing through a police cordon. His trump card was that Tory government minister, Allan Stewart, had been fined only £200 for brandishing a weapon against protestors on the M77 construction site. Upon refusing to pay the fine, he was sentenced to seven days imprisonment but released in less than that due to short-term prisoner policy.[80] It was from this protest movement that Tommy first met Rosie Kane, who he later praised as one of 'Scotland's foremost environmental campaigners'.[81]

The Save our Schools campaigns was supported in a high profile way by Tommy as a councillor through working alongside the parents and school kids to organise and mount occupations, sit-ins, blockades, demos, and lobbies of schools and councils. In this, he was accused of being leader of a rent-a-mob but, as he often responded, activists cannot start or lead a protest or movement that is already in motion. The campaign won a partial victory: 'In terms of the cuts, there are some schools and centres that were occupied and wouldn't be open today if that hadn't happened ... although the cuts budget was still passed'. These actions formed part of a wider backdrop of Tommy's activities inside and outside the council of opposition to cuts in old people's homes and leading a demonstration to encircle the city chambers which tried to stop the council setting a £43m cuts budget in 1996 and urged the setting of a 'needs budget' instead. Tommy remembered:

> We were arguing for a deficit budget, a needs budget, a budget that suits Glasgow and not the Tories ... that was popular ... our argument was that [in 1996] with the Tories so weak [we could actually do this] but it fell on deaf ears in Labour.

In 1997, the Save our Services campaign entered the political landscape of Glasgow in a dramatic way. Led by Tommy, and deploying the tactics of the campaigns a year before, it resulted in the occupation and blockade of city chambers by some 1,200 protestors and, thus, stopped the majority of councillors getting to the meeting to agree to £81m of cuts and a 22% council tax increase. In the weeks afterwards, the councillors reconvened and set the cuts and tax increase budget. Accusing the

Labour council of doing the Tories' dirty work, Tommy said: 'Labour councillors ... didn't have a backbone ... between them'.[82]

Some older battles also continued in 1995. One was against the removal of water from public control and the suspicion that this represented a precursor to privatisation and price increases. Tommy led successful actions to stop the first meetings of the West of Scotland water authority, proclaiming it to be unelected, unaccountable and illegitimate. He characterised this as a 'theft of Scotland's water ... [a] theft of Scottish water'[83] in a way that spoke to his uniting of radicalism and national identity. HoW called upon local authorities not to collect water bills for the three quangos given that the resistance of Strathclyde Regional Council, controlled by Labour, had only managed to go as far as stopping the use of private consultants in the transfer of water to the quangos. While his mother Alice was jailed for refusing to pay a fine for a breach of the peace at a warrant sale, Tommy was in court in Greenock over a breach of the peace for a protest at debt recovery through a warrant sale for poll tax debts in Greenock. He refused to accept a community order, arguing: 'We refuse to be branded criminals for defending the poor'.[84] He was released pending appeal as he won the argument to reduce the bail conditions given that he was a councillor who needed to see his constituents. When the appeal was heard in late 1995, he conducted his own appeal (as well as for Keith Baldassara), winning the commuting of a sentence of 30 days to a £150 fine – which he stated he had no intention of paying as this would be to admit that he had committed a crime. Then in April 1997, he was banned for life through a permanent interdict from obstructing sheriff officers from the firm in Greenock (that organised the Turnbull Street warrant sale) in their debt recovery activities for poll tax arrears. Tommy challenged this in court, representing himself. While he gained its revision, the interdict was still granted and costs awarded against him (which were recovered in 2002).[85]

As SML's sole councillor, Tommy began to develop and apply alliance building skills with other councillors that would stand him in good stead from 1999 onwards in the Scottish Parliament. He worked with SNP councillor, Kenny Gibson (subsequently an MSP), and even on occasion won the support of the Tory councillors for his motion of opposition to cuts in old people's homes. Of this, Tommy believed: 'It taught me that you have to be able to work with certain people ... just because I was on my own or there were just a small group of us we didn't not use the council ... we presented alternative budgets and rate rises ... we were constant pains in the arses to [Labour]'. Again, he focussed on housing stock and corruption under a Labour administration. He pointed out that only 13% of the 100,000 housing stock was of a comprehensive modern standard, concluding that 'we are heading ... [in the direction of] the level of sub-standard housing to match the 1920s and 1930s'.[86] He continued to argue against rent rises, and fought a long battle to expose corruption of a Labour councillor (who was a member of the finance committee) for not paying all the rent due on her council flat.

The Scottish Socialist Alliance

At the Socialist Forums – on-going meetings of various socialists in Glasgow – in 1995, Alan McCombes floated the idea of a Scottish socialist alliance whereby various existing socialist groups would come together to make something bigger of themselves, and in so doing create a presence that could gain representation in a future Scottish Parliament. The groups he made the overture towards were those like the Communist Party of Scotland, the Socialist Movement (of mainly Labour members) and the Liberation group within the SNP. In this overture, he gave an undertaking on behalf of SML not to dominate a Scottish socialist alliance by virtue of its numerical strength. The move towards founding a Scottish socialist alliance was spurred on by the inability of the Socialist Labour Party (SLP) – founded by Arthur Scargill on 1 May 1996 – to agree to autonomy for its section in Scotland, a position of self-determination for Scotland, and maintenance of existing membership of other organisations. Tommy recounted: 'When Scargill threw down the gauntlet of a new socialist labour party we were excited ... we wore Scottish socialist spectacles but we could take them off to see the broader picture and we're keen to be involved with Arthur'. For the SLP, the refusal to accede to these terms formed part of a wider phenomenon whereby Scargill and his supporters imposed a structure to allow them to maintain full control of the new party. This sounded the effective death knell – or still birth – of the SLP as potentially a major new force on the left. Looking back on this, and seeing this as a 'lost opportunity', Tommy commented:

> At the last meeting [of three to discuss founding the SLP], we turned up to discuss the constitution but we were presented with a constitution ... a fait accompli ... we were not accepting Scotland being a region and not a country ... I thought that Scargill was willing to work with others but I think he'd been so badly burnt by personal betrayals that it was his way or the highway ... the passage of time has been on our side as it's turned out to be a horrible mistake ... the way it was born and what it turned into ... indeed, some [in Scotland] that joined the SLP have now joined the SSP ... our tactics and strategy have stood the test of time.

The move by SML to become a broader-based socialist party had also led it to engage in more joint work with other groups and on terms agreed between them – as opposed to establishing its own version of particular campaign or asking others to work with it on its terms. One such instance was the campaign, led by Richie Venton, from 1995 to 1997 to support 500 sacked Liverpool dockers which involved fund raising and creating political pressure. This kind of activity built trust and working relationships between SML and others, putting meat on the bones of unity overtures. So the outward orientation and activity were crucial building blocks to creating a Scottish socialist alliance.[87] But of equal importance was the decision by SML to transfer its resources of staff, office and newspaper over to the SSA in an act which suggested that while politically SML would continue play a key role in the SSA, the SSA was not a continuation of the SML. This again was vital to cement the alliance. However, underlying all of this and what explains the ability of the alliance to be created was the coming together of political perspectives. In other words, the existence of trust and working relations was predicated on something bigger and more important. Trust and relationships would have easily broken down, and irreparably, if a bigger political bond of vision and goals had not existed. Tommy recalled the process and issues:

> Through a lot of the campaigns ... where we campaigned together ... there was an obvious gravitation towards bringing this left grouping together ... The idea of the SSA came about because we recognised we were in the same boat but we're not ready to declare our unity with each other ... [it was a case of] let's get together but not make it a party ... the humanising effect of the campaigns and meetings where we were doing things together made it clear that we had 80% of ideas that united us – that we had agreement with each other on – and the disagreements on the 20% weren't fundamental.

The tenth of February 1996 saw 400 activists come together to commit themselves to the idea of a common radical socialist alliance to work together in joint campaigns, where the whole would be greater than the sum of its parts. In seeking to take socialism out of its somewhat self-imposed ghetto, the SSA championed proportional representation for the forthcoming Scottish Parliament[88] on the basis it could get Tommy elected. Tommy's significance for the SSA was that he was a public figurehead around whom much of the radical left could unite, especially as the SML evolved from its strict Leninist-Trotskyist past, and as a councillor and leader of the anti-poll tax revolt he was the best placed individual from the far left to be elected to a future Scottish Parliament. More generally, the SSA supported self-determination, and declared that it would not stand against other socialists or in marginal seats where the Tories might win as a result of splitting the vote with Labour. In line with its disagreement with Scargill, the SSA operated on the basis of 'open affiliation' so members of existing socialist groups could maintain this membership. Tommy was elected the SSA's national convener and Allan Green, from the Socialist Movement, became a key player as its national secretary. The SSA was formally launched on 20 April 1996. The *Scotsman* predicted that such a rainbow coalition would dissolve in the sunlight.[89] The continuing rightward shift in Labour as well as Scottish Labour meant the 'market' was believed to exist for this new broad socialist party.

The first election the SSA fought was standing Rosie Kane in the Toryglen by-election for Glasgow City Council in August 1996, where 315 votes were polled, constituting 18.6% and third place. While this represented a highpoint, with the SSA not doing nearly so well in other subsequent council by-elections, the SSA had its first major outing in the 1997 general election. Standing on a tax the rich, renationalise privatised companies, a decent minimum wage, rent freezes and scrapping Trident warheads programme, it fielded candidates in all 10 seats in Glasgow and six elsewhere (including two in Dundee). The campaign slogan was 'Vote for the real bravehearts'[90] – following the success of the Mel Gibson film – and again showed the fusing of socialism and national identity into a form of Scottish radicalism. Tommy saved his deposit in a revised Pollok constituency, with 3,639 votes (11%) while Jim McVicar and Alan McCombes gained significant votes in Baillieston and Govan respectively.[91] Tommy recalled:

> In 1992, we got almost 20% in Pollok, and came second ... by 1997, we got 11% and came third ... but it was a really good result because the overwhelming mood was 'I agree with you son but we need to get rid of the Tories' ... I got a good vote because I was still the local councillor ... we ... raised the banner and did so in the very difficult circumstances of the rise of [new] Labour.

Allan Green recalled that although the SSA 'got gubbed' in this general election, Tommy 'spoke as though we had made a historic advance with his power and persuasion ... he spoke with conviction and passion even though what he said didn't tie up with events around us ... people knew he was doing this and it still lifted them ... it would be hard for someone to do that without the belief in what they were doing [and] because he is a good performer that didn't mean he didn't believe [what he'd said]'. But despite Labour saying Tommy was a 'busted flush' and that his 'star is on the wane',[92] he maintained his profile and presence.

On the future Scottish Parliament, he argued: 'There is no way what is on offer will satisfy the hunger of the people ... The Scottish people have a right to full democratic powers to decide their future, and that demands a parliament which is not in bondage to Westminster and an unelected House of Lords, or an increasingly unpopular monarchy'.[93] Rather, he argued for a vision of the Scottish Parliament as becoming a centre for action against poverty and low pay and for better public services. This was to raise people's sights and provide an alternative to the mainstream. In doing so, there was the inevitable risk that some would also see it as ill-advised kite flying and grandstanding because it was too many steps too far ahead to be realistic.

A Balance Sheet: Early to Late 1990s

Notoriety for leading high profile strikes and struggles is no guarantee of being able to make a political breakthrough as Tommy had been able to do. For example, the case of 'red' Roddy Slorach, the leader of Glasgow council social workers' unofficial strike in 1998, victimised union activist and SWP member who then stood in Glasgow Cathcart in the Scottish Parliament elections in 1999 was a case in point. Standing on a platform of tax the rich, welfare not warfare, a decent minimum wage, the right to work and a reduced working week, he came fifth and last, polling 920 votes (3.4%). To make a breakthrough takes consistently being at the forefront of major struggles (indeed, leading struggles), a certain type of personage, specific skills as well as a particular political perspective with a sizeable organisation pursuing this. This puts into context the sense that some luck of being in the right place at the right time is also involved, for being in the right place at the right time is not necessarily a matter of luck but choice. Tommy's jailing in 1992 gave him the basis of credibility not only to put himself at the forefront of struggles but also to help initiate, build and lead them. Often it was said that Tommy was jailed in 1992 for not paying the poll tax.[94] This was a useful myth that he did nothing to dispel. Tommy was now able to bring publicity and profile to issues because he was Tommy. And being Tommy was critically, as Ronnie Stevenson put it, being the same but different from other working class young men. In other words, being from the scheme but not a just 'schemie'. The decision to jail Tommy will no doubt have been seen in retrospect by the establishment as a mistake for it neither cowed him nor the continuing revolt. More than anything else, his jailing showed that he was prepared to put 'his money where his mouth was'. Thus, the *Sunday Times* argued 'his strongest claim as radical' was going to prison over fighting the poll tax.[95]

Personal Traits, the Media and Media Representation

Tommy's 'personable' and 'charismatic' public persona[96] allied to his tub thumping, plain-speaking skills of oratory continued to make a growing mark on politics and for socialism in Scotland and further afield. He had constructed a persona that interested and appealed to journalists, namely, social skills married to socialism. Thus, while the *Sunday Times* noted that Tommy 'does little that could not be described as politically motivated ... includ[ing] football [for fitness for political struggle]',[97] this did not make him uninteresting or too diffident. Rather, the folk hero and 'man of the people' characterisations demanded a certain level of earnestness and intensity but not to the point of being colourless and boring. Tommy even proffered humility and humbleness by showing self-deprecation: 'I've still got a lot to learn. I'm on the coattails of Maclean rather than in his boots'.[98] An extensive feature on him in the *Herald*[99] played this out, and made his answering machine message – that he was 'probably out fighting the Tories ... Remember, don't let the Tories and their rotten system get ye down. Let's stand up together an' fight for change and socialism' – the best known in Scotland.

The nature of his relationship with the media was not one of be smitten youth experiencing unrequited love. Instead, it was developed into reciprocation, where both chased each other. But this was after Tommy's hard work of chasing journalists first of all, constantly issuing press releases and making time for them. Tommy did not wait for journalists to contact him but sought them out and took initiatives for which he held hundreds of press conferences and issued thousands of press releases. Sometimes, he spoke to some journalists' own beliefs in social justice. More often than not he spoke as a tangible tribune of others. He started to become a 'rent a quote' where he offered quotes because he was asked and they were used because they were eminently quotable. Whether it was the working class being 'fed up of verbal soufflés and lack of action' from Labour[100] or 'There are 80,000 houses with no central heating. Tony Blair's Cool Britannia still means freezing [in] Scotland',[101] Tommy gave enlivening and colourful ripostes, showing that he had an eye for making hard hitting socialist-inspired comment. Putting all this together, from 1992/1993 onwards his actions and activities began to be covered in the press in the guise of Tommy being a minor celebrity, certainly more so than any ordinary councillor or political activist would justify. And although many of his claims and comments were over-the-top, there was a growing audience for the message he espoused. Initially, when media appearances were relatively uncommon, Tommy would discuss with Alan McCombes and others what he should try to get across and would be coached. However, from the late 1990s, this happened less for

Tommy developed his own skills and relationships with journalists. In this period, he also began to get some experience in writing short, pithy, agitational articles based around a foundation of facts and figures through his regular column, 'Tommy gives it laldy', in the SML newspaper and a few commissioned articles for the mainstream press.

Leadership

Although he often engaged in self-deprecation in public and talked in terms of the 'we' of SML, Tommy did on occasion recognise what the specific and considerable skills he brought to the table were. He told the *Herald*, using the football team metaphor: 'No everybody can score the goals, and strikers are no use without men at the back. The midfield is the powerhouse of the team, creating chances for the forwards and stopping the other team breaking through. I think that's where I belong'.[102] The practice of his style of leadership was, nonetheless, to be strong headed, single-minded and determined as Allan Green, SSA (and then SSP) national secretary recalled:

> [In] any lengthy discussions I had with Tommy, I was always of the impression that he had decided what he wanted beforehand and that I was there to be persuaded. I never felt that we were there to try to [jointly] work out what to do [and that reflected] the way Tommy thought about working with others that weren't from Militant. ... Tommy used to meet me in his office to tell me – that is what it was – that he was in favour of this or that. I never felt that we could bounce ideas off each other.

Gordon Morgan detected this style was 'a Militant trait' resultant from a culture of decisiveness and omniscience where 'a decision is made amongst the elite and then it is a question of selling it to others rather than broadening out the debate ... this commandist view [helps] cut through bureaucratic and administrative confusion [and sometimes the other methods] means you don't end up making decisions'.

Despite saying that he 'never had a grand plan in terms of standing in the general election, the council elections', the willingness to contest elections with him at the forefront was a conscious and deliberate political strategy in order to gain a wider audience. Alongside this, he continued to pioneer and advocate direct action, commenting: 'We were using these tactics well before they became sexy because they were used elsewhere in the world ... others on the left ignored us and then came to them late in the day' even if they had been used by others before.[103] Tommy's first formal leadership position in an open socialist organisation – of SSA National Convener – came about from Alan McCombes' initiative. In the first draft of the SSA constitution, there was no post of National Convener but Alan made the argument that Tommy in this position would be best able to use his profile to promote the SSA.

From Militant, he took the political orientation of aiming high and being ambitious. This revealed a central tension that would run throughout Tommy's political career. On the one hand, and as a socialist and leader of socialist political parties that wanted to both reform and revolutionise society but had little in the way of resources (financial, human, social) in a society dominated by hostile forces, he developed a set of policies and political stances that sought to inspire people with ideas and inspire them into action with these ideas. That necessarily meant the ideas had to be lofty and ambitious and where people looked to themselves, rather than others, to implement them. It meant talking up the possibility that change could, thus, happen and could be human made. However, on the other hand, to many this approach also seemed a tad far-fetched, unrealistic and unrealisable to say the least. In the absence of many successful mass collective actions – where the poll tax was only one even if a big one – this seemed all the more so. Notwithstanding his successes, more citizens seemed to view Tommy's ideas in this latter way than the way he wanted them to. But, of course, to cede ground to moderation and restraint would be to give up his firmly held political beliefs and, critically, his political brand. The questions now – as for all time later – were whether these would remain for a niche market or become for a mass market, and whether it was in the power of Tommy and his allies to determine which of these it would be.

Politics

Tommy's overarching politics meant that as soon as he finished attacking the Tories, he turned to pointing out that Labour was elected to defend people from the Tories but as soon as it was elected, instead of fighting the Tories' cuts and attacks, it raised the white flag of surrender and made and managed the cuts. Then he projected SML as 'real' Labour to open up his gambit for socialism as he understood and desired it:

> I want a social and economic system where the means of production are collectively owned and controlled, where need is the driving force of economics and not profit. We're no' talkin' about the local fish and chip shop or the newsagent round the corner [being nationalised], we're talkin' about the conglomerates

that decide what happens in our lives. What we should have is a ceiling and a floor, and within that make sure nobody falls below the floor or rises above the ceiling. ... I think it's inconceivable for us to argue we can't do it. Some might say I'm looking for some kind of Utopia. I would reply 'yes, why the hell not?'[104]

These idealist 'high politics' were complemented by and developed out of more mundane concerns:

In every campaign we're involved in, socialist change is what we're after. That's the big idea, that's what we're grasping for. But revolution isn't just one big act, it consists of hundreds and thousands of smaller actions in which you're always trying to raise the issues of justice and equality. Far too often people will blame this or that on an individual politician or a party. I think the most important thing is to try to promote awareness that it's the social and economic system itself that's to blame, and that we need a radical transformation of the whole system.[105]

He also told the *Sunday Times*: 'Common decency to me is socialism ... respecting other human beings to me is socialist therefore I can't separate my political outlook from my day-to-day activity trying to help people'.[106] Moreover, echoing the practicalities of community politics, he commented to the *Herald*: 'Folk formed human barriers outside the homes of people they had never met before – but they were determined to protect them from warrant sales. To me, it was a microcosm of a new society where ordinary people have power and are able to express and display their power'.[107] Later, and in a similar vein, he told the *Daily Record* that he supported community action – in this case a blockade against the erection of phone masks – because: 'Actions like this make communities what they are'.[108] Such views helped to show that some aspects of his socialism were somewhat more tangible and practical than many others on offer.

Conclusion

Tommy was a fortunate victim of historical circumstance in that the inability of the SLP to accommodate to the SSA led to the founding of the SSP. Had it not, the Scottish SLP would have been a wider but more varied terrain on which Tommy would have had to operate and do so alongside Scargill and rising stars like Bob Crow. While this may have been better for socialism, it would have made it that bit harder for Tommy to emerge in the way he did as an individual. This is all the more so when the joint-SSP/SLP list vote of 101,867 in the 1999 Scottish parliament election would likely have been boosted by the enhanced credibility of a united left and led to two other Scottish SLP MSPs also being elected in the Central and Lothian regions. The founding of the SSA and then SSP helped fill something of a dip in Tommy's fortunes for while being a councillor sustained him it did not maintain his elevation in the way the anti-poll tax revolt had. Indeed, after the fading of that revolt, Tommy was an individual without a sizeable body of people behind him. It took the decision of the SML to establish the SSA and then SSP to but that sizeable body of people back behind him.

Notes

1. As a result of one of these occupations in Glasgow in the summer of 1991, 180 hours community service was meted out to Tommy. And, in mid-1992 he was found innocent (along with others) of disorderly conduct in late 1991 in a demo against sheriff officers in Barlanark.
2. *Times* 31 May 1991.
3. *Herald* 24 January 1992.
4. *ATTR* p. 181. In his defence at the subsequent court case, he emphasised he tore up the interdict because of how it was served rather than being contemptuous of the court which granted it. This cut no ice with the judge. Interestingly, given his protestation about not swearing in the 2010 perjury case, he said in *A Time to Rage* (p. 204) of being accused of saying 'Fuck the interdict' – which formed a part of the evidence over ripping up the interdict – 'I can swear as good as anyone but not usually in public and not with scores of journalists and a couple of TV cameras in tow. Swear words have little places in speeches, though I can't help referring to bosses and certain members of the ruling class as bastards, because that's what they are'.
5. *ATTR* p. 187. Alan McCombes recalled that Tommy did not need to attend the protest nor rip up the interdict but it all made for a good piece of theatre which he applauded (*DTTSS* p. 16).
6. *Guardian* 2 October 1991.
7. *Independent* 2 October 1991.
8. *ATTR* p. 185.
9. 6 October 1991.
10. Ironically, he tore up the interdict after the warrant sale was cancelled.
11. The court in Parliament Square is where he would return in 2006 for his defamation action against *NoW*.
12. *ATTR* pp. 202–203.
13. *ATTR* p. 206.
14. *Herald* 29 January 1992.
15. Ironically, being at 'Hotel Saughton', meant Tommy – like other prisoners – was exempt from paying the poll tax for the duration of their incarceration. Now journalist (but then social worker who observed Tommy in Saughton), Phil Mac Giolla Bain recalls that although not required to wear a prisoner's uniform, Tommy was keen to do so, with this giving some basis to his belief that Tommy was putting on a performance

and acting out a character role while in prison (see his 'Citizen Sheridan' 24 December 2010 http://www.philmacgiollabhain.ie/citizen-sheridan/).

16. *ATTR* p. 207, 211.
17. *Herald* 7 March 1992.
18. In his time inside Saughton, Tommy saw both humanity and violence in the prisoners and their link to poverty and depravation. He was quick to make such points when given the opportunity by the media so that crime was put in its full, socialised context. While in prison, he received considerable correspondence, some of which were allegedly offers of sexual relations from women. It has been reported that he responded positively to these and engaged in so much correspondence with one of them that the letters needed to be retrieved (for more details on this see *DTTSS* pp. 21–22).
19. See also *ATTR* p. 196.
20. *ATTR* p. 226.
21. 15 December 1991.
22. *Herald* 24 March 1992.
23. *ATTR* p. 223.
24. *Herald* 11 April 1992.
25. Venton, R. 'The Battle for Pollok' in *Our Stand for Socialism* (Militant, 1992), p. 35.
26. See, for example, *Independent* 24 March 1992.
27. *Sunday Times* 22 March 1992.
28. *Independent* 7 April 1992.
29. *Herald* 11 April 1992.
30. *Herald* 11 April 1992.
31. *ATTR* pp. 223–224.
32. For an account of how the campaign in Pollok was used to successfully recruit 175 members, establish 6 more branches and lay down further root, see Venton, R. 'The Battle for Pollok' in *Our Stand for Socialism* (Militant, 1992).
33. One of those elected, Stevenson, had favoured standing in every seat in Glasgow (*ATTR* p. 232).
34. This success was recognised by independent observers. For example, Hearn, J. (*Claiming Scotland: national identity and liberal culture*, Polygon, 2000, p. 57) wrote: 'Under the charismatic leadership of Tommy Sheridan, SML had some striking successes in the impoverished public housing projects of Glasgow'.
35. While Tommy was inside Saughton, his flat in Linthaugh Road was used as the campaign headquarters for the two election campaigns. In recognition of the mess this made and of their close friendship, George and some others redecorated the flat for Tommy's homecoming (*ATTR* p. 230).
36. *Herald* 2 July 1992.
37. By contrast, the SWP took a rather abstentionist position, encapsulated in its slogan, 'Revolution, not devolution'.
38. *ATTR* pp. 247–248.
39. Milligan, T. 'Left at the Polls: the changing far-left vote' *Scottish Affairs*, 1999, No. 29, p. 12.
40. SML needed five councillors to be official group but was unable through acrimony with Labour to peel off one or two Labour councillors to achieve this.
41. This had echoes of Liverpool council in the mid-1980s under Militant leadership.
42. *Herald* 13 March 1995.
43. *Herald* 7 February 1997.
44. This led the council in mid-1994 to seek and gain an interdict against Tommy, Alice and two others to prevent them entering its finance offices.

45. However, it appeared that it was more difficult for SML as a political party to gain media attention (see *ATTR* pp. 252–253) and so for it, direct method of communication with workers and communities continued.
46. *Herald* 3 September 1993.
47. *Herald* 23 June 1992.
48. See *Herald* 10 June 1993.
49. *Sunday Herald* 6 May 2007.
50. See also Milligan, T. 'Left at the Polls: the changing far-left vote' *Scottish Affairs*, 1999, No. 29.
51. *Herald* 5 September 1992.
52. *Herald* 31 October 1992.
53. See *Independent* 5 September 1992.
54. See, for example, *Independent* 5 September 1992, *Herald* 9 December 1992.
55. *Sunday Times* 18 October 1992.
56. *Herald* 16 October 1992.
57. *Sunday Times* 23 August 1992.
58. *Herald* 12 August 1992. See also *ATTR* p. 235.
59. Later on, Tommy was still arguing: 'We are confident that the Scottish people will sink the Tory water boards' (*Herald* 3 March 1995).
60. *Herald* 29 January 1993.
61. *Independent* 5 September 1992, *Herald* 9 December 1992.
62. This spadework also included campaigning against dysentery, sell offs of council land and facilities to property developers, and the impact of Child Support Act 1993 on reducing benefits (see *ATTR* pp. 241–243). In this period, Tommy 'co-authored' a SML pamphlet with Alan McCombes called *Struggle, Solidarity and Socialism* which set out the tasks of socialists in Scotland.
63. *Herald* 16 Feb 1993.
64. *Herald* 1 March 1993.
65. Milligan, T. 'Left at the Polls: the changing far-left vote' *Scottish Affairs*, 1999, No. 29, p. 9.
66. *Herald* 7 May 1994.
67. *Scotsman* 1 July 1994.
68. *Scotland on Sunday* 16 June 1993.
69. *Herald* 7 May 1993.
70. See *ATTR* pp. 248–252.
71. 25 May 1994. Some 16 years later, Ian Bell would write a less than complimentary piece on Tommy's situation, showing his disappointment with Tommy's actions (*Sunday Herald* 30 January 2011).
72. He spent a short time in Barlinnie 1996 for his role in trying to prevent a poinding in 1994. He was sentenced to seven days for non-payment of a £150 fine but due to prison rules concerning holding short-term prisoners over weekends, he spent about two-and-a-half days in prison. Originally he was sentenced to 30 days for resisting arrest, but appealed to the Court of Session and the sentence was reduced to a £150 fine.
73. *Herald* 3 November 1994.
74. *Daily Record* 19 October 1994.
75. The reorganisation of local government in Scotland into unitary councils meant that SML's regional councillors were only in post for another year.
76. *Herald* 16 March 1995.
77. *Herald* 16 March 1995.
78. *Cf. ATTR* p. 232.
79. *Herald* 2 March 1995. This type of accusation would be made against Tommy again when he encouraged school students in Edinburgh to leave classes to join an anti-war

demonstration in 2003. What both events testified to was his ability to able to build a close relationship with school students.
80. He was also convicted on another charge related to another M77 demo in 1995, where he conducted his own defence.
81. *Herald* 28 September 1999.
82. *Scotsman* 11 March 1997.
83. *Herald* 30 September 1995.
84. *Herald* 4 August 1995.
85. *Scottish* Socialist Voice 8 November 2002.
86. *Herald* 18 December 1996.
87. The same was true of many of the joint-campaigns and their relative successes dating back to the poll tax but the difference with those of the period 1995 onwards was that SML had given up the idea of it being the only legitimate revolutionary socialist force.
88. Labour had committed itself to create such a parliament and was consistently ahead in the polls despite John Major, Conservative prime minister, continually putting off the general election – in search of his Tory augmenting 'green shoots of economic recovery' – to the last possible minute.
89. 12 February 1996.
90. *Herald* 22 April 1997.
91. Ironically, the SSA recorded in first substantive electoral advance when in 1998 Scots-born Hugh Kerr, then MEP for West Essex and East Hertfordshire, joined the SSA after being expelled from Labour. Of this, Tommy believed: 'When Hugh Kerr joined, it showed [us] gaining audience and respect outside the far left ... [if you like] the idealists not just the poor and downtrodden'. As a result of this developing relationship, Tommy remembered: 'Hugh introduced me to mobile phones ... we scoffed at them initially because of the yuppies but they became essential to organising'.
92. *Herald* 16 April 1997.
93. *Herald* 15 August 1997.
94. See, for example, *Daily Record* 14 September 2000.
95. 11 August 1996.
96. *Herald* 13 March 1995 and 22 April 1997 respectively.
97. 11 August 1996.
98. *Herald* 13 March 1995.
99. 13 March 1995.
100. *Herald* 9 December 1992.
101. *Daily Record* 11 December 1998.
102. 3 March 1995.
103. See *ATTR* for various cases of Tommy recognising this.
104. *Herald* 3 March 1995. This seemingly heterodox espousal of a role for small business under socialism would take on added significance when discussing Tesco in the 2003 Scottish Parliament elections (see later).
105. *Herald* 3 March 1995.
106. 11 August 1996.
107. 20 April 1999.
108. 14 September 2000.

4

The Golden Years

Introduction

The years 1999 to 2003 marked the great renewal of the radical, socialist left in Scotland, beginning with the election of Tommy to the Scottish Parliament and ending in the arrival of five other SSP MSPs. For the SSP, seats in parliament were not the be all and end all of its success – and neither should that be the only measure used to judge its success. But it did, nevertheless, indicate that a significant upturn in the ability of a socialist party to enter the main political arena had taken place, suggesting the SSP had become credible to a large swathe of citizens. For the first time in a generation, socialism had come out of the ghetto in Scotland, and Tommy was its key lieutenant. In no small measure was this success down to the combination of public recognition of Tommy, his tireless work and political skills. To take advantage of these and, indeed, to make them manifest, the army of activists and other leaders behind and alongside Tommy had put their shoulders to the wheel.

Death of SSA and SML

The last conference of SSA on 20 September 1998 took the momentous decision to launch the SSP on 21 February 1999.[1] In some ways, this was just a change of name for little new would happen in the intervening period. But in other ways, the creation of a party from an alliance was a sign of not only the maturing of a radical, socialist unity project but its intention to also grow and develop so that it became more than just the rearranging of the deckchairs on a socialist Titanic.

The SML conference to move towards creating the SSP took place in March 1998. This led to the parting of the ways between the majority (85%) and the minority (15%) where the CWI leadership based in London argued against a broad party of socialism (i.e. the SSP)

in favour of a cadre-based party which remained essentially as the
SML. Tommy recalled that these arguments were: 'trying to hold
onto an identity which had moved on ... [when there was a need] ... to
re-popularise the ideas of socialism [because while] in the 1980s inside
Labour socialism was already quite popular but what wasn't was a particular stand of Marxist socialism ... [Then the] popularity of socialism
had been lost ... [prompting] ... a battle over which road to go down ...
the term SML also sent out all the wrong messages to other socialists
that were looking for a new home'. SML took the decision to dissolve
itself just before the establishment of the SSP. Tommy recollected at
various points:

> When we dissolved SML, we never thought we'd not be in an
> organisation ... we saw ourselves as part of the new left rather than
> the new left itself ... we never had a problem about the idea that in
> a few years SML would be wound up or join something else ... we
> played a critical role in bringing about the SSA ... from Liberation
> to the Socialist Movement, the project was to create with these
> people something bigger than ourselves but that wouldn't be us ...
> Militant's argument was the SML should be the bigger party ...
> but we had to rebuild the whole idea of socialist ideas from the
> bottom up ... in the 1980s the argument was about how to deliver
> socialism, not what it means but after 1990 there was a 'new world
> order' and 'the end of history' ... we needed to be part of laying
> the new broad foundations for socialist ideas while the Militant
> was talking about the building of a revolutionary socialist party
> that appealed to a narrower base ... tactically and ideology there
> was a clash ...
>
> We'd by this time in our political development already moved
> to the recognition of the need for a broader organisation that
> could reconquer the summits of socialism rather than a narrower
> organisation that represented [just] a strand of socialism ... in the
> 1990s socialism had to be re-resurrected compared to the 1980s
> when the idea of socialism got an echo ... SML was an initial stab
> at broadening our appeal ... it wasn't just a cadre organisation ...
> when we started to work with others we had to overcome the
> problem of 'this is just Militant by another name', especially if
> the word 'militant' was retained ... it was also a problem retaining
> the name 'Labour' ... we understood the need to build a broader
> socialist party and that brought us into conflict with Militant in
> London ...
>
> SML was a necessary development in re-orientating the left, not
> just the revolutionary left ... a spur to change ... because [it] showed

more than anything else that there was an electoral alternative to the left [of Labour] ... that there wasn't any complete isolationism by standing ... electorally we were probably more successful electorally although that only tells you that events and objective circumstances determine success rather than subjective circumstances ... SML recorded six first-past-the-post victories – which the SSP hasn't equalled yet as it's had only two. SML showed that standing against Labour didn't mean you were consigned to the rubbish bin of hell where you'd never be seen again.

Finally, another reason Tommy explained, was: 'It became difficult to ask people to go to two sets of meetings [SML, SSA] and to run two organisations and do any of it properly'. Upon dissolution, most of what was SML reconstituted itself as an internal platform, namely, the ISM. But before the SML and SSA were consigned to the 'historical dustbin', they had shown their usefulness as well as that the holy trinity of the sins of reformism, electoralism and nationalism – as alleged by various far left and Trotskyist groups like the SWP – could be successfully navigated and countered in the building of a credible socialist force. But more than that both organisations showed that all three sins – especially where national aspirations are reconfigured as national identity – could be reconceived as means to propagate socialism and not threats to it. Although Tommy was a leading exponent of the dissolution of the SML and the creation of the SSA and SSP, he was not one of the behind-the-scenes negotiators. On his side, these were Alan McCombes, Jim McVicar and Ronnie Stevenson. Yet in the moves within SML towards founding the SSP, Tommy displayed much impatience. Richie Venton recounted that Tommy was rather 'fast and loose with principles' for he advocated the new party had no need of an internal platform representing the politics of Militant. Richie believed this indicated Tommy's disregard for subtleties and betrayed a depth of understanding. He recalled: '[Tommy] was premature because he wanted to use fiat and diktat as a means of imposing an ideological progression on the SSP which had not yet happened because the homogenisation of the SSP had not advanced sufficiently to justify dumping platform organisation and leaving those that would be looking for a home of Marxist ideas to the SWP amongst others'. Subsequently, Tommy did not play an active part in the ISM (although he was not alone in former Militant/SSA/SSP leading members in doing this). Later on, Allan Green, from a different political perspective, also detected this tendency: 'His determination to try to take radical, socialist ideas to a mass audience ... [was] a great strength, and potential weakness' because while it 'sometimes [led to] breaking down taboos and challenging the left about how to do this ...

collective restraint was [also] important on him because he was capable of going in directions that are not just about breaking new ground but breaking with socialist ideas'.[2]

Gaining More Critical Mass

The year 1998 saw Tommy taken more seriously by the mass media. For example, the two mass circulation tabloids from a Labourist stable in Scotland, the *Sunday Mail*[3] and *Daily Record*,[4] ran full length features on Tommy. The significance of this was while the *Herald*, *Scotsman* and *Scotland on Sunday* had done so before and in sympathetic ways, the *Sunday Mail* and *Daily Record* doing so allowed an audience with a wider and more working class constituency. This represented a key point in the crossover. In the *Daily Record* piece, the multi-faceted 'Citizen Tommy' persona was given more ground. This consisted of the good looking, sincere and affable working class rebel: 'Long, lean and handsome, deep tan, perfect complexion, the eyes are deep pools of integrity ... the Robin Hood of Scottish politics ... Tommy Sheridan is the trendy 1990s version of the Red Clydesiders ... [T]he Tommy Factor has been present in every people's protest in the last decade – warrant sales, council cuts, water charges, the M77'. His voicemail message on his mobile became almost legendary because of the number of times it had been replicated in the press: '[Sorry, I can't take your call right now but] I'm probably out fighting Blair and his new Tories'.[5] But so that he did not become reliant upon the potentially fickle 'goodwill' of the press, he became an inveterate letter writer to the *Daily Record* and *Herald* in this period. Shorter and longer letters for the two newspapers respectively kept his name in the frame on the issues he wished to speak out on and he appeared to be guaranteed publication by virtue of being both Tommy Sheridan and an elected councillor. Of this, Tommy said these were 'used to get our voice heard especially [as the letters' pages were a] vibrant arena ... to get the identity of SSP known and to raise socialist issues ... we used whatever means were available to get a platform ... and the *Record* allowed us to get to loads of people'.

The solicitation and courting evidenced by the features above showed Tommy continued with the strategy and tactics he developed for getting the best from the media: 'Unlike the rest of the left, I think the media is to be courted and used, not ignored and abused ... it is a horrible, horrible beast but it's one you cannot ignore and even though you'll never tame and control it ... if you just ignore it, it will savage you'. Tommy continued to build up his skills of working out who to deal with and how to deal with them. Compared to other party leaders and politicians, he was available to speak to them directly, allowing him to form these contacts and links. His skill here stemmed from an understanding that the means of delivering the socialist message had to be expanded beyond leaflets, socialist newspapers and strike support. Moreover, he believed in taking the struggle to one of the hearts of beast. In short, he advocated – and acted upon – trying to win the hearts and minds of citizens and in so doing build wider influence rather than the time served method of many Trotskyist groups of concentrating on membership recruitment and paper sales. In his television interviews, he was clear and well thought out in what he was trying to achieve:

> When it comes to the telly, I try to be as plain talking as possible and use phrases that summarise things you'd like to say in one sentence rather than a few. [That] I always try to be as honest and straightforward as possible is appreciated by people because they don't get straight answers from politicians.

Birth of the SSP[6]

To keep up the momentum established, the SSP announced an array of high profile supporters like actors Peter Mullan, Dougray Scott, Gary Lewis, Martin McCardie, Peter McDougall and David Mackay, novelists Iain Banks, Alistair Gray, James Kelman and Irvine Welsh, and playwright Peter Arnott, and former Celtic and Hibs footballer Jackie McNamara. Of this, Tommy commented: 'I had no qualms about pursuing people like Peter Mullan ... because, although people are not sheep, it is important to have credibility and legitimacy because people look up to those in the front-line ... I'm trying to broaden our appeal and deepen our ranks ... Do we approach them for publicity? Yes and no: we don't 'use' them because they want[ed] to do things for their party'. The pursuit of the likes of Peter Mullan, Davy McKay and Peter Arnott took place on the basis of already knowing them through their political activism and their politically-inspired work (like 'Harmony Row' about the poll tax). For example, Tommy knew Gary Lewis in the LPYS and Dougray Scott had also been in the LPYS.[7] To Tommy, there was a wider context for this collection of 'celebrity supporters': 'Some of the most creative minds come from the left – the passion and willingness to express a rage against a social injustice ... previously they would have naturally found their home in Labour but as Labour drifted rightwards these people became lost like Elaine C. Smith, Tony Roper and Ricky Ross'. But it was not just these left-wing 'luvvies' that gravitated towards the SSP. Maybe in echoes of Richard Holloway's comments, Father Steve Gilhooley – who also wrote a regular *Evening News* column – became a vocal public supporter around this time.

In regard of one of the most high-profile of these, Tommy said: 'Peter Mullan always used to make the point that up until the SSP he was politically homeless because he always believed in independence for Scotland and in socialism and the SSP was the first party to bring those together'. Some of the most obvious help that the actors were able to give was the making of SSP party political broadcasts. But it was not just 'the luvvies' that Tommy and the SSP pursued. Many press launches were also held to announce the welcoming of new recruits and defectors from other parties.[8]

At this time, a poll showed that up to 20% of the electorate might vote SSP in the forthcoming elections for the Scottish Parliament.[9] In Tommy's hand such polls suggested: 'There's no reason to believe that in next May's election we can't take five or six seats' as well as play a kingmaker role if the SNP and Labour tied with an equal number of seats.[10] Into 1999, some polls (including one commissioned by the SSP from System Three) showed the SSP had enough support to get more than one seat, with Tommy predicting up to 10 seats and, again, a balance of power role, and a historical parallel with the ILP.[11] Of his predictions, Tommy justified his rationale for doing so:

> There's a tightrope to be walked between being dishonest and misleading, on the one hand, and not dousing the flames of enthusiasm in your members and supporters [on the other] ... very few people want to back a loser so you have to inspire people that their efforts and their vote will count ... for 1999 that sound[ed] a bit over top especially because polls in Glasgow weren't looking good for us – though they were wrong as it turned out.

But in a one-off moment of caution, possibly to save himself from being hoisted by his own petard, Tommy told the *Scotsman*: 'Whether I am elected in May or not is not the question. What we have created is a party that can carry the torch of good, the torch of hope, the torch of socialism ... It was never a big ambition of mine to get elected, but there comes a time when you either have to put up or shut up. I was asked to stand for election, so I did. It's as simple as that'.[12] That one case aside, Tommy's dubious predictions were no doubt largely forgotten as a result of his star performance in the first Parliament.

Prior to the election, the SSP had 1,040 members in 36 branches,[13] having risen from around 600 in September 1998. Just after the May 1999 election, this had grown to around 2,000, suggesting that

in this case – in addition to Tommy's election and largely because
of it – the old adage that socialist parties do not just stand in elections for votes was true and meaningful. Shortly before the election,
the SSP agreed with the SWP an electoral arrangement whereby the
SWP would stand in four seats unopposed by the SSP in return for
not standing against the SSP in the other constituency seats and in all
the list seats.[14] The key list region for this arrangement was Glasgow.
Tommy recalled that the SSP 'always approached others on the left
for unity. ... What we were giving [to the SWP] compared to what we
were getting was a good deal ... we tried the same with the SLP but
they weren't for listening and neither would the CPB'. Come the election, the SSP secured 23,564 (1%) votes in the constituency seats and
46,635 (2%) in the list seats, crucially with 18,581 (7.2%) votes in the
Glasgow region, securing Tommy's election and confounding some
polls which predicted the SSP (as with the Greens) would not make
it past the 6%–7% threshold on the list seats in their target areas. In
the constituency election, Tommy secured 5,611 (21.5%) votes, coming third. The significance of the SLP turning down any cooperative
arrangement was that it secured 55,232 votes, outpolling the SSP in
five of the eight list regions. According to Tommy: 'Some of that was
to do with the miners and Scargill's name [especially in areas of former mining areas of central and south of Scotland and the Lothians]
but the amount of anecdotal evidence we came across that people said
they voted for us and they'd actually voted SLP [was considerable] ...
the evidence for this is that we beat them out of the park in the Euro-
elections two months later and by which time we were far better
known'. At the very least, an agreement to put the votes together
under a single socialist party in each list seat would have secured – in
all likelihood – more than another socialist MSP. In the June 1999
European elections, the SSP's share of the increased from 2% in May
1999 to 4% (39,720 votes) on a reduced 33% turnout.

The Workers' Wage

The policy of 'a workers' MP on a workers' wage' was not a new one for
Militant had pioneered its practice with its three MPs in the 1980s and
when a number of its members were elected as union leaders (like John
Macreadie in the Civil and Public Services Association in the 1980s).
SML promoted it thereafter. However, as the prospect of Tommy being
elected to the Scottish Parliament drew closer, it took on far greater
significance and helped establish both him and the SSP as a different
kind of politician and political party respectively. With increasing public

disdain for political corruption and politicians' personal aggrandisement, the workers' wage policy reinforced the view that Tommy would do what he said he would do, namely, be incorruptible and remain steadfast to his socialist principles. So, Tommy began raising the issue as early as possible.[15] He told *Scotland on Sunday*: 'Our argument is, if you are going to represent the average worker you should have a similar lifestyle. We say a worker's MP on a worker's wage and we've turned the slogan into reality'.[16] And, challenging what were seen as high salaries (even if these were lower than their Westminster counterparts), Tommy, with his usual colour, proclaimed: 'You mean, if we pay peanuts, we'll get monkeys? We've already got monkeys and we're paying over the odds for them'.[17] The workers' wage formed part of a wider position on wages. Way ahead of its time, the SSP advocated a maximum wage (of £70 per hour, with the minimum of £7 as a 'living wage'). Occasionally, some would attack Tommy on the workers' wage when they realised that rather than giving the money back to the taxpayer (as they had assumed), the money was given to the SSP. In 2001, Tommy's take home pay was £1200 per month with £1100 per month going to the SSP (along with his £370 councillor's monthly allowance and monies from TV appearances).[18]

Tommy Sheridan MSP

Tommy as the socialist tribune – or any other such appellation of prior to May 1999 – fully came of age when he was elected to the Scottish Parliament. Amongst 128 other MSPs, he could have easily got lost. As a lone SSP MSP, he could have avoided the parliament. In a parliament, he could have easily become just a parliamentarian. Ensconced amongst the politicians of the mainstream parties, he could have lost the anti-establishment fire in his belly. In the parliament, he could have become detached from the SSP. But not only did none of these happen. Rather, quite the reverse happened. He became the commonly acclaimed stand out MSP and parliamentary performer despite also being the hardest working elected politician outside the Parliament; he lost none of his righteous anger; he laid down a slew of bills; and he put the SSP in a position of lift-off as a mainstream *socialist* political party. Early on his only competitor for the mantle of 'colour and conscience'[19] was fellow MSP, Dennis Canavan. Quite quickly, Tommy came into his own, having no imitators or rivals on this score. His experience of negotiating agendas and committees and working on his own albeit by building alliances on Glasgow City Council stood him in good stead.

The Signing in Ceremony

The iconic image of the first Scottish Parliament is not of so-called 'father of the nation', Donald Dewar, speaking in the chamber or some such sight but of Tommy Sheridan, fist clenched, taking the oath of allegiance under protest and duress at the swearing in ceremony. The *Herald* believed the image became a 'legend'[20] and it adorned the cover of the co-authored book with Alan McCombes, *Imagine* (see later). It was not just the clenched fist of defiance but the wearing of a suit that constituted the iconography.[21] Tommy recalled: 'What I did from the outset showed that I might be in a suit but was not part of it ... I'm still a rebel ... it matters what you say and do, not what you wear or look like ... it did become an icon of that opening ceremony'.[22] But for some of the rightwing press, Tommy made himself into a 'playground ass'[23] while for the *Daily Mail*, Tommy 'act[ed out] his Trotskyite fantasies'.[24] Tommy took up the story surrounding this:

I was contemplating wearing jeans for the 1999 swearing cer-emony ... for all the 1980s and 1990s, I was the black bomber jacket and jeans guy ... I was always I thought smart and clean and presentable but I never wore a tie ... When I was elected in 1999, I had a dilemma about what to wear and what to do ... with the basis on which I was elected, I didn't want to lie by taking the oath ... if the Westminster system had been adopted I might not have taken my seat like Sinn Fein does ... but the Scotland Act entrenches the monarchy because if you don't swear the oath of allegiance within three months then your seat goes to the next person in line on the list or a by-election ... I think I did the right thing for the SSP ... and we didn't have the option ...

I was going to wear my jeans and shirt but not a suit or a shirt and tie ... I had a suit from a wedding and Gail bought me a white shirt and a red tie ... I phoned around people like George McNeilage, Richie Venton, Keith Baldassara, Alan McCombes ... they were two for shirt without tie and two for suit but it was my granny, Rose,[25] that was the one that won it because [she said] I was representing the working class so I should be as smart as possible ... and Gail said wearing a suit was like wearing a uni-form ... and I concluded it was more about what you do within the uniform than the uniform itself ... If I'd gone for the shirt and jeans at the opening, I'd have probably got slaughtered ... I think we might not have been taken seriously ...

That day I was up and away at six in the morning because I was going to a protest against the building of a dump in a working class area where the residents were out to block the road ... with all that going on I never really had the chance to think what I was going to say ... it was only when I was wait-ing there in line to take the oath that I began to form in my mind the words I want to express ... it wasn't written down ... I hadn't thought about raising my fist either but I knew I want to express my defiance ... I started my words and then raised my fist because it was not pre-planned ... I'd always been inspired by the Black Panthers.

So on the 12 May 1999 Tommy declared at the swearing in cere-mony: 'Before making the affirmation, I would like to declare that as a democratically elected socialist, my vision for Scotland is of a democratic socialist republic, where the supreme sovereignty lies with the people of Scotland, not with an unelected monarch. I there-fore make this affirmation under protest'. Initially, Tommy said he would not take the oath.[26] On the day, Tommy pledged allegiance to her majesty's 'hair and accessories' and not her 'heir and successors' according to the *Sunday Herald*.[27] Along with Dennis Canavan, he did, however, boycott the Queen's speech at the open ceremony, speak-ing at a rally against student tuition fees instead. Later in the day, and instead of attending any of the official celebrations, he attended an alternative one at the Jack Jardine Memorial Centre (see later) in Pollok, where he bemoaned that there was no public holiday to cel-ebrate the official opening of the Scottish Parliament nor any official celebrations outside Edinburgh. All this was press released so that Tommy's position on the matters was made evident. It was covered because he provided colour – the colour, red – to the proceedings.

Despite some criticisms from republicans that he should not take the oath, it became evident that he had to take it in order to be able to operate and so the comparison they made with Sinn Féin was not warranted. Once sworn in, the issue of where to sit took on some importance. Tommy, along with Dennis Canavan (MP for Falkirk West party) and Green MSP, Robin Harper, took seats at the front as they represented individual parties. Upon realising the significance of this for ease of being spotted by the Parliament's Presiding Officer to get called to ask question as well as media coverage, Labour and the Liberal Democrats tried to get the three MSPs ejected from the front row. Tommy threatened a sit-in along with the other two.[28] They won out, and Tommy said Jim Wallace, Liberal Democrat leader, should move nearer Donald Dewar so 'the puppet could be next to the puppet master'.[29]

Attitude to Parliament

For the Trotskyist left, one of the most serious errors to befall socialists in parliament is parliamentary cretinism. Marx and Engels defined it as the fatal delusion that a socialist society could be achieved exclusively by peaceful, parliamentary means. Although the experience of 'Red Clydesider' Labour and ILP MPs as well as Ralph Miliband's *Parliamentary Socialism* had reinforced this definition, parliamentary cretinism had also come to mean the unduly heavy emphasis on parliament as a site of agitation and propaganda eclipsing such activities outside it and to their detriment. So for Tommy, there was another important tension to be successfully navigated. That he was the only SSP MSP, however, meant that it would be difficult for parliamentary cretinism of the first sort to happen, accidentally or otherwise. But it would not be difficult for a single MSP to become ensconced in parliament as part of the hothouse of an elite club of self-important people, to think that what happened inside parliament was far more important than what happened outside it or to feel the need, because of being the only SSP MSP, to have to work in parliament all the harder and longer. One of the best known measures to avoid such pitfalls has been to be politically anchored in an oppositional ideology. Thus, Tommy explained:

> Dave Nellist and Terry Fields were better role models for me than Tony Benn because while he was an inspiration, they were 'ours' so I had ideas about how to perform by promoting your ideas and represent your class, communicate on their behalf and take on the rich and powerful because they were voiceless.

In practice, this meant being there for key votes and making as many speeches and interventions on selected issues as possible but not to the detriment of building the SSP and resistance outside parliament. Thus, Hassan and Lynch concluded that with one of the worst voting records in parliament, Tommy was still 'one of the undoubted stars'[30] of the parliament. Instead, Tommy was willingly used by the SSP to travel the length and breadth of Scotland speaking at public meetings, launching new SSP branches and the like. In his weekly *Scottish Socialist Voice* page, he recounted his hectic speaking itinerary and picketlines visits. His column entitled 'No sleep 'til socialism'[31] gave a good indication of his 'life in the day of' which began at 6am and ended at 11pm.

Political Tasks Inside Parliament

Underlying everything Tommy did in his first term as MSP was a strategy to capitalise on disillusionment with 'new' Labour, from those of an 'old' Labour disposition[32], as well as from new idealists, and prevent this mood drifting to the SNP. In doing so, the point was to show the SSP as radical and different but also credible and serious. It was the antidote to the mainstream political parties which had been colonised by neo-liberalism – the worship or acceptance of the 'free market' – in one form or another. Thus, he sought to use his exposure as a result of being an MSP to make the political case that socialism and independence could go together by taking every opportunity to demonstrate that the Scottish Parliament lacked the powers it needed to bring about radical social change. He was able to make hay doing this when Alex Salmond stood down as SNP leader in 2000 to be replaced by John Swinney (until 2004). The point was to allow the SSP activists to recruit members and gain an audience, and according to Jim Sillars,[33] this began to happen as he argued that the SSP was recruiting members and voters that the SNP used to attract. Of this time, Tommy said:

> If we were seen as 'old' Labour then that wouldn't be a problem because we would have then become a serious contender ... and there were some aspects of 'old' Labour that were very good ... and if people see us as an 'old' that the SNP used to be a radical, anti-establishment party, then that's good too ... but many people [increasingly now] see us just as the SSP because they've not known anything else ... and that's good too.

As a lone MSP, Tommy could have decided to be just a noise, proclaiming what he was for and decrying what he was against. He did this but if he had only done this, he would have been attacked by his political foes as a grandstanding MSP incapable of being constructive. So he showed, in the words of American president, Lyndon Johnson, that he could 'fart and chew gum at the same time' by being both a socialist voice and a socialist legislator. But, of course, 'want doesn't get' as requisite skills are required to achieve goals. Tommy had begun developing these as a councillor, so he sought out like-minded MSPs in order to construct the necessary alliances. He said of this time:

> At the outset, I didn't know many of the SNP – that only came through working with them. I didn't know Alex Neil but I had come across Kenny MacAskill in the anti-poll tax campaign ... we tried to come to arrangements with the Greens but it became

clear there was a middle class majority within them that said – in terms of any electoral alliances – what they lose in the middle class areas won't be compensated by what they'd gain in the working class areas. So I didn't hold out much hope there [with Robin Harper]. I asked Dennis Canavan to join [the SSP] before the 1999 elections and he did give it serious consideration ... so I knew I'd be able to work with Dennis although I had a fall out with him in 2000/2001 when he applied to rejoin Labour ... I was disappointed in him ... I didn't know John McAllion or Elaine Smith but through raising issues I started to make links with them and others ... I managed to build a consensus of individuals ... I started with issues I knew about like warrant sales and debt and then went on to the free school meals which was a radical anti-poverty and pro-health strategy.

While he made considerable headway here, he was kept out of the Social Inclusion, Housing and Voluntary Sector Committee he wished for given his interests. Instead, he was given membership on the Local Government and Transport Committee. Early on, Tommy recognised that he could deploy the resources at his disposal in a productive way: '[As with the council chamber] I learnt to use ... the Parliament by saying to the finance people, 'I want to come up with an alternative budget' and they would do all the work and come up with the figures ... you learnt to use other people's resources'.

One of the very visible hallmarks of Tommy's public pronouncements as an MSP was to excoriate the parliament and Labour for excess, waste, corruption and hypocrisy given the purported promise of the parliament to be 'about the people, with the people, for the people' as well as for Labour in Scotland to be the 'people's party'. Thus, he went to town on the expenditure on medals for the first MSPs, and attacked the 'stench of hypocrisy and arrogance'[34] of Labour over its position on PFI in the first main debate of the parliament and later on its connivance in ending free education. A few months later, he told parliament in a debate on Dewar's proposals for open and accountable government: 'It disnae matter how many times you reheat mince, it's still mince'.[35] When Tony Blair, then prime minister, proclaimed that 'the class war was over' as part of his 'new' Labour third-way ideology, Tommy had the temerity to ask 'so who won then?' in order to highlight that the capitalists still seemed to be in control. In 2002, he blasted Labour again, saying: 'PFI is not an economic imperative but a political statement'.[36] And, in line with the workers' wage, he continually attacked the rises in the salaries of MSPs which were consistently above those for most others and overwhelmingly accepted by the MSPs. He did not just criticise the extremely generous pension arrangement for disgraced former first minister, Henry McLeish, but took the lead in challenging it.

Early on he was recognised as 'a star of the Scottish Parliament'[37] and that he provided the only 'real colour' in parliament,[38] with *Scotland on Sunday* declaring he had 'star quality, a genuine charisma and conviction'.[39] Professor John Curtice, the leading psephologist, recognised that Tommy in parliament gave the SSP the 'crucial credibility it needs to act as an effective conduit for traditional Labour voters dismayed at their party's move to the centre'.[40] The question that was posed by the likes of radical SNP MSP Alex Neil but could not be answered in the affirmative for some time yet was whether this would be anything more than a protest vote. Neil contrasted the SSP as the 'party of protest' to the SNP as the 'party of power'.[41] Nonetheless, Tommy performed so well that there was discussion in Labour circles of avoiding the embarrassment of Tommy getting the first Members' Bill into law by submitting another to stymie it.[42]

However, Tommy introduced his *Abolition of Poindings and Warrant Sales Bill* on 24 September 1999. This was an obvious but, nonetheless, clever choice given his anti-poll tax activity. It showed Tommy continued to have a practical aspect to his politics and carried on working on longstanding concerns. He highlighted that 23,067 poindings and 513 warrant sales took place in 1998,[43] and batted back various attempts at exemptions from interested groups and championed those establishment voices that said warrant sales were inefficient, immoral and bad for public relations. His *piece de resistance* here was to point out Labour's policy since 1893 had been to abolish warrant sales without ever doing much about it. In another indication of his ability to work with others and harness their expertise,[44] the Bill was drafted by Mike Dailly of the Govan Law Centre (who also worked on Tommy's Free School Meals Bill). Later on, Tommy would deploy the services of two academics, Mike Danson and Geoff Whittam, to compile the groundwork for the case for the replacement of the council tax (the successor to the poll tax) with the income-based and redistributive Scottish Service Tax. So, Tommy thereby pioneered another Bill which further ploughed the furrow of the hated poll tax but at the same time showed his practical intent, and on an issue which struck a chord with low income citizens. In taking these initiatives, Tommy also showed not just an ability to work with other MSPs but to take the lead and gather them around him. The obvious examples were the co-sponsors of his bills and motions, namely, Dennis Canavan, John McAllion and Alex Neil. All this showed that Tommy well appreciated the need for a serious and considered approach – simply and only bawling and shouting from the stump was not part of his repertoire. In all this, Tommy managed to skilfully ride out the accusation of being law-maker and lawbreaker from the likes of Donald Dewar (who charged 'We can't pick and choose which laws to obey') by making it clear that his guiding principles were socialist beliefs and popular support for these.[45]

Drawing First Blood

Tommy's *Abolition of Poindings and Warrant Sales Bill* was passed on 6 December 2000 and received Royal Assent on 17 January 2001. It amended the *Debtors (Scotland) Act 1987* and was the first Members' Bill to be passed in the Parliament.[46] He recalled:

The battle of the bill was won in the Justice Committee ... if [it] had recommended opposition then it would have been defeated in Parliament ... whereas if the Parliament overturned the rec-ommendation of the committee supporting the principle of the Bill then it would have been the first time this happened in the life of the short Parliament and would have had enormous impli-cations because the heart of the Parliament was supposed to be these powerful committees that scrutinise bills ... indeed, there's been only one occasion when a committee's recommendation has been overturned [by 2004 on the Rural Affairs committee on fox hunting].

My work was largely in the committee, rebutting the sher-iff officers, debt recovery agencies and the Law Society and supporting the evidence of communities like the Govan Law Centre ... John McAllion and Alec Neil were helpful here ... What I found really absolutely reprehensible and a disgrace was that the supposed 'father of the nation' [Labour First Minister], Donald Dewar, not only opposed the Bill but got out of his sick bed [after a first heart attack] to try to rally the Labour MSPs at a specially convened meeting into line against the bill ... Elaine Smith, John McAllion and Johann Lamont were important in stopping this.

This was no easy feat, especially as Labour engineered delay in pro-gressing the Bill by sending it to the parliament's busiest committee. Tommy helped solidify an alliance of Labour rebels and the SNP by winning the support of three other parliamentary committees. Of the

Labour leadership's stance, Tommy believed: 'There was a political sectarianism against me ... they didn't want me to win something ... but there was also the establishment privileged outlook of so many of the MSPs which is about keeping the working class in line and making them pay their debts'. Passing the Bill was the major Labour backbench rebellion of the first Parliament. Even though many Labour MSPs did not want to support it because it was Tommy's bill, they felt they had no choice if they were to be true to their political pledges. Nonetheless, victory turned out to be pyrrhic, for Labour fought a rearguard action by delaying its implementation by a year because it said there was nothing to put in the place of poindings, the use of warrant sales increased before their scheduled abolition, and then the Act was repealed after the Labour-Liberal coalition passed the *Debt Arrangement and Attachment (Scotland) Act 2002*. Tommy believed the new alternative to warrant sales was merely 'warrant sales by any other name'.

Despite all this, much good did come out of the exercise. First, the *Sunday Herald*, for example, recognised: 'The SSP is still a marginal force in Scottish politics but Sheridan has become the parliament's first real celebrity. That can't be bad in a parliament burdened with charisma-free nonentities'[47] while the *Guardian* suggested Tommy had been 'a saviour for the Scottish Parliament' as he showed that the 'new politics' could happen.[48] Much of this was, to quote *Scotland on Sunday*, because 'Sheridan spoke with dignity, passion and anger' in the debates.[49] Second, Tommy's show of righteous rage over wealth inequality that was bound up with warrant sales allowed him the opportunity to lay down a motion on 30 March 2000 on one of his next major campaigns – on the Scottish Service Tax – and this led to a review of local government finance. Third, he then worked with Alex Neil and John McAllion on legislation to limit the power of arresting bank accounts and leaving debtors penniless.

Going for Second Base

Undeterred by his experience over warrant sales – but rather galvanised further by it – Tommy opened up a second front against poverty and its 'new' Labour apologists by introducing another member's bill on free school meals on 14 November 2001. Sponsored again by John McAllion and Alex Neil (as opposed to Robin Harper or Margo McDonald), the *School Meals (Scotland) Bill* compelled local authorities to provide free nutritious meals to all school children under its charge. Such a measure sought to tackle both poverty and poor diet which can produce such ill-heath as obesity and diabetes, showing again that Tommy's politics were not so easy to categorise as negative and grandstanding. To support the Bill inside and outside parliament, he built a coalition consisting of Unison, STUC, Child Poverty Action Group, BMA, SSTA and EIS teaching unions and ten other charities and NGOs. However, the Bill fell at the Stage 1 debate on 20 June 2002 by 74:37. Failing to get the support of the parliament's Education Committee was, Tommy said, 'a big blow' and the major factor in the vote. However, the Bill still had a positive impact in not only raising the issue but influencing the Scottish government to extend existing (but selective) provision of free school meals.[50]

Cult and Colour?

While the general consensus in the media was that Tommy had brought a combination of red and orange colours to the parliament – in light of his political perspective and fake tan, his hardline political opponents pursued the line of attack of the SSP being 'little more than a cult'.[51] Political bruiser and 'new' Labour attack dog, John Reid MP, claimed the SSP 'was in danger of becoming a personality cult for Tommy Sheridan'.[52] If there was any truth in these allegations, it was not being solicited as Tommy explained:

> Craig McLean [a photographer who was an SSP member] had the foresight to take two photos ... a relaxed one and a more for- mal one ... and Fiz [Felicity Garvie] kept on getting requests for signed photos ... so we did it because if you say no you look like an arrogant prick ... you cannot win either way so I think it was better to go with the flow ... with a wife, mother and sisters, I'll easily get slapped down if I get above my station.

And, when he was voted best dressed and sexiest MSP early on in the first Parliament, he said:

> You have to take it with a huge batch of salt and say well the competition wasn't up to much ... politics is Hollywood for ugly people ... it doesn't say much ... but you have to be willing to respond on this level because it normalises you and for many that is what they talk about.

Although there was a heavy emphasis in SSP material (like placards in Glasgow) on electing Tommy in 1999 and putting his name on the ballot paper as well in that election, other than in 1999 European elections and the south of Scotland region in the 2003 Scottish Parliament election, Tommy's name was not used again in this manner for subsequent elections while he remained within the SSP. Media commentators in attacking the so-called 'Tommy one-man band cult' were quick to play fast and loose with the actual usage of his name on ballot papers. In their hands, it appeared that his name was always used when longer pieces were written on Tommy and the SSP.

Uniting Populace and Parliament

Given the need to 'chew gum and fart' simultaneously, it was some feat of human endeavour on both mental and physical planes that, as Tommy recounted: 'The years 1999 to 2003 were a rollercoaster of a constant speaking tour ... I visited places in Scotland that I'd never been to before ... [being or not being in parliament] at the time ... wasn't an issue because we were taking so many initiatives inside and outside Parliament ... the Warrant Sales Bill linked in with what we were doing outside and nobody said Tommy Sheridan was or wasn't at a debate on Wednesday or Thursday ... I wasn't expected to be there ... I probably attended more than my fair share and always tried to make an intervention when I was there ... I was doing so much it wasn't an issue'.[53]

Out of the constant speaking tour, two importance consequences arose. The first was that the publication of *Imagine: a socialist vision for the twenty-first century* in 2000. According to Tommy,[54] it resulted 'from me discussing with Alan [McCombes] the common questions that arose at the meetings like what is socialism, is it possible in the twenty first century [and so on]'. With Alan playing the same role as Joan McAlpine, that is, *de facto* sole author but with Tommy's name being used, *Imagine* set out an argument and vision for a socialist society *per se* as well as in an independent Scotland.[55] Tommy gave the book its title and not much else. Indeed, Alan recalled: 'I did it all' with Tommy never claiming otherwise and being happy within the SSP to acknowledge this and thank Alan. Allan Green recalled: 'At the launch of *Imagine* at a hotel in Argyll Street, Tommy was completely open that the only thing he contributed to the book was the title ... it was completely written by Alan ... it was part of the division of labour ... and Tommy never claimed otherwise. The same was true of policy'. *Imagine* was not a work of high theory, leaving many issues about what a revolution might look like unaddressed. But that was its point, for it was to speak to people who were attracted to the idea of socialism and were relative novices. It did this job very well and sold well, receiving much positive response at public meetings.[56] The book was also a metaphor for the close political and personal relationship between Tommy and Alan, casting Alan as the theoretician and Tommy as the politician (see later). The second important consequence was that it was on some of these nights away from home that some of the allegations of unfaithfulness revolve (see later).[57] But back on the campaign trail, Tommy showed how he had moved away from the shibboleth of narrow party building of his former comrades in the CWI:

> ... one of the key things was to gain credibility rather than get people to join up ... you have to help them and build a relationship and then if there is evidence that they are interested you pursue that but you have to be careful not to exploit your position so the way to build a party is in the public arena.

In this sense, Tommy saw his role as being the messenger of the message or as Felicity Garvie put it 'the mouthpiece' who was out on the frontline. More generally, Tommy used the platform of speaking in parliament and being an MSP outside it to give attention to workers' struggles, thereby ensuring some greater degree of coverage of these in the media, and, thus, helping the workers' build leverage. For example, in parliament he highlighted the long running Glasgow library workers strike of 2000, the medical secretaries strike in 2001 (led by Carolyn Leckie) and the low wages of the workers that worked in parliament, visited numerous picketlines, spoke at countless strikers' rallies, and brought workers to parliament to argue their case in committee like those of the Continental tyre workers from Newbridge, Edinburgh. Sometimes this meant clashing with, and incurring the wrath of, national union leaderships when he argued their union had given the strikers insufficient support when the strike was unofficial. Visiting picketlines, especially very early in the morning, indicated to the *Evening Times* that, despite being an MSP, he had 'not forgotten his roots'.[58] But it was not just workers but also pensioner and asylum seekers that he played this role for.

There's Still Only One Tommy Sheridan

While newspapers continually talked of 'Tommy Sheridan's SSP' and the 'one-man band'[59] as if he had been Hercules in creating the SSP pretty much himself, Tommy not only tried to correct this distortion but rather hid his own considerable light under a bushel by presenting a public persona of self-deprecation. For example, in his introduction to *Imagine*, Tommy denied that he was due any special praise as an individual and highlighted the role of the collective instead. Similarly, he reflected:

> Every single movement needs it's leaders ... leaders do not deter-mine the movements ... I was elected and promoted as the leader of the SSA and now the SSP ... I was the best known, had a track record and it was obvious therefore it was that people would asso-ciate me with the SSA/SSP and vice-versa ... that was just the reality of the situation ... the media used to attack us for that but they wouldn't quote us unless it was me being quoted ... we had to take a hard decision that we wanted to have our voice heard ... after 1999 the one-man band stuff got amplified but so what? ... It was becoming the biggest one-man band in Scotland.

And, he said in his *Sunday Herald* column that 'without the commitment and hard work of over 2,000 members, the SSP would not exist and I certainly would not have secured a seat [as an MSP]'.[60] Later he told the *Guardian*: 'It is not about me. It is that socialism and the idea of solidar-ity is very strong and rich ... and the SSP is now the party which holds that banner high'.[61] While understandably trying to knock back charac-terisations like 'the party is all about its charismatic leader. Remove him and there is little left of substance or chutzpah',[62] Carolyn Leckie, for example, bent the stick a bit too far: 'If Tommy falls under a bus tomor-row, we'd have a wee wake. It would be a blow, of course. He's pro-moted the ideas of the SSP brilliantly but we have a party that has a very democratic structure, thousands of members, a very competent party that Tommy is part of, but, to be honest, he's just a cog in the wheel'.[63]

So, Tommy was unwilling to identify or recognise his particular leadership and other talents. In the light of events some five to ten years later, it is an interesting question as to whether this was an entirely gen-uine disposition or one constructed to fulfil the mantle of 'man of the people'. That said, his political friends and foes were somewhat wide of the mark with their observations.[64] Alex Neil believed: 'Without him, the SSP would be nothing ... If Tommy was run over by a bus the party wouldn't survive'[65] while the *Evening News* commented:

> None of the [other parties] ha[s] a leader to compare to Tommy – the handsome young rebel with a cause ... No matter how much they reject suggestions that their party is a one-man band, the Scottish Socialists are dependent upon Tommy's political nous and boyish charm. Without him, the SSP is nothing more than a collection of idealistic students, disillusioned old Communists and a handful of genuine believers like Colin Fox.[66]

Still Talking a Good Game

Tommy's tendency to engage in socialist spin – or just plain old 'talking up' as it would have been called at the time – was consistently evident after the breakthrough of May 1999. A System Three poll put the SSP's support up from 2% to 5% by late July 1999[67] and other System Three polls in October and November indicated that the SSP would gain a second list MSP seat if an election was to be called. Meantime, the SSP's vote – as a measure of Tommy's rising star – increased to 9% in these polls. In the midst of this, the SSP achieved third place, with 1,847 votes (9.5%), in the Hamilton South by-election following Labour MP George Robertson's appointment as NATO Secretary General. This was a very good performance given it was a Westminster seat, outside Glasgow and Tommy was not the candidate. Indeed, shortly before the election, Tommy predicted that the SSP would come third.[68] However, and following this, Tommy was not on the same solid ground when, basking in the light of this good performance, he flamboyantly predicted that the SSP would now become third force in Scottish politics[69] and 'the third force in working class constituencies' in Scotland.[70] And, similarly with the warm glow of the anti-poll tax revolt still to bask in, he frequently promised more such revolts such as over housing stock transfer in Glasgow[71] and the council tax.[72]

Gazing at the Stars

Tommy's penchant for making big, bold statements on a range of issues continued. Greeting the New Year in his *Daily Record* page he proclaimed: 'During the twenty first century, I am confident [that] ... genuine socialism will be reborn as an unstoppable movement in Scotland, Europe and eventually right across the globe'.[73] Later on, he predicted the SSP would reach the giddy heights of MSPs in double figures and hold balance of power in parliament.[74] Again, the perspective underlying these declarations was his belief in the power of inspiration to instil hope and confidence through transformational leadership (see earlier). He told *Scotland on Sunday*: 'I think many people have the ideals but they don't have the courage or the optimism to see them realised. They say: 'I agree with you but ...' If people agree with the ideals they have a duty to try and see them realised in their lifetime'.[75] He saw his job as being a medicinal remedy: 'There's a lot of feint hearts and soothsayers of doom and gloom on the left so we are a corrective ... The left has to have optimism because we are the David that has no right to win but we think we can ... we need to have that level of optimism but not one that becomes a delusional or fantastical optimism'. Yet, he did admit that he and Alan McCombes[76] are 'more the wild-eyed optimists' while Allan Green, Ritchie Venton and Keith Baldassara are 'enthusiastic when required but also realistic when necessary'.

Still Councillor Sheridan

Tommy continued to as serve as a councillor for Pollok until 2003, donating his councillor's allowance of some £6,000 a year to the SSP. He stood for re-election in 1999, winning the seat with 1,214 votes (44%). The rationale for doing so at the same time as standing for the Scottish Parliament was to maintain a presence in Pollok and to provide a fall back in case Tommy came up short in votes on the regional list. Still as a lone councillor, Tommy kept up his barrage of criticism on Labour corruption:

> In the council there were few areas that you can make an impact on your own so I exposed the huge junketeering and expenses claims and I opened that can of worms ... Labour used to use that to dampen down people with fire in their belly ... I shone a light on some of their darkest practices. I did it because it was wrong, it needed to be exposed and I could do it on my own.

He became a skilled tactician, challenging Labour on issues of democracy through substantive and procedural means. But he also continued to campaign against schools closures as well as the use of PFI to build and renovate schools, and was involved in the battle against the 'stock transfer' of council housing in Glasgow from the city council to the Glasgow Housing Association quango. He argued that Labour wanted this to get rid of the problem of council housing – specifically the cost of providing decent public housing – by this means and castigated its argument to tenants of 'money for repairs if you vote for transfer' as ideological blackmail. To publicise his actions as a councillor, he regularly put out press releases on the basis that if 'you don't offer them they will not be taken' and even though many were not strictly in his capacity as councillor, Tommy used to get secretarial staff at the City Chambers to type them. Not only was he charming in asking them to do so but they had considerable respect for him even if they did not support his politics. But Labour was also looking for a way to hit back against Tommy, whether underhand or not. So he was investigated for the heinous crime of giving council envelopes to anti-stock transfer campaigners so that information could be left for councillors in their pigeon holes. Under council rules, all such communications had be enclosed in envelopes. Tommy was exonerated, saying the 'lunatics have taken over the asylum'.[77] In August 2002, Tommy announced his intention to stand down as councillor – by not contesting the forthcoming election – so he could concentrate more on being leader (convener) of the SSP as it geared up for 2003 Scottish Parliament election, and the prospect of more SSP MSPs: 'I need to be organising them to be an effective opposition group as possible'.[78] Looking back on his ten years as a councillor, he believed his biggest achievement was to help improve housing, especially reducing dampness through ending flat roof council houses. According to Keith Baldassara, it was in his early days as a councillor that Tommy 'began to display the art of self-promotion: party promotion as well as self-promotion'.

Running an Office

At Glasgow City Council, Tommy had no dedicated administrative support. Ordinary councillors had to use the pool but as an MSP, he had the resources to employ an office manager in parliament and a case worker in the list constituency. He chose Felicity Garvie because she was a party member with a Militant background but more importantly had the previous experience of organising an office. Tommy remembered: 'I'd already decided before I got elected to approach Felicity because she was very efficient and competent ... she's been an absolute crutch to lean on and get support from ... much of my success was due to her organising my office'. Felicity recalled Tommy was 'glad to have somebody who wanted to do the job, was excited about it and had the skills to do the job ... he took a very hands-off attitude because I knew what was required to make him a success ... He had no expertise with a computer and couldn't type so I typed all his correspondence for him, looked at all his emails [and so on]'.[79] This role also involved acting as a gatekeeper (other than through his mobile phone) and, as Felicity recounted: 'Quite a lot of the time, I would write the response [to constituency and other enquiries] and just send it off in his name ... because he trusted my political instincts'.

In terms of the constituency worker, Tommy commented: 'Both Keith and George were able to be my constituency agent but George was involved in so many other things ... both of them allowed me to do what I do best which is communicate with people and take initiatives'. Having already come on the scene, former MEP, Hugh Kerr, offered his services for free as an aide and press officer for the length of the first parliament. Tommy was glad to take up this offer but it was one that was not without its problems. Being quite pompous and over-bearing, Hugh put many people's backs up and later there were sexual harassment allegations against him.[80] As Alan McCombes recounted, it was one of the few issues before 2004 that he and Tommy did not see eye-to-eye on. But for Tommy, Hugh had the virtue of unswerving loyalty as time would later show. Behind the scenes, Keith found Tommy to have a ruthless but focused streak after being told by Tommy to 'cherry pick out the [cases] that would give us coverage, profile and publicity ... then he effectively left me to it and didn't intrude on the casework [because] he hates casework ... he has grown to hate case work because it takes away from Parliament and what he likes ... hdidn't want to be a constituency MSP ... if there's a profile to a case he'll do it, if not he'll give them my number or the Citizens' Advice Bureau'. Alan McCombes confirmed this orientation: 'Tommy will turn up at the protest at the dawn raid [against asylum seekers] but won't do the casework'. What this indicated was that Tommy was determinedly focused upon using his skills to the best and biggest effect as a media operator.

Wielding the Journalistic Sword of Justice

Shortly after being elected to the Scottish Parliament, Tommy began writing a fortnightly column in the *Sunday Herald* (called 'left winger') and this lasted for most of 1999. The columns concentrated on sport and the politics of sport. Most pieces discussed the politics of football in terms of football as a business and how spin had taken over. But another example was one on Mohammed Ali the radical.[81] However, it was the weekly page in the *Daily Record*, which started in May 1999 with the by-line of 'the radical voice of politics' that allowed Tommy to impinge far more upon the mainstream psyche of the working class and on the basis of his chosen agenda. Reflecting on this point, Tommy commented: 'A quarter of a page in the *Herald* or the *Scotsman*, that they might give you, would be less effective than two paragraphs in the *Record* or *Evening Times* in terms of readership' although he did acknowledge as well that 'Given that there is this idea that you should only support the SSP if you are poor or dispossessed when in actual fact research shows that a lot of our support comes from educated professionals like social workers [and] teachers ... yes we want to appeal to the dispossessed but our message is for all in terms of all of those workers that need to sell their labour'.

For the next eighteen months, the page provided comment and analysis, interspersed with little titbits on ordinary folk so that the page was not always a case of 'in your face', direct and undiluted hard politics. The style was a combination of the *Record*, 'Tommy gives it laldy' in the SML's paper, his 'Inside the system'/'Behind the lines' column in the *Scottish Socialist Voice*[82] and Paul Foot's page in the *Daily Mirror* in the 1980s and 1990s.[83] So the articles railed for the 'satisfaction of need not gratification of greed' and against 'more and more wealth [being] now concentrated in fewer and fewer hands ... the new century demands a new society'.[84] He attacked Tory MP, Shaun Woodward, joining 'new' Labour as 'from Toryism to Tonyism ... the switch from Tories to New Labour ... for right-wing politicians or businessmen ... [was as easy as] trad[ing in] your Rolls-Royce for a Mercedes'.[85]

The general tenor was to highlight class contrasts (even though he seldom referred explicitly to class as such and more deployed the terms of 'rich and poor', 'them and us' and 'have and have nots'), to debunk the Blairite 'third way', and to take an issue or news story and use it as a prism by which to open up space to comment upon capitalism.[86] Part of his skill here was to be a story teller before getting to the punch line of the hard politics at the story's conclusion. Most often this was through a human story being told and then leading to the political point he wished to make. The use of the implicit language of class and class contrasts was reminiscent of Jimmy Reid's use of discourse and language in the UCS work-in (see later). The pages particularly championed working class people (as well as those from Glasgow and Scotland) as examples of what citizens are capable of and the dangers of success (like world champion boxer, Benny Lynch, in the 1930s). As often as possible, the pages tried to bring to readers some knowledge of Glasgow's radical past, and as would be expected he publicised demonstrations and meetings (including those of the SSP[87]). Judging from the letters' page called 'Voice of Scotland', the readers' response was overwhelmingly positive.

Looking back on his *Record* page, Tommy remembered: 'My purpose was to popularise socialism in as many varied ways by taking up as many varied issues as possible ... it was a great opportunity because it was the most widely read newspaper in Scotland ... I'm not sure that the working class that buys the *Record* and *Sun* are distinguishable now ... years gone by there was a conscious working class that bought the *Mirror* in England and, perhaps, the *Record* in Scotland because they were politically to the left of centre ... [even though] over the last ten years they've dumbed down to delve into the *Sun's* market'. In the *Record's* coverage of him at this time, overwhelmingly readers responded well and warmly to Tommy judged by their letters to the paper. This extended his reputation for honesty, integrity and principles. No matter what issues Tommy chose to write about, the fee for providing the copy – some £300[88] – was donated every week to the Jack Jardine Memorial Hall (now Community Centre) in Pollok to help meet its running costs. The fight to save the centre, then the Ladymuir Community Hall, was led by local community activist and former anti-poll tax activist, Jack Jardine, and so was named after him. It involved an occupation and then the running of the centre by local residents when the centre was axed by the city council.

Ironically, how the *Record* page came about was through an offer from the (Scottish) *Sun* to write a weekly column for it:

Originally, we were approached by the Sun and offered a column but we knocked it back and I've always agreed that I would never write for the Murdoch press because of the attempt at Wapping to smash the print unions ... Alex Salmond, Jimmy Reid and Jim Sillars wrote regularly for it following that ... which I thought was a disgrace ... they say that to avoid an audience the size that those newspapers have is stupid ... and they have a point ... at the time in 1999 when I was offered the column in the Sun, I immediately said no and then I discussed it with Jim Friel, President of the GPMU and Paul Holleran of the NUJ and they said they wouldn't have had an objection because they are now allowed to organise at [News International's plant at] Kinning Park and they also said they were having more problems with the Record at that time in terms of recognition and organising ... I suppose it's a political overhang that still leaves a bitter taste in the mouth ... I've done guest columns for them but never taken any money but if the Sun was to offer something now it would be difficult not to accept it because despite it being a horrible right-wing rag [... which also backed independence even though this was a market driven ploy rather than a serious commitment to it ...] 600,000 were buying it – as long as you had a guarantee of no editorial interference in your copy.

He continued that although *Record* editor at the time, Martin Clarke, 'was a Thatcherite manager ... he said to us 'I don't agree with your politics but at least you're honest unlike many other politicians' so they gave it a go ... they were pleased with the readers' response – it was the most responded to by readers – and showed that they were open to a range of opinions. When they were campaigning against the abolition of Section 2A [like abolition of Clause 28], I was campaigning for it including the use of the column ... if they had interfered with that I would have given it up ... Alan McCombes and I worked hard to submit the required number of words so there was no cutting ... I would edit Alan or Alan would edit me ... so there was no room for cutting ... at that time I couldn't have done it without Alan as I was on my own [in the Parliament] and there was so much [else] to do'.

But behind this are three lesser known facts. First, most of the time, Alan McCombes wrote Tommy's columns including in the *Sunday Herald*. Making the same point as he would in the 2010 perjury case, Alan recounted: 'I did virtually all his *Record* columns ... I could write authentically as his voice because I knew him so well ... I would write the column and send it in [without him seeing it] such was the level of trust and cooperation between us'. Initially with the *Record* column, Alan met with Tommy to discuss and edit Tommy's text. After a few weeks, Alan did the writing on his own. Second, it was upon advice from Alan McCombes that Tommy went to the *Record* and said he had the offer from the *Sun* and would it offer him a column instead. It was Alan's arguments about the dangers of writing for the *Sun* that outweighed Tommy's willingness to write for it.[89] The *Record* accepted this because of Tommy's stature and to spike the *Sun*'s guns. Third, Tommy had not always had a very good opinion of the *Record*, saying in 1994: 'It pretends to be a people's paper but is really just an establishment rag'[90] and he was scathing of it over the poll tax when it refused to cover the Federation's press releases. This changing nature of his relationship with the *Record* was to continue thereafter.

Part of the reason for dealing with these issues at length is found in the significance of Tommy's respective statements of 22 December 2010 in his summing-up speech and after being convicted of perjury on 23 December 2010 that: '[he] had fought ... the Murdoch press ... through-out his life'[91] and 'I have fought the power of News International all my political life, and I make no apologies for taking on the might of Rupert Murdoch' and in his plea of mitigation on sentencing on 26 January 2011: '[News of the World] is part of an organisation I have spent most of my adult life fighting'.[92] This indicated his willingness to bend the stick of truth to breaking point. Indeed, it would be truer to say that he had spent more time fighting the *Daily Record* and *Sunday Mail* (rather than the *Sun* and *NoW*) even if he did not always fight the *Daily Record/Sunday Mail* either (see later), that *having* to fight off the attacks of the *Record* was far more significant than fighting off the attacks by the likes of the *Sun* because the *Record* was a left-leaning paper, and he was not averse to writing for News International papers or being interviewed by them (see elsewhere).[93] But another part of the reason for doing so is to highlight that Tommy was prepared to take risky opportunities, even if it meant that he could come under the kind of scathing criticism that Ken Livingstone received for writing a column for the *Sun* in the 1990s. Thus, Richie Venton recalled: 'He wanted to do it [write for the *Sun*] ... he was quite prepared to go down that route ... his rush coincided with his desire to have personal and party publicity'.

Dealing with the Media

Even though it seemed Tommy was able to command considerable coverage[94] as the leader of the SSA/SSP and, thus, for the SSA/SSP, it is clear that it was not – in his view – quite the nature or extent that he wanted it to be.[95] Suggesting there was no particular conspiracy from on high, he recalled it was 'probably more that they ke[pt] us marginal because we [we]re marginal rather than a conscious strategy'. For this reason, and because 'there is this cosy relationship between politicians and the press ... [creating] a cosy business-friendly consensus which we are not part of', conscious and deliberate newsworthy actions had to be taken so that the more Tommy and the SSA/SSP did, the less they could be ignored. Tommy, in particular, managed to gain publicity and successfully bat back much of the accusation of being publicity seeking. He was quick to point out the double standards involved in these kinds of attacks on him because without generating publicity he and the SSA/SSP would be ignored by the media: 'Throughout my life I've always been attacked as a publicity seeking self-publicist but that is just water off a duck's back because we need to have people knowing about what we're doing – I adopt the Oscar Wilde approach that the only thing worse than getting talked about is not getting talked about'. In making this judgement, he had in mind the benchmark of the relationship he had with the *Evening Times* (see earlier) and this was testament to the bigger challenge of getting more favourable coverage (in quality and quantity) from the Scottish and British media. However, he did begin to build good working relationships with Murray Ritchie and Robbie Dunwoodie at the *Herald*. Keith Baldassara recalled: '[Tommy] held court every Friday in the Cuba Norte restaurant with individual journalists one after another ... he was 'the don' ... everything he did he press-released religiously ... like letters to others ... and got it to the press'. But because of the overall challenge, he took as many other opportunities as possible like the safe gig of broadcasting on *Scot FM*, when filling in for a DJ on holiday, in 1999. Of this example, he commented: 'You can't talk politics to everyone [straight off or at all] so it's good to be able to talk football because that leads into politics ... that normalises you with people'. And, he understood the point about delivery: 'I've learned presentation is important. Although the package is just as angry as it's always been, hopefully it's presented in a more accessible fashion. I'm calling for revolution, but I'm calling for it reasonably.'[96]

'Working Class Zero'

A new *Record* editor, Peter Cox, was not only the catalyst for ending Tommy's column in November 2000 but also the beginning of a long and concerted attack upon him and the SSP.[97] Tommy told the *Sunday Times* he was informed his column was dropped because it, according to the new editor, was getting 'too tedious'.[98] After he was arrested at Faslane in 2001, the *Record* labelled him 'PILLOCK No1',[99] and remarked in such a vitriolic editorial – 'Tommy, of course, would claim he is a people's leader. But he is not. Tommy is just a charismatic politician with a massive ego and a martyr complex'[100] – that the *Sunday Herald*[101] and *Scotsman*[102] commented upon this. The *Sunday Herald*[103] also suggested the assault was evidence of a coming election. But the high point of the assault was the whole of the front page of 23 March 2001, accompanied by an editorial, which attacked Tommy with the headline 'working class zero' over the SSP's policy to legalise cannabis. Thus, the text of the story ran: '[O]n the day the horrific extent of Scotland's drug problem is revealed, sun-tanned designer MSP Tommy Sheridan is trying to have cannabis legalised'. Just before this, the *Daily Record* had fulminated: 'Tommy Sheridan has worked hard on his 'man of the people' image. Now, he is the man AGAINST the people. 'Citizen, Tommy' is the master of gesture politics. Now, he has made a gesture that is cheap and petty – a two-fingered insult to the victims of drugs and their families. On the very day of the *Daily Record*'s great national march against drugs, he wants to hold a counter-demo calling for cannabis to be legalised'.[104] The *Record*'s 'war against drugs' also saw it allege that Tommy called for heroin to be 'legalised'. Rather, Tommy argued for addicts to have prescribed heroin and called for the link to be broken between cannabis and heroin by legalising the former. More widely, Tommy took the drugs issue seriously as he had seen firsthand how it had blighted his Pollok community. This led him to call for cannabis to be legalised for recreational and medical use (as opposed to being decriminalised whereby it would lawful to buy but not to sell thereby forcing buyers go to criminals), to support Margo McDonald on debating this openly and establishing a commission to review evidence, and to advocate giving heroin under controlled circumstances to addicts to reduce their dependence upon criminals.[105]

Behind the scenes, Labour's leadership had good reason to be increasingly worried by Tommy's growing stature and influence, and the prospect of an enhanced contingent of SSP MSPs at the next election (as psephologist John Curtice, with no political axe to grind, pointed out[106]). This was conveyed to the *Record* who acted to locate and attack perceived weak spots with gusto. To Tommy, the change was evident in a very practical way: 'I got the *Record* to get on board on the campaign against warrant sales but couldn't get it over free school meals because it wanted to be sycophantic with 'new' Labour'. From early 2001 onwards, and with its own campaign to rid communities of hard drug use, the *Record* was a constant and vocal critic of Tommy.[107] And if it was not outright attack, it was total neglect – with the *Daily Record* banning coverage of Tommy because he was 'sub-zero'[108] – so that it was not until nearing the campaign for the 2003 Scottish Parliament elections that Tommy and the SSP received any coverage in this paper (and which could be said to be in any way fair). For example, the *Record* disingenuously attacked Tommy on his claim of donating half his salary to the SSP.[109] Tommy consulted the NUJ over taking legal action for defamation on the 'working class zero' accusation but nothing came of it.[110] Tommy responded by saying the *Record* was the 'Daily Distort' which sought to 'denigrate and destroy through distortion and deceit'.[111] This cast an interesting light on Tommy selling his story to the *Record* in 2006 (see later).

Pragmatism

The Prussian politician, Otto von Bismarck, famously declared in 1867: 'Politics is the art of the possible'. Some hundred years later, the Situationists in France declared 'be reasonable, demand the impossible'. Navigating a correct course between the two for an elected socialist politician is a potentially fraught matter. On one side exists accusations of selling out, and on the other those of ultra-left isolationism. With Tommy making clear what his (socialist) principles were, the *Scotsman* commented: 'Sheridan should be a spin-doctor's dream, but for one fatal flaw: he refuses to compromise [saying] 'If you are idealistic it is difficult and you can lose your faith in ideas and get tired if you suffer too many defeats. But if you genuinely hold an ideology in your heart and your head regardless of the ups and downs, it is like a map that guides you through your political life and your personal life".[112] Later, he told *Scotland on Sunday*: 'I'll put up my hand immediately to idealism ... I don't accept it's a crime. Being involved in politics you should have ideals. If you don't ... [w]hat are you trying to achieve?'[113] while earlier he told the *Sunday Mail*: 'The most important thing for me is the mirror test ... Looking at myself in the mirror and knowing I have stayed true to my conscience. I'd rather die an idealist than sell my soul'.[114]

However, the *Sunday Herald* revealed that in his capacity of a councillor, Tommy was prepared to engage in hard, practical bargaining: 'It becomes clear that Sheridan, usually portrayed as an extremist and an ideologue, is one astute player. He will, he says, compromise socialist absolutes and deal with the private sector as long as it provides for the public. Afterwards he says he needs to be amenable to industry, as long as it means work for locals and two or three apprenticeships are promised. It is not his first choice, but is the best deal on the table at the moment. He stresses this often. He has learned it is essential to make compromises'.[115] Similarly, he worked with house builders, Beazer, to ensure the provision of low cost homes in Pollok in 2001. In Tommy's practice, there did not seem to necessarily be an insuperable tension between the two, indicating that, and to paraphrase Trotsky, revolutionaries can show that they are the best reformers (as opposed to reformists) for putting pressure on the companies or withholding cooperation to them can be used to gain some concessions from them.

In a similar way, Tommy applied the same *modus operandi* to creating coalitions inside and outside parliament and the compromises they sometimes involved. But by being a coalition creator, and deciding what to pitch and how to pitch it, Tommy was able to minimise any compromises and concessions.[116] However, any willingness to compromise did not go as far as seeking greater office and access to any corridors of power through the Labour Party. In echoes of Margaret Thatcher, the man was not for turning. He told the *Scotsman*: 'People tell me if I had kept my head down I could have done well within Labour ... But it would have been soulless power'[117] and *Scotland on Sunday*:

Yeah, I've heard that people had me marked as a Labour candidate of the future, but I couldn't and wouldn't be happy with power without principle, it's as straightforward as that ... Honestly, I look at some of those New Labour folk in Glasgow, and I can't understand how they can sleep easy with their consciences intact when their city is bedevilled with social ills, bad housing, terrible health problems, and when there are kids with no hope beyond the dole. Sure, it might sound melodramatic, but Labour has abandoned [its] grassroots, deserted the millions in favour of the millionaire visitors to Downing Street, and you've only had to listen to the cries of disenchantment tonight to realise that the SSP has a serious role to perform in the new millennium. Fact: we've earned 6% of the vote with 0.1% of the publicity. Tells you something, doesn't it?[118]

Reflecting back on his first term as an MSP and emphasising the need to be part of a collective inside and outside of parliament, he commented:

Dennis [Canavan] is a very talented individual, very good speaker, has a command of his brief but I think he's been severely handicapped by being on his own ... [he] has allied with people but he hasn't raised any bills ... he could have had a much wider impact by either being in the SSP or working as a group of independents ... I was often referred to as an independent MSP but I wasn't. I was an SSP MSP and had a party campaigning outside the Parliament with me ... the same wasn't true [as for Canavan] one year in for Margo MacDonald and John Swinburne (even though he is nominally part of a party).

Media Reception

It was not just political principles and ideology that kept Tommy on the socialist straight and narrow. What he was doing and how he was doing it became part of a winning formula. The *Scotsman* declared: 'It is impossible to doubt his sincerity and commitment to issues that have become distinctly unfashionable in the new Labour camp', adding this was aided by being 'deeply tanned, fashionably dressed and utterly charming'.[119] Meantime, the *Sunday Herald* called him 'articulate and passionate'.[120] It was for these types of reasons – and that he was doing what many wanted Labour to do – that the *Independent* commented he was 'eulogised by some journalists as the 'most gifted politician of his generation''.[121] Occasionally there were pieces which showed more than the one cherished side to Tommy:

Sheridan's capacity with the snappy quote has gained him the unfortunate reputation of a man who enjoys being in the public eye ... He became a martyr and a hero the likes of which the city has not seen since John Maclean. ... [but he] lacks the scary staring eyes or the saccharine edge ... [he] speaks in the measured accent of the educated working class Scot sounding as if he is trying to make sure he is understood by a foreign audience. It's like John Gordon Sinclair without the irritating boyish lilt. ... He manages to do so without the oily smack of posturing.[122]

In television interviews Sheridan always uses the personal touch, using the interviewer's first name frequently and earnestly. ... In person he seems just, well earnest. You want to know what his dad did and he wants to tell you about Marx's labour theory of value. After an hour you begin to feel you're talking to someone who's standing on top of a soap box. You admire his conviction. You agree with some of his principles. But you can't help wishing he'd lighten up. ... Sheridan's charisma is probably more powerful in public meetings when ideology can seem exciting, even romantic. In private conversation, ideology can seem a little cold. Sheridan, however, has a reputation for being 'good with people'.[123]

But snappy 'quotable' quotes outweighed any Schadenfreude or skin-crawling comments effect when he was able to come up with, as at the press launch of the SSP manifesto, such statements as: 'I usually reserve shirt and ties for births, deaths, and marriages. The only marriage you'd find in this election campaign is the marriage of the SNP with the big business agenda, which they have fallen for hook, line, and sinker. The only death so far has of course been the socialist soul of the Labour Party'.[124] Thus, the *Observer* opined he was: 'becoming the undoubted star of Scottish political scene, a gifted populist ... articulate and rational performer ... media star'.[125] All this meant that both what he did do as well as what he did not do were reported like taking part in a protest against the closure of Govanhill swimming pool and not playing in a football match between councillors and MSPs.

Fringe Issues and New Audiences?

The most regularly worn decoration on the lapel of Tommy's suits was a CND peace symbol badge.[126] If there was only one badge worn, it would be this one, indicating from 1999 onwards his very public commitment to unilateral nuclear disarmament, and scrapping Trident in particular. While this commitment existed well before then and he started attending the annual Faslance blockades in 1997, it took on an added significance by virtue of Tommy making it one of his key personal political commitments as an MSP. Politicians can have any number of individual causes but putting them amongst the foremost in their agenda marks the particular cause out as being more than a tokenistic one or an 'also ran'. Although he frequently raised the issue in parliament despite it being reserved business (for Westminster), the most obvious sign of this commitment was his preparedness to be arrested at Faslane in a collective attempt to (temporarily) close down the nuclear base. Again, this marked Tommy out as bold and different in his radicalism and socialism.

Tommy's series of arrests at Faslane began in mid-February 2000 at the biggest demonstration at the gates of the base for fifteen years.

He was arrested along with 178 others including Keith Baldassara, and charged with the public order offence of breach of peace as well as resisting arrest. Proclaiming he was 'proud to be arrested'[127] for resisting the obscenity of nuclear weapons, in November 2000 he represented himself and pled not guilty in court, citing the ruling of the International Court of Justice in 1996 that nuclear weapons were a breach of international law because they were indiscriminate, that is not discriminating between civilians, war combatants and the military, so this gave him the right to disarm Trident. He was, nonetheless, found guilty and fined £250. But he stated he had no intention of paying and proffered: 'If I disarmed a madman with a machine gun on the street I would be hailed a hero – the same should apply to anyone who tries to get rid of nuclear weapons'.[128] His insistence on not paying the fine was because to do so would be an admittance of guilt.[129] On going back to jail, Tommy said it would be 'like boarding [school] but with different accents'[130] and of the protest that led to his arrest: '[S]ometimes we have to stand up for our beliefs ... and sometimes we have to sit down for them',[131] showing he had some sense of humour despite facing the grimness of prison. He was sent to jail for five days on 17 December 2000. Gail also showed she had a sense of humour: she was miffed at his jailing in the run up to Christmas but made clear her support for Tommy and this cause, saying he's only going to jail 'to avoid the Christmas shopping' and it would give 'me more time to hide his presents'.[132] Of his time in jail, he said in a diary that was carried in three newspapers that being strip searched upon entering prison is the 'most humiliating experience'.[133] The significance of this for his fearlessness later in life is that he often said public speaking or being interviewed on television was nothing compared to that: 'If you can come through that, you can come through anything'.

He was next arrested on 12 February 2001 at Faslane – along with 379 others including George Galloway[134] – and charged with breach of the peace and resisting arrest. On 8 October 2001, he defended himself in a district court, using the same argument as before, and this time was found not guilty, establishing the right to peaceful protest. He was also arrested later in October 2001, for a breach of the peace along with 167 others at another Faslane protest, and then in February 2002 along with 111 others. In June 2002, the Crown challenged his not guilty verdict but Tommy knocked this back by defending himself at the Court of Criminal Appeal. Although he had many detractors, these actions and success established him as a foremost peace campaigner, giving him a crossover to many on the left but who were not socialists.

But it was not just what some regarded as the 'fringe' issue of nuclear disarmament that Tommy championed. He also showed a refreshing heterodoxy in his other 'fringe' causes, indicating a more rounded approach and well before many of these became fashionable or more mainstream for the wider left. These causes and commitments showed he had grown out his 'fringe'. Some like Colin Fox attributed this to moving in wider circles of the left outside the narrow far left.[135] So he was against fox hunting, for animal welfare (highlighting cruelty in circuses), for cheap public transport (including rail renationalisation) on environmental grounds, and backed parents seeking single MMR vaccinations for fear of triggering autism. He was also for gay rights, proudly telling of being on pride marches, and for legalising cannabis, saying: 'We don't promote drug use, either legal or illegal substances, but we oppose the criminalisation of those who consume hash'[136] and:

Lots of young people come up to me and ask me when I'm going to get cannabis legalised because they know about our 'free the weed' policy ... it strikes a chord with them and can open then up to discussing other issues ... but I've always gone out of my way to make it clear that we don't promote drugs and drug use.

In 2002, he helped organised a republican garden party on the day of the golden jubilee, laying down an amendment for Scotland's future 'as an independent republic where people are sovereign and are recognised as citizens, not subjects' to a motion in parliament welcoming the Queen's jubilee. In moving the amendment, he berated the monarchists:

[M]any MSPs, especially from the Labour and SNP benches, are squirming with embarrassment at the sycophantic, servile, fore-lock-touching motion they are being asked to support by their party leaders ... Keir Hardie might have worn a cloth cap and sported a big beard but he was a real modernising politician. He was 80 years ahead of Johnny Rotten and the Sex Pistols and more than 100 years ahead of our four main party leaders in Scotland today, who in the 21st century are still fawning after an institution that was already past its sell-by date in the 19th century.[137]

On various campaigns and issues, Tommy did not just issue supportive press statements, speak at their demonstrations and rallies or mention them in parliament. Rather, he played quite a leading role, as in the Scrap the Clause (Section 28) campaign, where he attacked Stagecoach boss, Brian Souter's, private referendum to support keeping it, saying it demonstrated the Americanisation of politics, where politics becomes a rich man's game. Without being too trite about it, he sought to gener-alise out from these issues to the bigger picture in his journalism.

Tommy also put a fair amount of time into miscarriages of justice. One early example of the latter was when he became coordinator, in late 1998, for the campaign to gain leave to appeal for the 1984 conviction of the so-called 'Ice Cream War' killers, Thomas (TC) Campbell and Joseph Steele, over the deaths of six members of Doyle family. In this capacity, he targeted Donald Dewar the Scottish Secretary as he had refused leave to appeal, as well as Henry McLeish, the Scottish Office Minister, with demonstrations outside, and occupations of, their offices. Tommy was asked to become involved in uniting the two families to get their campaign for justice back on track. Many thought Tommy should not get involved as both were criminals but he was convinced that they were innocent of this particular crime (with both not denying involvement in other crimes). After many appeals and interims releases, their convictions were eventually quashed in 2004 and permanent liberty granted. Reflecting on the issues involved, Tommy commented:

> Signing a letter, going to a rally, speaking at a rally and so on are easy but actually getting involved in the mechanics of a campaign or dispute is much more difficult [for me] because it demands a lot more of your time, effort and energy ... you have to prioritise your time ... in the Glasgow Two [Campbell and Steele] campaign, this was a working class campaign rooted in the east end schemes of Glasgow and it gave us the opportunity to show to some of the most dispossessed in Glasgow that we cared about things that were about them ... and it was harder to get people to come to Free the Glasgow Two campaign meetings than the Chhokar meetings [over the murder of Surjit Singh Chhokar] because it wasn't about a black guy ... there [was] also a middle class aspect to not coming to the Glasgow Two meetings.

And, for six weeks in 2001, he lived off the minimum wage in a campaign allied to the Child Poverty Action Group, providing weekly reports in the *Scottish Socialist Voice* on whether and how he managed to do so. In addition to his *Scot FM* one-off slot, Tommy stood for the rectorship of the University of St Andrews in 1999. It is the oldest university in Scotland, dating from 1413, and is well known for having not only more English students than Scottish but the *crème de la crème* of the children of the middle and ruling classes. It was no accident that Prince William attended it in the early 2000s and met, his future wife, Kate Middleton, there. Tommy believed standing provided the opportunity to speak to new audiences in an unrestricted way. Indicating there was also a sense of 'get it right up them', he said: 'At St Andrews, we won the first and second rounds ... but lost on the third round under STV which

was just as well because I couldn't have done the job and be an MSP ...
but we showed there was a leftwing constituency in that bastion of the
right'. In doing so he ran victor Andrew Neil, the rightwing journalist,
quite close. Later, in 2000, he declined the invitation to stand for the
rectorship at the University of Glasgow because there was a danger he
might win, making his workload unmanageable. In similar terms, he did
not shrink from accepting the invitation to address the professional debt
collectors at their Institute of Credit Management conference and putting to them his ideas for abolishing the current debt recovery regime.
But he was on more familiar ground when he was frequently invited to
speak to students in schools,[138] BBC's *Question Time*,[139] cultural events
like Celtic Connections as well as countless other meetings and rallies.
In addition to his regular columns, he wrote occasional articles for the
Sunday Times,[140] *Morning Star*, *Mirror*, *Sunday Mirror* and *Evening
Times*. He did all this because he believed, as the *Scotsman* said of him,
'audiences are like vitamins: habitual and necessary'.[141] Later, he commented that longstanding forms of socialist communication like public
meetings were ebbing away and new ones needed to be tried.[142]

Two Steps Forward, One Step Back?

In early 2000, a System Three poll recorded the SSP attracting 6%
on the list seats, which would give it a second seat in Glasgow and
some elsewhere.[143] This was followed by coming fourth (with 4.2%) in
the first by-election for the Scottish Parliament in March. Later in the
year, another System Three poll suggested Tommy would be joined by
another 3 SSP MSPs.[144] By the end of 2000, in the shape of the Falkirk
West (Westminster) by-election, the SSP completed a run of beating
the Liberal Democrats in eleven of fourteen contests by coming fourth
and saving its deposit with 5.1%. Into the new year, the SSP stayed on
5% for the Scottish Parliament list seats[145] with Tommy predicting six
to eight MSPs in 2003.[146] And, in the general election of 7 June 2001,
where Tony Blair and 'new' Labour were still overwhelmingly dominant, the SSP polled 72,516 (0.3%) votes across the 72 constituencies
in Scotland. Whilst this was very favourable compared to the votes of
the Socialist Alliance (57,553 representing 0.2% from standing in 98
constituencies) and the SLP (57,288, 0.2%, 114 constituencies), it was
nonetheless a setback because Tommy had boldly and frequently predicted getting 100,000 votes.[147] Characteristically, Tommy turned this
on its head by saying: '[I]f that's a failure, I can't wait to see a victory'.[148] He blamed the failure to reach that number on a poor turnout
and media censorship, reasoning:

> The advantages outweigh the disadvantages ... we have to raise
> people's sights ... we weren't going to lie to people ... we weren't
> going to win any seats ... but we needed to have a target for our
> activists to work for ... I think the gamble is worth it because you
> always have to inspire people ... to help create some momentum ...
> there's be a bit of you can't win if you say you're going to win
> seats or not win seats when you aren't [actually] going to [win
> any] ... you're likely to get slaughtered either way ...

Although this was not the best terrain for the SSP, being a Westminster
general election, there was still some disillusionment created by coming
so far under the target. But in this case, the mistake was not fatal as the
May 2003 Scottish Parliament elections would show, and indicated the
Scotsman's political antennae to be wonky when it proclaimed: '[T]he
SSP will forever remain on the margins ... moralistic, idealistic, unrealistic'.[149] And, although Tommy's considerable skills of persuasion were
unable to get either MSPs Dennis Canavan or John McAllion to join or
back the SSP in the period, there was something of a backhanded compliment when Labour scrapped its plans for elected mayors in Scotland
because of the danger of Tommy getting elected in Glasgow and burning
Labour's fingers as Ken Livingstone had done in May 2000 when he stood
for and won the London mayoral election as an independent (after failing to secure the Labour nomination). Staying level in the polls allowed
Tommy to continue to predict a tally of six to eight SSP MSPs in the 2003
election but, raising the stakes further, to this he added that this might
constitute holding the balance of power in Holyrood.[150] But more often
than not he stayed on the safer territory of just six to eight SSP MSPs.[151]

Scotland and Scottishness

Unlike the 'Brit left' as it is called, Tommy was keen to embody and
colonise Scottishness and Scottish national identity for radical, progressive and socialist ends. The former saw this as a form of nationalism
which was not only a stain on socialism but divisive and damaging of
working class unity either side of the border. What was particularly
interesting about Tommy's perspective were the following emphases:

> I'm a socialist first and Scottish second. My first love is for
> humankind. I'm for the solidarity of ordinary people through-
> out the world, regardless of race, religion, creed or colour. Yes,
> I am very proud of my roots. I'm a Glasgow[152] boy who loves
> Scotland. I am very proud of our reputation for friendship and

solidarity throughout the world. The phrase about us all being 'Jock Tamson's Bairns' is supposed to encapsulate that spirit of friendship and support for fellow members of the human race. ... Socialists fight for maximum unity of all working-class people. If we unite across national, racial and religious divisions we can secure decent wages, pensions, homes and hospitals.[153]

The way Tommy married these elements together was to talk frequently in terms of the kind of 'Scotland I want to live in'.[154] Indeed, he extended this to 'the kind of Scotland I want my daughter to grow up in' after Gail's pregnancy was announced. At root, what he was trying to do was shape the view of what it meant to be Scottish, pulling it away from shortbread and tartan and pushing it further towards social justice and egalitarianism. Thus, in the *Mirror* he argued: 'There is no doubt that Scots have voted for the sort of collectivist political values and principles that the Labour Party used to stand for'.[155] And so, in praising as a famous Scot Manchester United manager, Alex Ferguson, for his hard work and teamwork ethic, he did not flinch from criticising Ferguson's mistaken socialist support for 'new' Labour.[156] But sometimes in his rush to laud fellow Scots, he did not state the obvious. So when he commented on Sean Connery receiving a knighthood he rightly attacked the honours system but in saying: 'There is no doubt that Connery is one of the great Scots of the century',[157] he forgot to mention what one reader felt compelled in the letters' page to do:

> As an admirer of Tommy Sheridan, I was shocked to see him refer to Sean Connery as the greatest living Scot. Connery made his name and a lot of money acting in films where the real stars were the special effects and he made sure he kept most of his cash by becoming a tax exile. If we are looking for great living Scots, then we should not be looking at someone who also thinks it is okay to give women a slap now and again, but at care workers, hospital staff and all those working in the community for a pittance. Even Tommy himself is more deserving of the title than Mr Connery. – C. Halliday, Glasgow [158]

Overview

If the times prior to the 6 May 1999 were his 'salad days', the period from 6 May 1999 to 30 April 2003 was not just Tommy's political coming of age but also him becoming a household name.[159] As early as 2001, the *Evening News* believed he was visually the best known Scottish politician[160] while looking back over the course of the first parliament, the *Scotsman Guide to Scottish Politics* commented he had 'inspired more column inches than any other MSP save [the first three First Ministers] Donald Dewar, Henry McLeish and Jack McConnell'.[161] The *Sunday Herald* went so far as to say he was 'a peacock amongst penguins' in the parliament.[162] BBC Scotland political commentator, Brian Taylor, observed that in the first parliament, Tommy had been a 'remarkable individual'.[163] Mainstream observers were quick to point out that without the poll tax and proportional representation, the figure Tommy became was not possible. What these commentators were not so quick to observe was that without the socialist and social democratic traditions of Scotland (and Glasgow, Strathclyde and the Central Belt of Scotland in particular) and their oft fusing with radical notions of Scottish national identity and progressive visions of national self-determination, Tommy would not have so easily or widely emerged.[164] These were important facilitators (but not determinants). But equally well what these commentators were not so quick to observe was that Tommy as a tribune fitted the times very well in another way. So while the poll tax revolt was a successful social movement, it did not inspire or lead onto others on the same scale or with the same success, and in the same period the number of strikes in Scotland declined markedly as elsewhere.[165] Consequently, as lone councillor and lone MSP, Tommy provided a voice for the voiceless and became a fighter for others because they were not fighting for themselves.

That said, Tommy's ultimate reward was to play a major role in taking advantage of the conditions to furnish a greatly enhanced SSP presence on 1 May 2003 as well as to advance the cause of socialism in Scotland. As the 'uncompromising voice of Scottish socialism',[166] he was able to use his developed political antennae[167] along with his charm and star quality to help do so. He became a valued asset to the cause of socialism by taking it out of its partly self-inflicted ghetto and putting it on show to a vastly enlarged audience. This is no better demonstrated than in the backhanded compliment that many ordinary citizens[168] as well as politicians paid to him apropos 'I don't agree with his politics but I admire his integrity and conviction'. And this was achieved despite often being accused of playing gesture politics, talking in clichés and soundbites,[169] and wanting attention. It was also achieved despite being accused of political immaturity and infantilism. For example the *Evening News* dubbed him a 'rebel without a cause ... [with] adolescent economics' and these 'economic policies may be the politics of the sixth form'.[170] But the other side – the damaging side to the aforementioned backhanded compliment – was that others felt that Tommy could make a fine case *against* capitalism but not *for* socialism. Some of this was because while recognising the inherent problems of capitalism, they could not see a viable alternative because of the stains on the soul of socialism courtesy of the Soviet Union and Stalin. But some of this 'admire but not agree' was because even with the (relatively) large and growing forces of the SSP, the content of his arguments still seemed a bit far-fetched to more amenable minds. Although critics amongst his former comrades in the CWI (former Militant) accused him of political backsliding, he described himself as 'fully red-blooded socialist'.[171] But, unlike such far left critics, Tommy had found a productive means by which to apply his socialism in some very practical and nuanced but still aspirational ways. This made him able to engage as a socialist with wider numbers over a wider range of issues than ever before. Thus, for example, he argued that 'my vision is of a society where charity [i]sn't needed – but for now it is'[172] and he donated his journalist earnings to charity, showing that he understood that compassion was needed in the short-term, and this put him in a good position to criticise reliance upon it in the long-term. As an MSP, he rode the law maker-law breaker divide extremely capably, judging issues on what were matters of principle worth fighting for and how this might play out in the court of public opinion. The *Guardian* recognised him as a constructive and mature politician.[173] Others believed he had become almost statesman like. In all of this, his political courage was borne of a personal courage. His prodigious work rate was 'Protestant' rather than 'Catholic'.[174] The years 1999 to 2003 were his undoubted golden years.

Notes

1. See Patterson, R. 'Scotland's brave new world' (*Red Pepper*, May 2004) for an account of the SSP's evolution and growth and Gall, G. 'Radical left unity projects in Europe' (*Scottish Left Review*, January-February 2008) for an overview of similar left realignment projects in Europe.
2. Examples of the former were commercial adverts in membership packs and cheaper membership.
3. 12 July 1998.
4. 11 December 1998.
5. *Daily Record* 11 December 1998.
6. See Bennie, L. 'Exploiting new electoral opportunities: the small parties in Scotland' in Hassan, G. and Warhurst, C. *Tomorrow's Scotland* (Lawrence and Wishart, 2002) for a brief overview of the SML/SSA/SSP.
7. Other celebrities which Tommy knew like Tam Cowan and Elaine C Smith were brought into help launch campaigns like those over free school meals campaign in 2004.
8. These included two ex-Labour councillors on Glasgow City Council, Heather Ritchie and Carolyn Moore, in late 1998 and then former Labour MP Ron Brown and leading SNP postal union activist, Derek Durkin.

9. *Herald* 9 December 1998.
10. *Daily Record* 11 December 1998.
11. *Independent* 19 April 1999, *Herald* 10 April 1999, 23 April 1999, *Scotsman* 19 April 1999.
12. 19 April 1999.
13. *Herald* 10 April 1999.
14. The SWP would later join the SSP en masse in May 2001, becoming the *Socialist Worker* Platform within the SSP, after it belatedly recognised that being outside the SSP put it outside the main (socialist) drag and that its thesis that the SSP had succumbed to the dangers of nationalism and electoralism was unfounded. Some of this disdain was due to a residual antagonism and sectarianism towards Militant.
15. See, for example, *Herald* 23 May 1998.
16. 16 January 2000.
17. *Sunday Herald* 11 April 1999.
18. *Scottish Socialist Voice* 16 November 2001.
19. *Herald* 12 May 1999.
20. 15 December 1999.
21. In *ATTR* (p. 117), Tommy showed that he had the nous to not allow his opponents to attack him for what he was wearing when he wore a shirt, tie and trousers (as opposed to jeans, jumper and black leather jacket) when he appeared on German TV for one of his first major TV interviews.
22. Contrary to media assertion, his suit was not made by Armani but by Candidate. His suit for his 2010 perjury trial was from Burton (blog 29 September 2010).
23. *Press and Journal* 13 May 1999.
24. 13 May 1999.
25. In a long interview in *Scotland on Sunday* (16 January 2000), Tommy played to the extended family and respectful grandson themes by saying: 'I wasn't going to go against my granny'.
26. *Scotland on Sunday* 9 May 1999.
27. 16 May 1999.
28. See Daily Record 29 May 1999, Mirror 10 June 1999.
29. *Herald* 29 May 1999.
30. Hassan, G. and Lynch, P. *The Almanac of Scottish Politics* (2001, Politicos), p. 280.
31. *Scottish Socialist Voice* 22 November 2002.
32. In this context, Tommy said: 'If the Labour Party was doing what it was supposed to do, then there would not be a place for us' (*Guardian* 17 May 2001) and 'Labour has abandoned socialism and we have picked up that torch' (*Mirror* 4 June 2001).
33. *Sun* 13 June 2000.
34. *Herald* 25 June 1999.
35. *Herald* 7 September 1999.
36. *Herald* 1 October 2002.
37. *Sunday Herald* 26 September 1999.
38. *Sunday Herald* 23 May 1999.
39. 9 May 1999.
40. *Scotland on Sunday* 26 September 1999.
41. *Evening News* 25 September 1999. This was a little ironic given a Labour-Liberal Democrat coalition formed the government of the first two parliaments.
42. *Herald* 3 September 1999.
43. *Herald* 6 October 1999.
44. Tommy was also a diligent user of the Scottish Parliament Information Centre (SPICe) for facts and figures for making his arguments. He also used the research by Schlesinger,

P., Miller, D. and Dinan W. (*Open Scotland? Journalists, Spin Doctors and Lobbyists*, Polygon, 2001) to further embarrass Labour's over its 'lobbygate' scandal.

45. *Daily Record* 1 September 1999.

46. The Scottish Parliament can pass Executive, Committee, Member and Private Bills. As a single MSP and the SSP's only MSP, the Member's Bill avenue was the most appropriate route for Tommy to go down.

47. 30 April 2000.

48. 3 May 2000.

49. 30 April 2000. Tommy won the Spirtle of the Year award for Parliament because of his 'undoubted oratorical skills ... [where he] cleverly painted a picture of sheriff officers ... as "Rottweilers in suits" ' (*Scotland on Sunday* 17 September 2000) and this made him 'Parliament's most passionate orator' (*Herald* 16 November 2000). He was also voted 'people's parliamentarian' for two years running by Scottish People's Network Accolades from 2000.

50. Free school meal provision was introduced in 2007 and extended in 2010, both by the SNP.

51. *Daily Mail* 25 September 1999.

52. *Herald* 25 September 1999.

53. He did, however, take some flak for having, by late 2000, the worst voting record although he was there for all key ones. Although much of his absence was due to building the SSP, he did still have constituents to deal with despite being a list MSP. Alan McCombes (*DTTSS* p. 213) pointed out that Tommy was ejected from his one parliamentary committee for poor attendance.

54. See also Tommy's 'Introduction' to the *Imagine* (pages xiii–xx). Although, Tommy talks of the 'we' of himself and Alan in writing the book, Tommy was unashamedly public in his praise for Alan in actually writing the book, with himself playing the role of minor contributor. Interestingly, in the paper of Tommy's former comrades (*The Socialist*, 9 February 2001), the book was heavily disparaged.

55. While it was overly harsh to suggest that Tommy's contribution to *Imagine* was little more than suggesting the title, it was wrong of opponents to label him a theorist not a doer (*Sunday Herald* 19 November 2000) because it was the doing that meant he did not have the time to be an equal partner in writing *Imagine*.

56. Former Trotskyist, now SNP supporter, and then *Scotsman* associate editor, George Kerevan, wrote that while Tommy was a 'tanned Trotskyist ... [who] says what he means which is a joy to behold ... Tommy's socialism is utopian guff ... [a] social-worker vision of socialism' (*Scotsman* 17 November 2000) while Alison Rowatt (*Herald* 25 November 2000) believed: 'Imagine is socialism for the cappuccino generation – it's quick, easy, has lots of froth, and makes the blood rush to the head. It's no bad thing for that, but ... most readers will stick to the hard stuff of *realpolitik* until Mr Sheridan comes up with something easier to swallow'. The review by Tom Brown (*New Statesman* 11 December 2000) was less harsh.

57. At this time and for a large part of her time as a stewardess, Gail worked on long haul flights, necessitating time away from home.

58. 9 August 2002.

59. See, for example, *Sunday Times* 19 March 2000, *Sunday Herald* 19 March 2000, *Herald* 20 March 2000, *Scotsman* 18 April 2000 (*cf. Herald* 25 September 1999).

60. 16 January 2000. As it turned out, this may have been written by Alan McCombes (see later).

61. 14 July 2001.

62. *Herald* 25 September 1999.

63. *Herald* 2 November 2002.

64. The issue, as time proved, was not whether the SSP would survive, but the nature of its survival. In this period, it was assumed the most pressing crises the SSP would face would be internal ructions over reform and revolution, and over the prospect of joining a coalition with the SNP to form a government.
65. *Scotland on Sunday* 16 January 2000.
66. 24 February 2000. Often, Colin Fox would try to make light of the press attitude: 'Sometimes we are eclipsed by Tommy's superstar status – and his suntan' (*Evening News* 4 April 2000).
67. *Herald* 2 August 1999.
68. *Daily Record* 22 September 1999.
69. *Daily Record* 25 September 1999.
70. *Herald* 25 September 1999.
71. *Guardian* 6 September 2000.
72. *Evening Times* 7 September 2000.
73. 1 January 2000.
74. *Daily Record* 9 August 2000.
75. 16 January 2000.
76. Given that many of his newspaper columns – where many of the quotes come from – were written by Alan McCombes (see below), it may be thought that it was Alan that was the exuberant 'talker upper' but the tight working relationship between him and Tommy and Tommy's statements elsewhere testify to Tommy's willingness to talk in the same way. Thus, to judge Tommy was also to judge Alan in this regard.
77. *Evening Times* 8 August 2000.
78. *Herald* 12 August 2002.
79. Evidently, Tommy did not learn much from his Cardonald College course. Colin Fox recalled that initially Tommy was so 'technologically-challenged' that he thought the mouse for a computer was used directly upon the screen. In his 2006 trial, Tommy had to be instructed by the judge, Lord Turnbull, on how to use the court computer (*Sunday Times* 6 August 2006). Being unaccustomed to computers lay largely in Tommy's preferred and staple medium of communication being direct by phone or in person. Felicity Garvie recalled: 'He would give anybody and everybody his mobile phone number … he made himself available to everybody … and he hardly turned anyone down that wanted to conduct an interview with him, including students, because he wanted to speak to anybody that was interested in our ideas'.
80. From interviews with Felicity Garvie and Carolyn Leckie.
81. *Sunday Herald* 5 September 1999.
82. This column ended with the election of the 5 other SSP MSPs in 2003 and its replacement with 'Holyrood news' in which the 6 SSP MSPs reported on their work (usually two per week in a turn and turn-about situation).
83. See the collection of these in his *Words as Weapons: Selected Writing 1980–1990* (Verso, 1990) and *Articles of Resistance* (Bookmarks, 2000). In late 2004 during his interviews, Tommy suggested that I organise and edit a collection of his *Record* and *Mirror* articles similar to the aforementioned Paul Foot books. Despite doing some initial work on this, discussion at the 2005 SSP conference and follow up a meeting on 9 September 2005 with him, Tommy did not commit the time to progress the project in terms of selecting the pieces and getting Mirror Group Newspapers to waive copyright.
84. *Daily Record* 29 December 1999.
85. *Daily Record* 22 December 1999.
86. See, for example, *Daily Record* 5, 23 February 2000, 22 March 2000. The use of particular forms of language which eschew explicit reference to class for a more productive implicit and subtle inference of class echoes that of the vocabulary and

discourse used by Jimmy Reid in the UCS work-in (see Foster, J. And Woolfson, C. *The Politics of the UCS Work-In: class alliances and the right to work*, (Lawrence and Wishart, 1986) and 'How workers on the Clyde gained the capacity for class struggle: the Upper Clyde Shipbuilders' work-in, 1971–2' in McIlroy, J., Fishman, N. And Campbell, A. (eds.) *British Trade Unions and Industrial Politics: the high tide of trade unionism, 1964–79* (Ashgate, 1999), pp. 297–325).

87. One of the conditions of Paul Foot's column was that he was not permitted to use it to publicise the political party of which he was a member, namely, the SWP. Interestingly, this was not a condition for Tommy, and not just because he was known for being a politician and not journalist. Rather, it suggests that Tommy had greater standing and, thus, leverage. And, following from this, there was no censorship or editing of his copy so long as it was to the required word count.

88. Showing his and Alan McCombes' unfamiliarity with the higher banding for personal income tax, Tommy – as an MSP earning at this time some £40,000 – was hit with a big tax bill because the £300 was paid to him before being donated. After this, the fee was paid direct to the centre.

89. See also *SSP All-members Bulletin* 'Crisis in the party: the fight for the truth', August 2006, p. 4. Tony Benn, one of Tommy's political heroes, was offered a column in the *Sun* on 9 June 2000 but refused it because he did not want to become know as a 'Sun columnist' (see Benn, T. *Free at Last: Diaries 1991–2001*, Hutchinson, 2002, p. 609).

90. *ATTR* p. 210.

91. *TST* 22 December 2010. This was repeated by Tommy's lawyer, Aamer Anwar, during the *NoW* phone-hacking scandal when he said Tommy 'had spent his adult life fighting the Murdoch empire' (*Press Association* 13 July 2011).

92. By contrast, Solidarity ('Who is pulling the strings?' Solidarity website, 16 December 2007) argued a much wider *raison d'etre* by claiming Tommy's 'only crime, the real reason that the NotW have gone after him, is that he has spent his entire adult life speaking truth to power'.

93. *NoW* (2 January 2011) pointed out that he frequently cooperated with it in the past. Moreover, he also played a charity football match in Wishaw in June 2003 wearing a shirt which prominently featured the *NoW* logo (*NoW* 26 December 2010).

94. One indication of this was that he wrote fewer letters to the press after becoming an MSP.

95. For example, he wrote to the *Herald* (28 March 2000) criticising its lack of coverage of the SSP.

96 *Scotland on Sunday* 16 January 2000.

97. Not long after, Tommy gained a *Sunday Mail* column of not only fewer column inches but on a monthly basis and more sports-based. It did, however, provide another source of income for the SSP.

98. 26 November 2000.

99. 13 February 2001.

100. 13 February 2001.

101. 14 February 2001.

102. 2 April 2001.

103. 11 March 2001.

104. 3 March 2001.

105. *Sunday Herald* 10 October 1999

106. *Scotsman* 25 September 1999.

107. This was ironic given the *Record's* favourable coverage to proposals to legalise cannabis in 2000.

108. 16 May 2001.

109. 23, 25, 26 March 2002. See also 23, 30 October 2002.

110. George McNeilage believed that one of Tommy's motivations for considering action was as a shot across the bows of any newspaper thinking of printing any stories about his sex club visits. He also did not take legal action against odious slurs on him by the *Sunday Mail* (30 March, 6 April 2003) and the then First Minister, Jack McConnell, despite saying he would (*Guardian* 7 April 2003, see also *DTTSS* p. 99).

111. *Scottish Socialist Voice* 20 July 2001.

112. 19 April 1999.

113. 16 January 2000.

114. 12 July 1998.

115. 11 April 1999.

116. In addition to Alex Neil of the SNP, Tommy also worked with his fellow SNP MSPs Sandra White and Lloyd Quinan.

117. 19 April 1999.

118. 9 May 1999.

119. 19 April 1999.

120. 13 June 1999.

121. 24 April 1999.

122. *Sunday Herald* 11 April 1999.

123. *Scotland on Sunday* 16 January 2000. The *New Statesman* (29 January 2001) commented on his 'po-faced earnestness' too.

124. *Herald* 13 April 1999.

125. 18 June 2000.

126. One seasonal accompaniment to this was the white poppy which he took a lot of stick for.

127. *Herald* 15 February 2000.

128. *Sun* 15 November 2000.

129. *Scotsman* 11 May 2000.

130. *Sunday Herald* 19 November 2000.

131. *Evening Times* 18 December 2000.

132. *Herald* 15 December 2000.

133. *Sunday Herald, Sunday Mail, Scotland on Sunday* 24 December 2000.

134. While Galloway (*Sunday Times* 4 March 2001) said, in complementary terms, that Tommy was younger, better looking and more leftwing, in his *Mail on Sunday* columns (for example, 4 March 2001) he often made snide, critical remarks against Tommy.

135. But such heterodoxy did not always reach into all corners of the legacy of Tommy's thinking. For example, when Motorola closed its Scottish plant in 2001, Tommy argued on *Newsnight Scotland* that it should be nationalised. However, this was at a time when there was a massive glut in microchips, indicating a lack of political imagination which would have allowed him to say the plant should have given over to making socially useful products or the workforces' skills used elsewhere rather than allow the *de facto* deskilling of Scottish Executive's retraining programme to take place. Such imagination was not without precedent given the 'swords to ploughshares' thinking evident in the Lucas aerospace and Vickers engineering workers' plans in the 1970s (see Beynon, H. and Wainwright, H. *The Workers' Report on Vickers* (Pluto, 1979) and Wainwright, H. and Elliot, D. *The Lucas Plan – a new trade unionism in the making* (Allison and Busby, 1982)).

136. *Herald* 17 December 1998.

137. *Press Association* 16 May 2002.

138. He estimated he carried out about a dozen school visits per year to give talks at the request of staff or students.

139. His first appearance on this was in 2001.

140. 13 October 2002.
141. 16 May 2000.
142. *Guardian* 15 August 2007.
143. *Herald* 17 January 2000.
144. *Herald* 8 August 2000.
145. *Herald* 15 January 2001.
146. *Guardian* 17 May 2001.
147. See *Sunday Herald* 11 February 2001, *Guardian* 17 May 2001, *Herald* 18 May 2001. Although Tommy correctly predicted the SSP would become Scotland's fifth political party, this was still a slip back from putting the Liberal Democrats into fifth place in the by-elections.
148. *Scottish Socialist Voice* 15 June 2001.
149. 12 February 2001.
150. *Morning Star* 21 March 2002.
151. *Evening Times* 1 October 2002.
152. In the first parliament, he argued in that the new parliament building to be located in Glasgow – not so much for reasons of 'Glasgow nationalism' but in order to distribute jobs and resources away from the richer Edinburgh.
153. *Daily Record* 3 May 2000.
154. *Daily Record* 19 January 2000.
155. 4 June 2001.
156. *Sunday Herald* 16 January 2000
157. *Daily Record* 29 December 1999.
158. *Daily Record* 9 January 2000. Sean Connery (*Mirror* 8 March 2003) 'returned' the compliment by saying of Tommy and the SSP: 'That's the spirit one wants to see. They're all shit scared of anybody that's going to create any waves'. Ironically, Tommy would have been unaware of Connery's fleeting sympathy for workers' plight in his 1967 *The Bowler and the Bunnet* (*Sunday Herald* 23 January 2011).
159. An unusual measure of this was that a photograph of Tommy could sometimes be seen in the house of Archie the Inventor in the popular children's BBC television series, *Balamory*, which aired between 2002 and 2005.
160. 11 January 2001.
161. *Scotsman Guide to Scottish Politics* (Scotsman Publications, 2004), p. 216. Somewhat ironically in 2001, Tommy was (involuntarily) entered into *Burke's Landed Gentry*, and said the rest of the usual entrants need not fear for their lives, only their wealth and land.
162. 19 November 2000.
163. Taylor, B. *Scotland's Parliament: triumph and disaster* (Edinburgh University Press, 2002), p. 228.
164. See Gall, G. *The Political Economy of Scotland: Red Scotland? Radical Scotland?* (University of Wales Press, 2005).
165. Gall, G. *The Political Economy of Scotland: Red Scotland? Radical Scotland?* (University of Wales Press, 2005), chapter 2. Examples like the Scottish nursery nurses, thus, stood out like the proverbial sore thumb (see Gall, G. 'Women workers as trade unionists in Scotland' *Perspectives*, 7:7–10, 2004 and 'Assessing the outcome of the Scottish nursery nurses' strike' *Frontline*, 14:14–17, 2004).
166. *Herald* 2 June 2000.
167. See *Scotsman* 8 August 2002.
168. For example, two members of the public in the public gallery of the Scottish Parliament commented: 'He says what he means, doesn't muck about or play to the gallery. He's sincere' (*Scotsman* 25 February 2000). Countless letters over the years in the *Daily Record* and *Herald* also testify to this perception.

169. Part of his ability to convey his arguments to mass audiences was by these means including those of alliteration and rhyme (like the 'creed of greed') so not all would agree with this criticism. However, in using alliteration – like describing a report on council tax collection as 'shabby, shoddy and shallow' (*Herald* 10 February 2000) – he did not get lambasted as Neil Kinnock's did where Kinnock was tagged the 'Welsh windbag'.

170. 17 April 2001, 25 October 2000.

171. *Evening News* 3 September 1999.

172. *Sunday Mirror* 20 February 2000.

173. 10 May 2003.

174. See Weber, M. *The Protestant Work Ethic and the Spirit of Capitalism* (Penguin, 2002).

5

The Big Breakthrough

Introduction

In a play on the title of a well-known book, the *Scottish Socialist Voice* greeted the election of a veritable team of SSP MSPs with its front page headline of 'The Joy of Six'.[1] The joy would be very intoxicating but also very short-lived. It ended on 9 November 2004, this being the SSP's '9/11'.[2] But before moving to the event which set off the train wreck extraordinaire, it is worth not forgetting the 'golden' year and a half from 1 May 2003 and what the *Sunday Herald* called 'Britain's first experiment in legislative Trotskyism'.[3] Tommy pronounced: 'a new political force is being born in Scotland'[4] and that 'we're going to shake up Scottish politics over the next four years and put socialism back on the political agenda'.[5] The breakthrough was certainly helped by proportional representation but it was not just the result of proportional representation for a political force capable of taking advantage of it was also necessary.[6]

Ironically this time, Tommy was almost bang on the money when predicting in 2003 that the SSP would win between six and seven MSPs in 2003.[7] On one occasion when he suggested four MSPs was 'more realistic', the *Guardian* saw this as 'talking down his party's chances'.[8] However, he was well adrift in predicting the SSP would have between twenty to twenty five MSPs in 2007,[9] and be in a power sharing arrangement with the SNP in 2007.[10] Nonetheless, as late as autumn 2002, the *Herald* doubted whether Tommy, despite being 'both populist and respected' and 'a politician of some principle', could go beyond being 'a supreme single-issue campaigner' in order to see the SSP becoming a collective force at Holyrood.[11] That doubt was easily removed on 1 May 2003 when the SSP became more than a 'one man band' operating out of its Glasgow citadel, vindicating the strategy of the SSP and Tommy's orientation on Labour and the SNP (see before). Tommy could then rightly say: '[A] new political force has been formed – and that force believes the wealth of Scotland belongs to the people of Scotland'[12] while the *Scottish Socialist Voice* proclaimed the SSP's vote as 'the biggest vote for a party to the left of Labour in Scotland's history'.[13] The SSP gained 118,764 (6.2%) across the 73 constituency seats and crucially 128,026 (6.7%) across the eight regional list seats. The latter secured the 6 MSPs and the SSP was not that far away from winning an MSP in the Highlands and Islands, Mid Scotland and Fife, and North East Scotland seats and a clutch of councillors where it came second in 19 seats. In Glasgow, Tommy secured 6,016 votes (28%, a 6% increase) in the Pollok first-past-the-post constituency contest,[14] and was head of the regional list for Glasgow which secured 31,116 votes (16%, an 8% increase) which saw him and Rosie Kane elected. In all of this, there was some good natured banter. Upon being elected to Glasgow City Council, Keith Baldassara joked that he was the only elected SSP member to have won through 'first-past-the-post' while Rosie proffered: '[W]e're Mr and Mrs Socialism ... now, at least Tommy will have some company [in Parliament] ... it will be just like double trouble'.[15] In characteristic bombast and flamboyance, Tommy declared: 'We will be mounting a campaign that will engulf Scotland ... We are going to put socialism back on the agenda not just in Scotland but across Europe'.[16] The only downside to the 2003 celebrations was that the Greens, without much in the way of grassroots organisation, achieved one more MSP.

Run-Up to the Breakthrough

In a major interview with the *Sunday Herald*, Tommy identified that his major strengths were flexibility and heterodoxy:

Any politician who isn't willing to adapt, to be flexible, will be condemned to irrelevancy. ... Principles and ideals are very important, but the method of communication will change over time. What I've learned from my early days is that social revolution isn't one act. It's not the Bolshevik revolution all over again. In the past, socialists like me were hamstrung by the absolutism and purism of dogma. If you didn't believe in the first four congresses of the Bolshevik Party, [then] you weren't a real revolutionary. But that's pish. It represents nothing to anyone. What people want to know is what you'll do here and now. And then what other parties lack is what they would do tomorrow, a vision, what it is they stand for.[17]

One indication of being flexible and heterodox was in another major interview with the *Herald*.[18] At the launch of the SSP's election manifesto, he retorted: 'I don't know if you've noticed the bags under my eyes after all the sleepless nights I have had worrying about them'[19] when asked about the rich leaving due to SSP tax proposals. But he then provided a less flippant and more considered response to the *Herald*.[20] Asked about the likely flight of capital if the SSP won a share of power as well as whether there would be nationalisation of the likes of Tesco, Tommy responded by saying there was already divestment (i.e. offshoring) going on now before stating:

> I don't think there's a need to nationalise Tesco right now. What I think there's a need for is to impose on Tesco proper wages and employment conditions ... What we would be doing is regulating business. You don't have to own it, you just regulate it ... We very much believe in a mixed economy ... our mix is different from New Labour's mix. Labour would like to add a wee drop of whisky to the Atlantic ocean and say that's a mixed economy. We think that's wrong. We think there's a larger role for the public sector to play. It is worth making the point that 99.9% of business in Scotland is small business. When people say to me 'Are you business-friendly?', I say 'Yes, we are very small business-friendly'.

Rather than trying opportunistically and disingenuously not to frighten the horses, this appears to be more to do with innovative thinking for a former Trotskyist, and which would bring him into conflict with his former CWI comrades.[21] Tommy had made clear that attaining socialism was a process not an event (like a revolutionary insurrection) and not necessarily about workers' soviets (see later). Similarly, he spoke 'the language of class war'[22] but without using the term 'class' as such.[23] But, given that there are at least two sides to most tales, these characteristics of being transparent, flexible and knowing how to position and present issues would take an unusual and interesting turn of direction come 9 November 2004. Yet for the moment, ignorance being bliss was the case. All was rosy in the garden.

After losing his *Record* weekly page, Tommy gained one in the *Mirror* in January 2003. Arguably this was a better fit for the *Mirror* had a more leftwing political tradition than the *Record* by virtue of opposing the Iraq war, supporting the firefighters in their 2002–2003 dispute and the miners against pit closures in the 1992. However, it also had a much smaller circulation as well and this may have inclined him to take up other opportunities as they arose like writing a 'new year's message' article in the *Sun*.[24] In contrast to Rosie Kane writing her own columns for the *Sunday Mail* for the period 2003–2007, Tommy's column was either written by himself or the SSP press officer, Eddie Truman until the political split (as Alan McCombes had taken on other roles). Nonetheless, the *Mirror* page – as with his *Record* page before – comprised politics and chitchat, with his fee being given to good causes (which were announced each week on the page). He was both populist and popularising, but Gail was now a more prominent feature of the chitchat. Tommy's other writings in this period were in the *Morning Star, RMT News* and *Big Issue (Scotland)*.

Against this backdrop, Tommy was a peace warrior against war in Iraq which began with the invasion on 20 March 2003. He steadfastly argued it was a war for oil, there was money for this war but not a war on poverty, and that if removing dictatorships was such a key issue then why had there not also been invasions of Indonesia and the like. One of his memorable jabs against 'new' Labour in parliament was: 'Wake up and smell the oil!' Moreover, he was prepared to risk the inevitable and widespread wrath when he stated he did not support British troops in what they were doing and that they should mutiny and come home.[25] Similarly, he took pelters for encouraging school kids to walk out of school in protest over the beginning of the invasion. For the many against the war, Tommy was able to use the credibility he had earned from being a peace campaigner who was prepared to go to jail for this to lead the opposition. Indeed, in 2003, he was in court again arising from his arrest at Faslane in February 2002. He defended himself, pointing out the irony of being charged with breach of the peace for campaigning peacefully for peace. Being found guilty, he refused to pay the fine and was jailed for four days in August 2003. Upon being sent down and redolent of his 'specialness' to her, in court his mother tellingly shouted to him: 'Keep walking in the light'.[26] Tommy recounted his time in Barlinnie, saying it made him feel 'dirty, knackered and apprehensive'.[27]

In the fight against 'new' Labour, Tommy had lost none of his incisive hard-hitting, thinking on one's feet skill. So when attack dog, John Reid MP, as chair of the Labour Party, told Scottish Labour's annual conference: 'I've been in politics for a long time – I can remember when Tommy Sheridan was white', Tommy shot back with: 'I've been in politics for a long time, I can remember when John Reid was a socialist'.[28] And as an enduring sign of Tommy's personal appeal, at an SSP eve of the election rally in the Assembly Rooms in Edinburgh, an ordinary member of the public left before the rally started when this person realised that Tommy would not be speaking as billed. No amount of Colin Fox lauding the merits of the other speakers that night could change the mind of this person.

Gang of Six

While pollster projections of 'just' four seats immediately before the election proved untrue, Tommy was full of praise for the SSP's leading candidates including Rosie Kane, Carolyn Leckie, Frances Curran and Colin Fox.[29] When Rosie Kane promised: 'I'm going to bring something different, something colourful to Parliament',[30] Tommy was perfectly comfortable in commenting: 'She will brighten up the Parliament and bring a real working class perspective to Holyrood'[31] because he argued the other parties 'served up ... the same grey porridge ... in different coloured bowls'.[32] Tommy then profusely praised all his new MSP colleagues.[33] It was not long before media and political opponents returned to using the term 'Trot' as one of abuse. Into this breach stepped George Kerevan, with his prediction: 'Like any centrist formation [which equivocates between reform and revolution], the SSP is inherently unstable and will likely founder when the Trots start to fall out with each other'.[34] Like any other lesser or better informed commentators, the rationale for the prediction was way off beam for while there were tensions between the various platforms in the SSP, these never came close to splitting the SSP. And, as for the mix of new personalities, Tommy happily lauded Rosie as 'a kind and wonderful person ... her heart is so big and her compassion so huge'.[35]

Both *Evening Times* and *Herald* hinted early on that the women SSP MSPs may make trouble for Tommy by stealing his limelight and putting him in the shade.[36] They were not wrong in this, especially in the case of Rosie Kane. The salience of this is that, contrary to what Tommy asserted in his 2010 perjury case, if there was anyone who had an interest to 'do' somebody 'in', it was him 'doing in' Rosie, not vice-versa because Rosie showed signs of becoming the star – in her own right – of the parliamentary show. But contrary to press reports that Tommy was annoyed that Rosie was getting more attention, there is little evidence of Tommy having this view much less doing anything about it at this point because there was no tension of that sort (contrary to what Tommy argued and asked a number of his witnesses to give testimony on).[37] This was because the attention Rosie was receiving was very much based on her as a colourful, garrulous working class woman who championed certain issues and in certain ways. In this regard, Tommy was not in direct 'competition' with her as he played to the characters of the elder statesman and the more serious and austere politician. Indeed, the *Scotsman* believed Tommy remained a 'superb parliamentarian' in contrast to his five new SSP colleagues.[38] Yet, depending upon the demands of his political and legal fight from 9 November 2004, he engaged in various twists and turns where he created political and personal myths.

Just as importantly, Tommy was still able to command column inches of coverage such that the *Sunday Times* identified him as a 'brand'[39] and he made the top one hundred of the *Guardian's* most influential members of opposition.[40] The coverage was not just of his socialist political message but also of the stories of which he believed had a humanising nature on him as a socialist politician. So with some artistic license, he not only solicited the coverage of the following but got two bites at the cherry with two different accounts. In an exclusive in the *NoW* entitled 'Waverley station is Tommy's Water-loo', he experienced an 'embarrassing gaffe' and 'had to be freed from a locked train after spending too long in the loo. ... Last night Tommy claimed he'd rushed into the toilet after spilling coffee on himself ... He said 'When I tried to get off I couldn't get out. The doors were locked'.[41] Writing in the *Mirror* a few days later, he was without the coffee spill or the loo in 'I'm an MSP, Get Me Out Of Here!' ... as I tried to get off the 6.15pm Edinburgh to Glasgow train, which was in perfect working order when I boarded at 6.02pm but had taken ill by 6.06pm. There I was, sitting with my extortionately-priced ham and cheese baguette, thinking I was really lucky to get a seat, when I realised the train was going nowhere. I tried the electric doors. No electricity. I tried to shout from the window. It wouldn't open'.[42] And, elsewhere he showed the political nous to always make it seem that each conversation with a member of the public was a fresh and new one even though he'd had the same conversation countless times before. He was also renowned for asking for directions, when he did not need them, just in order to speak to as many people as possible.

Responsibility of Influence

Tommy, as SSP national convener, was acutely aware that in his own words 'with seats comes responsibility [and] it's less easy to dismiss poor showings'. With 6 MSPs, it was inevitable that media and opposition political party scrutiny and criticism would increase for the SSP was now gatecrashing the established parties' party and in a position to change and affect the law. Indeed, a chance meeting on a train in 2003 between George Kerevan, *Scotsman* associate editor, and Alan McCombes confirmed this, as Kerevan explained the SSP was now seen as a threat by the mainstream political parties and would come under scrutiny because it had had an easy ride so far.[43] Tommy observed:

> Now that we have a bigger group then you cannot get away with [not being in Parliament] because we are a group and not just a lone MSP ... and we have to manage that tension otherwise the press will have a go at us ... it's funny when the report came out we were shown to be among the hardest working [in Parliament]

because it didn't surprise us but it did surprise them ... we have had
to have our eye more on the Parliament because the expectations
of us are greater with six than with one.

Tommy also understood that with genuine influence there was an obligation to be politically more measured and less rash than before. But
in what now seems as a bizarre turn of events, Tommy – assisted by
Hugh Kerr – held meetings with the leading regional list candidates
prior to election to ask them whether they had any 'skeletons in their
closets' that the SSP leadership should be aware of because, if elected,
they would be put under intense media scrutiny.[44] The initiative was a
good one as forewarned is often to be forearmed but given that Tommy
had already been in parliament, was an experienced media operator and
was the interviewer, it appears he was not subject to the same process.
Whether this would have led to any admissions on his part must be as
open to doubt as whether this would have then allowed the forthcoming
fall-out to be any less significant or damaging. The supreme irony was
at this very time, according to Keith Baldassara, Tommy had just admitted to him going back to Cupids in Manchester.

The issue of responsibility of influence also related to controlling
others' expectations of the SSP's performance, so as to not create any
hostages to fortune. In a rare admission of error, Tommy believed:

In the 2004 Euro election, I think it was a mistake in retrospect
to the raise the prospect of 100,000 votes and winning a MEP as
clearly and as unconditionally as we did ... we prompted these
and they were possible so they were taken more seriously than the
one about the 10 MSPs [where I responded to a poll] ... what we
failed to do was to look at the wider situation of a Euro election
where we weren't the only anti-Iraq war party ... we raised expectations so much that going to 6% didn't look like a good result
for us ... we have to be a bit more sophisticated ... for the 2005
general election, we have to realise that our appeal as a Scottish
Socialist Party is going to be by its very nature diluted and we
have to be prepared to handle that.

Although that change of heart could not be put to the test because of the
SSP's implosion following 9 November 2004, it seemed that the closer
proximity to greater influence was making an impact upon Tommy's
political perspective. Of course, that did not apply to the means he chose
to deploy to fight for his political life thereafter. But more immediately,
there was some sense that the shine was beginning to come off Tommy
and the SSP with the European 2004 election when the SSP gained only

61,356 votes (5.2%). This was because, other than in by-elections, the curve was nearly always upwards but what made this case more serious than the 2001 general election prediction (of 100,000 votes but only getting 72,000) was that the SSP now had six MSPs. However, it was not quite a case of the wheels coming off the SSP bandwagon. That would happen shortly thereafter. Still at this point, Tommy understood the terrain was getting a bit trickier to traverse:

> I'm the Convener of the party so I have to take the plaudits when it goes right as well as the brickbats when it doesn't go as well as it could ... and I'm expected to think about the wider development of the party ... that's what being part of the leadership means ... we need a party of people that are thinkers and doers ... so I have to take the rap when we don't achieve that.

Still the Socialist Tribune

In his second term as an MSP, Tommy continued to raise new and innovative issues to supplement his hardy perennials. So in addition to campaigning against the M74 extension in Glasgow, the deportation of asylum seekers and the privatisation of the Calmac ferry service as well as supporting the nursery nurses strike, he made the major fist of any MSP or campaign in taking up the cudgel against the fraud and corruption embodied in the Edinburgh allowance scheme, whereby MSPs could get the Parliament to effectively pay their mortgage on a property in Edinburgh and then pocket the difference between the price they bought it for and the price they sold it for (which was not inconsiderable in a rising Edinburgh property market).[45] Bearing testimony to Tommy's panache, not only did he ensure considerable publicity for his searing criticisms but he was able to do so more easily and more ably than any other critics. Some of this was due to his forcefulness and boldness. But choosing the allowance scheme was a cute move because it was an obvious case of exposing 'pigs' with their 'noses' in the trough and was led by a socialist, thus making popular overtures to a much wider constituency. To develop his list of innovative and heterodox campaigning issues, he supported the fishing communities of north-east Scotland in their battle against European Union quotas,[46] promoted the opening of the cannabis cafe, Purple Haze, in Leith in Edinburgh and maintained his staunch republicanism, boycotting the queen's speech with the effect he was dubbed a 'Ronseal Republican'[47] for doing what he said on the tin.[48] However, it was a considerable personal disappointment to Tommy that his bill to abolish the council tax and replace it with Scottish Service Tax did not catch fire inside or outside parliament to the extent he wished. For example, it gained the support of the PCS union but not Unison[49] and attracted just 2,000 marchers to its cause on its national demo.[50] Although able to re-introduce it in the 2003–2007 Parliament, Tommy was unable to see his prediction that the council tax would become another poll tax come true. This was because, as he later seemed to acknowledge, the council tax did not affect working class people in the same way at the same time and they did not have such ability to refuse to cooperate.[51] Tommy, with the support of the RMT union, launched on 31 May 2006 the *Provision of Passenger Services (Scotland) Bill* which sought to renationalise the railways in Scotland. However, it was quickly ruled out of order for dealing with reserved (to Westminster) business. There were still occasions when Tommy engaged in direct action. One of these was a protest outside an immigration detention centre in Glasgow on 21 November 2005 when campaigning against dawn raids on asylum seekers, where he was arrested and charged with breach of the peace for chaining a fridge to the gates. Come the trial, he represented himself and was given a not proven verdict.[52] His *Mirror* column ended in December 2005 when, in protest over job cuts of journalists on the titles bringing into doubt the continued quality of the papers, he resigned his position. Overall, Tommy continued to champion campaigning on 'bread and butter' issues like housing and minimum wages, indicating his understanding that given the state of working class consciousness, confidence and organisation, it was important to lead on these kinds of basic issues in the here and now rather than focus upon permanent revolution, soviets and workers' power in the way off, distant future.

Although Tommy continued to lead from the front, he was still self-deprecating in public about his considerable leadership skills. The most he would proffer in press interviews was: 'Every movement needs its leaders'[53] and he was dismissive of being accorded second place in the *Sunday Herald*'s poll of the ten greatest living Scots.[54] In the *Mirror*, he stated the 'real great Scots' are those ordinary people that struggle to survive in poverty and hardship.[55] However, subsequently he more fully reflected:

> I think what I do best, if I'm good at this at all, is to take ideas and popularise them by hopefully making them relevant to people's lives ... the style that's wanted is short paragraphs and few of them ... I think I'm better now because I used to write long sentences and long paragraphs, writing the way I spoke ... I've never felt the need or requirement to write long theoretical pieces

because I've always been around individuals who I trusted and collaborated with that were better at it than me ... it's a bit like a football team where if someone is better at scoring goals you put them at the front and you play at the back supplying the ball ... you cannot have a team all of centre forwards.

So Tommy was able to make the pitch to people, either in person or print. He and the SSP then relied upon activists to try to recruit and integrate them into a coherent force.

Six Leaders Better than One?

At face value, six SSP MSPs should have ended the media's and political opponents' ability to characterise the SSP as a 'one-man band' which would fall apart if Tommy was 'hit by a bus'. Even the politically sympathetic *Mirror* still argued: 'For many, Sheridan is the SSP'.[56] The success of having six MSPs signalled that the SSP had entered – even if only momentarily as events would show – the wings of the Scottish mainstream political stage. And while it was wrong to keep using these hackneyed tabs, it would also be erroneous to assume that having six MSPs implied there would be necessarily a far more united, collective leadership in parliament or elsewhere. Although it was collectively agreed that each SSP MSP would have a major bill to lay before parliament – often those that Tommy had attempted without success to do so between 1999 and 2003 – there were disagreements over how and when to act collectively. Tommy proposed an occupation within parliament when he was threatened as a party leader with being removed from having a front row seat[57] and wanted a deputy SSP leader and a whip elected to be more like the other political parties.[58] He was given short shrift by his fellow SSP MSPs on these issues. The dispute over Members' Support Allowance, which provided administrative and constituency resources, was another indication of this. There were different views about the way in which it should be collectivised and distributed with the axis being between Tommy, Colin and Rosemary on one side and Carolyn, Frances and Rosie, on the other. There were divisions over the protest that led to the suspension of Colin, Rosie, Carolyn and Frances from parliament in June 2005.[59] The four MSPs, in a peaceful protest, interrupted First Minister's Question Time in the parliament to highlight that, contrary to undertakings, parliament had failed to secure the right to demonstrate outside the Gleneagles Hotel (in Scotland) where the G8 group was meeting. While there was already much ill-will at this stage (see next chapter), interestingly given his earlier advocacy of the occupation tactic, Tommy believed the protest was rather infantile.[60] There were also strains over what the relationship of parliament and party was and should be, and these were as much between the MSPs as they were with Tommy. Frances, Carolyn and Rosie felt stifled to different degrees in and by parliament, wanting to maintain an orientation on (outside) communities. The difference with Tommy was that he believed in being a 'serious' parliamentarian which demanded more orientation on, and time and effort in, parliament in terms of a political strategy. Some personal working relationships were sometimes strained for other reasons. For example, Rosemary Byrne felt socially excluded.[61] But this arose largely because she could not start work as an MSP immediately (having been a head teacher who had to give longer notice of leaving) so relationships were begun by the time she arrived. Rosemary was also relatively unknown outside the Central Belt, had a 'head teacher' mentality, and Carolyn, Frances and Rosie would tend to socialise with each other when they stayed in Edinburgh mid-week while Colin and Tommy tended to return to their homes. Some of the new MSPs felt Tommy should have guided them more by showing them the ropes when they entered parliament because he was an old hand. By contrast, Tommy felt – for their own good – they should learn these themselves as he had done. The partial root of all of these strains was that the SSP was ill-prepared for having 6 MSPs because it had spent so much of its efforts on the campaigning and election trail and was not sure it would, on the day, do that well so it had not given time to planning how to operate as a parliamentary group. Neither had it given much time to think about how to go about building collective leadership which productively married parliament and party together. As soon as the breakthrough happened, the MSPs were chasing their tails to cope with the demands on them so time for much needed quiet contemplation on these issues was sparse. These tensions were not, however, the ones referred to in Tommy's defence in 2010 and the importance of this brief consideration is five-fold.[62]

First, while there were tensions before November 2004, these were not due to either a nascent or fully grown anti-Tommy faction as he alleged in court in 2010. There was certainly no jealously of Tommy from the new MSPs as Colin, Carolyn and Rosie quickly developed their own individual and independent media profiles. Of the three of these, Rosie was clearly the new rising star of the Parliament. Meantime, Frances was less comfortable with the media's gaze. Indeed, if there was any jealously at all, it was more likely to be from Tommy who may have felt that his 'crown' had been stolen by some young Turks.[63] Second, there was not a united collective leadership in Parliament by which to withstand the assault from Tommy. It tended to be the case that Rosie, Carolyn and Frances coalesced together with Tommy, Colin and Rosemary as three different outriders. When the crisis unfolded after November 2004, Rosie, Carolyn and Frances formed one group (and were members of the United Left), with Colin operating independently, and Tommy recruiting Rosemary as a malcontent with Rosie, Carolyn and Frances. Third, when working relationships broke down irretrievably, this was as a result of the faction fight Tommy initiated, and not before. The ability of Tommy to generate a sense of intrigue in Parliament in regard of the other MSPs, particularly Rosie, Carolyn and Frances, was facilitated by the nature of the SSP being increasingly dominated by its parliamentary group as well as by Tommy carrying out his relationships directly with journalists. Fourthly, while the SSP had an influential EC and NC and was broad and pluralistic, political authority in the party was still concentrated amongst a troika of Tommy, Alan McCombes and Allan Green, the national secretary, and within the Glasgow citadel. This led to another tension whereby, for example on one occasion, Colin Fox recounted he complained to Tommy about the SSP being effectively run by this troika with others being shut out or sidelined. Tommy told him: 'Tough, that's politics. If you don't like it, then go off and do something about it'.[64]

Lastly, it was Tommy that was more likely to have had to adjust to the new working environment than the other five MSPs. This was because while he was party leader and had been not just an MSP already but a lone MSP with a large degree of autonomy, the new MSPs had nothing comparable to change from – having never been MSPs before – and their collective weight meant Tommy had less latitude than before. For example, every Tuesday at 11am when parliament was sitting, there were SSP MSP group meetings. Frances Curran believed: 'The biggest culture shock in 2003 was for Tommy ... he wanted to be in charge and dictate what we would do and when ... he wanted be in the driving seat politically ... when we said we wanted to discuss things collectively he wasn't very happy ... [what made things worse] is that Tommy wouldn't operate informally ... it always had to be through formal committee structures [to have a discussion with him]'. Carolyn Leckie recalled: 'It was clear he had difficulty adjusting ... he hated group meetings, he hated disagreements and not getting his own way. It's difficult for everybody to adjust to change'. Meantime, Colin Fox concurred that Tommy 'found it difficult to adapt' and was not an obvious team player. This chimed with how Felicity Garvie saw the situation:

A fundamental weakness is that he's not a team player ... [so] when the other five were elected, I think it was a severe dent to his personal profile and position as the leader of the party, the only

SSP MSP and so on. You can call it personal pride or vanity but I think he enjoyed being in that position … it was a shock to him and I don't think he ever accepted that … or that the other five were talented individuals with their own strengths and skills, their own track records … He's been used to being top dog, well before 2003 … so his nose was out of joint.

Alan McCombes looked back on this aspect, saying: 'I didn't see it at the time but Tommy had a difficulty in readjusting to the change in 2003 … it disorientated me … it disorientated Tommy as well … he had got use to being the sole public voice'. But it was also true that as Tommy was an 'old hand', the others were novices and none of the six had worked closely together before, Tommy still had some space and nous to carry on as before. Just as important as these aforementioned considerations was that any notion of a plot against Tommy would have the difficult task of replacing him – following 'Elvis at Las Vegas' as Colin Fox put it when he did – as well as dealing with the subsequent mess. Moreover, it was difficult to talk of a leadership – as opposed to national convenership – takeover because the leadership in the form of the non-CWI/SWP majority on the SSP EC was the same leadership before and after Tommy resigned as national convener. All this indicates the notion of a plot was rather fanciful (see Chapter 6). Tensions between the MSPs did not constitute the basis of a plot against anyone, and not against Tommy. Where there clearly were tensions was between the largely ex-SML SSP leadership and the SWP and CWI platforms. The tensions existed bilaterally between the leadership and the two individual platforms as well between the two platforms, making for an often difficult cocktail albeit one that was not too unstable given the numerical superiority of the ex-SML leadership's support base.

Relations with Rosie

In public, Tommy's relations with Rosie were cordial and warm. In the *Mirror*, Tommy commended Rosie for her hard work and bravery[65] but behind the scenes, things were not quite as they seemed. When Rosie suffered a serious bout of depression and exhaustion in late 2003, leading her to take time off work, Tommy praised her publicly, saying: 'I will support her every step of the way … She's tired herself out by working too hard and worried so much about her cases'[66] and 'I applaud Rosie for having the courage to admit her mental health problem'.[67] Upon returning to work, Tommy said: 'It's crucial Rosie eases her way back into work. She must not give too much of herself too early'.[68] But behind the scenes, Tommy wanted Rosie to resign as an MSP and have her 'place' taken by the next on the Glasgow SSP list.[69] Alan McCombes felt 'this was strange because she'd become a celebrity [and] it wasn't as though we were coming under pressure that he was responding to'. Tommy was also annoyed with Rosie's extensive involvement in work with asylum seekers, because according to Keith Baldassara and Alan McCombes, Tommy felt it was a time-consuming business that ultimately had no votes in it at the end of the day (as asylum seekers are not entitled to vote) and was not popular with other voters. So while Tommy was prepared for politically campaigning on the issue, it seems he did not think it warranted the extensive case and support work that others thought it needed. Instead, he believed that the focus should be upon the progressive elements in the housing schemes who believed in wealth redistribution and public services but who could be conservative on race, gender and sexuality, and that causes that could undermine this milieu were not to be pushed too strongly. But again, none of this constituted the basis of a plot or faction fight.

Self-Deprecation

Tommy often paid tribute to Alan McCombes as being 'the brains, thinker and strategist' as at the SSP 2004 conference, indicating that he gave people their full due, at least in public. But Alan and other attendees at an SSP teambuilding event for SSP MSPs and their parliamentary staff recalled a different side to Tommy. Asked by the facilitator to rank themselves on a scale of one to ten on how they were doing in their jobs, most headed towards the lower numbers while Tommy scored himself without hesitation at ten. Alan recounted: 'Tommy was right up to number 10, absolutely no hesitancy, having no doubt or problem displaying it ... I don't know whether he felt he had to show strength and was scared to show weakness'. Earlier, Tommy had organised a meal for the MSPs at an Italian restaurant several months into the 2003–2007 parliament. Frances Curran recalled: 'We went along expecting to share our experiences as it had been a big change in all of our lives. He sat at the top of the table ... we all went round the table saying honestly and openly how difficult it had been. When it got to him, [it was] 'It's all fine' ... We were all thinking 'Gail can't be happy because you're never home ... Don't you want to talk about these pressures in your life?' He wasn't prepared to talk openly but he wanted to hear everything we wanted to say and then tell us how to put it right'.[70] Of the meal, Carolyn Leckie recalled: 'We talked about the changes and challenges and how we're feeling then when it came to him, it was 'Everything is fine'. I said to him

'But surely, you've been in here since 1999 [on your own] ... it must be difficult for you to adjust?' He said: 'Everything is fine, everything is brilliant ... we've got six MSPs ... he just stuck to that line like he'd give a TV interviewer. It was almost as though [that response] was for an audience ... where he was being watched'. Rosie Kane's view was that Tommy was intelligent enough to 'not to say 'I am the way and the light' but he is cleverly able to lead people to form that conclusion about him ... he encourages people to say that about him rather than him to say that about himself ... most of us would be embarrassed to do that and say stop it ... but Tommy would say 'Thanks, pal''. This chimed with how Colin Fox saw Tommy here: 'He might be humble about his achievements but he would never allow others to be humble on his behalf about his achievements. He is astute enough never to be seen to have to defend himself ... he gets others to do it – that's loyalty and high regard'.

Moving to the Populist Right?

After resigning as national convener and until early 2006, Tommy concentrated on making sure he would be re-elected as an SSP MSP. This involved focussing on issues which predominated in Glasgow especially such as knife crime,[71] airguns[72] and drink driving and responding with calls for with zero tolerance and tough mandatory jail sentences. This came from Tommy's thinking that the left was good in developing policies against injustice but not so on those who were victims of crime. He also made a fist of campaigning against the Edinburgh allowance for MSPs and to change charity law after financial scandals. At other times, not being national convener and parliamentary group leader allowed him more freedom to support some particular causes such as rights for fathers or the NatWest Three case of financiers being extradited to the USA for charges in relation to Enron's collapse when neither their employer nor the Financial Services Authority alleged any wrongdoing. Tommy's line was 'justice is justice or it's not justice at all'.[73] Many activists in Glasgow like David Archibald, Frances Curran,[74] and those in the SSY[75] saw such initiatives as evidence of Tommy moving to the right whereby either his political antennae had become wonky or his political compass had changed. Allan Green believed these initiatives constituted 'populist, superficial ways of proposing answers to deep-rooted social problems'. Alan McCombes was not one of them: 'I don't see a really big change in him ... he was trying to raise issues that he couldn't when he was convener because it might cause more problems' while Colin Fox believed Tommy was trying to give the left a 'kick up the arse' in order to force it to look at issues afresh. Meantime, the SSP Republican Communist Network platform also deduced Tommy was beginning to become a 'celebrity populist politician' with rightward moving tendencies. [76]

Balance Sheet

Accountability

Tommy had a track record in leading from the front, of doing what he thought was right for the SSP sometimes without necessarily getting agreement or consulting with others or as widely as some thought he should. Sometimes, he would declare his position and then seek support for it, rather than vice-versa. This grated with some but the tendency was more noticeable when Tommy was part of a parliamentary group (which even his staunchest supporters like Ronnie Stevenson and Jock Penman admitted). Such examples occurred over trying to recruit Campbell Martin MSP to the SSP after he was expelled from the SNP (and where the issue of the 'workers' wage policy in regard to him was not finalised) or approaching members of a Glasgow branch to stand down in favour of former SNP and independent MSP Dorothy Grace Elder as an SSP candidate when she was not an SSP member and without going to the SSP EC. Yet, at the same time, these matters must be held in regard of the situation where the SSP did not have policy on every issue and eventuality and MSPs often had to respond on the hoof to questions and issues. Moreover, there are other instances when Tommy would wait to see how the cards would fall out on an issue and when he would win party members' support without making them feel bounced into endorsing an earlier decision. And, Colin Fox's take on Tommy's style was not so much that he was unaccountable as more independent minded. So Tommy's leadership had different characteristics. Certainly, until late 2004, if this kind of accusation of lacking in accountability could be levelled at Tommy, it could also be levelled at others, most notably the two other members of the troika. But what gives such accusations of unaccountability (and, hence, an individualistic streak) their axe to grind is that after late 2004, SSP members began to consciously or unconsciously re-evaluate Tommy in a different light to that which they shone on him before. This meant that members looked back upon particular instances and concluded they should not – unlike before – be ignored or dismissed or that their significance now was different.

Skills and Attributes

The ability to 'make things happen' continued to be one of Tommy's fortes even if the context of having five other SSP MSP colleagues around him made this seem different from before. His access to the media and his persuasiveness on an individual level allowed him to maintain his profile for his chosen causes. This made it easier for him to be able to work with others outside the SSP in terms of building alliances and deploying their expertise. But it was also because he had established a political and moral authority that commanded wide respect and because he showed that he was able to engage in a willingness to think in an open, heterodox way, so jettisoning much of the heritage of orthodox Trotskyism. Tommy continued to be what some considered to an inveterate self-publicist. On one occasion, he was leaving the old Scottish Parliament as a lobby of striking nursery nurses was taking place outside. Realising that he would have to walk out with other people to go past the strikers or to greet them, he turned and went back into the building to then re-emerge several minutes later on his own in order to be fully recognised by the nursery nurses and to gain their applause for supporting them. This vignette could be read in one or more of at least three ways, namely, Tommy wanted to ingratiate himself with the strikers for his own benefit; Tommy wanted to clearly demonstrate to all the strikers his support; and Tommy wanted to win support amongst the strikers for the SSP's position on the strike within Unison whose leadership was hostile to the SSP and its position. So, the salient questions surrounding this kind of activity are whether it was solely for his personal and psychological aggrandisement or for the furtherance of the socialist cause, or for both purposes which happily and fruitfully coincided.

Nous

Alan McCombes recalled: '[O]ne thing that Tommy was quite obsessive about was the media ... somewhere along the line, Tommy became very media savvy and media conscious'. Indeed, Paul Routledge noted that Tommy 'plays the media like a violin'.[77] This meant, Alan McCombes believed, 'All of what Tommy did would be depend on the value of it to the media ... something that might be intrinsically valuable because it would be getting something done would be less important than that which would get media coverage ... that sounds harsh but sometimes it's about making a calculated decision when you have limited resources and you want to make an impact'. This is why Tommy spent considerable time cultivating relationships with journalists in order to work out what initiatives journalists would be most amenable to and then work on them on that basis, making the presentation of the initiative as attractive as possible. But it was also because Tommy understood the pressures journalists were under to file copy in under-resourced newsrooms. He also did not not return calls.[78] In particular, Tommy developed some relationships more than others. He developed firm relationships with STV's political editor, Bernard Ponsonby,[79] and Brian Currie at the *Evening Times*.[80] This was because STV was not prone to the same political pressures of maintaining impartiality (and, paradoxically, being mindful of its paymaster) as the BBC was. STV also had a more working class feel and audience. A consequence of this concentration of effort was that Tommy had less time to do other things and this locked him into doing certain other things. Related to this media nous was a social nous as well. Tommy was able to develop relations with the likes of RMT general secretary, Bob Crow – which helped lead to eight branches of the RMT in Scotland affiliating to the SSP in 2003–2004 – because he was prepared to be charming and diplomatic even at the cost of sidelining the SSP's industrial organiser, Richie Venton, who Tommy felt would be too hardline and demanding. Lastly, Tommy would do things like offering to run people home so he could get them on their own and put an argument to them. Nonetheless, some detected there was a downside to how Tommy's media strategy affected the SSP. According to Colin Fox, the SSP MSPs, thus, became too willing to 'speak on everything ... giving crude one dimensional answers ... [so that] ... we ended up being 'Jack of no trades, master of even fewer' ... [and] rent-a-quotes' with the affect they lost credibility while the SSP itself put an emphasis on 'publicity and profile rather than campaigning and developing political strength so that it had high visibility but there wasn't much behind it'. Consequently, the argument was that the SSP could not engage with issues on the ground because it did not have the intelligence and troops there to do so.

Conclusion

Between 2003 and 2007, Tommy continued to be the leading proselytiser of the socialist cause. For the far left, though, it was not revolutionary enough. Rather, it was socialism-lite or worse such as left nationalism or plain old reformism. But road- and stress-testing the pitch showed that it was the level most appropriate and suitable for the times. This was because in many ways, Tommy was a dab hand at reading the popular mood – which is not to say that he always necessarily played it safe. He was a risk taker. Yet, if the times had been more fertile, there is no doubt Tommy would have upped the pitch and ambition so that those who criticised him as a backslider from a purist stance of socialism mistake the interplay of strategy and tactics for principle and ideology. That long-time collaborator, Alan McCombes, believed 'the SSP wouldn't have got to its highpoint without Tommy but Tommy wouldn't have got to where he is without the SSP' indicated the complex inter-relationship between leader and led, suggesting that Tommy's huge contribution had to be understood in the context of many other lesser recognised leadership figures and activists. In all this, Tommy's nous in courting the media was critical. But here, he was extremely fortunate as Joan McAlpine put it: 'There's a lot of male journalists that wouldn't see past him. They think he's still the best thing since sliced bread and a breath of fresh air'. This meant that because he gave them colourful copy in a world of grey politics, they seldom questioned his exaggeration at the time he made it, nor took him to task subsequently for unfulfilled or overblown promises. Instead, they came back for more and gave him an easy ride.

Yet looking back on these years from the vantage point of 2011, the highpoint of 1 May 2003 all the more appears as a temporary and transient phenomenon. The SSP, led for the most part by Tommy, did not make a lasting, sizeable or positive material impact upon politics in Scotland or upon the lives of ordinary citizens, the poor and the marginalised. What the SSP promised in those years before late 2004 was the potential to deliver more in the years to come. Of course, it was never given the opportunity to try to do so. But if it had, in the 2007 and subsequent Scottish parliament elections, it is reasonable to suggest it might then have held onto a reduced but, nonetheless, significant size of parliamentary representation. Doing so would have provided it, and Tommy, with the foothold from which to be able to be part of, take advantage of, lead and further a number of political developments like the resistance to the crisis of neo-liberalism and age of austerity.[81] The following two chapters explain why such an opportunity never arose.

Notes

1. 8 May 2003.
2. Although it was widely reported in the perjury trial of 2010 that Colin Fox referred to this as the SSP's '9/11', the original derivation for the phrase came from Gall, G. *More Revolutionary Witticisms of Colin Fox, Carolyn Leckie and Rosie Kane MSPs* (Flying Pickets' Press, 2005), p. 4.
3. 30 December 2007.
4. *Evening Times* 2 May 2003.

5. *Herald* 3 May 2003.
6. Gall, G. 'Is the party over?' *Red Pepper*, April 2006.
7. *Evening News* 18 February 2003. In this respect, the *Herald* (23 April 2007) was wide of the mark when it commented: 'He has in the past been realistic about his electoral claims'. However, just before the election, Tommy spread bet by saying a good result would be a 100% increase, a 400% increase would be a 'spectacular breakthrough' and an 800% increase would amount to a 'political earthquake in Europe' (*Holyrood* 23 April 2003).
8. 7 April 2003.
9. *Evening News* 22 February 2001.
10. *Sunday Herald* 23 February 2003.
11. 20 August 2002.
12. *Scotsman* 2 May 2003.
13. 8 May 2003.
14. He was just 3,341 votes behind Johann Lamont of Labour, winner of the seat. Of his vote here, he pronounced at the declaration: 'I give notice ... it is time to redistribute wealth across Scotland. What's happening tonight ... is that a new political force has been born' (*Herald* 3 May 2007).
15. *Scotsman* 2 May 2003.
16. *Mirror* 3 May 2003.
17. 23 February 2002.
18. 30 April 2003.
19. *Scotsman* 2 April 2003.
20. 30 April 2003.
21. This is in line with his preparedness to be pragmatic (see earlier).
22. *Guardian* 7 April 2003.
23. Ironically, the use of the term 'class' is less politically problematic in Scotland than it is in the rest of Britain because of the pronounced tendency of those of an objectively middle class position to still subjectively defined themselves as working class – see Gall, G. *The Political Economy of Scotland: Red Scotland? Radical Scotland?* (University of Wales Press, 2005), chapter six.
24. 6 January 2004.
25. This was provided by the occasion of the Nazi jibe against Tommy by the *Sunday Mail* (30 March 2003). This would have provided a sound basis on which to take a defamation case against the newspaper. Instead, and despite threatening to take such action (*Guardian* 7 April 2003), Tommy dealt with the issue in his *Mirror* columns of 9 and 23 April 2003.
26. *Herald* 29 August 2003. Upon being sentenced and led away on 26 January 2011, both the *Daily Record* and *Sun* reported the next day that a supporter shouted to Tommy: 'See you in heaven'
27. *Sunday Herald* 31 August 2003, *Scottish Socialist Voice* 5 September 2003.
28. *Scotsman* 25 March 2003.
29. See, for example, *Sunday Mirror* 2 March 2003. Tommy had previously praised Carolyn Leckie as an outstanding union leader (*Scottish Socialist Voice* 15 February 2002).
30. *Press Association* 2 May 2003.
31. *Press Association* 2 May 2003.
32. *Times* 3 May 2003.
33. *Scottish Socialist Voice* 10 October 2003. .
34. *Scotsman* 5 May 2003. Kerevan was a member of the International Marxist Group (the British section of the Fourth International) between 1972 and 1980 and was a SNP list candidate in the Lothians in the 2011 elections (*Scotsman* 10 August 2006, 28 January 2011). This political past gave him an insight into the split but his disdain for his former fellow travellers often marred the understanding that resulted from these insights (see *Scotsman* 10 August 2006).

35. *Mirror* 8, 12 December 2003.
36. 9 May 2003.
37. *Mail on Sunday* 21 September 2003. Also see later. Of course, there was banter around the issue. Felicity Garvie, parliamentary assistant to both, joked: 'Tommy's getting jealous. It's her diary that's filling up ... I have taken more calls about Rosie since the [2003] election' (*Holyrood* 27 May 2003). A tension between Tommy and Rosie (see later) was over an entirely different matter.
38. 3 May 2004.
39. 31 August 2003.
40. 10 September 2003.
41. 8 June 2003.
42. 11 June 2003.
43. Alan McCombes relayed this to an SSP NC in late 2003 and recounted this meeting in *DTTSS* (p. 59).
44. Rosie Kane speculated there might have been a darker side to this, namely, to gain sensitive information on leading comrades (see also Note 70, this chapter).
45. See Sheridan, T. 'Out-of-pocket expenses must not get out of hand' *Sunday Herald* 23 April 2006. Here, Tommy proposed that the register of members' interest was revised to include benefitting from the scheme.
46. This involved travelling to Peterhead where Fiona McGuire lived.
47. *Herald* 5 September 2003.
48. Tommy was also one of the main speakers at the launch of the republican Declaration of Calton Hill on 9 October 2004 (http://en.wikipedia.org/wiki/Declaration_of_Calton_Hill).
49. Although Unison did support the SSP proposal of returning non-domestic rate setting to local authorities.
50. *Scottish Socialist Voice* 30 April 2004.
51. See *Daily Record* 1 April 2009.
52. *Herald* 1 April 2006.
53. *Herald* 30 April 2003.
54. Indeed, he was less than taken with my suggestion that I start the biography with this accolade.
55. 26 January 2004.
56. 26 April 2003. But it was not just journalists that made the SSP the personal property of Tommy. Academics like Murray Pittock (*The Road to Independence? Scotland since the Sixties*, Reaktion Books, 2008, p. 161) also referred to 'Tommy Sheridan's Scottish Socialists'.
57. See *Evening News* 4, 7 June 2003.
58. Richie Venton interpreted one driver for this as overcompensation for Tommy now having to be part of a group of six.
59. Tommy was absent by virtue of his paternity leave while Rosemary Byrne was absent due to a family bereavement. However, Rosemary subsequently indicated her unease with it (*Holyrood* 11 September 2006). The protest was met with a draconian response, with the four MSPs being suspended without wages for three months and banned from the Parliament and their offices. As Colin Fox remarked this was for 'all for holding up a piece of paper and delaying First Minister's Questions'. Subsequent and more serious transgressions – for example, by Wendy Alexander over election expenses – were not dealt with so harshly, suggesting there may have been an element of retribution in the punishment.
60. But it was many steps too far to claim as political commentator, Iain Macwhirter, did: 'Much of the antagonism [of the emerging split after the 2006 court case] arose because of Sheridan's apparent willingness to 'play the game', become a real politi-

cian [and] use his media skills to get the party taken seriously ... [compared to t]he other SSP MSPs [who] seemed more interested in staging student occupations and walkouts' (*Herald* 9 August 2006).

61. Rosemary told *Holyrood* (11 September 2006): 'I was coming in as the one outsider...'.
62. Indeed, the major tension in the SSP between May 2003 and October 2004 was over the relationship of national self-determination, independence and socialism, and on which the division was between the SWP and CWI on the one side and the rest of the SSP on the other (see Gall, G. *Socialism, 'the national question' and the Independence Convention in Scotland* (Edinburgh, 2003). Another tension existed over the degree of autonomy of regional organisers *vis-a-vis* the SSP EC and their place on the EC.
63. Carolyn Leckie believed Tommy was discomforted by Rosie's media attention, suggesting he persuaded Gail and Alice to complain about it. But also see earlier.
64. Richie Venton was also of the opinion that this troika existed although Allan Green was not of this view (see Chapter 3).
65. 6 August, 3 December 2003.
66. *Mirror* 8 December 2003.
67. *Evening Times* 8 December 2003.
68. *Sunday Mail* 11 January 2004.
69. See also *NoW* (30 January 2011) for a further account of this.
70. Frances Curran suggested that there may have been a darker side to the meal because: 'It has only become clear to me [recently] ... that it's always been a trait of Tommy's [to gather information on people in order] to be manipulative ... he does play divide and rule by denigrating [some] and buttering [others] up. ... That process has become much more visible ... now ... [before] ... it was behind the scenes or this issue or that'.
71. See his 'How do we tackle knife crime in Scotland?' in *Whose Justice? The Law and the Left* (SLRP, 2006), pp. 23–26. As lead editor of this collection, his chapter was put together by myself from his earlier journalistic pieces on the subject (e.g. *Scottish Socialist Voice* 20 January 2005) and then edited by him in order to not cut into his other commitments. Unfortunately, I was unable to get Tommy (or other SSP MSPs) to agree to contribute a chapter on this basis for the collection I edited called *Is there a Scottish Road to Socialism?* (SLRP, 2007) because of involvement in other more pressing matters of the time. In his pursuit of gaining a hearing with working class youth over knife crime, Tommy developed a relationship with reformed gangster, Paul Ferris (see, for example, *Sunday Times* 8 October 2006, 11 January 2009) that many found distasteful and dubious.
72. See, for example, *Evening Times* 18 December 2006, 22 January 2007.
73. How much his 'Pollok nationalism', as Colin Fox put it, was important to him having a personal link through Gary Mulgrew, one of the accused, is not clear.
74. Curran, F. 'Party rises from the rubble' *Socialist Resistance*, December 2006, p. 10
75. See 'The truth about Tommy Sheridan' SSY website, 23 December 2010.
76. See Armstrong, A. 'The Sheridan perjury trial' *Emancipation and Liberation*, 20, 2011, p. 27, 'A critique and exposure of Tommy Sheridan's *Daily Record*' and 'The SSP has reached the crossroad 'manifestoes' (both) *Emancipation and Liberation*, 13, 2006.
77. *The Bumper Book of British Lefties* (Politicos, 2003), p. 204.
78. This only became a feature of his behaviour around the issues of his personal life and ensuing faction and legal fights when he either did not want to comment or wanted to make a story have a longer shelf life by holding back his comment for the next day.

79. His relationship with Ponsonby would serve him well in the period of late 2010/early 2011.
80. The *Evening Times* remained a working class paper (compared to the higher brow of its sister title, the *Herald*).
81. Such issues will be fully explored in Gall, G. *The Scottish Socialist Party – the rise and fall of a new political force* (Welsh Academic Press, forthcoming).

6

Tommy Sheridan
vs
News of the World

Introduction

Following the unparalleled wall-to-wall media coverage of what turned out to be a spectacular victory against *NoW* in his defamation case in the summer of 2006, Tommy must have then run Sean Connery a close second as the most famous Scot in the world, or to the general public in Scotland at least. It was commonly and rightly described as the 'defamation case of the decade' involving sufficient drama and salaciousness to keep the media and public hooked for its entirety. To some on the left, this victory against *NoW* – and by implication News International – cemented Tommy as the quintessential working class hero of modern times in Scotland. To others on the left, it marked the most significant advance in the political degeneration of a figure who had at one time been the foremost socialist in contemporary Scotland. One way or the other, he became Scotland's most famous socialist in recent living times but the reasons for this and their significance were the points of fierce debate. Symbolically, 'Tommygate' would run from 9 November 2004 to 26 January 2011.[1]

The essential basis of Tommy's 2006 court case strategy was three-fold. The first part was, as he said on the McNeilage tape: 'They have been told it's me but they can't prove it'. In his own inimitable terms, he repeatedly said "They've got fuck all".[2] The second was that *NoW's* 'allegations'[3] if not challenged and overturned – in Tommy's own words – "will destroy me". The third was that if *NoW's* 'allegations' were not challenged and refuted, then further allegations about his sexual behaviour which were already circulating in Glasgow would be published by it or other papers because the media would conclude he would not challenge these in court. In other words, it would be open season on him. Tommy concluded that on this three-fold basis, he could and must win the case. He only ever conceded that if there was a smoking gun of indisputable photographic or other evidence about visiting Cupids sex club in Manchester would he desist from taking the defamation action against

NoW.[4] Personally and politically, Tommy decided he could not afford to let *NoW*'s stories stand. Underneath all this was that Tommy considered himself to being bullied – as he told the 2006 defamation civil trial, *NoW* 'will never get me to bow my head ... [it] may hurt me but [it] will never destroy me politically'.[5] In order to construct the foundation of his campaign, when most SSP members – including his supporters – knew the 'allegations' to be true, an elaborate fabrication needed to be used, this being that he was engaged in a principled political stance against the anti-union, anti-working class, anti-socialist *NoW*. The subterfuge that this involved could not be openly admitted and neither could the various twists and turns needed to keep his political and legal campaign on track.

And so was set in train a civil war within the SSP whose quintessential basis was, again, threefold; a) whether it was worthwhile or correct to lie to try to save Tommy as a socialist politician; b) whether Tommy was critical to the success of socialism in Scotland; and c) whether certain notions of honesty and integrity were part of socialist morality. The results were Tommy won his case and the SSP was split asunder. To convey some idea of the way in which the membership of the SSP of some 2,000 to 3,000 members reacted, around 500 left to join Solidarity, Tommy's new political formation. This included the SWP, CWI, Sheridanistas and independents. The remainder stayed with the SSP although the majority of these were inactive and a considerable proportion of these then let their membership lapse.

This chapter examines the twists and turns of the events and faction fight leading up to the 2006 court case, the case itself and the subsequent political fallout. These twists and turns and the issues and debates that raged around Tommy's political and legal strategy were like icebergs – partly open to public view but with much more below the waterline and, thus, neither fully seen nor fully understood.[6] Before examining them, it is interesting to note that Tommy broke with two revolutionary socialist shibboleths by taking his course of action. The first of not using the capitalist courts was thrown out the window by Tommy and his supporters (although Militant had used the courts against expulsion of its members from Labour in 1983).[7] Arthur Scargill, for example, adhered to the argument that socialists could not get justice in capitalist courts because of the role they play in enforcing capitalism and the costs involved. Rather, Scargill thought the court of public opinion and that of his membership were more important. By contrast, George Galloway has shown a radical could do so and win on many occasions but some would question whether that changes the equation for socialists. The second was that of 'don't lie to the class' meaning that to be honest and taken seriously by the working class, socialists should always state things as they are and not as they want them to be. For example, during the Eleventh Session of the Dewey Commission – officially titled the

'Commission of Inquiry into the Charges Made against Leon Trotsky in the Moscow Trials' – on 16 April 1937, Trotsky stated under questioning: 'I believe that the Marxist, the revolutionary, policy in general is a very simple policy: 'Speak out what is! Don't lie! Tell the truth!' It is a very simple policy'. Earlier, Tommy recalled this as 'Trotsky said the first rule for a revolutionary is to see things as they are'.[8]

Origins of the Crisis

The bare bones of the origins of the crisis are that in late 2001 a story was circulating that Tommy had attended the Cupids sex club in Manchester and a freelance journalist was trying to sell the story. Tipped off by Nicky McKerrell, Alan McCombes confronted Tommy but he denied the story saying he would not be so foolish or reckless to do this and damage his reputation, and it was just gossip. A little later, Keith Baldassara picked up on the same story from local sources in Pollok. Keith then confronted Tommy who, on this occasion, did not deny the story and assured him that there was nothing to worry about. Later in 2002, Keith was alerted to the story of the Moat House hotel sex party and the 'night of madness' there following loose talk by some of Tommy's friends. The event on 14 June 2002 was the night before Andy McFarlane's wedding to Gail's sister. Then, in November 2002, Tommy warned Keith that having returned to Cupids, the media had been alerted to this, leading Keith to meet with Alan.[9] At a subsequent meeting with Alan, Tommy denied any involvement at the Moat House and argued while he had been foolish, the Cupids story would not get out and he would not visit a sex club again. Unaware that the latest visit was with Anvar Khan, Alan accepted Tommy's argument and agreed to keep a lid on this for the best interests of Tommy and the SSP ahead of the 2003 election (and with only Tommy, Keith and Alan aware of the issues and decision). Then, in February 2004, George McNeilage picked up on a story circulating in Glasgow that Tommy had visited sex clubs. He confronted Tommy, with Tommy confirming this was true. When the story of the unnamed swinging MSP broke on 31 October 2004, Tommy did not deny to Alan it was him. A meeting with Alan and Keith on 1 November reached an impasse with Tommy rejecting their advice and stating categorically he would deny and fight the 'allegations'. Shocked by his intransigence, Alan arranged an informal meeting of some SSP EC members on 6 November to which Tommy was invited to put his case. The thinking was that it would be better to deal with such sensitive matters informally for both the SSP and Tommy. Tommy refused to attend so a special meeting of the EC was called for 9 November 2004. Contrary to Tommy's later claims, if there was anyone that, to use Tommy's terms, brought him down or did him in, it was not the 'coven of witches' and radical feminists but three longstanding collaborators, Alan, Keith and George. George would play a more important role later in 2006.

The '9/11' Meeting

Twenty one members attended the four hour SSP EC meeting including Tommy and Barbara Scott, the minute taker. Tommy explained on the McNeilage tape: 'They want[ed] me to come to a meeting to explain myself and this is where I make the big mistake. A fucking huge mistake. A humungous mistake. I got to the meeting. There's 19 people sitting around a fucking circle, sitting on desks, sitting on chairs. The atmosphere you cut with a fucking knife, man. I then make the biggest mistake of my life by confessing something in front of 19 people. What am I doing confessing to these cunts?' Barbara Scott's handwritten notes recorded Tommy's contribution:

> 2 visits 1996/2002 with close friends, mistake reckless etc. ... For 2 yrs someone been trying 2 sell the story to newspapers Met KB + AMc last Monday – asked 4 opp 2 fight this on own, ask to refer to TS, not lie but give no comment. Confident no proof of participation. Don't think should have to be hostage 2 fortune – Believe there's no evidence – but no guarantees. Askin 4 opp to prove I'm right. If proof then he would resign + apologise but not prepared when there is no proof. Fallen out wi Alan Mc over this. Don't deserve sympathy but do deserve opp to fight it – will deny allegation, take advice from NUJ + solicitors. Libel law – need to prove guilt not innocence. Some people may feel loss of confidence – for each comrade 2 decide. If by Feb cdes don't have confidence then will stand down at conference – citing family reasons. If now – gift horse 2 enemies of party. Not prepared to walk plank made by NoW. Prepared to take blame if presented with incontrovertible evidence.

They then recorded Alan McCombes contribution:

> Most painful discn between me + TS Politics – very difficult pol. decision, not about personal life. Chronology – 1st knowledge of this – 2001 ... someone tryin 2 sell story 2 media about swingers' club in Manchester. Confronted TS – denied absolutely – believed

that KB phoned a year later – not urgently – friends had informed that TS had taken part in swingers' club. Raised again wi TS – this time admitted, asked not 2 say anything cos no evidence existed – no poss that people there would tell. AMc + KB agreed 2 do that – although concerned about potential timebomb – TS image is of a family person etc. Startling contrast wi club. People will forgive sexual misconduct – but not the leader of party lying about it + refusing 2 take consequences. Asked TS to manage it in the media – as soon as named in press – 2 apologise, resign as convener, spend time wi wife etc. But TS refused – wanted participation in a cover-up. …. Most damaging part of Monica Lewinsky affair was the public denial. Political suicide to deny it in the press. This could wreck the political project we're on. Enemy got loaded gun. We need 2 take it off them. Don't want to participate in a cover-up. While TS convener we'll be on a time bomb.

Tommy's response is recorded as:

Reiterated – 1996 + July 2002 only visits. Nothing in 2001. … If deny and proved to be a liar – doesn't think that will happen. Political question different. Don't accept should admit. Cdes shouldn't comment on private sex lives. Won't be forced by NoW to take course of action. Ask cdes 2 be objective – if I'm wrong will go down.[10]

Tommy also suggested that the SSP fighting *NoW* over its claims against him would allow the party to make good political capital and the damages won would come to the SSP.[11] When the notes of the full minute were written up, it recorded:

Tommy Sheridan's contribution: The meeting began with an introduction by Tommy Sheridan. He responded to a recent article in the News of the World which alleged that a married MSP had visited a swingers/sex club in Manchester in the company of a female journalist who had now written a book about her lifestyle. Tommy admitted to the meeting that he had in fact visited the club on two occasions, in 1996 and 2002 with close friends. He acknowledged that this had been reckless behaviour and had, with hindsight, been a mistake. He reported that he had met with Keith B and Alan Mc and asked them for the opportunity to fight this on his own and for other party members if questioned about it, to either give no comment or refer all questions to himself. He said he was confident there was no

proof in existence that he had visited the club. Tommy said he was
not prepared to resign as Convener unless proof was revealed to
exist. His strategy was to deny the allegations and in this regard he
had already taken advice from NUJ solicitors. He also stated that
it was up to each comrade to decide if they had lost confidence
in his Convenership. If he did not still have the confidence of the
comrades by the February national conference, he was prepared
to stand down at that time citing 'family reasons'. He stated his
belief that to stand down immediately would be a gift horse to the
enemies of the party.

Alan McCombes' contribution: Alan McCombes then gave his
account of the issue. He stated that this was the most painful discussion he had ever been part of and that himself, Keith B and
Tommy S had worked together for over 20 years with no previous trace of acrimony. Alan stated that he had first been made
aware of this incident in 2001 at the annual Socialism event when
Nicky McKerrell had informed him that someone was trying
to sell a story to the media about the club in Manchester which
involved Tommy. Alan asked Tommy about it at that time, and
Tommy denied the allegations absolutely. However a year later
Keith B had contacted Alan because mutual friends had told him
that Tommy had visited such a club. Alan and Keith had raised
the issue again with Tommy who had this time admitted that it
was true and asked them not to reveal it further as there was no
evidence, and no possibility that anyone involved would tell anyone. Alan and Keith agreed although they had concerns about
the potential time bomb. When the News of the World recently
ran the story, Alan immediately realised the unnamed MSP was
Tommy. Alan's feeling is that to go to this type of club with a
journalist is reckless, irresponsible, and politically damaging to
the party. He is not concerned about any perceived moral issue,
but feels there are conflicts with the party's evolving positions
on issues such as pornography, prostitution, lap-dancing etc.
Alan felt that the public would forgive sexual misconduct, but
not the convener of the party telling lies about this and refusing
to face up to the consequences. Alan had asked Tommy to manage this issue in the media as soon as he is named as the MSP
involved in the story, apologise and resign as convener, citing the
reason as wanting to spend more time with his family. However
Tommy had refused to do this, instead wanting Alan and Keith
to participate in a cover-up. Alan voiced his concern about the
NUJ being involved in this, as their help had been enlisted with
false information. He cited the Bill Clinton/Monica Lewinsky

affair and pointed out that the most damaging part of that to Bill Clinton was the public denial. He felt it would be political suicide to deny these allegations in the press. Tommy's refusal to comply with this advice led to Alan and Keith talking to other comrades, however Tommy refused to meet with this group and began acting independently of the party, for instance arranging the Rose Gentle demonstration at the weekend unilaterally. Alan finished by asking Tommy again to tell the truth and stand down as Convener, and not to ask the Executive to participate in a cover-up.

General discussion

... Tommy left the meeting at 20:15 after the following [five] comrades had contributed ... Before he left, he repeated that he did not believe there was any evidence which would prove him to be lying. He did not accept that he should admit the visits to the club and felt that no-one should comment on private lives. He said he would not be forced into a course of action by the News of the World. The discussion continued after Tommy left ... Without exception all contributors disagreed with the strategy of denying the allegations. All felt that this would be the most damaging strategy for the party. The general feeling was that this was a bad situation, and that the "least worst" option must be found. All agreed that it would be better if Tommy changed his mind about denying the allegations.

The following proposals were put forward:

1. Tommy to be given until 10:00 tomorrow morning (Wed 10th Nov) to resign as Convener and the story to be run in the Voice, thus giving the party the upper hand rather than waiting for our enemies to fire the bullet
2. Tommy to be given until Saturday 13th Nov to resign, thus giving him the chance to think it over and talk to his family etc
3. Tommy to stand down at February conference citing family reasons
4. To comply with Tommy's strategy of denial

There was a vote. Option 1–7, Option 2–9, Option 3–0, Option 4–0

For the purposes of clarity, a unanimous endorsement of Option 2 was sought and obtained. It was agreed that Colin and Frances would speak to Tommy tonight if possible and no later than tomorrow morning (Wed 10th Nov). He will also be asked to withdraw his First Minister's Question tabled for Thursday 11th Nov. The EC will meet on Saturday 13th rather than the planned Sunday 14th meeting to plan the announcement of Tommy's resignation, first to the party membership and secondly to the press. ... The meeting closed at 22:30.

As normal this SSP EC meeting was minuted as per the SSP's constitution of the party with no requests at the meeting from anyone (including Tommy) for this rule to be set aside. There was no discussion of Fiona McGuire – the substance of further allegations in *NoW* on 14 November 2004 – at this meeting save that by Duncan Rowan, the north east of Scotland SSP organiser. Owing to a leak to the *Daily Record*, the EC's hand was forced so it released the following statement at 12.45am on 11 November 2004:

Tommy Sheridan has resigned as national convener of the party with immediate effect. Tommy has played an outstanding role in the development of socialist politics in Scotland over the course of two decades and has become one of the most effective party spokespersons in UK politics. Tommy Sheridan's track record in fighting for the cause of the working class is undisputed. ... Whether it was on striking workers' picket lines or his championing of the abolition of the council tax, Tommy Sheridan brought to Scottish politics a unique voice that spoke up for those who had no voice in the elitist world of establishment politics. 15 years at the frontline of political struggle would take its toll on anyone. For the first four years of the Scottish Parliament, Tommy battled alone as the sole MSP, for 6 years he has led the party and as a larger than life public figure has come under intense personal pressure and scrutiny. These pressures have recently been aggravated by changes in his personal circumstances which have been widely reported. Faced with these pressures Tommy has decided to take a step back from the frontline of political struggle. He has issued a personal statement explaining in more detail his reasons for standing down. The SSP Executive understands the pressure Tommy is under and accepts his decision to resign as national convener and is confident that he will continue to play an important role in the continued success of the party and the movement that he played a central role in bringing to the position it is today.

In a further statement on 14 November 2004, the SSP EC said it 'completely dismisses the rumours that have circulated in the press that

Tommy's resignation was provoked by a leadership challenge, a factional power struggle or any other form of internal in-fighting ... We understand that recent allegations in a Murdoch newspaper may be the subject of a future libel action by Tommy Sheridan and consequently the Scottish Socialist Party does not wish to comment on matters concerning the allegation'. The same line was taken in the *Scottish Socialist Voice*.[12]

So the lines were drawn in this battle royal. Tommy wanted support – or certainly no opposition – when still SSP leader to fight allegations that were not untrue. The rest of the SSP leadership, having rejected Tommy's two proposals (options 3 and 4) by 16:0, said it 'would have supported Tommy 100 per cent in any battle to clear his name. But [it was] not prepared to back a Jeffrey Archer or Jonathan Aitkin style libel action to prove a fiction'.[13] Since Tommy insisted upon taking his defamation action on 10 November 2004, his resignation was sought and gained. The issue was not about sexual morality, private lives or invasion of thereof but political strategy and truthfulness. The SSP EC said many times over: 'If the allegation had been false, we would have supported Tommy 100 per cent in any battle to clear his name [in political and legal action]'.[14] Tommy's strategy was based on lies to defend a manufactured reputation about his personal life. Investigative journalist, Paul Hutcheon,[15] was consistently clear from the outset that the dispute was about how to handle the situation, with the SSP EC asking Tommy to deal 'differently' from how he was proposing to do so, namely, suing *NoW*.[16] At the 24 November SSP EC 2004, Tommy requested that the EC minute not be distributed as per normal. This was agreed. And at the 27 November 2004 SSP NC, which endorsed the EC position requesting his resignation by 85:20 and 93:10, Tommy did not challenge the existence of the minute or its nature. Indeed, its status at this meeting was made clear – it existed but would not be distributed[17]. Interestingly in terms of what was to come, Tommy told the *Daily Record* of the 9 November meeting: 'I have never lied to the Executive of my party'[18]. On the 15 November, Tommy began proceedings against *NoW*, and having failed to receive either an apology or a retraction within a week, issued a writ for defamation on 23 November 2004.

NoW's Motivation

There was no doubt that *NoW* attacked Tommy with its stories of 31 October and 14 November 2004.[19] But rather than assume in an *a priori* or self-evident way that the rationale for *NoW*'s motivation was already known, it is crucial to ask the questions of 'why?' and 'on what basis?' *NoW* decided to run the stories, and the criteria employed for answering these are several (being a socialist, being a leader, being a socialist leader, being a public figure and so on). Another question is whether there was a conspiracy against Tommy by *NoW*. While the paper was no friend of the left, the basis of its brand and market niche was to print 'tits and bums' and 'kiss and tell' stories (as Tommy acknowledged in the 2010 case[20]) regardless of who the stories were about (as do many other tabloid papers). The only stipulation concerns whether the persons concerned are high profile enough to guarantee interest and sales. The fodder for this is, thus, celebrities, politicians and public figures. Tommy admitted this on the McNeilage tape, saying '... the *News of the World* makes a living out of fucking salacious stories about people'.[21] He was a celebrity, politician and public figure, as a result of being the leader of the SSP, an MSP and so on as well as one who cultivated the media with material on his private life in order to develop a certain persona. But the particular axe *NoW* had to grind against Tommy was for being a hypocrite given he espoused himself as the faithful, devoted and clean living partner and husband. That Tommy was a leading socialist was by no means incidental or unwelcomed for *NoW*[22] but it was not central to the rationale for printing the stories. As pointed out elsewhere (save arguably the case of Fiona McGuire[23]), Tommy had given *NoW* both the opportunity and the means by which to attack him by his hypocritical and reckless behavior. It was a revision of history to conclude *NoW* had always 'had it in' for Tommy, for Rupert Murdoch's reported comments about bringing down the 'commie bastard'[24] no matter the cost took place in a News International executive meeting came *after* Tommy won his defamation action as Tommy[25] and Solidarity[26] admitted (and not before as his mother alleged[27]). Clearly, Murdoch and *NoW* were smarting from their expensive and public drubbing. But Tommy significantly over-egged his pudding by claiming the attack on him was because he was a socialist fighter but he needed to do so to curry political favour inside and outside the SSP. This was because he was not defending himself from charges of sedition, contempt of court or conspiracy as John MacLean, the Pentonville Five dockers or the Shrewsbury Three building workers had, when challenging employers and the state.[28] Rather, he was prosecuting *NoW* for defamation on matters of his personal life. Indeed, the paper which had attacked him most – save the time he was a columnist for it – was the *Daily Record*. Its criticisms were not only made at the time when it was the largest selling (daily) tabloid but these were mounted from a position of being a centre-left paper. Both of these made its attacks more damaging than those by *NoW*.

Tommy's case for a politically motivated attack and conspiracy against him would have had more grounding if *NoW*'s stablemates, the *Sun* or *Times*, had carried out the alleged attack and conspiracy.[29] Not only were they printed six days a week allowing them to respond to events in a way that they could more easily and effectively carry out such attacks and conspiracies but they (especially *the Sun*) had proven track records in doing so – in a way that *NoW* did not. For Tommy, that did not seem to especially matter. He sought to make no differentiation between any of the News International newspapers, and invoked the battle fought by the print unions against derecognition and deunionisation at Wapping in 1986 as evidence that *NoW* was anti-union, and thus, anti-working class (even though this contradicted his assessment of the papers when he was offered a *Sun* column). He, thus, tugged on instinctive left political heartstrings. Tommy pushed other political buttons like suggesting it was a 'no brainer' for socialists to support him against *NoW* and to defend him from *NoW*. He posed this in terms of 'which side are you on?', conflating his struggle with that of workers *per se* and for socialism *per se*. For Tommy, in this regard as in many others in his faction and legal fight, it was a case of 'needs must'. He used the political and emotional appeal of these arguments to mask what he had done originally and what he would do in his faction fight. These constructs were ones that many supporters were prepared to mimic with a hitherto unknown ferocity against those that did not agree with the argument, with what Tommy had done or that it was an 'either or' choice. Once the battle between him and *NoW* (and News International) had begun, Tommy effectively backdated this evidence to validate his new claims but in doing so contradicted himself. So for example, he issued a statement after a NC meeting in November 2004 in which he said: 'I would like to take this opportunity to confirm that my resignation as national convener has nothing at all to do with internal power struggles. There is not and never has been any internal squabbles or back-biting about a leadership challenge'.[30]

Recklessness

The visits to Cupids in Manchester in 1996 and 2002[31] were "reckless" to use Tommy's own term not because they involved sex, group sex or any number of other sexual practices. Human sexual proclivities are wide and varied, and as explained later, are a matter of personal taste which should not be judged by other parties unless they are coercive or exploitative. Here, one person's 'depravity' is another person's 'pleasure'. Rather, the visits were reckless because Tommy had established, deliberately, a public persona which ran contrary to these activities and did so for political gain. To be shown to be otherwise was to risk being labeled a hypocrite which was highly likely to be a death knell to a politician who traded on integrity and honesty as Tommy so obviously did – and as he acknowledged.[32] If he had wanted to engage in such sex acts and fear no valid political repercussions, he should have not created his clean living, monogamous persona and he should have gained Gail's explicit and genuine agreement to do so. Despite being in Manchester, the club was not far enough away from Scotland that Tommy stood no chance of being recognised because he was so well known, and the 'code of honour' among swingers for maintaining anonymity was not strong enough to protect him. And, in an era of the internet and saturation news, it was unlikely that Tommy could not be recognised no matter where he was. Indeed, he was reported to have panicked when he was recognised by some fellow swinging Scots, and despite the so-called vow of silence that swingers engage in for mutual protection, he asked for his name (which he stupidly signed in as) to be erased from the club's signing-in register. The visits were also reckless because they could be substantiated through CCTV evidence and cell phone analysis of which masts mobile phonecalls were made through. But the visits were doubly reckless because they were made with Anvar Khan, who was not only a journalist, feature writer and celebrity interviewer but at the time of the 2002 trip worked in these capacities for the Scottish *NoW*. The two had a sexual relationship after flirting with each other in Saughton jail in 1992. Khan visited him to conduct an interview, saying said he had 'devilish charm' and that his 'je ne sais quois is legendary'.[33] It was a measure of Tommy's belief in the loyalty towards him that he thought his four fellow participants on his last known visit would be "solid" and would not disclose any details. But it was also a measure of what ends Tommy would go to when he told Keith Baldrassara and Alan McCombes at their 1 November 2004 meeting, according to Keith: 'I can destroy Anvar Khan'. Upon hearing this, Keith felt numb, saying: 'What do you mean you can destroy her?' Tommy, he recalled, responded: 'She deceived me ... I've been deceived so fuck her'. The recklessness also had other dimensions. Tommy had become the singular public face of the SSP and this would remain so despite of the election of five other SSP MSPs so that damage to him would inevitably mean collateral damage to the SSP. And as someone who the establishment would probably like to politically decapitate if given half a chance, he was giving them a full chance.[34] In this regard, there is an analogy where thoughtful shop stewards realise they should not give their employers opportunities to get rid of them through bad timekeeping or theft of company property.[35]

That Tape

The infamous video of George McNeilage's meeting with Tommy was dated 18 November 2004.[36] George had previously met Tommy in his car to discuss the issues, recounting that Tommy said: "We all make mistakes in our lives '... and I said what you're doing ... [is] madness ... given your position'. George told five or six others of this conversation but it was Tommy's refusal to meet with these people to discuss the issues that led to the tape.[37] George felt angered and let down by this refusal so the idea of secretly recording the meeting was to allow those denied an audience with Tommy the opportunity to hear Tommy put his side on the story under questioning from George. In the 2010 court case, it was revealed that Tommy had phoned and texted George to say he was only a few minutes away from getting to the house where the meeting was taped. After Scottish *NoW* editor, Bob Bird, was shown the video in his boxer shorts – to make sure he was not wired – George put the price of the tape at £250,000 (of which £50,000 was for local community projects). Verification and bargaining led to an agreement which George commented was for an 'ironic' sum.[38] This would later be revealed in 2010 to be £200,000, the sum Tommy was awarded by the jury from *NoW* in his defamation case.[39] George sold the tape for 'danger money' because he had already received a visit from Tam McGraw, a significant underworld figure, before the court case and which he believed was at the behest of Tommy. George expected more once he went public with the tape. Whether it was because of lack of nerve, not wanting to be called a grass, thinking Tommy would not win his defamation action, believing that the tape did not record or anger at the 'scabs' accusation against the SSP witnesses, the tape surfaced in 2006 because George went back to look at it. The tape ends abruptly because George erased the latter part as it dealt with a conversation about Alice and Gail which, in order to protect them, he did not want made public.[40] George recalled Tommy saying as he left his house 'things will never be the same again ... and that the 'black arts' have begun' as they did with the story slipped to the *Mirror* on Alan McCombes and Carolyn Leckie's relationship.[41] When the tape became public, Tommy's reaction was that it was concocted using spliced segments of his own voice[42] but by his 2010 perjury trial, he argued it comprised an actor mimicking him with a pre-arranged script. Similarly, his claims of the makers of it changed between 2006 and 2010.

Why Tommy Fought

This chapter's introduction laid out the basic lines of why Tommy engaged in his fight with *NoW*. The SSP EC gave him the options of a) ignore the allegations, leaving them to become tomorrow's fish-and-chip papers;[43] b) go to a sympathetic newspaper like the *Daily Record* or *Scottish Mirror* to defuse his imminent revealing and to show some

contrition; c) issue a 'non-denial denial';[44] d) say 'no comment'; or
e) say there were a personal matter which he and his wife would deal
with privately so, effectively, 'butt out'. The SSP EC also made it clear
that it was a reckless, kamikaze strategy to not only deny the stories
but also sue for defamation on allegations that were true and this would
open up a can of worms, all with the effect of seriously damaging
Tommy, the SSP and the cause of socialism. The leadership argued it
was a no-win situation, going so far as to suggest oblivion was being
stared in the face. This was sound advice and may have allowed Tommy
to take a step back from the leadership before returning to it at some
point in the not-too-distant future. It would have badly rocked the SSP
but not destroyed it. It certainly would not have pressed the nuclear
button which Tommy did with his strategy of defiance and defamation
action. For example, Richie Venton believed: 'He totally miscalculated
that it would destroy him if he admitted it because there would be three
types of reaction: 'That's disgusting and I want nothing to do with you';
'Well, that's his life, it's up to him'; and 'What's the address? Give me
some of that'. We're not living in the age of Profumo and it's not the
1970s ... His misjudgment is rooted in his fixation with fame and public
approval ... and [the legacy] of him being the chosen one when he was
a child' while Colin Fox argued: 'He grievously overestimated the damage it would do him politically when he stated 'This will destroy me'.
It didn't do Galloway any harm ... Even if he lost the court case, that
wouldn't have destroyed him. It might have made him look stupid and
a shagging machine. It would have been the financial costs that would
have destroyed him [not the allegations]'. Moreover, Richie Venton
recalled that he and Colin Fox repeatedly advised Tommy not to go
ahead with the court case because *NoW* would bring to the table other
material to 'blacken your character' in order to 'claim you don't have a
character to defame'.

But, paradoxically, there is still the possibility that Tommy was more
right to take the defamation action than those that advised him not too.[45]
This possibility arises because one of Tommy's fears was that there was
so much more material that could possibly come out about his sexual
activity and what this then said of his personality type – being much
more than Keith Baldassara and Alan McCombes knew or could know.
Indeed, George McNeilage recounted in the 2010 perjury case that
Tommy told him: 'I can't put my hands up ... If I do that the floodgates
will open. I have to take this to court'.[46] By this, Tommy meant that his
mask of respectability and credibility would be torn off to reveal the
type of person he actually was and the type of behavior he regularly
engaged in. Thus, the logic here in taking the case against *NoW* was
to fire a shot across the bows of any newspaper in order to say that if

they printed any further such material, they would have to contend with legal action. All this was because Tommy believed such stories, if unchallenged could "destroy" him because such a large part of his reputation was based on the combination of honesty and integrity, on the one hand (as he admitted in his defamation trial[47]), and being the devoted and faithful partner and husband on the other. It may have also been because the fresh material may have destroyed his marriage with Gail, thus, ripping up the foundation of his image as a devoted and faithful partner and husband. So, Tommy felt forced by his circumstances to take the action. This may have been the reason why he told *Scotland on Sunday* he had taken the action, in a kind of Orwellian doublespeak, 'primarily' for Gail[48] and that he was taking it for the sake of his family[49] even though it risked bringing other things to light.[50]

There were occasions beforehand such as *Daily Record's* 'working class zero' attack when Tommy could have taken a defamation action but did not. The *NoW* stories showed just how significant Tommy felt them to be for his cultivated persona. At least with the *Daily Record* attack, he could luxuriate in the reputation of being attacked for his politics. Alan McCombes recounted Tommy said if left unchallenged he 'would be politically destroyed and could never recover'[51] and Allan Green recalled: 'Tommy's main starting point was that the swingers' club story would, according to him, finish him politically ... he took the view that if he was going to be finished by accepting the story the only chance of him not being finished politically was by going down this road of challenging [it]'. Thus, with his back against the wall, he felt he had no option but to take this course of action. It was Monte Carlo or bust. In the light of what *NoW* was to reveal after his conviction and sentencing, this calculation may well have proven correct.[52] This casts new light on the discussions between Tommy, Alan McCombes and Keith Baldassara on Monday 1 November 2004 as Alan recounted them:

> He told Keith and Alan that he 'could win this', and would 'destroy' Anvar Khan. He insisted that if this story came out, he would be not just politically damaged, but would be 'totally destroyed' and could never come back. Keith and Alan strongly disagreed, arguing that, especially if Tommy handled the allegations with dignity and a degree of contrition, any damage would be temporary. People respect those who are prepared to take responsibility for their own actions. They would forgive, and over time forget, private indiscretions.[53]

And on the McNeilage tape, Tommy reports Keith saying of him at the 9 November 2004 meeting: 'I don't know whether this is all he's been involved in'. This shows the sense that to live by the sword of creating a media image based on a conventional morality of integrity, clean living and monogamy also entails being prepared to acknowledge that one can also be wounded or killed by this self-same sword. The problem was for the SSP that Tommy was not prepared to fall on this sword – his sword. There is also the no small matter of whether Tommy was prepared to admit to Gail and his family that his sexual behavior of before his relationship with and marriage to Gail had not since continued after these. On the McNeilage tape, Tommy mentions that his sisters Lynn and Carol remonstrated with him saying: 'You better not be doing this all again' and in the 2010 trial, George recalled Tommy stated: 'I can't go to Gail'.[54] Then there was the aspect that Tommy was "not prepared to be destroyed by these people" meaning a rightwing tabloid newspaper who he felt was bullying him.[55]

But this perceived need to fight is only one third of the explanation of why Tommy fought. The other two thirds are the combination of precise nature of the allegations and existing evidence, and the ability to fight back. Before examining these, it is worth recalling that Tommy repeatedly asserted that his case would not come to court but he needed to keep the pressure of the threat of action on in order to gain an apology or retraction. He also made it clear that if this did not happen, he would drop his case.[56] However, as time progressed these statements and calculations were changed as *NoW* proved more resistant than he anticipated. Thus, different twists and turns were made within the framework that Tommy was not prepared to compromise or back down.

When Anvar Khan's story headlined 'Married MSP is spanking swinger' was published on 31 October 2004, it was written in a way which deliberately changed dates and details to hide Tommy's identity and these aspects contradicted the material of her forthcoming book, *Pretty Wild,* which she was using the story to publicise. Tommy deduced that he could challenge the story because she had undermined its integrity by this divergence. Indeed, he said on the McNeilage tape that she had 'made a cunt of herself' and would do so again when in court. Then when the Fiona McGuire story – 'My kinky 4-in-a-bed orgy with Tommy' – broke on 14 November 2004, Tommy decided to act on this because this story had no basis in fact, according to him, and had so many inexactitudes that he could successfully attack it and, thereby, successfully attack the veracity of the Anvar Khan story as well.[57] Thus, by going for *NoW*'s weak spot he thought he could sink all their stories. A *NoW* story reported on 21 November the 'real' reasons for Tommy's resignation. The other side to the coin here was that Tommy believed that if there was incontrovertible evidence of the Cupids visits, it would have been used before 2004, that is, in the run up to the May 2003 Scottish Parliament election.[58]

The final third part to understanding why Tommy fought was because he had the wherewithal to do so and because he was able to create the alliances necessary to facilitate this. This is much more than, as he admitted, being 'very bad' at 'accepting advice'[59] and comprised of a number of elements. His oratorical and media skills are recognised and analysed elsewhere so are not dwelt upon here other than to say he gave some of the most impassioned performances of his career in this internal party dogfight,[60] operated in a very clever Machiavellian way by only telling supporters what he thought they needed to know,[61] deployed different arguments with different people,[62] and used his close and direct relationships with journalists to gain favourable media coverage (meaning that he operated outside party structures). The defiant and audacious nature of his personality was also critical to providing him with the cerebral and psychological resources to do what he did. He told me at the 28 May 2006 NC: 'If I'm going to go down, I'm going to go down fighting'. To him, it was better to go down fighting no matter the cost than accept – or not challenge – the 'allegations' against him. In all of this, he not incorrectly expected kneejerk support from other socialists because his fight was against *NoW*, part of News International, because there was a debt of loyalty to him as a leading socialist fighter and so on. Indeed, his argument was that it was the duty of socialists to support him against *NoW* even if he had lied and had to lie to win his case. He traded on all these facets as well as the analogy that union members should defend their shop steward when in difficulty.[63]

However, because Tommy was a national figure, spending most of his time in parliament and with journalists or the senior party echelons, constructing an alliance with local activists was no mean feat. His discussions with local activists before late 2004 tended to be fleeting and perfunctory. In Glasgow, his main points of contact were with the likes of Richie Venton, the local organiser, rather than the branch activists. Even where he spoke at local branches, it was still the case of dipping in and dipping out very quickly. None of this was compensated for by being active within the ISM.[64] But the ability to construct the alliance was all the more remarkable given two other aspects. The first was that because most of the political battles he fought were not inside the SSP but outside it (and with other political forces) and that because Tommy had not been a major player in the split with the CWI or the negotiations over bringing together the SSA and SSP, he was not versed in the ways of internal faction fights and other such organisational methods. In other words, Tommy seldom played a significant internal role in the SSP, with Allan Green commenting he did not 'try to organisationally dominate the party ... [he] was not interested in internal organisational matters unless there was a problem ... he wasn't involved in the mechanics of the organisation'. The second was that because Tommy sought to remain as popular as possible with all sections of the SSP and, thus, often waited to declare his position one way or the other in internal debates until after it became clear which way the wind was blowing, again he was not well versed in the ways of fighting for his position within the wider SSP membership.[65] Moreover, where 'his' position was fought for within the SSP, it had been fought for by others like Alan McCombes after he, Alan and Allan Green had made a decision. But the more important psychological aspect here was that Tommy was no longer operating in his 'comfort zone' of being popular. This would have internally unnerved him, at least initially.[66] Nonetheless, he did have some foundations and skills with which to construct his alliance. The most obvious was the sense of loyalty to him as a person that he could call upon, especially as he remained popular with most within the SSP and had not had major fallings out with them. Another was that he had gained the skills of alliance building and agenda setting while working as APTU federation chair and as a lone councillor and parliamentarian. A further skill was that Tommy was a planner as Felicity Garvie recalled: 'Once ... Tommy had a concrete idea about how [a] goal should be achieved ... he thought the steps [out], could plan ahead and foresee the consequences of th[e] action and that's what made him so good in the libel case ... that was exactly the skill he needed'. Before examining the nature of the alliance he built, it is worth recalling that unlike most far left permanent political formations (like the SWP and SPEW), the SSP permitted platforms and dissent as legitimate so that Tommy did not face this extra obstacle.[67] Moreover, Tommy believed that since he had resigned as national convener, he now had an absolute right to pursue his chosen course of action. Indeed, this seemed to him to be the *quid pro quo* for resigning.[68]

A number of Tommy's key individual and previously unaligned supporters, like Graeme McIver, Gary Fraser[69] and Gordon Morgan, tried to dissuade Tommy from taking his defamation action for reasons of opening up Pandora's box and a can of worms, and the risks involved. With his own frequent experience of defamation actions and litigation, George Galloway was another of these.[70] They were unsuccessful but then went on to support Tommy because once he had made his decision, he was able to convince them and they were able to be convinced. The former related to his powers of persuasion, particularly portraying his fight as a principled socialist one, and use of his track record and legacy to give him political authority and leverage. Supporters found him very forceful and persuasive, and some fearing susceptibility to these powers agreed only to go away and think about the issue for fearing of being bounced into a decision there and then. In this, Tommy had not only a Svengali-type power but also 'Clinton-esque ability'[71] to give the person not only his undivided attention but make them feel they were the only person on earth for whom he had attention at that moment in time. The latter related to their willingness to defend what they saw as the most valuable public asset to socialism in Scotland, and what they wanted in terms of Tommy's greater ability to be returned to parliament than any other SSP MSP. Steve Arnott believed, for example, 'If we are going to win votes we need Tommy'.[72] Most, if not all, of Tommy's supporters and court witnesses, therefore, knew the 'allegations' to be true yet continued to back-up Tommy's lies in court and elsewhere. Ironically, these activists then often felt compromised by their part in events that they felt they could not stay in the SSP and were compelled to join Solidarity. Indeed, with the onset of a perjury investigation and charges, some strands of the reasons for their support of Tommy grew immeasurably in that they were now compromised by the part they played in a conspiracy and were sucked into Tommy's vortex.[73]

Of the major internal platforms (or constitutionally legitimate factions) inside the SSP, the SWP was numerically the dominant one. It took the position of supporting Tommy for a number of reasons over and above the 'defend a socialist fighter' line.[74] But this was not before it argued that he should not take a defamation case[75] and agreed that his willingness to take such a case necessitated his resignation. But within a week, its line had changed to:

It is with sadness we note his resignation … follow[ing] a series of salacious 'reports' about his personal life. Even if there was a grain of truth to any of this, so what? What consenting adults do in their personal lives is their own business, providing they don't hypocritically try to impose Victorian values on the rest of us.[76]

There was enmity on the SWP's part towards the SSP leadership, and Alan McCombes and Frances Curran in particular, over the party's direction in its anti-war and anti-capitalism work as well as its general orientation. The SWP characterised the SSP as having degenerated politically.[77] By siding with Tommy and then jumping ship with him to form Solidarity, the SWP hoped to be able to influence it to be, in its terms, a less narrow party-building and a broader 'movementist' project.[78] The SWP also believed that Tommy was such an important asset to socialism in Scotland that his star should not be squandered and that in his defence the ends justified the means.[79] Like the CWI, the SWP was accused of being opportunist by some who pointed out how fierce a critic it had been of Tommy before late 2004 in regard of his alleged nationalism and reformism. Both the CWI and SWP defended their actions by arguing that they showed extreme principled-ness by defending someone with whom they had significant criticisms of.[80] Whatever the merits of these arguments, Tommy knew which forces to approach, what buttons to press and what to offer them in order to build his support base.[81] This can be all the more seen for the CWI criticisms[82] of the SSP were quite at odds with those of the SWP. The CWI believed that the SSP had dropped any Marxist orientation and was suffering as a result. Its leadership also had a personal enmity towards Alan McCombes and Frances Curran for leaving the CWI in order to establish the SSP as a broad socialist party. An irony is that the CWI initially also argued that Tommy was misguided to take the defamation action.[83] Nonetheless, the CWI position was that Tommy had to be defended no matter what he had done: 'Tommy Sheridan may have been found 'guilty' in a capitalist court of law. But for socialists he is innocent of any crime against the interests of the working class'.[84]

If the non-aligned individuals had not given their unqualified support to Tommy, it would have been numerically and politically very much harder for Tommy to construct the alliance he did. Thus, Tommy would then not have won the motion at the 28 May 2006 NC for the SSP to give him 'political support' against *NoW* and drop the defiance strategy of not handing in the minute. Nor would he have been able to go from meeting Allan Green and Colin Fox on 12 May 2006 where he argued for defiance, citing it as a labour movement tradition, to arguing the opposite. The non-aligned supporters gave some weight of numbers and some social weight for although many activists were aligned to platforms many were not and most members were not either, thus, critically giving Tommy's case the semblance of being correct and reasonable. This applied especially to those that gave evidence in the 2006 court case like Jock Penman and Graeme McIver. In a nutshell, without their support, the alliance with the CWI and SWP would have not only been too slight numerically but it would have looked too odd as well. Some have concluded that these individuals in particular share a large burden of responsibility for effectively allowing Tommy to do what he did. However, there is an extra dimension here as well. The tactical ineptitude of a number of individuals associated with the United Left and radical feminism within the SSP was very helpful for Tommy in allowing him to show his opponents to be as he alleged them to be, namely, crackpot feminists, Tommy haters, personally vindictive, politically deluded and so on.[85]

Some concluded from Tommy's actions to construct his coalition that he was immoral or amoral or that the only right he was defending was the right – his right – to hypocrisy.[86] By contrast, it would be truer to say he had a different morality rather than having none and, thus, one that clashed with others. This morality was of 'who dares win' and 'will to power', backed up by his particular version of what constituted loyalty (see later). It was not so much that Tommy would not take responsibility for his actions and tried to evade them as Carolyn Leckie[87] and Alan McCombes[88] believed. Instead, and contrary to his initial admission of 'I've made a mistake and I need to pay for that mistake' (McNeilage tape), he tried to shape and determine what the consequences might be and how they might be meted out. It seemed Tommy subscribed to the principle that the truth is what you make it and that one of the spoils of victory is to write its history. The morality of those that supported Tommy varied and in not all cases were individuals, willingly or not, consciously or not, operating with all the available information to hand. Nonetheless, his supporters gave legitimacy to Tommy's methods which included deliberate distortions,[89] lies and character assassinations and employed some of these tactics themselves.

Finally, it should be borne in mind that Tommy felt such betrayal by Alan McCombes, Keith Baldassara and Frances Curran that he was all the more unwilling to yield to their demand to drop the court case. He reasoned that if he did, he had no chance of winning the fight over his future to return to the party leadership because the allegations against him would still stand and 'victory' would be handed to them, now his opponents. Indeed, according to Richie Venton, Tommy scoffed at the offer of a fighting fund to help him pay his legal fees – which could bankrupt him and lead to his ejection from the Parliament – if he dropped the case for: 'He laughed in my face because he said half the party wouldn't make a donation [to it]'. This indicated the depth of animosity towards Tommy after 9 November 2004. With his mind frame of bloody mindedness and no escape route, he would not back down. In this regard of the internal faction fight, he saw he was left with no option but to fight.

Balls of Steel

Tommy's brazen sense of fearlessness and defiance was described by Colin Fox as 'having balls of steel'. Gail also admitted he had 'balls'.[90] Others like, Keith Baldassara, said he had 'nerves of steel'. Either way, they were hugely evident in Tommy's campaign to win his political and legal fight. Tommy was determined to prove black was white and white was black depending on the needs of his hour. First there was trying to overturn the events of the 9 November 2004 SSP EC meeting where he told not two or four people but a whole room of people that he had visited Cupids and then resigned as a result of this admission and how he proposed to respond. Second, there was the production of a fake minute of the 9 November 2004 meeting which has been assumed by many was the work of Tommy or his close supporters. For example, Alan McCombes in the court case testified under questioning from Tommy that this minute 'was your concoction'[91] as did elsewhere the SSP Republican Communist Network platform.[92] The added dimension to the audaciousness was for this minute to appear at a time when the SSP had taken a decision to provide Tommy some protection and not aid *NoW* by not circulating the (actual) minute with Alan McCombes having gone to jail to protect it as SSP property.[93] Amongst many reasons, the fake minute was necessary to fight a possible charge of perverting the course of justice over destruction of the (actual) minute. Third, there were various examples of brazenness like arguing in a meeting with Allan Green and Colin Fox on 12 May 2006 to not hand in the minute and then some two weeks later at the 28 May 2006 NC arguing the reverse, and after reading the (real) minute at the 12 May 2006 meeting saying it would not "fatally" damage his case (giving some inclination of what he was prepared to then do).[94] Fourth, to not only suggest the McNeilage tape was a fake but it was one made up by *NoW* and the SSP together using at first spliced tapes (2006 court case) and then an actor (2010 court case). Fifth, his endless number of media interviews, especially the television ones, where he maintained his innocence in the face of all the evidence to the contrary – not just by denials but by constructing elaborate untruths and lies. Sixthly, his performances in two courts of law where he cross-examined and eyeballed former lovers and comrades and character assassinated them. In the 2006 case, Tommy constructed the fabrication that the 11 SSP members were guilty of "the mother of all stitch ups" against him and of perjuring themselves in court to do so. All of this involved perjuring himself and others in a necessary but desperate gamble. And, lastly, there was the Orwellian doublespeak of the *Daily Record* front page: 'I'll destroy the scabs who tried to ruin me'.[95] Of course, there were more minor components like being willing on countless occasions to reignite the flames of the battle by, for example, issuing his open letter on 28 May 2006.[96] In doing so, he knew that he would sustain further damage to his reputation as the media reprinted all the material about his private life again but he saw this as a short-term sacrifice in order to try to gain a longer term goal.

Panicked into Resigning?

Tommy resigned as national convener on 10 November 2004 following his insistence on taking his defamation action while still national convener. The argument by Tommy and his supporters, like the SWP, was that the SSP leadership was panicked into taking the action it did, namely, of forcing Tommy's resignation. They believed it should have stayed its hand and waited to see what happened rather than taking such precipitous action (and this was especially so when the Fiona McGuire story emerged). Thus, *Socialist Worker*, for example, argued:

> The obvious response would have been to say that Tommy has never stuck his nose into other people's personal lives or lectured them on morality—unlike David Blunkett—so why should he be judged by the News of the World? The story would have quickly died a death, and it cut little ice with tens of thousands of SSP voters. But the SSP leadership panicked, and urged Tommy's res-ignation. That panic derives from seeing things too much in terms of media perceptions rather than how grassroots party support-ers view things. The argument that the party cannot back Tommy because it cannot support a possible libel action brought by him does not hold up. You can broadly defend someone without being drawn into the details.[97]

The Socialist Party of England and Wales made the same argument using different terms: 'they [the SSP EC] buckled under pressure'[98] with Philip Stott adding the SSP EC 'took fright … made a colossal error of judge-ment … because Tommy has had huge political authority in Scotland … and because the nature of the allegations … were not particularly impor-tant, even if proved true [because] they were consensual relations'. Later, Tommy decided to publicly run with this argument, saying: 'In retro-spect, we probably allowed ourselves to be panicked by the News of the World'[99] and 'Perhaps I was panicked [into resigning], however at that time … I thought it was the right thing to do'.[100] Behind closed doors, he argued in a private meeting with David Archibald in March 2005, accord-ing to the latter: '[T]he Executive had made a cunt of the situation … [and that] he'd be vindicated as nothing [i.e., no conclusive evidence to date] had emerged'.[101]

However, there were four problems with this kind of 'don't be pan-icked' argument. The first was Tommy was not prepared to take this very course of action which *Socialist Worker* outlined which was to effectively ignore the stories (as he was urged on 9 November 2004). Indeed, he very quickly initiated proceedings. The second was that given the Anvar Khan story and what else was known about Tommy's sexual activities to his close comrades (which did not include the SWP or CWI), it was more than likely there would be further damaging stories to emerge. This meant even ignoring them would become increasingly problematic. The third was that Tommy, in seeking to disprove what was true in a court of law, fundamentally changed the whole situation.

The fourth was that while Tommy had not 'lectured on morality', he had created his own moral edifice which was at stark variance with his private and sexual behavior (see below). Nonetheless, both the SWP[102] and CWI[103] were critical of the *tactical* decision of the SSP leadership. This would change to being critical of the strategic and principled nature of the decision as Tommy continued his political and legal campaigns.

Counter-Intuitive

The forcefulness of Tommy's aforementioned political case, and his forceful delivery of it, is highlighted by asking a number of questions. Why did he resign if the Cupid allegations were not true, and if there was not something to them? Why would there be a political problem for the SSP if he was suing against allegations that were false? Why would the SSP protect its minute from the court if it was trying to 'do' Tommy in (as judge Lord Turnbull highlighted in the defamation trial[104])? Moreover, removing Tommy as national convener and in such circumstances as those of November 2004 was clearly a move which would have huge and detrimental implications for the SSP, so there are a number of other obvious questions to ask: why would so many leading activists help destroy their own party, and one they had so patiently spent so much time and effort building up over the years and held so dear?; and, why would they put at risk their own livelihoods as MSPs and party workers (and for which they had accepted low wages)? Indeed, in these circumstances, one might have expected there to have been a rush to cover up for Tommy in order to preserve the SSP and its leadership given that trial witness and SWP member, Pat Smith agreed with the *NoW* QC that Tommy was the 'goose that laid the golden egg'[105] and that for many 'Tommy Sheridan was the SSP'[106] while Alan McCombes also commented that the SSP 'killed the goose that laid the golden eggs'.[107] The argument that others were jealous of Tommy holds such little water in these circumstances.[108]

The Mother of all National Councils

The 28 May 2006 special SSP NC meeting was always going to be a fraught one. Tommy had sounded some people out for a split in early May 2006 as he was unsure of winning a majority at this NC but the response was not heartening.[109] The 14 May SSP EC had passed a motion calling upon Tommy to withdraw his case[110] but there were diametrically opposed motions to be discussed at the NC with one calling upon the

SSP to give Tommy full political support in his fight against *NoW*. And, the 9 November 2004 SSP EC minute became subject of intense debate and legal significance as Tommy's trial approached after a lull in the internal strife. *NoW* asked in court on 10 May 2006 for the minute and Tommy refused, leading *NoW* to cite successfully – after objections from Tommy failed – Colin Fox, Frances Curran and Alan McCombes before the court.[111] The SSP strategy of defiance of not handing in the minute led to Alan McCombes being jailed for 12 days for contempt of court (of which he served three) and landed the SSP with a £30,000 legal bill (to compound its existing financial woes). At the same time, Tommy asked Allan Green, according to himself and Colin Fox, for the minute to be destroyed at the Golden Pheasant meeting. When the lawyer for the SSP saw the pleadings from *NoW*, it became clear that *NoW* did not have "fuck all" and was not intent upon settling out of court. As many had predicted, the danger of a defamation action was that new material (other than that which was in the original articles) was brought to bear like that concerning Katrine Trolle and the Moat House hotel orgy.

The May NC meeting was packed out and when Tommy entered the lecture hall at Glasgow Caledonian University, there was a 'spontaneous' round of applause for him organised by his supporters. The meeting had been preceded by the passing of his supporter Martin McCardie's motion (then distributed from his MSP email account once passed) at his own SSP Cardonald branch meeting on 15 May 2006 to destroy the minute.[112] Tommy then distributed his 'Open letter' to the NC meeting, and beforehand everyone attending was acutely aware that the *Sunday Herald's* front page that day was devoted to the faction fight – the revelation of an affidavit by the paper from a then unknown senior SSP member was assumed to be a recounting of the detail of the 9 November 2004 SSP EC meeting. With the defamation case looming, Alan McCombes in Saughton jail for contempt of court in not handing in the 9 November 2004 SSP EC minute – indicating the SSP did not want to assist *NoW* – and mounting party debts being run up as a result of the 'defiance' strategy, all hell did break loose. The air was thick with recrimination and accusation on all sides. Tommy's open letter – which was simultaneously released to the media[113] – launched a full-frontal attack on his political foes. It talked of 'internal [party] decay over the last 18 months' (i.e. from November or December 2004) where 'an unsavoury cabal at the core of the leadership ... [is] more interested in pursuing personal vendettas ... than conducting the class struggle'. Tommy then went on in the open letter to overturn what he had previously agreed and accepted in regard of the 9 November 2004 minute.[114] In the letter, he then moved onto argue the case of capitalist – i.e. *NoW* –

victimisation of a socialist – i.e. him. The point of a plot since November or December 2004 was made on three other occasions and a dig was made at some like Carolyn Leckie for allegedly wanting to turn the SSP into 'a gender obsessed discussion group'.[115] Looking back on the NC, there were mixed views on what the open letter symbolised – with some believing it was a leaving declaration after months of Tommy not attending previous EC meetings (on the purported basis that he had been legally advised not to). Others like Alan McCombes believed it was the first outing of the fabrication that Tommy would use in his defamation action, and was thus targeted towards those that would be the jury members.[116] Moreover, Tommy was reported to have only attended the NC once he was convinced that he might have the numbers to win. However, such views were often forgotten given the outcome of the NC that day.

In his speech, Tommy mounted a breathtakingly audacious and vicious attack, even going so far as to accuse Catriona Grant of endangering the life of his (as yet) unborn child with her comments.[117] He performed a somersault by appealing for the minute to be handed over, at no time suggesting it was not the real one (and he did not allude to a fake minute having been already handed over to *NoW* and its legal team).[118] He cleverly played the role of helping to save the SSP from itself by calling for the minute to be released so as to bring to an end the mounting legal costs the SSP was bearing. The SSP EC motion asking for support for its 'defiance' strategy was defeated by 82:67. As time was running out for the vote to be taken on a motion calling for Tommy to be given 'full political support', and leaders of the anti-Tommy faction were stalling for time to prevent a vote being taken, Alice Sheridan went off to speak to the cleaners to furnish an extension to the duration to the meeting by getting the cleaners to agree to do their work in the lecture hall a little later. In that extended time, Tommy and his supporters won the key motion by 81:60. This was the beginning of the split in the SSP even though it was not known at the time. The vote committed the SSP to doing something the majority of the leadership opposed. It was a measure of Tommy's oratorical skill and the error of the SSP's defiance strategy that he managed to win a majority at the meeting despite earlier not believing this was possible. Tommy then wrote to the *Scottish Socialist Voice* alleging those who 'took, kept and alerted the press to the existence of a dodgy record or minute of a private and confidential discussion … dragged the Party into a court case they should not be part of and [showed] their desire to do in Tommy Sheridan … The current crisis is not 'precipitated' by Tommy Sheridan but by a group of individuals who have acted in a duplicitous, anti-democratic and anti-socialist fashion'.[119] Shortly afterwards, the United Left group was formed on 11 June 2006 to defend what it saw as the soul of the SSP which it believed was under threat from Tommy and his supporters.[120] This precipitated the establishment of the SSP Majority by Tommy's supporters on 24 June 2006.[121] By late June 2006, the United Left statement had 156 signatories (or supporters) and the SSP Majority statement 306 signatories (or supporters). By 29 July, these numbers had increased to 161 and 335 respectively, growing to 167 and 345 by 7 August and to 173 and 363 by the 22 August.[122]

Refusing to Play Second Fiddle

Although Tommy supported Colin Fox to succeed him as SSP national convener on 13 February 2005 and aligned his supporters behind him,[123] this position of support was not to continue. Tommy's support for Colin Fox was as much to do with Alan McCombes being the other contender for the position as it was positive support for Colin Fox. In other words, Tommy wanted to see the candidate that was not Alan McCombes succeed because he believed Alan McCombes had 'stabbed' him in the 'back'. Colin Fox won the election by 252 votes to 154. Notwithstanding some supportive comments,[124] Tommy began to act in a way that showed that his support for Colin was transient and temporary. Tommy's then friend, Peter Mullan, popped up on *Newsnight Scotland*[125] to say that Colin was not cutting the mustard and Hugh Kerr and Rosemary Byrne publicly pitched in with the same line too.[126] After the May 2006 NC, there was an attempt to show unity between Colin Fox and Tommy but it was clear Colin was unable to prevent Tommy from acting as Tommy intended.[127] Then, Tommy did an interview on STV[128] effectively saying that he wanted to be leader again and another on *Newsnight Scotland* saying he regretted resigning as convener.

As the court case drew nearer, Colin recounted that Tommy asked him as the SSP national convener 'to send a statement to his solicitor saying that the minute [wa]s false, that he had not admitted to visiting a swingers' club and that those people who said that he had attended were mistaken'.[129] As national convener and of independent internal standing, Colin would have been a considerable asset to Tommy for the minute of the 9 November 2004 SSP EC was becoming ever more important. Colin recalled: 'He said 'My lawyers say these minutes will kill me so I have to cast doubt on their accuracy and authenticity'. His lawyers said he needed at least two or three people to do this. Then it became a numbers game'. So in addition to the 'whose side are you on?' tact, Tommy used three arguments in particular as Colin recounted in meetings at the Beanscene café and Jurys Inn hotel in Edinburgh.[130] The first concerned the issue of evidence:

He ... says, in a court of law, it's not about the truth, it's about proof – 'If they can't prove it, then it didn't happen. And they've got nothing'. I said 'What do you mean they've got nothing?' He said: 'They can't prove I was with this woman or that woman'. I said 'Well, were you?' He said: 'That not the point. The point is whether they can prove it'. I said 'In the world I live in, that is the point, an important point' ... I saw his statements that it was all about proof as an admission that these things did happen and that they were true.

The second concerned telling the truth:

He said: 'To our people, to our class, to people in the schemes, you never go to the cops and you never grass on your own side. You'll be seen as a 'grass''. I picked him up on the use of the word 'grass' and said: 'That's an interesting use of the term because no one disputes they're telling the truth – it's about a moral dilemma about whether they go to the cops or not. ... By calling me a 'grass', you're effectively admitting that what I'm saying is true'. ... Implicit in the grass [allegation] is that someone is telling the truth. It's not about people telling lies to the police to fit [someone] up – that's a conspiracy.[131]

The third concerned:

We had a conversation where he said that if I lie for him in court, he'd back me for national convener again and we'd have a dual leadership ... If I don't, he said he'd come back and take the convenership off me.

When Colin did not agree, Tommy told him 'You've picked the wrong side'.[132] Colin also surmised that if Tommy won his forthcoming court case, Tommy would in any case mount a challenge for the convenership. In the course of these discussions, Tommy told Colin that he had come clean about his sexual escapades to his mother and Gail. Both Richie Venton[133] and Steven Nimmo[134] were also asked by Tommy to go to court and lie for him.

The Trial

Given *NoW* did not cave in – as Tommy expected[135] – because it maintained its stories were 'substantially true', the defamation case of the decade began on 4 July 2006 in court six at the Court of Session in Edinburgh and ended on 4 August 2006, lasting 23 days. Tommy was suing for up to £200,000 plus costs for articles published in late 2004 and early 2005 which he alleged made false and defaming statements about him being an adulterer and a swinger who engaged in orgies. In law, it was for *NoW* to prove the allegations true not for Tommy to prove they were not true. The arguments he used were developed and tested in the run-up to trial, whether that be within the media[136] or within the SSP (and would remain the same ones used in 2010). These were based on the principle that the case was not about truth and lies but about what could and could not be proven in a court of law. Rather than cast doubt on the evidence, Tommy's strategy was to cast doubt on the process by which evidence was gathered and presented and cast doubt on the character of the witnesses.

The writ for defamation led principally on the Fiona McGuire story because it was by far the weakest aspect of *NoW's* case (as was proven to be in court in 2006). Tommy also sought to lead on the Anvar Khan story. This was because in the former, there was no corroborating evidence (of specific dates, sightings, texts, phonecalls or hotel bills etc) and in the latter no specific MSP was named. Moreover, in both it was admitted by *NoW* that the details had been 'sexed up' under so-called journalistic license,[137] and that the corroboration of each story was the other. Indeed, as the trial progressed, the *NoW* QC increasingly avoided dwelling upon the McGuire story and concentrated instead on Katrine Trolle (to whom *NoW* had been alerted to by Duncan Rowan) and the minute of the 9 November 2004 meeting. *NoW* also brought in the Moat House hotel orgy material. *NoW's* reliance upon evidence other than that concerning McGuire and Khan indicated that defamation cases inevitably lead to a general examination of the person and their character. Tommy attempted to refute the stories by pointing to inconsistencies as well as impugning the integrity of witnesses by way of their financial (McGuire, Khan and the Moat House witnesses, Anne Colvin and Helen Allison) or political motives (SSP EC members). The trial saw *NoW* call 24 witnesses and Tommy ten. Of *NoW's* witnesses eleven were SSP EC members who attended the 9 November 2004 meeting (Carolyn Leckie, Rosie Kane, Colin Fox, Allison Kane, Keith Baldassara, Barbara Scott, Catriona Grant, Alan McCombes, Jo Harvie, Richie Venton and Allan Green). As many of them pointed out, they were unwillingly in court and were there because of the action initiated by Tommy.[138] Tommy called four SSP EC members who were present at the 9 November 2004 meeting (Rosemary Byrne, Graeme McIver, Jock Penman and Pat Smith) along with two other SSP EC members who were not present at this meeting (Steve Arnott and Mike Gonzalez).

As had become something of a tradition, but never in such a spectacular situation or with such high stakes, on 14 July Tommy sacked his legal team so that he could represent himself (from 18 July). He was then assisted by his two sisters, and by novelist and supporter, John Aberdein. Tommy's stated reasons for doing so was that he was unhappy with his QC being absent (at the House of Lords) and his junior counsel made a serious mistake of wrongly accusing a witness of fraud. In addition to these, however, it seemed Tommy had decided that he knew the arguments and case he wanted to pursue better than anyone else and was, thus, better able to articulate and prosecute them. Concurring, his QC later admitted this was a 'very political move ... [that] worked well for him'.[139] Whether this was because the following day, Gail Sheridan was the next witness is not entirely clear. What is clear is Gail played a key and starring – almost theatrical – role when cross-examined by Tommy (as he admitted[140]), saying with tears that if the allegations were true: 'You would be in the [river] Clyde with a piece of concrete tied round you and I would be in court for your murder' and 'You are like a monkey, so anybody rolling an ice cube round your body would end up with a hairball in their throat. ... When he takes that off there is more hair on his body than there is on his head'.[141] Gail made a big play of being proud of Tommy, and portrayed herself as the feisty – rather than downtrodden – partner.[142]

Tommy's professed willingness to "destroy" Anvar Khan was meted out on her and other former sexual partners, showing he would take no prisoners and show no compassion. He argued he was being persecuted by *NoW* because of his leftwing beliefs,[143] that he had passed the most important test of Gail believing him[144] and the real reason he stood down was because legal action against *NoW* could bankrupt the SSP.[145] Thus, he claimed he was the victim of a political 'battle for the heart and soul of the SSP [where] this courtroom has become an arena for that battle'.[146] He was supported by SSP Highlands and Islands organiser, Steve Arnott, with the latter proffering that it was 'mass delusion'[147] that led the 11 SSP EC members to recollect Tommy admitting the Cupids visits. Tommy called the 9 November 2004 SSP EC minute 'dodgy' as he argued its contents only came publicly to light in May 2006.[148] In all of this, he cleverly used his skills of alliteration – of being addicted to 'scrabble and sunbeds' not 'champagne and cocaine'. Tommy's summing up speech was brief – at 85 minutes – compared to that of *NoW's* QC at six hours. The latter was meandering and contained errors whilst Tommy's was strong and passionate, emphasising that his life and career were in the jury's hands and that the life of his wife and unborn child had been threatened by *NoW*.[149] The media variously reported the speech as 'barnstorming' and 'spellbinding'. John Aberdein believed it was 'the greatest speech ever given by a Scottish politician'[150] while journalist, Paul Hutcheon, believed it was 'the best speech of his career'.[151]

After 160 minutes of deliberation, the jury found in Tommy's favour by 7:4 and awarded him the maximum damages (of £200,000).[152] Despite evidence to the contrary, the jury believed Tommy. Or did they? It is never entirely possible to second guess the rationale for a jury's decision but it is certainly possible that rather than Tommy convincing the jurors that he was innocent of what he was alleged to have done, the jury believed he had been defamed or wronged because he was a socialist, the aggressor was *NoW*[153] and they did not want Tommy to lose[154] and be "destroyed" to use Tommy's term. In this sense, the verdict may have been rather more against *NoW* than for Tommy because Tommy convinced the jury *NoW* was guilty rather than that he was innocent by putting *NoW* on trial.[155] For example, Lorna Martin, *Observer* Scottish correspondent concluded that Tommy 'didn't focus too much on disproving the specific claims in the articles'.[156] Essentially, he argued a political rather than legal case where the actual facts of his behaviour became almost an irrelevance.[157] Sometimes, this meant ignoring the alleged sexual misdemeanours because of the belief that something far more important was at stake.[158] Others like Richie Venton observed Tommy 'challenged the jurors to think: 'Would I be so crazy and stupid to go to orgies just down the road from where I live and in my home city? Would I be so stupid to go to sex clubs when I was married with my well-known face?'... It paid off because [while] there was hostility to *News of the World* ... the jurors must of thought: 'This fella isn't stupid. He's an intelligent, articulate, powerful character. Surely, he wouldn't be that stupid?'[159]

Along the way, Tommy put *NoW*'s gutter journalism and its unscrupulous journalistic practices in the dock, used his oratorical prowess to its full, and deployed Gail to stunning effect. What was particularly of use to Tommy was that in both the Anvar Khan and Fiona McGuire stories, *NoW* had deliberately 'sexed up' the stories.[160] However, it was not just his performance in court that Tommy relied upon but his political campaign of fabrication prior to the court case. Without the latter, no amount of brilliant performance in court would have been enough. Additionally, maybe the jury was unwilling to find for *NoW* because it would have meant bankrupting Tommy and, thus, ejecting him from parliament. The jury recommending the unprecedented size of the award against *NoW* – which Tommy was required to name[161] – suggests all of the above came into play in some way or another. But Tommy was far from being certain of victory. His strategy was highly risky not only given that the Cupids 'allegations' were true, that by sacking his legal team he queried his 'no win, no fee' arrangement,[162] and that Lord Turnbull instructed the jury that it had only to believe one witness for *NoW* to substantiate its case.[163]

Thus, he handed over his share of the Paisley Road West house to Gail on either 6 or 12 July 2006, fearing its loss[164] and signed an exclusive and lucrative financial deal with the *Daily Record* (see below) on the eve of the verdict. But more than that, he did not expect to win. All this belied his bravura of "they've got fuck all'. Thus, on the morning of the verdict and looking 'grim'[165], he was bracing himself for the worst: 'Regardless of today's verdict, I am one of the most fortunate men in the world in that I have such a beautiful and loyal wife and such a beautiful and loyal family. That makes me one of the luckiest men in the world'.[166] The night before he told friends: 'I am hoping for the best but preparing for the worst'.[167] Awaiting the verdict, Tommy was 'downbeat'.[168] And, he was barely able to speak when verdict came in at 3.48pm.[169] Indeed, his face upon leaving the court – and before he made his victory speech – portrayed shock (while Gail's portrayed a sense of disbelief too). The reaction on the street was as much one of non-political interest in sexual proclivities as it was of a socialist triumph for a socialist. For example, in a television *vox pop* on the verdict, a woman pensioner in a Glasgow street thought Tommy must be innocent because: 'Why go out for mince when you can have steak at home?' Elsewhere, there was often support for his victory but incredulity at the suggestion that he had told the truth. In his victory speech outside the court, Tommy said:

> We have over the last five weeks taken on one of the biggest organisations on the planet, with the biggest amount of resources to pay for the most expensive legal team, to throw nothing but muck against me, my wife and my family. Well, brothers and sisters, today's verdict proves working class people, when they listen to the arguments, can differentiate the truth from the muck. The working-class people on the jury who have found in our favour have done a service to the people of Scotland and have delivered a message to the standard of journalism that the News of the World represents. They are liars and we have proved they are liars. ... I want to finish, brothers and sisters, by saying one thing. Gretna have made it into Europe for the first time in their lives, but what we have done in the last five weeks is the equivalent of Gretna taking on Real Madrid in the Bernabeu and beating them on penalties.[170]

The intensity and heartfelt[171] nature of Tommy's court performance in 2006 and his victory speech were not the result of resisting the truth being traduced by untruth, with Tommy cast as the victim in this. Instead, they came from his belief that it was betrayal of and disloyalty to him – by Anvar Khan, Katrine Trolle and those that would not sweep the 'allegations' under his carpet – that had brought him to be in the position of fighting for his personal and political lives. His anger at their disloyalty to him – as he saw it – was genuine if entirely misplaced.

Chinks in His Armour

Tommy made a few minor mistakes of protocol in representing himself.[172] He also sought to describe some evidence as a bent as a 'ten bob note'.[173] Given that such notes did exist, a 'nine bob note' would have been more appropriate. Yet these were inconsequential compared to being revealed as being willing to lie and compared to his inconsistencies about the nature of the alleged plot against him.[174] Under questioning from the *NoW* QC, Tommy admitted that it was acceptable to lie for political reasons[175] such that when he argued he was going to expose *NoW* as 'the real hypocrites and liars',[176] the fact that he used the term 'real' suggested that he considered his lies not to be worthy of that same term. In court, Mike Gonzalez testified there had been hostility towards Tommy 'since' November 2004[177] while Tommy variously stated there has been a plot against over the 'last two years'[178] over the 'last 18 months'[179] and before November 2004.[180] Indeed, the *Herald* reported: 'Lord Turnbull asked Mr Sheridan why his colleagues should create the minute 18 months ago then try to keep it out of court if it was part of their conspiracy'.[181] The problem with this was not only the inconsistency of when the alleged plot started but that if it had started in November 2004, it could be merely a reflection of the reaction against his intended course of action and that it did not constitute a plot. Equally critical was that Tommy's victory was predicated on trying to destroy the credibility and authority of the SSP leadership. What he did not seem to bank upon was that it would fight a rearguard action after the court case. But the sense of chinks in his armour was wider than just the mechanics of the court case – important though they were. So Tommy was now operating – as alluded to earlier – without being part of a road-tested small team of close collaborators that could check excesses and smooth rough edges.

Socialist Scabs

Tommy negotiated an exclusive deal with arch *NoW* stable rival, the *Daily Record*, for his story. The deal was £20,000 and expenses of being put up in a Renfrewshire hotel for interviews that would fill a

week's worth of the paper.[182] Tommy chose to ignore what he had earlier said about the *Record* being an 'establishment rag'[183] and the attack
it previously made on him as the 'working class zero'. He also seemed
to forget the relish the *Record* would have – as a Labour supporting
paper – in printing stories which helped further undermine the SSP.[184]
The *Record* deal led to the infamous 'I'll destroy the scabs who tried
to ruin me' headline on 7 August 2006 in which Tommy accused the
11 SSP EC members of lying and perjuring themselves. Whether the
deal was a financial contingency plan in case he lost, just a way of
capitalising financially and politically on a possible victory or both,
Tommy went on the rampage, showing no humility or grace. But calling the 11 SSP EC members 'scabs'[185] and 'political scabs'[186] and 'collaborators with the enemy'[187] was a strategic blunder for this further
polarised the situation inside the SSP and prevented any possibility of
a truce or Tommy's hoped for return as national convener or heading
the SSP Glasgow list.[188] The view amongst the United Left became
that it would be better to lose seats in the forthcoming election than
win them with Tommy at the helm.[189] The court victory and the 'scabs'
allegation also precipitated Barbara Scott handing into Lothian and
Borders police her handwritten minute of the 9 November 2004 SSP
EC meeting on 7 August 2006, saying: 'I need to clear my name. I did
not commit perjury, neither did the 10 other SSP witnesses who told
the truth, the whole truth and nothing but the truth'.[190] On the BBC
Scotland documentary, *Sex, Lies and Socialism*[191] and in a letter to all
SSP members,[192] Tommy tried to side step the error of his accusation
by changing his terms of attack to 'political scabs' in recognition of the
error in calling the eleven 'scabs'. However, he immediately nullified
this by saying that they, in a play on the Militant Tendency, had joined
'the Murdoch tendency'.[193] And in another reference to the political
importance of his public persona as the devoted and faithful partner
and husband, he told the documentary: 'I said the *News of World* would
never break me politically and they never will. And they never will
break us as a couple either because our love is unbreakable'. Later in
the *Herald*[194] and on BBC Radio Scotland's *Off the Ball*,[195] Tommy
made another characteristically non-apology apology when he said
that he had 'let himself down' by using term the scab and using it publicly. In *The Rise and Lies of Tommy Sheridan*,[196] he said he should not
have used the term 'scabs' and, rather, the term should have been kept
for use in meetings. Finally, he again made a non-apology apology,
saying: 'I damaged my dignity by lowering myself to the level of the
name-callers'.[197] Nonetheless, Tommy's use of the term again testified
to his anger at being put in the position of fighting for his political and
personal life as a result of what he believed was personal betrayal by

close comrades: 'In the couple of days after the verdict I felt so angry ... When somebody takes that position [of testifying against me] ... it's a loss'.[198]

The Split

On 13 August 2006, Tommy and some 70 supporters met. Their mood was rather downbeat and there was some discussion of the possibility of leaving the SSP[199] even though the talk just days earlier had been of retaking the SSP.[200] However, it was not until 27 August that the decision was taken to leave by Tommy and the same group of supporters. On 25 August 2006, Tommy left the SSP parliamentary group. This was the precursor to not only leaving the SSP but establishing Solidarity. What was the basis of the split? It was not about big political ideas, political strategy or political policies like how to achieve socialism and the role of the revolutionary party in this – as it had been with the CWI over a decade earlier – but about working relationships of trust and respect, and political practice, *modus operandi* and notions of morality (even if others like the SWP saw their support for Tommy differently).[201] But more than anything else it was that Tommy could not guarantee that he would make the top of the Glasgow SSP list. Anything less than this would bring into doubt being returned as an MSP in 2007 (regardless of whether he was national convener). If his victory against *NoW* had been achieved on the basis of truthfulness and honesty (and, thus, not tearing apart the SSP), not only would Tommy have secured the top spot on the list but he would have been re-elected as an MSP. Nevertheless, Tommy jumped the gun somewhat in leaving because the United Left was also discussing leaving the SSP.

But he had undermined any possibility of him staying and the United Left leaving as a result of his 'scabs' outburst and its impact on the August 2006 NC and the October, brought forward, annual conference.[202] Indeed, for Tommy, this outburst backfired badly. He said he would like to return as SSP convener, and would put himself up for election against Colin Fox, the incumbent, if he received 'upwards of up 25 or 30' branch nominations.[203] In the event, he got less than a dozen (which was less than he secured when standing for SSP co-chair in 2006), indicating that his support was weak. This indicated that his backing in the SSP was far, far less than the 'at least 70% support among the party membership' which his supporters claimed.[204] Meanwhile, the biggest branch in his home city of Glasgow passed a motion of no-confidence in Tommy and two other branches (Cumbernauld and Kilsyth, and Dumbarton) passed motions calling on Tommy to resign from the

SSP. So, despite the alleged groundswell of opinion for Tommy within the SSP after his defamation victory as well as his supporters claiming they were the 'SSP Majority', the reaction to the 'scabs' outburst further undermined his support base and, thus, may have been what led Tommy to waiver about standing for the national convenership and the top of the SSP Glasgow list – for it added to the problems he would encounter in having to revisit all the issues from 9 November 2004 onwards in these internal elections. At the final SSP Majority meeting on 27 August, there was near unanimity to stay and fight at the October conference but Tommy argued for breaking and won this, suggesting that issue of working relationships and the ethics of lying were more important for him than any alleged political differences. Subsequent justifications about the degeneration of the wider political culture of the SSP unconnected with 'Tommygate' were rather expedient and disingenuous.[205] They were retrospective, post-hoc rationalisations. The inability to secure sufficient branch nominations for a credible leadership bid was one of the key developments as was his inability to be elected to head the Glasgow list for the SSP. Solidarity was launched on 3 September 2006 at a meeting which had originally been planned to be a discussion of whether there should be a split and the launching of a new party.[206] Indeed, in a letter to members, Tommy asked members to come to the meeting to 'have your say on these matters'.[207] But the hurried decision to launch Solidarity then saw Tommy declare that Solidarity would have 1,500 members within six months[208] and would target citizens that did not vote.[209] The essential difference between the SSP and Solidarity was Tommy, leading Rosie Kane to joke that come the 2007 elections Tommy had produced the Solidarity manifesto by copying the 2003 SSP one.[210] The additional irony here was he was as much an author of that manifesto as any other leading member at the time.

Outmaneuvering His Opposition

With hindsight and perfect 'twenty twenty' vision,[211] it became clear that Tommy outmaneuvered and outplayed his opposition within the SSP before deciding to leave and set up Solidarity (although that in itself indicated the limits to this outmaneuvering and outplaying).[212] The outmaneuvering and outplaying resulted from both what Tommy did and from what key SSP leaders did and did not do. In other words, naively as it turned out, they gave him unnecessary latitude, and allowed this to happen.[213] It mattered not that several years down the line that Tommy was convicted of perjury because the colossal damage had been done to the SSP by then and a jail sentence could not undo that. Indeed, although the

SSP believed its position on Tommy had been vindicated, the SSP as a party was far from vindicated as the 2011 Scottish Parliament elections showed.

The now key leadership troika of Alan McCombes, Frances Curran and Carolyn Leckie believed – in Alan McCombes' words – that Tommy was 'a walking, talking timebomb who could be blown up at any time in the future'.[214] This was because he had already told lies that they believed would come undone. It was also because there were known to be other allegations circulating about his sexual behaviour over and above those published by *NoW* in October and November 2004 which it was believed would cause further damage to Tommy because they would show him to be a liar and hypocrite and because of Tommy's insistence on suing *NoW* for defamation.[215] As a result of this, the most appropriate strategy to deal with Tommy would have been expulsion from the SSP in order to wholly dissociate itself from him. The basis of this would have been not only for bringing the party into disrepute as a result of confirming that he would take a defamation action on matters that were substantially true but also in recognition that Tommy was not someone that would abide by the decision of the SSP EC.[216] Remaining an (SSP) MSP of Tommy's stature meant that he continued to have the ear of the media to fight his fight. There is no doubt that this action would have torn the SSP apart and diminished it in the way that did subsequently happen for there was no easy way out of 'Tommygate'. If there was to be a saving grace of cutting Tommy adrift in this way and at this point, it would have been to have done so on the SSP leadership's terms, and to do so as far in advance of the 2007 Scottish Parliament elections as possible, even if the SSP would be seen as the 'party that did Tommy in' (which was until late 2010 how many did see the SSP). This decisive act may have given some time to stabilise and renew the SSP, albeit on a much lower level of influence and organisational coherence (for attaining a replay of 2003 was no longer on the cards in the situation the SSP found itself in).[217] Such an action would have necessitated the publication of the 9 November 2004 EC minute and before the close of 2004. As it was, the manner in which the SSP leadership dealt with the situation ensured that the faction fight with Tommy lasted from late 2004 through to late 2006, and was essentially lost to Tommy (even if all including Tommy were ultimately diminished by it). In that time, the faction fight almost totally consumed the SSP. After 2006, the damage of these years could not be undone and was further compounded by the 2007 electoral wipeout of the SSP (and Solidarity). Subsequently, Alan McCombes reflected that: 'Whether, in retrospect, we should have brought out all the facts into the public domain is a legitimate point of discussion. It would certainly have allowed us to move on and would almost certainly have forestalled the catastrophe of July 2006 ... Perhaps the party would be in better shape if we had gone open at the time, rather than emphasise respect for Tommy's privacy'.[218] He then argued that the SSP should have withdrawn the (parliamentary) whip, and even membership, from Tommy.[219] But instead, the SSP leadership gave Tommy the rope to hang it with.

First, it allowed Tommy to set the public terms of his resignation as national convener by providing his own (false) rationale. The agreement was Tommy's immediate resignation in return for him choosing the reason. In his statements on 11 November, Tommy said it was because he was becoming a dad and, to be a 'good socialist dad', he could not remain SSP leader given the time constraints this would place upon him.[220] The SSP repeated the general thrust of this in its 11 November statement and when questioned maintained the matter was private (like Alan McCombes on BBC Radio Scotland's *Good Morning Scotland* the morning after Tommy resigned). Not only was this completely fictitious and counter-intuitive for a politician and party based on honesty and integrity but worse than that – as the story had no credibility for the resignation came pretty much out of the blue with no evidence of prior ructions or discussions – the media was rightly suspicious, especially with the proximity to the 31 October 2004 *NoW* story. The salience of this was that Tommy could then spin that there was a plot to oust him to an already alerted media (as the *Mirror* did from early on).[221] Moreover, the choice of the SSP, through its *Scottish Socialist Voice*,[222] not to explain matters merely added to the confusion and the ability of Tommy in due course to strike back.

Second, the other side to the compromise agreement that Tommy was forced to resign as SSP national convener if he was to take a defamation action was that once Tommy had resigned as national convener, he then had the right – by this agreement – to take his defamation action. This was a short sighted action on the part of the SSP EC because it gave Tommy some moral high ground about taking the action and did not address the longer term issues, reflecting the mistaken belief that this would be the killer blow against Tommy. In other words, it was firefighting and crisis management which would come back to haunt the SSP EC. As moves towards court action progressed, the sense of righteous indignation and betrayal felt by Tommy at being forced to resign (see Chapter 8) was then heightened by the subsequent attempt by the SSP EC to take away the very *quid pro quo* of what he had been forced to give up for this. The double sense of being spurned merely spurred Tommy on.

Third, both the EC (9, 14, 24 November 2004) and the NC (27 November 2004) agreed not to distribute the 9 November 2004 EC minute to the NC or wider membership, creating ample room for 'dark arts' to be practiced in arenas of membership ignorance like the red herring of claiming a minute should never have been taken and it represented a political conspiracy against Tommy. Circulating the minute could have spiked Tommy's guns very early on for there not only would have been a true record of the meeting but a public record *per se*, thus, preventing Tommy from being able to question its authenticity and existence as he later did.[223] As the court case of 2006 grew nearer, publicly releasing the minute may have been even more devastating to Tommy. Neither would have been without major controversy and division for the SSP was in a 'damned if you do, damned if you don't' situation which either way Tommy would have tried to use to his advantage. The strategy of trying to protect Tommy's privacy and the privacy of internal party affairs led to the SSP EC being branded 'moral commissars' by Iain Macwhirter[224] even though prior and concurrent reports in the *Sunday Herald*[225] clearly showed the dispute with Tommy was not about the morality of the substance of the allegations but about how to politically deal with them. Another version of this was George Galloway's charge of 'Trotskyite Calvinism'[226] and 'a bizarre Scottish Trotskyite sect in the grip of a Wee-Free brand of feminism'[227] or George Kerevan's 'sexual prudes'.[228] Later trying to protect the privacy of internal party affairs also gave Tommy the latitude to launch his plot theory because it always looked like the SSP had something to hide or was trying to hide something. Fourth, by not releasing the minute, the self-confessed party of truth, honesty and integrity[229] of 2006 was shown not only not to be prepared to divulge the whole truth but every attempt to deal with the consequences of not releasing the minute further complicated matters, raised further questions and further tarnished the SSP. These could only be dealt with by releasing the minute. Such conclusions were reached later by both Alan McCombes and Carolyn Leckie.[230]

Fifth, the sworn affidavit given by Alan McCombes to the *Sunday Herald* in November 2004[231] as a result of the paper's insistence to verify the decision taken by the EC on 9 November 2004 to ask Tommy to stand down immediately – but which contained no details about Tommy's sex clubs visits or the minute – was intended to torpedo Tommy's fabrication of a plot to bring him down. Instead, it was used by Tommy' supporters to stunning effect at the SSP NC of 28 May 2006. The NC voted to ditch existing SSP policy and support Tommy. The front page of the *Sunday Herald* that day was headlined: 'Revealed: secret record of meeting that felled Sheridan and led to imprisonment of SSP official' and indicated that an unnamed but senior SSP official had given the affidavit. It did not contain new or substantive information concerning 9 November 2004 (although that was not known at the time) but stimulated an extraordinary meeting of a Highlands SSP branch at a service station on the A9 on the way down to the Glasgow meeting that day where an emergency motion was passed condemning the affidavit which was then presented and passed as an emergency motion to the NC. This set the tone for the defeat of the SSP EC leadership at that NC. No one except Alan McCombes (and Carolyn Leckie[232]) knew who the affidavit was from but it was assumed to be from a critic of Tommy trying to point a loaded gun at Tommy's head, thus contravening the self-imposed ordinance that no one from the SSP should speak to the media about 'Tommygate'. The fact that Alan McCombes was in jail at that time of the NC, defending the SSP's right not to be forced to hand over its minute to the court and, thus, *NoW* (and, therefore, protecting Tommy) became, in the fever of the meeting, irrelevant at best and at a liability at worst (given that the legal costs incurred in the 'defiance strategy' of not handing in the minute could bankrupt the SSP). The affidavit could not have been used in this way if the minute had been circulated as normal and rather than clarify matters, which was the intention, it muddied them. Indeed, the affidavit would not have been needed if the minute had been circulated. Ironically, the affidavit had been intended as an insurance policy against Tommy's course of action by stating that the details would be put in the public domain if need be.

Sixth, it was a mistake not to seek to overturn the key votes for Tommy and his supporters of the 28 May 2006 NC at the subsequent NC. With these votes, those within the SSP decrying Tommy's fast approaching defamation action could be met with the easy and robust retort that the SSP had given Tommy its support. Querying that statement made Tommy's opponents look like only agreeing with party democracy so long as it led to the right outcome (no matter the extraordinary nature of the 28 May 2006 NC). Indeed, as Alan McCombes recounted, it was 'a serious tactical mistake'[233] to not do so. He suggested that taking the 18 June 2006 SSP EC motion (which was passed) to the following NC on 25 June 2006 would have, in effect, overturned the decisions of the 28 May 2006 NC because to oppose the EC motion would have meant openly calling for witnesses to lie in the forthcoming court case. But in the SSP EC, it was believed best to try to avoid another rerun of the inflammatory and traumatic 28 May 2006 NC, especially, as Alan McCombes put it, because the passed EC motion calling on cited SSP witnesses to tell the truth in court would be sufficient. This motion stated: 'In response to direct questions in court, those cited should not lie or commit contempt of court' and was passed by 17:2 with one abstention.[234]

Tommy campaigning against the poll tax outside the Scottish Labour Party recall conference in Govan, 1988.

Addressing a protest to stop a pounding in Lasswade, Midlothian.

Tommy addressing the first Scottish Anti-Poll Tax Federation conference.

Tommy and Gail

Tommy with SSP candidates for the 1999 Scottish Parliament election.

With actor Peter Mullan on demonstration in Glasgow

Tommy with Colin Fox during the 2003-2003 firefighters' strike.

Addressing the Calton Hill 'Independent Scottish Republic Declaration', 9 October 2004.

Tommy celebrating the election of Colin Fox as SSP national convener, Perth City Halls, 13 February 2005.

Tommy outside the old Scottish Parliament building in October 2002.

By these actions alone, Tommy was allowed the latitude to go on the offensive and begin laying the foundations for his 'tower of lies', to use Alan McCombes' phrase of a Dundee SSP meeting of 16 November 2004.[235] Furthermore, members were vulnerable to Tommy's arguments in the absence of such information from the minute. With Tommy's far better access to, and friends in, the media, it was his arguments that members and the wider public heard most widely. The fact that Tommy dealt directly with the media, unlike other party leaders, was a considerable advantage here. These strategic errors were compounded by the strategy of refusing to hand over the (genuine) EC minute of 9 November 2004 to the court prior to Tommy's defamation case. This allowed Tommy to give some credence to the fake minute. None of this is to detract from the fact that it was Tommy that was the creator and instigator of the train wreck the SSP then became. Neither is it to ignore that this was a wholly unprecedented situation to be in where the learning curve was almost vertical or that hindsight is a great thing. Equally well, the SSP leadership found itself between a 'rock and a hard place' over, for example, the minute. If it handed it to the court, it would be accused of state collusion. If it did not, it faced bankruptcy. (However, this situation was a result of keeping the minute secret.) Yet, as the phrase, 'all's fair in love and war' testifies to, the SSP leadership fought a war where it misguidedly kept one of its hands tied behind its back. The SSP leadership lacked the killer instinct that Tommy had – it lacked his *modus operandi* of 'who dares wins' and 'will to power'. It had compunction where he had none.[236] It was slow to realise this was a fight to the death. It ended up in the worst of all worlds – split, reduced in numbers, pilloried and ridiculed in the media press, and standing accused of killing the goose that laid the golden egg but with no comeback.

The wider context to understanding the outcome of this civil war concerns the nature of the SSP. It necessarily played to the rules of the media game of having one recognisable leader before and after Tommy's election to the parliament. To not have Tommy as *de facto* leader given he was the party's only MSP would have been lunacy. However, it is not as simple as then merely concluding that the SSP put all its eggs in one basket until 2003 as the media often did. There were many other capable individuals at a senior level but the party at that point was run by a very small collective leadership. Essentially, and up until early, 2003 it was run at this level by the troika of Alan McCombes, Allan Green and Tommy. This meant that come the mother of all internal battles, there were too few individuals of stature to provide a sufficiently large counter-weight to the pro-Tommy forces. More widely, the layer of cadres underneath the EC was insufficiently large, organised and developed to act independently and withstand the barrage from Tommy. And, underneath these, the members were equally not sufficiently developed in terms of consciousness to do so either. The slow disintegration of the ISM platform was an aspect of this. So while the SSP was not a vanguard party of the Leninist model, its leadership was a tiny, centralised vanguard with extremely high levels of political authority. Matters were little changed by the election of five other MSPs in May 2003.[237] Indeed, as the centre of gravity of the SSP moved into the Parliament following this, the degree of separation of the leadership from activists and members was maintained if slightly reconfigured and extended.[238]

Conclusion

Tommy risked everything in taking his defamation action and then representing himself. This showed the extent to which he knew his public persona would be wrecked by the unmasking of his sexual proclivities. He risked his personal and political future by taking the case, and by sacking his legal team (and, thus, dispensing with the 'no win, no fee' arrangement), he risked his financial future too. Bankruptcy would have led to his ejection from the Scottish Parliament. Tommy not only celebrated his victory in his usual bombastic terms of a modern-day David versus Goliath battle but he also hailed it as a victory against lies, hypocrisy and press intrusion and for workers, trade unionists and socialists. Thus, the *Mirror* greeted Tommy's victory with its front page headline of 'Working class hero'.[239] Meanwhile the *Sun* entitled one of its articles on his victory as 'A working class hero ... but finished in politics'.[240] Unfortunately, there was rather more substance to the *Sun's* observation than Tommy and many others thought at the time. Even if the perjury investigation was not set in train, the intense wall-to-wall media coverage of his sexual activities of November 2004, May 2006 and July-August 2006 meant that the 'red in the bed' (rather than 'reds under the beds') stories would damage Tommy. And maybe he realised, that in his own words, 'throw enough muck ... [and] some of it would [be] bound to stick'.[241] Indeed, one political commentator observed that despite winning his 'credibility was very seriously wounded'.[242] For a politician whose reputation was based on honesty and integrity, this was not good. But for the moment, it seemed that David's victory over Goliath by 7:4 was enough to allow Tommy to continue as Scotland's foremost socialist politician. He took the further risk of establishing a new political party just eight months before the next Scottish Parliament elections. For him the SSP's destruction to allow all of this was just collateral damage. One of the many ironies for the SSP was that most on either the pro- or anti-Tommy wings of the party thought its first major crisis would be over the conditions for entering a coalition government with the SNP. The danger Tommy faced was that even if he won the case his reputation for honesty and integrity could, nonetheless, be undone.

Notes

1. Arguably, 'Tommygate' ran from before 2004 given the circulation of stories about him on the grapevine. It will no doubt run until after 2011 as well (see Conclusion).
2. This quote from Tommy was not gained directly from him but from others (and whose veracity was corroborated through triangulation). Other quotes from Tommy which were sourced in the same way are indicated by double inverted commas.
3. The term 'allegations' is placed in inverted commas for the Cupids visits are not allegations but attested facts.
4. This was said to a number of then close comrades like Alan McCombes, Keith Baldassara, Richie Venton and Colin Fox and repeated at the 9 November 2004 SSP EC meeting (see minute of that meeting)'.
5. *Herald* 22 July 2006.
6. The issue of why there is a case for examining the private and sex lives of Tommy Sheridan is made in Chapter 8. See Archibald, D. 'Carry on comrade? No, hold on a minute' *The Drouth*, 21, summer 2006, for another account of some of the events and issues.
7. Militant at the time regularly discussed using the courts to defend itself given the attacks it came under in the media. This component of its political culture helps explain why the argument of not using the capitalist courts on principled grounds was not strongly debated over Tommy's actions. On at least seven occasions between 1983 and 1986, Militant used the courts or lawyers to defend itself (see Crick, M. *The March of Militant* (Faber and Faber, 1986)). The reason why the SWP jettisoned its longstanding belief that socialists cannot gain justice in capitalist courts is explained elsewhere in the chapter.
8. Former Militant member, Alex Wood, recalled: 'Militant excused its dishonesty about its own existence by stating that it told the truth to the working class but lied to the enemies of the working class within the Labour bureaucracy' (*Scottish Review* 20 January 2011). It may be inferred that Militant's political philosophy permitted certain types of lying.
9. Some of this detail is recounted by Tommy in the McNeilage tape.
10. The denial of a visit in 2001 is intriguing as Tommy had previously told George McNeilage and Keith Baldassara, amongst others, that he had visited Cupids then. For example, George recalled that at small party of close friends, he spoke to Tommy about Cupids, with Tommy saying: 'I was fucking stupid, man … I was there in 1996 and 2001 … I was fucking daft'. In the 2010 perjury trial, Barbara Scott recounted: 'He said that it was him and that he had gone to [Cupids] … but that it had not been on the dates that they said in the newspaper, that it had been two different dates …' (*Herald* 5 October 2010, see also *Herald* 30 October 2010). Alan McCombes shed some light on the issue of 2001 and 2002 (see *DTTSS* pp. 163–164).
11. Later, Tommy would also claim he was fighting the fight against *NoW* for others who were voiceless and powerless (*Scotsman* 5 August 2006, *Herald* 19 August 2006).
12. 19 November 2004.

13. *SSP All-members Bulletin* 'Crisis in the party: the fight for the truth', August 2006, p. 6.
14. *SSP All-members Bulletin* 'Crisis in the party: the fight for the truth', August 2006, p. 6.
15. *Sunday Herald* 14 November 2004, 28 May 2005, 1 January 2006, 29 January 2006, 21 May 2006, 6 August 2006, 26 December 2010.
16. Of course, Tommy could not discuss or debate the terms of this dispute in public for it would torpedo his fabrication strategy (see later).
17. *Herald* 27 November 2004.
18. 15 November 2004.
19. These are the key dates of publication because once a defamation action was initiated by Tommy the nature and dynamics of the battle significantly changed so that far more was then at stake and the terrain of the battle changed too. Thus, for example, material like the Moat House sex party was brought in. These points were all the more true once Tommy won in 2006. To put it bluntly, *NoW* was after revenge *after* being turned over, and this would likely be true no matter who had achieved this.
20. *Herald* 13 November 2010.
21. The progenitor of the latterly broadly Sheridan supporting Socialist Unity blog, Andy Newman, wrote: 'I have never believed that the News of the World specifically targeted Sheridan because he was a socialist. They went for him just because he was a politician and they could, and it would sell newspapers' ('The power of the Murdoch empire' *Socialist Unity* 3 January 2011). He also argued in this article: 'I have always argued though this [i.e. suing *NoW*] was a mistake'.
22. *Cf. Scotsman* 6 October 2006.
23. See below.
24. *Guardian* 4 October 2006. Tommy was actually the source of the original claim, saying: '... after the court case Mr Murdoch himself at a meeting said he didn't care how long it takes, he wants that little commie bastard destroyed' (*Guardian* 4 October 2006). His evidence was that a source at the BBC has told him of Murdoch's comments at that meeting (Rogers, N. 'A tale of two rallies' *Weekly Worker* 7 September 2006). Nonetheless, Lynn Sheridan subsequently restated the case of perennial victimisation on the occasion of the implosion of *NoW* in early July 2011: 'We [the Sheridan family] have said all along that the News of the World were out to get Tommy ...' (Defend Tommy Sheridan Campaign website statement, 8 July 2011) even though the Defend Tommy Sheridan Campaign (website, 19 July 2011) then stated the meeting took place after Tommy's 2006 defamation case victory (but added that the embellishment that the meeting was specifically held about Tommy and was attended by all editors and reporting staff at *NoW* and associated titles). Alan McCombes questioned what evidence there was for the original claim (see *DTTSS* p. 242).
25. *Guardian* 4 October 2006.
26. 'Who is pulling the strings?' Solidarity website, 16 December 2007.
27. *Herald* 27 January 2011. Gail Sheridan (*Scotland on Sunday* 25 February 2007) also proffered that *NoW* had been after Tommy for years.
28. See also Osler, D. 'The fall of Tommy Sheridan' (David Osler blog, 23 December 2010).
29. The information from George Kerevan (see Chapter 5) about the SSP being seen as a threat is not *prima facie* evidence of a conspiracy against Tommy because not only was it about the SSP rather than him but the attack, Kerevan said, would come from the political parties, Labour in particular, who were now going to pay the SSP more critical attention after they felt the SSP had had an initial easy ride.
30. *Sunday Herald, Sunday Mail* 28 November 2004, *Scottish Socialist Voice* 3 December 2004.

31. According to Keith Baldassara and George McNeilage, Tommy told them he had been to Cupids in 1996 and 2001 but he subsequently denied the 2001 visit to the 9 November 2004 meeting. The 2006 and 2010 trials hinged on visits in 1996 and 2002. The 2001 visit was corroborated to Keith by Gary Clark.

32. Tommy told the court: 'I am a socialist politician who believes he has a reputation for honesty, integrity and hard work' (*Guardian* 3 August 2006).

33. *Herald* 23 June 1992. Alan McCombes believed Tommy introducing information about his relationship with Khan was 'a pre-emptive strike' (*DTTSS* p. 78).

34. Just for the avoidance of any doubt, this is not the same as saying there was any plot or conspiracy initiated by *NoW*, the establishment or the state to 'get' Tommy as he and his supporters alleged for, as explained in the chapter and elsewhere, there was no concoction of evidence regarding Cupids etc for the purpose of 'doing in' Tommy.

35. In this regard, Stephen Smellie, longstanding socialist and union activist (see *ATTR* p. 71) believed Tommy was 'in the privileged position of being able to represent his class ... [as a result of] the efforts of hundreds of comrades who worked hard to advance the socialist case ... With this privileged position came responsibilities [including] *conducting yourself appropriately* [emphasis added] and remembering that you are a comrade among equals, not a personality above others ... He didn't live up to these responsibilities and betrayed his privileged position by believing that his behaviour and his personal position was above criticism from his comrades and that his personal interests, profile and position were more important than the cause he represented' (personal correspondence 15 June 2011).

36. The taping is not completely without precedent. First, Tommy attempted unsuccessfully to clandestinely tape a meeting with the then leader of Strathclyde Regional Council, Charles Gray, during the early 1990s (*Herald* 28 March 2007). Second, Derek Hatton taped a meeting with Neil Kinnock so that when Kinnock presented a version of the meeting afterwards to the media that bore little resemblance to the one that had actually taken place, Hatton was able to expose him (see Hatton, D. *Inside Left – the story so far,* Bloomsbury, 1988, p. 108.)

37. *Herald* 9 October 2006. See also McNeilage, G. 'You traitor! Why I'm mad at Tommy' *NoW* 1 October 2006, p. 7.

38. *STV News* 9 October 2006.

39. Underestimating the significance of the tape, Tommy believed the payment was £20,000 (*Herald* 4 October 2006). In an exchange on *STV* (9 October 2007) with Tommy, George McNeilage revealed only that it was an 'ironic' figure.

40. Tommy attempted to use the fact that the tape was edited in this way as an indication that it had been tampered with, so calling into doubt its veracity, in his 2010 perjury trial (*Herald* 9 November 2010).

41. Tommy's charges of hypocrisy against Alan and Carolyn for having a relationship since 2000 while Alan was married and not separated (until 2003) missed the point: neither were public figures of Tommy's standing, nor party leader (and with a certain cultivated image).

42. *Channel 4 News* 3 October 2006, *Daily Record* 4 October 2006, *Herald* 19 October 2006.

43. Ironically, the *Sun* (13 October 2011) commented: 'If when the Scottish Socialist maverick was confronted about whether he'd been up to naughties at sex clubs he'd had the courage to say yes, to look his accusers in the eye and tell them to grow up, to shrug that everyone had consented and no one had got hurt, the whole scandal would have been a two-minute wonder'.

44. An example would be to say: 'I will treat the allegations with the contempt they deserve'.

45. Tommy's willingness to take action over 'allegations' about his sexual behaviour can be contrasted with his unwillingness to take – and absence of – legal action on previous occasions (see Chapters 4 and 5). It may be concluded that Tommy believed – for reasons outlined in this chapter – that these 'allegations' posed a greater risk to his reputation and influence than any other of the accusations (see Chapters 4 and 5).
46. *Scotsman* 5 November 2010.
47. *Daily Record* 3 August 2006.
48. 12 August 2007.
49. *Sunday Herald* 29 January 2006.
50. George McNeilage (*Herald* 6 November 2010) recounted that Tommy told him that he had to take the defamation action 'because it blocks anything else coming out'.
51. *Sunday Herald* 26 December 2010.
52. These relate to stories of sexual relationships with Laura Smith and Marion McGinlay (*NoW* 26 December 2010, 30 January 2011) but could also relate to the allegation that a well-known football manager was a participant in Tommy's sexual adventures (*Daily Record* 24 December 2010). Alan McCombes believed there were other cases but he thought these unlikely to become public as the women concerned did not wish to become subjects of media attention and scrutiny.
53. *SSP All-members Bulletin* 'Crisis in the party: the fight for the truth', August 2006, p. 5.
54. *Scotsman* 5 November 2010.
55. Further analysis of Tommy's motivation for taking the defamation action is to be found in Chapter 8.
56. Tommy admitted that the threat to sue *NoW* was 'just bravado' until he heard of the 'no win, no fee' system (*Daily Record* 7 August 2006). This was introduced to him by the National Union of Journalists (of which he was a member) and its lead organiser in Scotland, Paul Holleran, who was also a witness for Tommy in both the 2006 and 2010 court cases.
57. Alan McCombes cast doubt on Tommy's denial of knowing Fiona McGuire (*DTTSS*, pp. 166–173). Colin Fox recalled that at various times in conversations with Tommy, Tommy moved from stating he had never met McGuire to he had met her once to he had met and spoken to her on several occasions.
58. While such swinger stories about Tommy had been circulating amongst the media long before they appeared in print (*Herald* 6 July 2006), the 2006 and 2010 court cases revealed that there was resistance from Fiona McGuire and Anvar Khan to providing the kind of evidence the *NoW* wanted for them, thus, delaying their publication.
59. *Independent* 27 July 2007.
60. His performance at the special SSP NC of 28 May 2006 was exceptional for his purposes. Here, and on many other occasions, he touched nerves and pressed buttons that appealed to rather un-progressive political traits amongst some SSP members.
61. For example, he maintained to most of his supporters that he was fighting on the grounds of the Fiona McGuire story and did not mention that he would also introduce the Moat House events (see *DTTSS* p. 178).
62. For example, he tried different tactics with each of the six activists' signatories of a letter to *Scottish Socialist Voice* (25 August 2006) in individual meetings with them in 2005. With Nicky McKerrell, it was a more political tact (against *NoW*) and with Liam Young and Jim McVicar, more the force of 'inherent' male human heterosexual nature.
63. This analogy, however, does not seem to extend to personal misdemeanors which could taint the union if they were defended. In these situations, it has been wiser to elect a new steward and move on (as workplace unions have done).

64. As Tommy regarded it as unnecessary, he was not active within it. It was also the case that many ISM members agreed with Tommy that it was not appropriate for the SSP national convener to be an active in a particular platform.

65. One example was the debate over equal representation for women in the selection of election candidates – the so-called '50:50' debate.

66. Thereafter, he appears to have settled psychologically speaking on being on a permanent (internal) war footing.

67. The SSP's plurality and polyarchy, unlike democratic centralist organisations like SML, arguably made it easier for an individual like Tommy to operate in the post-November 2004 period because he could make pitches to different extant groups and sections.

68. See *Daily Record* 7 August.

69. An activist in Edinburgh who became the key independent supporter of Tommy in the Lothians before and after the split. He and others including Steve Arnott (formerly of Militant and the ISM) would form the *DGS* network to give non-CWI/SWP aligned Solidarity members a collective voice and focus. *DGS* began as an online magazine on 1 May 2008.

70. *Sunday Herald* 2 January 2011. On his 24 December 2010 radio show, Galloway said: 'He lied about his sex life and sexual proclivities ... As I advised Tommy at the time ... if you have slept with any other woman, then your libel case will fail ... libel can only work if your contention is that the statements made in the article have lowered your reputation. But if you are an adulterer ... then you cannot claim that the false allegation that you slept with Miss A has ruined your reputation, because you have no reputation in that respect. ... So, I think they do it, they [politicians] sue, to defend their political position. They would be far better saying, 'This is untrue ... but I am not suing because to do so would be to open up the entirety of my personal life" (see also *Sunday Herald* 2 January 2011). This contradicted his *Daily Record* (27 December 2010) column on his 'reasonable doubts' over the conviction.

71. *Independent* 25 May 2001, *Herald* 2 November 2002.

72. *Scotland on Sunday* 6 August 2006. He repeated this again later (*Herald* 9 August 2006).

73. This raises questions about how far his supporters were prepared to go to cover for him in terms of their morality and political reasoning despite the fact they knew the 'allegations' to be true. Some of their critics asked would they have supported Tommy if he had been a rapist or murderer.

74. See Gonzalez, M. 'The split in the Scottish Socialist Party' *International Socialism*, 112, 2006.

75. See *Sunday Herald* 13 August 2006. Prominent SWP member, Richard Seymour, commented: '[M]ost of his defenders consider that this [taking the defamation action] was a crazy thing to have done' *Lenin's Tomb* blog, 23 December 2010.

76. *Socialist Worker* 20 November 2004.

77. In its third Internal Bulletin for its 2008 conference, the SWP Scottish Steering Committee argued: '[I]n many ways [the splits'] origins lay in internal conflicts among members of the Militant group ... The split with Sheridan was the pretext [for] ... a deep and insoluble political disagreement over the kind of political strategy appropriate to this period'.

78. These were the SWP's primary criticisms of the SSP before the split. This desire proved not to be the attainable in the SWP terms by late 2007 (*Herald* 22 December 2007) and thereafter Solidarity became little more than a 'defend Tommy Sheridan' organisation.

79. Esme Choonara, the then SWP full-timer in Scotland, argued at the 27 November 2004 NC that socialists should, on principle, lie to the media.

80. In subsequent Scottish and British publications, the CWI rather the SWP gave more favourable regular and extensive coverage to the 'vendetta' against Tommy.
81. According to Keith Baldassara, when the SSP gained 6 MSPs, Tommy said he 'would do in the SWP' as the party would be financially independent.
82. See Stott, P. 'Lessons from the SSP experience' *Socialism Today*, April 2006.
83. Philip Stott cited reasons such as courts being difficult arenas to gain justice in and the superior resources of News International. He also believed Tommy should have made 'no comment on the allegations and left it at that'.
84. Socialist Party Scotland press release, 23 December 2010.
85. Some examples are the phone message to Tommy wishing his mother died from cancer on 3 October 2006 (*Mirror* 2 March 2007, *TST* 4 November 2010), burning an effigy of him at an SSY camp (*Mirror* 25 August 2006), threats of violence (like 'You're a dead man!') and violence at the Lothian's SSP region members meeting in Dalkeith on 5 August 2006 (see also *Herald* 7, 8 August 2006), threats of violence towards an NUJ full-time official, on-line threats of violence (*Sunday Herald* 6 August 2006), violence between two prominent United Left and SSP Majority supporters in Musselburgh (*Sunday Herald* 20 August 2006) and the taunting of a child of Graeme McIver, Solidarity national secretary, that his father was going to go to jail for perjury. This was followed by the alleged taunting of Gail Sheridan at the Glasgow North East by-election count in November 2009 of Gabrielle growing up with an absent father.
86. *SSP All-members Bulletin* 'Crisis in the party: the fight for the truth', August 2006, p. 3.
87. *Herald* 21 July 2006.
88. *Sunday Mail* 12 June 2011.
89. For example, Tommy claimed in a pre-recorded interview on *STV News* 23 December 2010 that the SSP EC discussing lying was an indication of the political conspiracy against him which involved constructing and telling lies. While it is true that the EC did discuss lying, the discussion was whether the EC members should be prepared to enter a court and lie for Tommy. The discussion concluded that EC members should not be prepared to do so.
90. *Scotland on Sunday* 25 February 2007.
91. *Herald* 3 November 2010. In *DTTSS* (pp. 128–130) Alan further suggested Tommy was the culprit.
92. See Armstrong, A. 'The Sheridan perjury trial' *Emancipation and Liberation*, 20, 2011, p. 27.
93. In the 2010 court case, Charlie McCarthy stated he had a conversation with Tommy in which he suggested the (actual) minute be given to Tommy and that Tommy had 'jumped on that' and said he would produce a 'basic minute' that contained only who had attended the meeting and what decisions had been made' (*TST* 4 November 2011). McCarthy made the same points in his internal SSP statement of 12 August 2006 (see also *NoW* 20 August 2006). McCarthy was not a member of the United Left and as he made clear he was politically close to Tommy. The connection between Tommy and the fake minute may also be highlighted by it being 'grammatically poor' (*Sunday Herald* 26 December 2010) and his open letter of 28 May 2006 being of a similar state. In the latter, the syntax was appalling, 'principle' was confused with 'principal' thrice and Alan McCombes' last name spelt as 'McCoombes'.
94. It seems logical to conclude that calling for the minute to be handed in necessitated rubbishing it and the furnishing of a fake one (when one considers which party would stand to benefit from such an event).
95. 7 August 2006.

96. Allegations of witness tampering and intimidation (*Sunday Herald* 20 May, 6, 26 August 2007) did not lead to charges. See also *DTTSS* pp. 180–181.
97. 4 December 2004.
98. *The Socialist* 10 August 2006.
99. *Daily Record* 7 August 2006.
100. *Politics Scotland*, STV 1 June 2006.
101. Later, and from a different perspective, writer and activist, Kevin Williamson, asked a similar question in his letter of resignation from the SSP (21 August 2006).
102. *Socialist Worker* 20 November 2004, 4 December 2004.
103. *The Socialist* 27 November 2004.
104. *Herald* 22 July 2006.
105. *Evening Times* 25 July 2006.
106. *Evening Times* 25 July 2006. Steve Arnott believed Tommy was 'the key that unlocks the door'.
107. *The Rise and Lies of Tommy Sheridan*, BBC Scotland 23 December 2010.
108. Long-time Tommy collaborators like Keith Baldassara, Alan McCombes, Richie Venton and George McNeilage had shown by their actions they did not seek the limelight and had consciously chosen 'behind the scenes' roles. This is because there is a division of labour where people gravitate towards their strengths, often influenced by their type of personalities and their own wants.
109. This became apparent with reports of these soundings emerging. Richie Venton also recalled: 'Philip Stott and Peter Taaffe met with Tommy prior to May 2006 and persuaded him not to leave the SSP but to put a fight up to expose the 'methods of the cabal' which led to the open letter. The CWI boasted of this in one of their circulars'.
110. *Sunday Herald* 21 May 2006. See Alan McCombes' account of that EC (*DTTSS* pp. 123–124) and the following one on 21 May 2006 (*DTTSS* p. 126). The motion was passed by 14:0.
111. *Sunday Herald* 21 May 2006.
112. *Sunday Herald* 4, 11 June 2006.
113. The release to the media may have also been done with an eye to influencing the jury in his forthcoming defamation action.
114. But his open letter at least admitted the minute existed even if he claimed not to have seen it.
115. This led to a two page response from Carolyn Leckie 'Equal fights' (*Sunday Herald* 4 June 2006) which made the case for feminist socialism, and articles like that by Grant, C. 'Naming women's oppression' *Emancipation and Liberation*, 14, 2007.
116. *DTTSS* p. 141.
117. Through a procedural vote, Tommy was allowed to address the meeting for 10 minutes (while other speakers in the debates were allowed three minutes each).
118. It is interesting to speculate why Tommy called for the minute to be released. This may have been because he believed he would be able to convince the jury it was 'dodgy', that it would be spiked with the fake minute, that it would not "fatally damage" his case and because he believed he could then blame the SSP leadership for helping bring him down. The result of the fake minute was that *NoW* was able to cite 13 SSP members as witnesses for itself. Tommy wrote to all SSP members on 9 June 2006 appealing for support on the basis of 'class solidarity', and was injuncted from further communicating with potential witnesses again (*Scotland on Sunday* 2 July 2006).
119. 9 June 2006. It is interesting that Tommy recognised the 9 November 2004 SSP EC meeting as one which comprised 'private and confidential discussions'.
120. The precursor to this was the 'February 2006 network' which was established in February 2006 (Patterson, R. 'No more heroes' *Red Pepper*, October 2006).

According to Patterson, it 'met every few weeks ... discussed what was happening, shar[ed] stories and theories and ha[d] a good bellyache about it all'. When the United Left was established, it saw itself, Patterson argued, as 'the SSP-within-the-SSP'. An SSP Unite Left leaflet (June 2006) stated it emerged from 'informal meetings' and 'a non-platform platform meeting' at the SSP conference on 5 March 2006.

121. The media picked up on the Orwellian doublespeak and Monty Python-esque irony of names like United Left and SSP Majority. They would shortly also do so with Solidarity. In parliament's toilet humour, Solidarity was named the 'Solids' to match the SSP as 'Trots'. At other times, Solidarity was referred to as 'Squalid-arity'.

122. This indicated that the vast majority of the 2,000–3,000 SSP members were undeclared, with the consequence that the majority stayed with the SSP for being an SSP member was not synonymous with supporting, or being a member of, the United Left.

123. Tommy stated: 'I have no intention of seeking a return to [the] job' (*Scottish Socialist Voice* 25 March 2005).

124. See, for example, *Sunday Herald* 29 January 2006.

125. 22 August 2005.

126. See, for example, *Sunday Herald* 28 August 2005.

127. In early June 2006, George Galloway and Peter Mullan both publicly waded in for Tommy by criticising Colin Fox for being a political lightweight.

128. *Politics Now* 1 June 2006.

129. *Herald* 8 October 2010.

130. As recounted in the next chapter, the charge of attempting to suborn Colin was dropped in the 2010 perjury case for lack of corroborating evidence, with Alex Prentice QC stating 'the withdrawal of the charge is not a reflection on the credibility of Mr Fox [as a witness]' (*Herald* 3 December 2010).

131. Earlier, Tommy had argued: 'You never call someone a grass unless you've very good evidence' (*ATTR* p. 133) when he was called a 'grass' over the 31 March 1990 anti-poll tax demonstration in London.

132. Tommy repeated this accusation after the trial: 'Colin Fox has chosen the wrong side' (*Herald* 7 August 2006).

133. This was recounted by Colin Fox where he recalled that pro-forma letters had been created by Tommy for himself, Richie Venton and Steven Nimmo. See also note 134 in chapter 7.

134. Steven Nimmo, SSP Lothians regional organiser, was asked in a meeting in Burger King at Waverley station in Edinburgh about ten days before the trial to lie. He said he almost felt pulled by the strength of Tommy's argument but refused to countenance lying in court, particularly for fear of the consequences of committing perjury.

135. At a meeting with Allan Green and Colin Fox on 12 May 2006 at the Golden Pheasant pub, Lenzie, Tommy argued that *NoW* was about to concede and the minute should not be handed over. Here, he also argued that he was 'in too deep' financially to stop the defamation case – which jarred with his statements about only being able to take the case, in the absence of legal aid, because of the 'no win, no fee' arrangement. Tommy also argued as late as 1 July 2006 that *NoW* would settle on the steps of the court before the case began. It has not become apparent what the financial consequences were of dispensing with his 'no win, no fee' arrangement.

136. See, for example, *Evening Times* (2 March 2005) with regard to Gail.

137. See before on Anvar Khan making a 'cunt' of herself according to Tommy on the McNeilage tape.

138. Refusing a citation to appear as a witness was not an option on account of legal coercion. Neither was refusing to answer questions on the grounds of contempt of court. At the SSP EC of 18 June 2006, members were instructed to tell the truth in court by a vote of 17 for, two against and one abstention. Tommy had long stopped attending EC meetings but his sister, Lynn, sometimes did.

139. *Sunday Herald* 27 May 2007. Other legal experts concurred with this, stressing his force of personality and oratory – as opposed to legal acumen (*Scotsman* 5 August 2006).

140. *Daily Record* 5 August 2006.

141. Gail also had the gift of the gab and 'showmanship' as she had earlier demonstrated when she said of opting for a Caesarian for the birth of Gabrielle on 30 May 2006 that she was not 'too posh to push' but 'too smart to suffer' (*Scotsman* 1 June 2005).

142. Gail's ability to perform was highlighted by Tommy (*Mirror* 8 September 2004) when he talked of Gail's invitation to perform in a play, saying: 'You'd think she was bloody Bette Davis, Jane Seymour and Doris Day rolled into one. She even insists I call her a thespian'.

143. *Herald* 25 July 2006.

144. *Daily Record* 3 August 2006.

145. This was an obvious fiction because it was Tommy, not the SSP, taking *NoW* to court.

146. *Herald* 22 July 2006. The political basis of this battle was never explained for there were no significant political differences between Tommy and the SSP leadership.

147. *Herald* 27 July 2006. Steve Arnott then went on to suggest the delusion extended to another 139 people (*Radio 4* 5 August 2006).

148. *Daily Record* 22 July 2006. This contradicted his earlier statements in regard to the minute in 2004, which testified that it existed and was genuine.

149. It is a matter of conjecture whether a much shorter summing up would have benefitted Tommy in 2010.

150. *Sunday Herald* 6 August 2006.

151. *Sunday Herald* 6 August 2006.

152. One juror was retired so that he or she could go on holiday. The remaining jury comprised six men and five women.

153. Solidarity ('Who is pulling the strings?' Solidarity website, 16 December 2007) expressed this point as well. So did Bob Bird, editor of the *NoW* Scottish edition when he wondered whether the jurors disliked *NoW* more than Tommy (*Sunday Herald* 8 October 2006). The *Scotsman* (5 August 2006) suggested the outcome was rather more a defeat for *NoW* than a victory for Tommy.

154. This was also the view of advocate, Robert Skinner (*Sunday Mail* 6 August 2006).

155. Even though the formal case was one of Tommy attempting to show that he had been defamed, the trial effectively became one of whether he was guilty or not.

156. 'Tommy: a sex opera' *Journalist*, October 2006. *Journalist* is the magazine of the National Union of Journalists.

157. One small indication of this was that he addressed the jury as 'brothers and sisters' in his closing speech (*Herald* 3 August 2006).

158. It was testament to the strength of Tommy's performance and the buttons he pressed with the jury that it was willing to ignore the evidence of his sexual liaisons with Katrine Trolle despite her testament in the witness box, evidence to corroborate this (such as telephone records and two other witnesses) and because he could not show that she had either a political or financial motive for giving her testimony. A number of senior legal figures in Scotland also supported this line of analysis (*Scotland on Sunday*, *Sunday Herald* 6 August 2006).

159. On 2 August 2006, Tommy made these very points in his summing up (*Scotsman* 3 August 2006).
160. See *Daily Record* 5 August 2006 for Gail's reaction to these.
161. Precedent had, however, been set in this regard in previous defamation cases in England (*Observer* 8 August 2006). The highest previous award in Scotland was £120,000 (*Daily Mail* 5 August 2006).
162. To give an idea of the cost of taking action, if Tommy had lost his legal bill would have amounted to some £250,000 (*Daily Record* 5 August 2006) or £350,000 (*Sunday Times* 6 August 2006). Indeed, the *Mail on Sunday* (6 August 2006) believed Tommy would be in debt to the legal team he sacked to the tune of £100,000 which would not be covered by *NoW* meeting his legal costs as a result of the award against it.
163. *Herald* 4 August 2006.
164. This protection only works if bankruptcy is avoided for five years thereafter.
165. *Scotland on Sunday* 6 August 2006.
166. *Evening News* 4 July 2006.
167. *Scotland on Sunday* 6 August 2006.
168. *Sunday Times* 6 August 2006.
169. *Times* 5 August 2006.
170. In this, he continued his political victimhood strategy by suggesting all the jurors were working class when he would have had no clue as to their social class. However, this would not have mattered given the high propensity for members of the middle class in Scotland still to call themselves 'working class' (see Gall, G. *The Political Economy of Scotland: Red Scotland? Radical Scotland?* (University of Wales Press, 2005), chapter six.
171. This included weeping twice.
172. *Herald* 5 August 2006. Others are documented in the *Sunday Times* (6 August 2006) concerning the calling of witnesses.
173. *Herald* 20 July 2006.
174. If the media, prosecution and police had looked at previous coverage of Tommy's public and reported statements, this and many of others of Tommy' inconsistencies would have been identified. Moreover, if the SSP had been infiltrated by the security services, these inconsistencies would have also become apparent.
175. *Observer* 23, 30 July 2006.
176. *Scotsman* 25 July 2006.
177. *Evening Times* 26 July 2006.
178. *Sunday Mirror* 13 August 2006.
179. *Daily Record* 7 August 2006.
180. *Herald* 22 July 2006.
181. *Herald* 22 July 2006.
182. The deal with the *Record*, even though the money was said by Tommy to have gone to Gail, sits rather uneasily with the claims by his mother and supporters that Tommy 'could not be bought' (see, e.g. *Herald* 27 January 2011). Indeed, in a long interview with the *Sunday Times* (5 August 2007), Tommy expressed regret at doing this deal whilst at the same time saying: 'I've never done an exclusive deal in my life'. On other occasions, Tommy said the money would also be used to fight *NoW's* appeal (e.g. *Scotsman* 9 August 2006). But just as importantly, it invalidated his claim that stories that were bought were necessarily not truthful.
183. *ATTR* p. 210.
184. Indeed, the *Daily Record* (5, 7 August 2006) pretty much declared the party was over for the SSP. The significance of Tommy selling his 'story' to the *Record* is

also to be found in his attack on the CWI for releasing a statement to the media in 2001 – and which was carried by the *Record* (17 January 2001) – which attacked him. Tommy wrote to Peter Taaffe, condemning Taaffe and the CWI, for committing a 'cardinal sin' of putting 'disagreements ... within the socialist movement ... in the hands of the anti-working class, anti-democratic anti-socialist press and media. ... You don't run to our enemies when you fall out with socialists' (in *DTTSS* p. 35).

185. *Sunday Mail* 6 August 2006.
186. 7 August 2006. Once free of internal SSP considerations, Tommy freely labelled the 11 EC SSP 2006 trial witnesses and SSP as 'collaborators' (*Daily Record* 4 October 2006) with Murdoch which was as derogatory as 'scabs'.
187. *Daily Record* 7 August 2006. However, it should be noted that internally Tommy and his supporters had already stated that any SSP members that enter court to testify as a result of a *NoW* citation would be scabs, grasses, traitors and collaborators.
188. A good indication of this was that on 7 August 2006, as one of the defamed 'scabs', Colin Fox phoned some forty key supporters of Tommy in the 'SSP Majority'. He recounted that 'not one of his supporters stood by his claim or his conduct on this'. These included Steve Arnott, Mike Gonzalez, Pat Smith, Jock Penman, Rosemary Byrne, Jim Byrne, Lynn Sheridan, Gill Hubbard, Philip Stott, Sinead Daly and Gary Fraser. Frances Curran failed in her defamation against the *Daily Record/Sunday Mail* because the judged ruled the 'political scabs' attack was not on Frances' 'private character ... but rather on her political decisions and political loyalties' (*Daily Record* 27 March 2010).
189. See *Herald* 8 August 2006.
190. *Herald* 8 August 2006.
191. 7 August 2006.
192. Sheridan, T. 'A personal message from Tommy Sheridan' 5 August 2006.
193. *Herald* 8 August 2006.
194. 19 August 2006.
195. 19 August 2006.
196. *BBC Scotland* 23 December 2010.
197. *Sunday Herald* 20 August 2006.
198. BBC Scotland *Off the Ball* 19 August 2006 (as reported in *Sunday Express* 20 August 2006).
199. See *Scotsman* 14 August 2006, *Press and Journal* 17 August 2006.
200. *Herald* 9 August 2006. For example, an SSP Majority letter (8 August 2006) to all members, and signed by Tommy, called upon supporters to organise themselves for the 27 August 2006 NC and the brought forward annual conference (of October 2006).
201. The key issue of morality and ethics here concerned lying, and its why, when and wherefore. Tommy and his supporters believed that lying in a capitalist court against a capitalist was acceptable socialist practice and not equivalent to lying to workers. In this regard, Steve Arnott believed it was an honour to testify for Tommy in 2006 and that there was only 'one socialist truth', namely to stand on the side of a socialist against the enemies of socialism (Rogers, N. 'A tale of two rallies' *Weekly Worker* 7 September 2006) while Peter Mullan (*Sunday Times* 27 August 2006) believed the 'truth ... can never [be] divorce[d] from its context' thus legitimatizing the telling of untruths. In 2006, Tommy spoke at the Paisely SSP branch and used the simile of asking for support for his denial strategy to maintain himself as a leading socialist to that of not 'shopping' – or abetting the prosecution of – a striking miner who had thrown a brick at the police. (This approach was rejected at the branch.) Critics of

Tommy and his supporters argued not only that truth and integrity were rather more absolutes than this but lying in this arena was tactically inept and naive. However, the issue was not always as clear cut as Colin Fox made clear in court with regard to the operating in the court of public opinion (see *Scotland on Sunday*, *Sunday Herald* 6 August 2006). See also Chapter 8 on the relationship between means and ends.

202. The conference was brought forward from March 2007 at the request of Tommy. This was agreed by the SSP EC in order to try to bring closure to the situation for elections for all national office bearers are held at annual conference including those of national convener and members of the SSP EC.

203. *Daily Record*, *Herald* 7 August 2006.

204. *Scotland on Sunday* 6 August 2006.

205. Coverage of the split again indicated the inability or unwillingness of the media to seriously probe the issues. Instead, they uncritically took their cue from Tommy's statements.

206. *Scotsman* 19 August 2006, *Sunday Herald* 20 August 2006 (see also *Socialist Worker* 2 September 2006). Tommy pronounced Solidarity 'will exist as of tomorrow' (*Herald* 2 September 2006). He also informed the media of Solidarity's founding before the CWI and SWP had time to discuss amongst themselves whether to join, effectively, bouncing them into doing so.

207. Sheridan, T. 'The future of socialism in Scotland' 16 August 2006.

208. *Daily Record* 4 September 2006.

209. *Herald* 2 September 2006, *Observer* 3 September 2006. This seemed a rather desperate means of justifying room for two socialist parties in Scotland. It was also rather bizarre as socialist parties seek to target – in elections – the most class conscious of workers, these being the ones that are sufficiently conscious as to vote.

210. *Herald* 5 April 2007.

211. While some of the leading protagonists like Alan McCombes and Frances Curran had prior experience of faction fights, these were over programmatic issues and political ideals. Such experience did not necessarily lend itself quite so easily to engaging in a faction fight which was devoid of such content (even if the organisational means of doing so were more similar).

212. Interestingly, if Tommy had believed in his own fabrication at the time of late 2004, he would have jumped at the occasion of the SWP seeking to give him an opportunity to regain the national convenership by supporting the debating of its motion at the 12 December 2004 NC (see *Sunday Herald* 12 December 2004).

213. There was disagreement within the SSP leadership about how to best deal with Tommy. On one side, Alan McCombes, Frances Curran, Carolyn Leckie and Keith Baldassara believed the best way to neutralise Tommy's potency was by isolating him from other members (albeit not by expulsion). On the other side, Colin Fox and Richie Venton believed that a constructive dialogue was the best way to get Tommy to compromise (e.g. *Sunday Herald* 30 January, 6 February 2005). Ironically, neither was able to deal with Tommy as he was determined to continue his course of action, showing how ill-informed some analysis was. For example, Mark Hoskisson argued Tommy should have stayed on as SSP leader after agreeing not to go to court and instead mount a campaign to say his sex life was his business and no one else's ('Personality of politics?' *Permanent Revolution*, 2, 2006, p. 32). It is an overstatement to suggest that it only takes one person to pursue a court case but not much of one for Tommy needed (just) a few witnesses but not many.

214. *SSP All-members Bulletin* 'Crisis in the party: the fight for the truth', August 2006, p. 2. Alan McCombes was the bulletin's author (see also *DTTSS* p. 225).

215. Alan McCombes believed some of this would be dependent upon the women concerned wishing to enter the public arena and have their sexual past scrutinised in it.

216. For example, within days of the November 2004 NC Tommy began challenging what was agreed with the EC with his 'What side are you on?' argument and by casting doubts the EC's statements. Calls for expulsion – and other forms of disciplinary action – only emerged in August 2006 (*Cumbernauld News* 17 August 2006, *Herald* 11, 18 August 2006).

217. Following from this, any possibility of the SSP renewing itself would have had a head start on 2011 when the SSP began an internal debate on what it was for and what it should seek to do.

218. *SSP All-members Bulletin* 'Crisis in the party: the fight for the truth', August 2006, p. 7, p. 12. The same point was made in an Executive Committee statement to the SSP special conference of 5 February 2011. Alan McCombes reiterated more strongly his feeling of regret at not being more open in *DTTSS* (pp. 81, 91, 110).

219. *BBC Radio Scotland* 'Good Morning Scotland' 24 December 2010. Disciplinary action against Tommy was never taken or even mooted (*Herald* 21 August 2006).

220. In the *Sunday Herald* (29 January 2006), Tommy returned to the fatherhood argument for the first time since November 2004, giving the impression that he choose to resign on 10 November because of it.

221. 12, 18 November 2004. It was not a coincidence that the *Mirror* led here given that Tommy was a columnist for it and had a number of (his) loyal supporters on its journalistic staff.

222. 19 November 2004.

223. *Sunday Herald* 29 January 2006. Alan McCombes and five other EC members at the 9 November 2004 meeting voted in favour of releasing the minute (via the *Scottish Socialist Voice*) under option 1. Catriona Grant as SSP co-chair advised the minute be made open to members at the time (*Sunday Herald* 6 August 2006). However at the 14 May 2006 SSP EC, a motion to circulate the minute to members (and then had the minute to the court) was defeated by 13:2.

224. *Sunday Herald* 21 November 2004.

225. 14, 21 November 2001.

226. *Scotsman* 5 June 2006.

227. *Daily Record* 27 December 2010.

228. *Scotsman* 18 November 2006.

229. These themes became those of the SSP 2 September 2006 national rally held immediately prior to the launch of Solidarity. Both were held in the same room, a mere 21 hours apart, in the Central Hotel in Glasgow.

230. See interview with Alan McCombes in late 2006 ('Lessons learned and looking to the future') and Leckie, C. 'The SSP, Tommy Sheridan, democracy and women' both in *Frontline*, 2/2, 2006. Allan Green also agreed with this retrospection. Later, Alan McCombes alluded to this in an interview about his account of the events in *DTTSS* (*Scottish Socialist Voice* 10 June 2011). He also admitted to making other mistakes, tactical and otherwise (*DTTSS*, p. 156, p. 312).

231. See *Sunday Herald* 28 May 2006, *Herald* 23 October 2010.

232. Her awareness of it emerged during the 2010 perjury trial. Alan McCombes denied he was the author of the affidavit at the 18 June 2006 SSP EC and, under instruction from the EC, wrote to the *Sunday Herald* seeking confirmation – which it duly did – that it only had possession of the affidavit and not a copy of the 9 November 2004 SSP EC minute (Minutes of SSP Executive Committee Meeting, Sunday 18 June 2006, 1pm Calton Centre Edinburgh, and Green A. 'Info re Emergency Resolution agreed at last NC' 23 June 2006).

233. *DTTSS* p. 155.
234. Minutes of SSP Executive Committee Meeting, Sunday 18 June 2006, 1pm Calton Centre Edinburgh. Those voting for this motion included CWI member, Sinead Daly, and Graeme McIver and Jock Penman (who were both witnesses for Tommy in the 2006 and 2010 court cases). Those voting against were Gill Hubbard of the SWP and Lynn Sheridan. One SWP member, Penny Howard, abstained. Tommy had left the meeting before the vote was taken.
235. *Sunday Herald* 21, 28 November 2004.
236. For example, the *Sunday Herald* (21 November 2004) reported: 'Last week McCombes said he believed Sheridan had behaved honestly and honourably 'in his own terms' ... I believe that Tommy has been honest in relation to how he sees it'. By contrast, at the 28 May 2006 NC Tommy argued for handing in the minute even though he had argued for it to be not handed in a meeting with Allan Green and Colin Fox on 12 May 2006. This U-turn was mimicked by his supporters in the CWI and SWP.
237. The winding down of the SSP's forward momentum became evident in June 2004 when it failed to gain the election of an MEP which it believed it could. For a wider analysis of the problems emerging in the SSP, see Gall, G. 'Hitting the buffers?' *Scottish Left Review*, January/February 2005 and 'Party context in retrospect and context' *Frontline*, 2/2, 2006.
238. After Tommy's departure, the SSP engaged in soul searching to find a way of preventing another 'Tommy'. It decided internal structural changes were the most effective way to do this but this failed to comprehend that internal and external political cultures were more culpable and these could not be significantly amended by such structural changes. Carolyn Leckie's (*Herald* 2 November 2002) comment that the SSP's democratic structures made Tommy but a 'cog in a wheel' was not re-appraised.
239. 5 August 2006. The *Scotsman* (5 August 2006) also observed that Tommy 'climbed back on the plinth marked 'working class hero'' and Andrew O'Hagan believed Tommy was confirmed not just as a 'folk hero' but as a 'national hero' (*London Review of Books* 17 August 2006).
240. 5 August 2006.
241. *Scotsman* 25 July 2006.
242. Trench, A. *The State of the Nations, 2008: Into the Third Term of Devolution in the UK* (State of the Nations Yearbooks, 2008), p. 28.

7

Triumph and Tragedy

Introduction

While Tommy won his defamation case, it quickly turned out to be a hollow and pyrrhic victory. Not only did *NoW* launch an appeal on 11 August 2006[1] but, in his summing up, Lord Turnbull commented that as the two sets of testimonies 'for' and 'against' were so contradictory, conflicting and divergent that one side must be telling lies. Furthermore, a member of the public made a complaint of perjury on 5 August 2006.[2] This set in train the preliminary perjury investigation which began on 2 October 2006, becoming a full one on 20 February 2007, and led to Tommy being charged with perjury on 16 December 2007 (and Gail on 19 February 2008).[3] The subsequent perjury trial put on hold the *NoW* appeal as it was suspended pending the former's outcome but which was re-ignited in early 2011 then put on ice again as Tommy appealed his conviction.[4] But before all that happened, Tommy failed to be re-elected to the Scottish Parliament. And, his defamation victory brought more damaging stories out of the woodwork (regarding Laura Smith, Marion McGinlay and an unnamed other woman[5]), testifying to two famous libel lawyers' comments that: 'If you are going to take a libel action, then you had better make sure your cupboard is free of skeletons' and 'Even when you win, you lose'. After the verdict, the media continued to report on the 'allegations' aired in the defamation case in a way that lent many of them increasing credibility and which continued to damage the victor. Given the key rationales for taking the defamation action – to scotch the original Cupids 'allegations' as well as any other ones concerning Katrine Trolle and the like and to also fire a shot across the media's bow on printing any further allegations about his sexual behavior – Tommy failed in a major way to achieve his objectives. All this made his celebration of 4 August 2006 rather short-lived. Indeed, choosing the analogy of Gretna FC was not a good one for it was dissolved due to massive debts in the summer of 2008, and one letter writer to the *Herald* compared Tommy to world class footballer, Zinedine Zidane, because the latter was 'an iconic individual blowing a reputation built up over years by an irresponsible act'.[6] This chapter examines the period of the birth of Solidarity in 2006 to Tommy entering Barlinnie prison in 2011. The arguments that Tommy used to resist the charge of perjury both inside and outside court were essentially the same arguments he used before but his prosecution of them became even more brutal and warlike and their strength became supercharged as he fought for his political life.

Solidarity

Solidarity was the daughter of a shotgun marriage, born on 3 September 2006 at a packed and sweaty rally of 600–700 people in Glasgow.[7] In a speech that *Socialist Worker* characterised as rather 'downbeat', Tommy argued: 'We may collectively as socialists never realise our dream. We may never deliver the type of society we have burning away in our hearts, but can we say in unison that we will fight with all our ability to discover that type of world regardless of the obstacles?'.[8] Before and after, Tommy variously claimed Solidarity would have 700 members within six months,[9] both 1,000 and 1,500 members within a few months[10] and that it had recruited 700 SSP members,[11] with the SSP regions in the south, north and north east of Scotland mostly going over to it.[12] Previously unfriendly and indifferent to each other political forces of the Sheridanistas, independents, CWI and SWP were thrown together. For example, Tommy was previously no particular admirer or close colleague of Rosemary Byrne but that was put into abeyance.[13] Political and personal expediency of the hour threw disparate forces together. The uniting issue was Tommy – more specifically, it was the view that what Tommy did in his private life was entirely up to him as long as it was consensual and that Tommy was the rock around which the limpets of the genuine socialist forces could not only cling but survive and prosper because Tommy was the most likely of all the SSP MSPs to be re-elected.[14] In Steve Arnott's words: 'Tommy is the key that unlocks the door, he's still the major pole of attraction ... the best chances of building a unified left party in the short-term are with Tommy Sheridan at its centre'. In these circumstances, the figure of Tommy was necessarily elevated to a new height because it was again 'Monte Carlo or bust'.[15] Privately, almost no one in Solidarity at this time denied that Tommy had visited Cupids[16] but the fault line with SSP members was over whether lies should be told and be told to cover for him. A number of SSP members joined Solidarity because they felt compromised by the role they had played in the faction fight and court case. They did not anticipate that such actions would lead to a split – rather, they thought they were fighting for their preferred version of the SSP. It is in this light that the justifications for the split should be seen. There were internal criticisms over the orientation of the SSP from the SWP and CWI, in particular, but until Tommy suggested breaking, there was no talk of those issues that were subsequently used as post-hoc political rationalisations for the split actually leading to a split. Indeed, Tommy did not raise these issues before 2006. The split institutionalised and exacerbated the fault line. Tommy's willingness to split was dependent upon him not being able to personally and politically dominate and lead the SSP as he had done. He proffered this in terms of leaving the trouble behind, starting afresh, and being able to concentrate on politics. For example, he told BBC Scotland: 'If I and others had stayed and fought within the SSP, then by the time of the October conference, we would have inherited a carcass. Because the blood-letting is so deep and so serious that it really is an animal that has run out of steam. It has run out of breath'.[17] In convincing others to join him, Tommy deployed the full force of his persuasive personal and political powers.

In the many rallies Tommy spoke at to launch and build Solidarity, the attendances were large[18] but that did not necessarily translate into recruits and new activists,[19] intriguingly suggesting Tommy's appeal was more as an individual socialist rather than as Solidarity leader,[20] and that his appeal as an individual was as much about his celebrity as it was about his socialism.[21] Indeed, for some attendees there seemed as much attraction to see Tommy as some kind of circus show. Just as importantly, behind all the huff and puff of Solidarity as 'Scotland's socialist movement', it was neither a movement nor a considerable political force.[22] Nor was it a unified party, being made up of the major component of the SWP whose major orientation was the anti-war movement, with the CWI being a minor component which advocated party building based on an explicit commitment to socialism.[23] But this reality did not dent the upbeat talk of looking:

> ahead with confidence and optimism. We continue to grow and become stronger in every region, city, town and village in Scotland, establishing ourselves as the only principled party of the left in Scotland ... we aim to return an MSP in every region of Scotland and a councillor in every local authority. ... 2007 will be the year of Solidarity, the year of fighting back.[24]

The goal of winning 8 MSPs was made at Solidarity's launch and its manifesto launch for the Scottish election on 4 April 2007. Tommy was confident of being returned and Solidarity winning a number of seats[25] even though at that point Solidarity was registering 1% or less in the polls.[26] Part of the problem, according to Solidarity's own commissioned polling, was that voters did not know Solidarity was led by Tommy. Once this was recognised, the commissioned polling suggested voter support would rise somewhat.[27] But there were other issues as well. There was the damaged nature of Tommy and socialism in Scotland as a result of the events of 2004 and after. Tommy proclaiming the Solidarity election broadcast – of him often 'ranting' in his car – as being 'raw and honest' did not overcome this. Neither did George Galloway's vocal and visible support – Tommy was, according to him, the 'most popular, most charismatic, most capable leader on the left in Scotland' and 'a working class hero'.[28] But there was also the matter that Solidarity was not just a young organisation born into inhospitable circumstances. It was also that compared to SML, it was not a unified, embedded cadre organisation that had been built through grassroots struggle. Well attended election rallies with rapturous applause did not translate into the necessary members or votes.

Not Gorgeous George

While 'gorgeous' George Galloway was a vocal and highly public supporter of Tommy, it was another George that was ultimately more significant to Tommy. When the George McNeilage tape emerged, Tommy responded with: 'Another Sunday, another pack of lies. The News of the World's vendetta against me continues ... [it] is a badge of honour'.[29] Tommy gave a number of explanations for why he would not pursue another defamation action against *NoW* for publishing the tape. Whilst saying he was considering an action,[30] he earlier said he could not afford to and he would not be able to gain another 'no win, no fee' deal to do so after sacking his legal team in 2006.[31] He also told *Channel 4 News* there was no point suing *NoW* when he could not get his £200,000 damages from the paper.[32] In responding to the tape, Tommy stated: 'I haven't spoken to Mr McNeilage for at least two years. I don't intend to speak to Mr McNeilage for the rest of my life'[33] but this pledge did not last long. On 9 October 2006, the two went head-to-head on STV's *Scotland Today* news bulletin[34] (with three days of exchanges in the 2010 perjury trial). Claiming: 'I would not be surprised if the state is involved [in the making of the tape] ... When the history of this whole episode is written about, I think you'll find that MI5 certainly was involved' did Tommy no favours.[35] This and the tape itself were highly damaging to him and Solidarity in the run up to the 2007 elections. But Tommy tried to turn the tape to his advantage by deepening his fabrication of victimhood, this time with Gail's role far more prominent. Thus, he deliberately conflated cause and effect by saying: 'Just as they [NoW] will never break me politically and they will not break Solidarity, they will not break Gail and I's relationship either because our sort of love can't be broken'.[36] The release of the tape formed part of a *de facto* rearguard action by some SSP members against the cause and effect of Tommy's defamation trial (including the 'scabs' outburst). Other examples were the public handing into Lothian and Borders police by Barbara Scott of her handwritten minute of the 9 November 2004 SSP EC meeting on 7 August 2006,[37] the public statement by six SSP members of Tommy's confession to them,[38] and an exclusive media interview with Katrine Trolle before leaving to return to Denmark.[39] Indeed, Alan McCombes ventured that a state of 'total war' existed within the SSP.[40]

Down But Not Out

Although he did not show any hurt and despair in front of cameras at the election night count, Tommy was deeply wounded by losing his seat in the 2007 Scottish Parliament elections.[41] Defiance and pride in the form of a fixed smile kept the tears away then but he was in tears about the result when speaking to close supporters away from the media glare. Later, he told the *Daily Record*: 'I'm battered, bruised and bloodied – but still breathing'[42] and Gail said he was 'gutted'.[43] As head of the Solidarity list for the Glasgow list constituency with 8,544 votes, Tommy was some 2,200 votes short of picking up the last list seat there in order to make the vital 5%-6% threshold. This was in stark contrast to his frequent predictions of Solidarity winning more than one seat and him being re-elected.[44] Indeed, the *Herald* believed with a combination of 'local hero status ... which his defamation case ... may well have boosted' and 'his ability to reach beyond normal politics [he] is the best chance ... for avoiding a hard left wipe-out'.[45] No matter that Tommy may have suffered disproportionately from the historically high number of spoilt ballots papers,[46] the blow was a massive one because, since leaving the SSP and establishing Solidarity, his political strategy had been based on him being the only one of the former six SSP MSPs to be returned to parliament, thus, clearing the way for himself – and Solidarity – to become the leading socialist force in Scotland. The hope was that a new socialist political force could be built around him as the SSP had done so between 1999 and 2003. Ironically, despite not achieving this, Solidarity still proudly proclaimed itself to be 'the only credible and viable socialist party in Scotland ... [being] united and determined to carry the torch of socialism in Scotland forward'.[47] Tommy proudly proclaimed Solidarity was now the biggest and best socialist force in Scotland. Solidarity said of itself that it 'emerged as Scotland's leading party of the left ... After only a few short months in existence the Solidarity vote totaled twice as many as the other left parties combined'.[48]

All this was the last refuge of the damned in a night that saw not only any radical socialist presence wiped out from the parliament but the combined Solidarity and SSP vote in the list constituencies come in at only a third of what the SSP achieved in 2003.[49] Yet, it was one that was entirely predictable in a number of aspects. So while radical socialists are well known for staring disaster in the face and calling it a triumph instead because they refuse to give succour to their political opponents, claiming – as Tommy did[50] – the court case and split had no effect on the result was not credible. Instead, Tommy proffered that the reason was that all the small parties were squeezed by the polarisation between the SNP and Labour. While this did happen, it neither explained why the Greens maintained two seats (down from seven) nor why Margo MacDonald retained her seat. But more than anything else, this explanation ignored the force of acrimony of the split and the loss of credibility of the radical left all around.[51] All were brought down by it. Moreover, since late 2004 Tommy was known more for fighting allegations over his personal life than for fighting for socialism. This meant his 'record as a fighter on behalf of his class' was no longer 'impeccable' as Solidarity maintained.[52] Using Tommy's name on the ballot paper for Solidarity was clearly not enough.

The political miscalculation of believing that a phoenix could easily and quickly rise from the ashes was further confirmed and deepened by subsequent electoral forays. This was all the more marked given that Tommy still commanded extensive media coverage whenever he stood. For example, he was able to feed media speculation with a 'Will I stand? Won't I stand?' line for the Glasgow north east by-election on 12 November 2009 prior to his confirmation as the Solidarity candidate. In the event, Tommy came fifth, being beaten by the BNP and losing his deposit with 794 votes (3.9%). But he declared: 'All in all Solidarity can be pleased of its campaign'.[53] In the general election of May 2010, he came fifth and lost his deposit in Glasgow south west with 931 votes (2.9%). In the June 2009 European elections, he stood on the No2EU ticket as the second on the list for the Scottish constituency. No2EU gained just 9,693 votes (0.88%).[54] The only chink of light was that Ruth Black was elected a councillor in Glasgow in the local elections in May 2007 but she then defected to Labour in late 2007, ironically leaving the much atrophied SSP as the only of the two parties to have a councillor

(Jim Bollan in West Dumbartonshire). Despite the odd overture for the SSP to join with Solidarity in a new electoral alliance under the RMT union-led Scottish Trade Unionist and Socialist Coalition banner,[55] there was no prospect of such moves. And, Solidarity as a political project became less of a viable and distinct entity for Solidarity did not always stand under its own banner in elections, its unity of thought and action primarily existed around defending Tommy,[56] and its CWI-affiliate established itself as the Socialist Party Scotland (SPS) in 2010. In the 2011 parliament elections, Solidarity stepped aside to clear the way for George Galloway to stand as the leading left candidate in the Glasgow regional seat. This was only after some considerable acrimony with Galloway when Tommy declared that Gail would stand as the lead Solidarity candidate[57] after Galloway had declined Tommy's offer of Gail standing second on the list to Galloway in a left slate.[58] Galloway declined Tommy's offer because he did not want his candidacy to be a referendum on Tommy's conviction for perjury, and said Solidarity was too leftwing and pro-independence.[59] Gail's candidacy was withdrawn[60] and a deal hammered out which saw Galloway lead the 'George Galloway (Respect) – Coalition Against Cuts' party list, with Solidarity in the form of SWP and SPS members underneath him on the slate.[61] However, Solidarity stood under its own banner elsewhere in Scotland with 'abysmal'[62] results. Gaining just 2,837 votes across seven regions – which would have been a bad result in just a single region in 2007[63] – it was clear that, to paraphrase Tommy: 'The people of Scotland decided Solidarity was not an important part of the future of Scotland'.[64] Solidarity was not shown to Solidarity by the people of Scotland,[65] and its future looked decidedly downbeat and shaky. A meeting on 22 October 2011 in Glasgow initiated by SPS union activists to stand a slate anti-cuts candidates – rather than Solidarity candidates - in the 2012 council elections indicated ever more that Solidarity had become a defunct organisation. A report of this meeting by Philip Stott[66] indicated there was no opposition to this from within Solidarity, and certainly not from its largest formal component, the SWP. Indeed, discussions took place within Solidarity after the May 2011 elections about winding solidarity up. After a plea from Tommy, it was agreed that further discussion to reach a definitive conclusion would be deferred until he was released from prison.

Celebrity Politician

From the ending of the 2006 court case to the 2010 trial, Tommy's allies always pointed out that a key reason why he should be supported was that he had been the leader of the successful poll tax revolt and had fought Thatcher and the Tories.[67] While that assertion that he was such a leader is not open to any doubt, in the period 2006 to 2010 Tommy became far better known for his celebrity activities than any socialist or political activity[68] – with the effect that these eclipsed this former reputation because they did not build upon or reinforce it. Indeed, an analysis of press coverage of Tommy from November 2004 shows more column inches were dedicated to his private life and celebrity status than campaigning political activities. So, for a younger generation who may not have known of his anti-poll tax fame and the like, the celebrity – rather than even 'celebrity politician'[69] or 'personality politician'[70] – was more likely to be the Tommy they saw. The use of the phrase 'The best fighter money can't buy' on his Solidarity election leaflets to describe him did not, thus, strike the chord it once did.[71] Inhabiting the world of celebrity-dom comprised being a participant in *Celebrity Big Brother (CBB)* 2009 for a reputed fee of between £25,000 and £100,000,[72] fighting charity boxing matches,[73] playing celebrity football matches, having his picture taken topless by the renowned photographer, Harry Benson, hosting a number of chat shows at comedy festivals,[74] and feeding the media with stories about these and other aspects of his personal life.[75] His public persona was not the socialist fighter of old and he devalued that with these activities. Even where media coverage was not directly solicited, it still reinforced this new reputation. For example, the media coverage of the 'Will he? Won't he?' enter *CBB* in 2007 concluded with the *Daily Record's* headline of the front page main story of 'Tommy turns down TV offer'.[76] This was not, Tommy said, because it was wrong in principle but wrong in timing[77] as it would damage his reputation as a serious politician in the run up to the 2007 election.[78] All this indicated the media was now far more interested in Tommy the sex scandal persona compared to the politician who promoted a bill for the re-nationalisation of the railways at the time.

The odd chinks of light in this were his *Big Issue Scotland* columns between 2008 and 2009 and his weekend radio shows on Talk107 between December 2006 and April 2008. Here as 'Citizen Tommy', he was allowed the free rein that he could not get on *Celebrity Big Brother*. But Talk107 had a small audience in the east of Scotland and was shut down due to losses incurred as a result of never being able to break out of its ghetto. But at least this brought in some income after he lost his seat and could not get other employment. For example, he tried for the post of political editor of the *Sunday Mail* in the summer of 2007. Between 2007 and 2008, Tommy undertook a Masters in Social Research at University of Strathclyde with a dissertation on military-funded research in universities.[79] This was undertaken with hope of beginning a lecturing career.[80] However, he then began an accelerated LLB law degree at the University of Strathclyde but pulled out from it in early March 2009 to concentrate on his legal defence which took up some three days per week of his time.[81]

Just as there is a valid argument for courting the media as Tommy had previously done in the 1980s and 1990s to promote the socialist cause, there is also a valid argument that with celebrity-isation of politics, socialist politicians need to be careful not to exclude themselves from this arena when trying to promote their political platform.[82] Although the argument that young people are apathetic and not interested in politics is vastly overblown, new and unusual opportunities to have a conversation with them should not be spurned. So there was a valid argument for socialist politicians entering such fora. But, extreme care has to be given to considering on what basis socialist politicians are invited – and willing – to participate in these arenas. Colin Fox alluded to this when he argued Tommy 'has become a celebrity, he has courted it and he has been successful at it. But being a celebrity in itself is not the issue or necessarily a bad thing, it's how you use it and for what ends, whether you pander to it, play to it and feed it'. It was inconceivable that Tommy would have been invited on to *CBB* without the allegations about his sex life, just as it was that he would be given as much time as he wanted to use the programme to broadcast his political views. *CBB*, as with *Big Brother* itself, is about putting people in an enclosed space where, being only concerned with the minutia of their own personalities, they end up fighting amongst themselves like ferrets in a sack. Tommy's involvement with the celebrity-isation of politics deepened the celebrity at the expense of not just the politics but socialist politics in particular. Although he managed to avoid the ignominy of George Galloway,[83] he appeared out of his depth with a younger generation,[84] and any radical or socialist is brought down by appearing on *CBB* – whose *raison d'etre* is making contestants ferrets fighting in a sack – as his own supporters made clear.[85] Viewers' comments on the *CBB* website were favourable to Tommy – but to him as an individual person and not as a politician or socialist.

More widely, it was not that his *CBB* appearance or the chat shows were completely devoid of political content in terms of what he was able and chose to talk about. Rather, it was far more the case that the content concentrated on him as an individual and as a minor celebrity following his 2006 court case. His Edinburgh Festival chat show revelled in his notoriety as a supposed swinger, and he invited on his celebrity friends and acquaintances. Yet even on Talk107, Tommy became a commentator rather than an actual leader or organiser of resistance. What lay behind Tommy's orientation on the media was the perspective that, to quote Oscar Wilde: 'The only thing worse than being talked about is not being talked about'. Here, keeping his name in the public realm did not hinge too much upon what the issue for coverage was. It was almost that all publicity was good publicity.

Perjury Probe

Tommy talked down the possibility of a perjury inquiry despite Lord Turnbull's comments. First, he argued there would be no perjury investigation, claiming that committing perjury was not exceptional and hardly ever prosecuted. Then he argued that if there was to be a perjury investigation, it would be of the other side in the defamation case.[86] Along the way he told *Newsnight Scotland* he had 'nothing to fear' and denied he had any 'personal problems' in his life,[87] and said he did not lose sleep over the inquiry, believing that those who did lie (i.e., not him and his supporters) should not be jailed but receive community service.[88] In the course of this, any criticism of Tommy by his former SSP MSPs was put down by him as 'beneath contempt' and 'lies'. He reserved his utmost venom for Carolyn Leckie, branding her a liar.[89] Tommy and his supporters continually pointed to the cost of the inquiry[90] but this could not detract from the situation that considerable legal and moral sensibilities had been offended by a serving (elected) politician taking *NoW* to court and winning £200,000 in damages as was subsequently proven on the basis of knowingly lying in court in order to do so. Critically, perjury was used to prosecute, not defend.[91] But after an eighteen month investigation, Tommy was charged with perjury on 16 December 2007.[92] Solidarity's reaction was that the charge was the result of a 'colossal vendetta by the Rupert Murdoch empire ... which is rooted in [Tommy's] role as leader of the anti-poll tax movement'.[93] When, on 3 March 2008, Tommy and Gail appeared in private at Edinburgh Sheriff Court charged with perjury, neither made any plea or declaration, and both were released on bail. Thereafter, Tommy hired Donald Findlay QC, arch-unionist and Tory, to represent him while Gail hired Paul McBride QC, adviser to the Tories on crime and justice policy after defecting from Labour. Legal aid – of up to the amount spent by the prosecution – was made available for paying for these QCs and for solicitors. On 27 January 2009, Tommy was served with the indictment for perjury and subornation of perjury.[94] Scottish legal magazine, *The Firm*, reported this came after mounting speculation in legal circles that the case may have been about to be dropped ahead of the Crown's deadline for proceeding (of March 2009) on the grounds of perceived benefit to the public interest, reliability of key witnesses and potential embarrassment of a 'not guilty' verdict.[95]

A preliminary hearing was set for 26 February 2009 at the High Court in Edinburgh. *The Firm* reported: 'Senior sources within the Crown Office ... claimed that Lothian and Borders Police placed them under 'incredible pressure' to proceed to bring prosecutions against Tommy Sheridan and Gail Sheridan'.[96] However, Lothian and Borders police stated that since submitting its report to the Procurator Fiscal in March 2008, it had no further involvement and the Crown added the case was being dealt with 'in the usual way'.[97] The next day, 13 February 2009, the Supreme Courts announced the 26 February hearing had been postponed for three months. Then, on 7 May 2009, a further two month postponement was announced so the hearing due on 11 May was rescheduled for 13 July 2009. This was held but at a further preliminary hearing on 26 October 2009, the start date for the trial was put back from February 2010. This pattern of delays continued and was lengthened when in late September 2009 Tommy dropped Findlay and hired Maggie Scott QC after Findlay had recommended Tommy accept a plea bargain.[98] Tommy refused the offer of an 18-month sentence for pleading guilty and the charges against Gail being dropped. This seemed to be because of his belief that he could win and that if he accepted the bargain it would create problems for him standing in the 2011 parliament elections and practicing law.[99] The initial delays were at the behest of the Crown, the later at the behest of Tommy,[100] who sought on occasion to halt any trial on the basis of media coverage prejudicing a fair trial.[101] Each and every one of the ten or so preliminary hearings were widely covered by the media as well all the associated developments.[102] As a result, the political arguments – of vendettas, witch hunts, conspiracies and persecution – that Tommy would use in his trial were all well trailed.

Crown versus Tommy Sheridan[103]

The opening day of what would become a 48-day trial stretching over nearly twelve weeks was reported by the *Herald* as being 'destined to be the biggest criminal trial of the year and promises a potent mix of celebrity, politics, and allegations of sordid sex and lies'.[104] With up to 200 potential witnesses to be called and some 270 pieces of evidence under consideration, the criminal trial was no mere re-run of the 2006 civil trial as the stakes had been raised considerably with the prospect of a jail sentence for a guilty verdict. After being sworn in, the jury, comprising 13 women and two men (with one juror, a woman, subsequently discharged on 15 December), heard evidence from 43 prosecution witnesses (of which 26 were current and former

SSP members) and 26 defence witnesses (of which 17 were former SSP and now Solidarity members). Some of the witnesses on the prosecution list were called for the defence. The charges against Tommy were two-fold: committing 18 counts of perjury in his defamation case in 2006 and attempting to persuade a witness, Colin Fox, to commit perjury. Gail was also charged with seven counts of perjury related to providing evidence to substantiate statements made by Tommy. The breakdown of the perjury charges related to denials of visiting Cupids, admitting visiting Cupids, having sexual relations with Anvar Khan and Katrine Trolle, the Moat House sex party, and the existence of the 9 November 2004 minute. In what had echoes of 2006, on 11 October Tommy sacked his QC, Maggie Scott, after she made too many errors, and began representing himself on 14 October.[105] To James Doleman, Scott was 'forensic and calm in her questioning, Mr Sheridan is far more passionate and inquisitorial'.[106] It was not just that Tommy had represented himself in 2006 and also on many other occasions and had begun some training in law. It was more to do with 'fighting for his life', as Tommy put it, and being an alleged victim of 'persecution, not prosecution'.[107] Consequently, it seemed again that Tommy believed he was the best placed to pursue the strategy and fabrication he had himself authored and invented. But the cost he bore was a high one. He asked for two weeks' preparation time before beginning to represent himself. He was given two days. Consequently, he was working late every night preparing for the following next day after having worked the full day in court. This and trying to withstand direct provocations[108] from witnesses took a toll on his health, requiring medical examinations and some days off ill in November.

Tommy's strategy was in many ways that of a time-served QC who seeks to pick holes in the prosecution case by bringing into doubt the veracity of pieces of evidence by implication (rather than by directly contradicting evidence) in order to prove the case against the defendant is dubious rather than prove the defendant is innocent.[109] The most obvious example of this concerned the dates of visits to Cupids and not the visits themselves. The tests were of whether there was sufficient reasonable doubt and whether the credibility and reliability of witnesses was sufficient. This takes on a special dimension in Scotland where in addition to the 'guilty' and 'not guilty' options, there is that of 'not proven'. Yet because Tommy was representing himself, there was no room to distance himself from the methods that he used – which would have been the case when represented by a QC – and Tommy was a politician not lawyer by profession so this created additional rankle. However, Tommy's strategy was also quite different on at least three counts from before. First, he chose not to give evidence himself and, thus, avoided being cross-examined.[110] Second, his underlying defence was a political one where he sought to sway the jury with material that was tangential and tendentious to the legal case but which the judge, Lord Bracadale, allowed so the case could be seen to be fair as well as be fair. He created a sideshow of potent distraction with his charges against *NoW*, Lothian and Borders police and the SSP of, respectively, conspiracy, vendetta and political civil war and factionalism.[111] And third, in fighting an alleged grand plot, there was no better way to fight – and fight with bare knuckles – than to have the 'victim' represent himself.[112] He again showed his 'balls of steel' in cross-examining former comrades – even recalling some to do so.

His strategy can be broken down into its respective elements. First, deny having been at certain places and deny having said certain things, supported by defence witnesses. Given that many of these instances were meetings with just two people (i.e. Tommy and another) or where Tommy and his defence witnesses outnumbered the other person, it was the situation of one word against another without much in the way of corroborating evidence. The obvious examples are the meetings with Colin Fox and Nicky McKerrell, where Tommy was aided by his sister, Lynn. Second, and following from this, brand prosecution witnesses liars and character assassinate them, especially by making insinuations about their past convictions and thespian aspirations. The obvious examples are SSP members (but George McNeilage and Keith Baldassara in particular). The irony here was that – as before and in an Orwellian manner – prosecution witnesses were branded liars for refusing to lie for Tommy. Third, prey upon innocent and not so innocent inconsistencies, differences and discrepancies in and between witness testimonies and statements of the 2006 and the 2010 cases as well as any other recorded statements. For example, Tommy tried to create doubt about basic events not by necessarily showing evidence that he was elsewhere but by picking upon inconsistencies in little details that were at the margins of these events. Fourth, fabricate, distort and exaggerate political tensions, personal disagreements and the existence of the United Left (with the effect of backdating their existence to 2004) even though Tommy himself earlier acknowledged the United Left existed only since June 2006.[113] Tommy cited that a political civil war within the SSP led to the prosecution witnesses telling lies in 2004–2006 so that they were compelled to continue to do so again in the 2010 trial.[114] However, other than accusations of jealousy, he never provided an explanation for why this political civil war existed in the first place.[115] Fifth, cast doubt and undermine the evidence and testimony of Anvar Khan, Katrine Trolle, Anne Colvin and Helen Allison by focusing upon financial offers and payments given by *NoW* to them. Such offers and payments (in particular) do not necessarily and inevitably undermine or compromise their credibility and reliability for citizens might take a number of views, *inter alia*, they should be paid to compensate them for the exposure they will then experience or that a newspaper which seeks to make profit out of them should not do so without paying. And, it has to be remembered that the £20,000 Tommy received from the *Daily Record* in 2006 did not necessarily or inevitably invalidate the content of the week's coverage that it paid for.[116] Sixth, cast aspersions over the mental health of Anvar Khan, Gary Clark and Fiona McGuire. Seventh, turn events on their heads by ripping them out of their original context. So, for example, the SSP EC 'defiance strategy' of not handing in the 9 November 2004 minute became one of conspiracy to commit contempt of court which was then used to explain why so many members of the SSP EC were then standing in court, (allegedly) committing another conspiracy by saying Tommy admitted at the said meeting to having attended Cupids twice. Meantime, that the SSP EC discussed (and rejected), upon Tommy's continual requesting, lying for Tommy became in Tommy's hands that the SSP EC – or those that stated he had admitted attending Cupids – were, thus, capable of lying in court.[117] Another example was that the informal meeting that Tommy was asked to attend (but refused to) prior to the 9 November 2004 SSP EC became a secret conspiracy meeting. Eighth, use the fact that people – especially when they become court witnesses – seek to cover up and not divulge information about illicit sexual relations for no other reasons than (self-perceived) guilt, shame and embarrassment for themselves and their families in order to create the impression of ulterior motives of a conspiracy against him. Subsequently telling lies and half-truths to avoid full exposure does not necessarily negate the existence of the original act of sex. Ninth, question dates in an attempt to show they were wrong rather than showing Tommy did not do what he was alleged to have done on a certain other date. Tenth, call witnesses like Andy Coulson whose evidence had no bearing on being at Cupids or upon Katrine Trolle in order to mount a political attack upon *NoW* as way of trying curry favour with, and sway, the jury by appealing to their likely political sentiments. Lastly, attack his former political organisation, Militant, and its members as being clandestine with the effect that they could not be trusted to tell the truth – although he did not raise the same questions to those of his defence witnesses like Philip Stott or Jock Penman who also had been Militant members.[118]

Additionally, the McNeilage tape was rubbished by virtue of profuse swearing, breaks in speech and so on to the effect that the voice was not Tommy's.[119] Tommy and his witnesses argued this could not be him because he was far more eloquent and did not swear. He claimed: 'I'm a relatively eloquent man who doesn't swear very often'.[120] However, he does swear frequently (see various chapters) and the situation that he found himself in – that is when and where the tape was made – was very different to that of his chosen terrain of being the public orator so his speech pattern was different. Thus, it was a private conversation between two old friends and Tommy was under the intense pressure of fighting for his political life as a result of his own actions. And, Alex Prentice QC questioned why, if the tape was made by Alan McCombes *et al.* or *NoW*, over ten aspects of its 'script' were used when they were clearly critical of McCombes *et al.* and *NoW*, were corroborated by other evidence and not challenged by Tommy or were hostages to bad fortune. In Prentice's words, the tape was the 'solid foundation' of the case.[121] Alan McCombes revealed after the trial that Tommy had sought to have the McNeilage tape barred as inadmissible, indicating that the tape was genuine.[122] Consequently, Tommy was then forced into his desperate attempts to undermine the veracity of the tape. So although evidence of voice authentication was barred after the Crown slipped up on a procedural irregularity under the 'Cadder ruling' (requiring that a solicitor is present when evidence is taken from an accused), Tommy did not attempt to call any experts in the field to verify that it was not an authentic and contemporaneous recording of his voice. Tommy only went so far as to try to call comedian, impersonator and acquaintance, Des Mclean, to show that his voice could be mimicked.[123]

The (real) minute of the 9 November 2004 was branded 'dodgy and distorted' and a 'United Left factional account'[124] (even thought the United Left did not exist until June 2006[125]) by Tommy while the fake minute was not barred as in 2006 even though it had the fatal error of only recording 18 attendees rather than the 21 that did attend. The trial revealed that behind the scenes Tommy had asked then friend and SSP national treasurer, Allison Kane, to 'rattle a few cages' on the 18 to 19 November 2004 to ensure that (formal) minutes of the 9 and 14 November 2004 SSP EC meetings were not produced from Barbara Scott's handwritten minutes,[126] and that Tommy also asked Allan Green, SSP National Secretary, to destroy the 9 November 2004 minutes on 26 November 2004.[127] Tommy then accused these defence witnesses of lying even though the withholding of the minutes had been to protect his privacy.

The calling of defence witnesses[128] from 3 December 2010 saw a number of Solidarity members, friends of Tommy and family relations testify, *inter alia*, that Tommy had not admitted to attending Cupids and that any extant minute showing otherwise was fake (e.g. Jock Penman, Pat Smith, Rosemary Byrne, Mike Gonzalez, Charlotte Ahmed, Steve

Arnott, Graeme McIver), that Tommy was in Glasgow at the time he was alleged to be at Cupids in 2002[129] or at other sexual encounters (e.g. Carol Allan (his sister), Allan Brown, Jim Monaghan, Brett Harper), the McNeilage tape was a fake (e.g. Ian Fitzpartrick, Philip Stott, Steve Arnott, Jim Monaghan, Lynn Sheridan)[130] and that there was a plot to 'do Tommy in' within the SSP from May 2003 onwards as a result of factionalism based on jealousy and feminism (e.g. Hugh Kerr, Gordon Morgan, Jock Penman). However, their evidence – or as might be thought 'mass delusion' to recall Steve Arnott's memorable phrase from the 2006 court case – did not shoot any silver bullets for Tommy. Moreover, it might have been expected that those defence witnesses not connected to the SSP or Solidarity would have provided robust, convincing evidence as they had no political axe to grind one way or the other. The veracity of this, like that from his brother-in-law, Andy McFarlane, was cast in doubt as the prosecution was able to suggest that these witnesses were in court out of a personal loyalty to Tommy.[131] Logically, given the outcome of the trial, there are grounds for believing that Tommy and these witnesses may have committed perjury.[132]

Again, Tommy successfully showed that *NoW* was very far from being squeaky clean, hoping this would cast further doubt on the veracity of the allegations against him. Specifically, he made the argument that because his mobile phone details had been found in the procession of Glenn Mulcaire, who was sent to prison in 2007 for phone-hacking while in *NoW*'s pay, he was also likely to have also had his phone-hacked, and this showed that *NoW* was out to 'get him' and in doing so would lie and use dishonest means. However, whether his phone was hacked or not was immaterial to the case for it did not relate to earlier incidents at Cupids (1996, 2002) and did not override his admissions of those. Similarly, the claims of a conspiracy by *NoW* against Tommy may have some substance but they only relate to the period after he won his defamation action when *NoW* was smarting from defeat. For example, claims of a *NoW* journalist that Tommy was being monitored by *NoW* relate to late 2006[133] and the bug found in his car relates to 2007 (although it was found not to be viable despite Tommy stating the police told him it was[134]).

In all of this defence, while the charges Tommy made against *NoW* may or may not have been true, they did not relate to whether he had or had not attended Cupids and had or had not admitted visiting it. This was the sense in which he tried to pull political heartstrings and press political buttons. In order to make sure the court was not added to the list of alleged conspirators, the judge, Lord Bracadale, twice allowed Tommy to have time off to prepare his case once he had decided to represent himself, take time off for medical reasons of exhaustion and health checks, and to use the lectern – and not the dock – to address the jurors from. But more than that, Lord Bracadale allowed Tommy to call witnesses and present evidence that were tangential and tendentious to the charges of perjury against him. For example, the calling of Andy Coulson on phone tapping did not relate to whether Tommy had or had not been to Cupids or admitted that he had or had not been there.

On 25 November 2010, two charges of attending and having sex at the Moat House were withdrawn as the key witness here, Matthew McColl who organised the event, refused to answer certain questions for fear of revealing the identity of his then girlfriend and was shown to be evasive and inconsistent in answering others as he tried to prevent inquiry into his sexual affairs. In conversations with others like Keith Baldassara, Tommy admitted to being at the Moat House party but not participating. Two other charges of Tommy falsely accusing two women, Helen Allison and Anne Colvin, of lying in court when they said that he was at the hotel with Andrew McFarlane were also dropped. At the same time, two charges were dropped against Gail. Shortly afterwards, the remaining charges relating to the Moat House were also dropped against Tommy, leaving twelve charges, as were further charges against Gail. On 2 December 2010, the charge of trying to persuade a witness to commit perjury was dropped – the Crown stating this was because there was no corroborating evidence[135] – as were three further charges against Gail. On 17 December 2010, all the remaining charges against Gail were dropped after the Crown stated that it was no longer in the public interest to pursue the case against her and that her personal circumstances had been taken into consideration. By 20 December, only six charges remained against Tommy. To be acquitted of the charges was a major victory although that did not provide a definitive rebuttal of the allegations and accusations surrounding those events for their withdrawal appeared to be for reasons other than the events did not take place such as lack of credible and reliable evidence presented in court.

And although it is not unusual for the prosecution to drop some charges during a trial,[136] the speed and extent with which the Crown dropped charges against Tommy and Gail merits explanation. The charges against Gail, although never put to the test, were probably both a bargaining chip against Tommy and a way of preventing Gail giving evidence for Tommy. The Crown said they were dropped for reasons of the public interest and taking into account Gail's personal situation (of being a mother of a young child), suggesting they had served both purposes.[137] In the case of Tommy, the Crown did not appear to have done its homework by testing Matthew McColl, the organiser of the Moat House sex party, for he was so obstructive and evasive for the Crown's case that it was left with no option but to withdraw these charges. The tactical ineptitude of a number of individuals associated with the United Left faction and the radical feminist school of thought within the SSP was very helpful for Tommy in allowing him to try to show his opponents to be as he alleged them to be. Thus, Tommy was able to at least put forward his (unconvincing) thesis that not only was there a 'plot' against him from November 2004 onwards but it pre-dated this as well. Indeed, this was a particular feature of his 2010 defence. Although Tommy relinquished his opportunity to be cross-examined so that the prosecution could not raise such issues, it was an indication of the weakness of its knowledge of internal party affairs that the creation of the United Left was not pinpointed to June 2006 (or that it was dissolved on 20 January 2007) or that there had long been concerns about Tommy's behavior that never materialised into a 'plot'. Those Solidarity members that were court witnesses for Tommy were consciously complicit in the last throw of the dice of a 'conspiracy' to prove that black was white and vice-versa. They were 'willing sinners' as they made his defence possible in both the legal and political terms he fought on. In his lengthy four-hour summing up speech (and his plea for mitigation for the sentencing hearing), Tommy fired both barrels. He mixed high emotion with political dogma and ever more relied for sympathy upon his line of the vendetta against his family and what the consequences of conviction would be for them.[138] In directing the jurors, Lord Bracadale reminded them: 'This is not a political court – you do not judge people on their politics … It's not your function to judge the sexual morality … Put out of your minds any feelings of sympathy you may feel'[139] in an attempt to focus them on the evidence presented before them.

Denouement

After six hours deliberation, on 23 December 2010, the jury found Tommy guilty of willfully and knowingly making false statements under oath on the remaining charges (but with one deletion and one amendment).[140] In doing so, it judged that Tommy was the MSP in the *NoW* story of 31 October 2004. In essence, the jury found he had visited Cupids, had admitted this to the SSP EC on 9 November 2004, and had sexual relations with Katrine Trolle while married. The media's conclusion was that he was a liar, cheat and hypocrite. The significance of being convicted for perjury was not just about telling lies but rather, and critically, telling lies to win a case. Just as with the 2006 case, it is difficult to know exactly why the jury reached the verdict it did and what were its particular reasons for this. It is entirely possible that each juror came to their individual decision for a different reason or set of reasons from others. However, it is also the case that the broad outlines of the prosecution and defence cases were ones that were recognised and evaluated by the jury collectively. It appears, on the one hand, the key pieces of testimony and evidence leading to conviction were from Gary Clark and Katrine Trolle as witnesses with no axes to grind and, on the other, comprised the McNeilage tape and the 16 witnesses at the 9 November 2004 SSP EC. Their strength was not undermined by Tommy's strategy of calling witnesses liars, for merely calling them liars did not establish that they were liars. But the verdict of 8:6 indicated that Tommy very nearly pulled-off a victory. This would have been an incredible feat had he managed to do so because his defence on the basis of evidence was thin and threadbare to say the very least given that there was no plot or conspiracy to bring him down as he alleged and that no evidence of this – consequentially – existed. One juror moving from their guilty decision would have led to a tie and the threshold for a verdict of guilty of a simple majority of the (original) jury of 15 would not have been reached. But as with the 2006 case when it mattered not that four jurors did not believe Tommy had been defamed, ultimately, it mattered not that six jurors did not believe Tommy had committed perjury. That said, it is a testament to the strength of Tommy's strategy, especially with many weak witnesses, that he won six jurors to his side, with three of these being in tears when the verdict was announced, and one woman juror on her Facebook page saying her fellow jurors were 'dirty low life b[astards]' for finding Tommy guilty and 'hoped they choke in their fckn sleep, scum bags they are'.[141] These jurors appeared to agree with the basis of his case, namely, that he should not be found guilty in spite of evidence, suggesting they saw him as a victimised socialist politician. In an interview, Tommy claimed that he would appeal the conviction on the grounds that his human rights had been infringed because he had not received a fair trial due to prejudicial media coverage during and before the trial and this had influenced the jury.[142] This involved something of a somersault given that he claimed after his 2006 trial that 'working class people, when they listen to the arguments, can differentiate the truth from the muck'.

Tommy remained defiant as ever.[143] Before, during and after sentencing on 26 January there was no public remorse, no contrition, and no admission of guilt (although he was reported to have cried uncontrollably in his mother's arms before meeting the assembled media outside the court on 23 December 2010[144]). Indeed, after conviction, he issued notice of taking action against *NoW*, the Metropolitan Police and Glenn Mulcaire over phone-hacking issues.[145] Posted on his blog[146] afterwards, he wrote: '[T]he fight isn't over yet. ... Right now, I am the target and I am being made to pay,'[147] 'my mood is dented, but not broken'[148] and

'We [Solidarity] have a proud and spotless banner'.[149] This was followed by a statement from him read out at a public meeting in his support: 'To those who lied and collaborated with the police and the News of the World to imprison me, he says, I may be in jail right now but in January [2012] I will be free. The collaborators and liars will be in prison for the rest of their lives – prisons of guilt, prisons of shame'.[150] Later, of *NoW* and News International he wrote 'their collective lies have helped convince a jury, by the narrowest of margins, that I and not they were guilty of lying under oath'.[151]

The closest he came to any remorse, contrition or admission was when he accepted in his pleading that he was a defendant who was not being wrongly convicted due to perjury and that on his blog from prison he commented: 'remember that every sinner has a future, and every saint has a past'.[152] However, he negated these with other statements before and after. In his mitigation pleading, he was careful not to explicitly protest his innocence but this was only a legal nicety.[153] Upon being led away to Barlinnie as prisoner 32057, Tommy proclaimed the sentence of three years was 'a fucking result'.[154] The tariff for perjury was three to seven years, with most legal commentators expecting five years.[155] His delight was because the circumstances of rejecting a plea bargain before the court case, pleading not guilty, being an elected politician at the time of committing perjury, and taking offensive (not defensive) action against *NoW* which necessitated an extensive and premeditated fabrication all suggested a longer stretch. Lord Bracadale, it seemed, did not seek to make much of an example of Tommy. His mother commented: 'God love you, son, how broad are your shoulders because you've taken on the manky Murdoch empire'.[156]

Solidarity condemned the sentence as: 'barbaric ... draconian ... [and] vindictive ... reinforc[ing] the widespread view that this is the culmination of a brutal vendetta carried out by the rich and powerful against Scotland's most prominent socialist [- a] socialist who has earned their hatred for his uncompromising defence of working class people for the last 25 years'. Tommy had only intended to appeal the sentence if it was longer than three years. After his conviction, there was talk of an appeal based on procedural matters involving, *inter alia*, certain witnesses being exempted from giving testimony (Fiona McGuire, Glenn Mulcaire), *NoW* withholding certain emails (claiming these were lost in storage transfer[157]), and the judge barring Tommy from calling certain witnesses (like impersonator, Des Mclean) and misdirecting the jury[158] as well an appeal based on new witnesses coming forward to validate his claim to have not visited Cupids in 2002.[159] But the case of the lead witness and Solidarity activist here, Fatima Uygu, subsequently fell apart when it was revealed she lied about the date of her birthday – which was central to her claim.[160] Tommy's lodging of a right to appeal was granted a six week extension on the basis of its complexity.[161] It was then lodged on 19 May 2011 claiming that Tommy was denied a fair trial, contrary to the European Convention of Human Rights, as a result of pre-trial publicity.[162] However, it was rejected on 10 June 2011 by Lord Wheatley because it did not contain 'arguable grounds of appeal'.[163] Leave to appeal this decision was given, and an extension given to the time it was required to be lodged by.[164] However, on 2 August 2011, Lady Paton, Lord Hardie and Lord Emslie sitting at the Court of Criminal Appeal in Edinburgh found the case for the right to appeal was 'not arguable'.[165] The court also rejected the argument from Tommy's solicitor, Aamer Anwar that the decision on the right to appeal should be delayed until the conclusion of the enquiry by Strathclyde police, called 'Operation Rubicon', into *NoW* witnesses potentially perjuring themselves in Tommy's 2010 trial. In response, Aamer said: 'This is not the end. We will consider the outcome and may appeal to the Supreme Court and … the Scottish Criminal Case Review Commission'[166] and that a fresh appeal may be based on the 'missing' *NoW* emails that were not available during the 2010 trial.[167]

Conclusion

In sentencing Tommy, Lord Bracadale stated: 'By pursuing, and persisting in the pursuit of, a defamation action against the proprietors of the *News of the World* you brought the walls of the temple crashing down not only on your own head but also on the heads of your family and your political friends and foes alike. You were repeatedly warned by the comrades that it would come to this'. This was as good an analysis as any for Tommy had initiated the process by suing *NoW* on 15 November 2004 and reinforced this with his statement that: 'If I'm going to go down, I'm going to go down fighting'. But it also highlighted, to paraphrase Martin Luther King, that 'no lie can last forever' so that achievements based on lies are like houses built on sand. But what Lord Bracadale's analysis did not allude to was that once Tommy protested his innocence there was no way back for he had to continue to do so because he became locked in by the logic of his own case. He was in too deep for reasons explained in the last chapter. Lies necessarily begat more lies. This meant the advice of 'once you're in a hole, stop digging' was not appropriate. He became a victim of the very thing he advocated when he told the *Big Issue (Scotland)*: 'Karl Marx's watch phrase was 'doubt all things'. I think you should always look underneath the surface'.[168]

Before Tommy received his new appellation of 'disgraced' politician and 'disgraced' former MSP, he ended up being a street fighter but not in the streets he first fought on but in a court of law. Not only did he play politics but he played dirty, lifting a veil of honesty and integrity from his head. Looking back at his glory days, one is struck by the multiple ironies of comments like 'you can't but think this man has got to be too good to be true but he seems whiter than white'[169], 'few question his sincerity'[170] and 'at least has the quality of believing in what he does'.[171] Initially, Tommy had been seen as the new Derek Hatton but, in this chapter of Tommy's life, the comparison broke down for, in 1993 after a lengthy trial, Derek Hatton was exonerated of corruption charges during his time as deputy leader of Liverpool City Council. The humiliation of being jailed for perjury was then compounded in May 2011 when Solidarity was beaten by the SSP in the number of votes obtained in the seven regional list constituencies they went head-to-head by a factor of more than 2:1 and in only one region – South of Scotland – did Solidarity outpoll the SSP.[172] Without 'Tommygate', a not disunited SSP could have hoped to be on a par with the Greens with two MSPs and eight councilors in Edinburgh and Glasgow between 2007 and 2012.[173]

Notes

1. The appeal was to be based on six different grounds and the submission of new evidence (*Herald* 12 August 2006). Some like Paul McBride QC doubted that an appeal was permissible on the basis on the verdict being perverse (*Herald* 5 August 2006). A date was set for the hearing of the appeal for December 2007 (*BBC Scotland* online 13 February 2007).
2. *Mail on Sunday* 6 August 2006, *Herald* 7 August 2006. The police were obligated to begin inquiries into the complaint made by the member of the public.
3. Gail's father, Gus Healy, Pat Smith, Jock Penman, Rosemary Byrne and Graeme McIver were also charged in February 2008 with committing perjury at the 2006. These charges were subsequently dropped late on in the 2010 trial.
4. This was to be held before three judges and not a jury. The basis of the appeal involved issues which were dealt with in the perjury trial (see *Sunday Herald* 9 September 2007). It was delayed due the perjury investigation taking precedence (see *Herald* 26 September 2007). Before the delay, the *Guardian* (15 August 2007) detected in Tommy's interview comments that he was preparing the ground for being defeated. After the closure of *NoW* on 10 June 2011 and the elapse of the five year period which triggers bankruptcy protection, it is unclear whether the case will ever be heard. Either mischievously or ignorantly, both the *Scotsman* and *Daily Record* (15 October 2011) reported that News International had never lodged its appeal (even though this was not the case) as result of statements from the Sheridan camp as a part of a story about Tommy raising funds to take News International to court to get his £200, 000 damages. Ironically, Tommy would need to move to end the suspension of the holding

of the appeal if he wanted to have it struck out. This would then bring forth the danger that the appeal was heard and won by News International, thus, not only depriving Tommy of his £200,000 damages award but making him liable for costs (subject to any bankruptcy protection).

5. *NoW* 26 December 2010, 30 January 2011, 6 February 2011. By late 2011, Tommy should no signs of taking libel or defamation action against these stories. The same was true in regard to the publication of *DTTSS*.

6. 9 August 2006.

7. The irony of Tommy stating: 'I like Tom Nairn's use of the phrase 'post-sectarian left' to describe the SSP because we've managed to ditch a lot of that baggage and look at things and people as they are' will not be lost on observers.

8. *Socialist Worker* 9 September 2006. It may have been this speech – using these words – that encouraged Alice Sheridan to sign unprompted and unannounced the Matt Monroe song 'The Impossible Dream' at Solidarity's launch. Tommy did not appear to enjoy the serenade.

9. *Evening Times* 2 September 2006.

10. Sheridan, T. 'Solidarity forever' *Red Pepper*, October 2006, p. 28, *Scotsman* 4 September 2006.

11. *Daily Record* 6 September 2006. While Solidarity did recruit members other than those who left the SSP in the split, such claims looked highly doubtful. *Socialist Worker* (11 November 2006) reported membership had 'grown to around 600 members'.

12. Tommy's belief that the likes of Peter Mullan would support Solidarity in the way that they supported the SSP did not come to pass (see *Sunday Herald* 20 August 2007) even though Mullan directed the 2007 election Solidarity party political broadcast.

13. *Cf. Holyrood* 11 September 2006.

14. While in such bare knuckle fights previous antagonisms are momentarily put aside, expediency is not the same as opportunism, crass or otherwise.

15. Thus, Solidarity was Tommy-centric in its lamp posters, ballot papers (i.e. 'Solidarity – Tommy Sheridan'), posters, leaflets, manifesto cover, election broadcast, press work and media photo opportunities. This made it ever clearer that the point of Solidarity was to re-elect Tommy. Indeed, Pat Smith, lead Solidarity candidate in the Lothians, reported early on in the election: 'Members will be travelling to Glasgow to help create a buzz around the campaign to get Tommy Sheridan MSP re-elected' (*Socialist Worker* 31 March 2007). The figure of Rosemary Byrne as co-convenor was to provide a fig leaf for Tommy's dominance. In these circumstances, critics scoffed Solidarity was 'Tommy Sheridan's new fan club' (*Daily Mail* 12 February 2007).

16. The blogger, *A Very Public Sociologist*, and member of the Socialist Party until early 2010 recounted: '[W]hat's more most of my comrades believed he [i.e. Tommy] had done it [i.e. lied in court] too' ('Tommy Sheridan: tragedy and farce' 23 December 2011).

17. 3 September 2006.

18. In all, a thousand people attended the 10 launch meetings for Solidarity (*The Socialist* 9 November 2006).

19. At the first Solidarity conference on 4 November 2006, some 250 attended.

20. It was believed that Aamer Anwar, Tommy's solicitor, was asked by Tommy to consider standing for the leadership of Solidarity but declined.

21. The positive effect of the defamation victory was less than Tommy would have wished. For example, he came fifth and last (with 8%) in the 2006 Scotscare poll of 'Great Scots' (*Press Association* 24 January 2007).

22. This, clearly, is no exoneration of the SSP either given its atrophy.

23. This tension was evident early on for, at Solidarity's first annual conference, the SWP was prepared using its force of numbers to try to veto the adoption of the proposed constitution for Solidarity (which would have left the organisation in limbo). Credit should at least be given to the SWP – in this sense – for standing by its view for other individual Solidarity members appeared to choose not to raise points of criticism of Tommy given they had been thrown together and were in a 'batten down the hatches' situation. However, both the SWP and CWI had to agree to a formulation of national self-determination for Scotland that was very far from their own. The close vote of 119:111 over Solidarity's name reflected these divisions (see Gall, G. 'Scotland's socialists' *Morning Star* 13 November 2006). See also Morgan, G. ('Solidarity: Scotland's socialist movement' *Scottish Left Review* November/December 2006) on the rather far-fetched view of Solidarity as 'the movement of the movements'.

24. Solidarity New Year Message 31 December 2006. Tommy used more measured language in his new year's address (*Socialist Worker* 13 January 2007).

25. *Sunday Herald* 31 December 2006, *Newsnight Scotland* 26 April 2007.

26. See, for example, *Herald* 23 November 2006 and *Scotsman* 27 November 2006.

27. *Herald* 18 January 2007. An opinion poll commissioned by Solidarity was used to suggest it would win seven MSPs (*Mirror* 19 January 2007). The same poll was used more accurately in the *Herald* (18 January 2007) to suggest Solidarity 'could win up to six seats'.

28. *Guardian* 26 April 2007.

29. *Scotland on Sunday* 8 October 2006.

30. *Herald* 13 October 2006.

31. *Herald, Guardian* 4 October 2006. Similarly outlandish statements were made on *Newsnight Scotland* (3 October 2006) and *Channel 4 News* (3 October 2006).

32. 3 October 2006.

33. *Times* 4 October 2006.

34. See report in *Herald* 10 October 2006.

35. *BBC News online* 3 October 2006. Colin Fox responded to the MI5 claim, saying: '[Tommy's] statements get more bizarre each time he speaks. His most recent claims to be a victim of an MI5 and CIA plot are utterly fantastic. You're not sure if it's MI5, MFI or Ikea. It's ridiculous. Who needs MI5 wrecking the socialist movement when Tommy Sheridan is around?' (*Newsnight Scotland* 3 October 2006).

36. *Daily Mail* 4 October 2006. He had made similar statements after his defamation case. For example, he told the BBC documentary *Sex, Lies and Socialism* (7 August 2006) that *NoW* 'would never break me politically and they never will. And, they never will break us as a couple either because our love is unbreakable'.

37. Some ambiguity still surrounds this handwritten minute – not in terms of its existence and authenticity but what was done with it for Allan Green stated that it was 'probably destroyed' (*Scotsman* 9 August 2006) in the defamation case (see also *Daily Record* 7 October 2010) while Barbara Scott in the 2010 trial stated the handwritten minute was in her handbag during the 2006 case (*Daily Record* 6 October 2010). Earlier, according to *NoW* (20 August 2006): 'Barbara said that during the trial she did not have the notes from which the minute was written. But after the trial ended it was revealed that she had discovered them'.

38. Although originally carried in the *Scottish Socialist Voice* 25 August 2006, it was the subject of a news story itself (e.g. *Observer, Scotland on Sunday, Sunday Herald* 13 August 2006).

39. *Observer* 13 August 2006

40. *Herald* 11 August 2006.

41. Ironically, not being elected may have saved Tommy from even greater humiliation come the outcome of the perjury trial because this would have led to being ejected from parliament.
42. 19 June 2007.
43. *Sunday Herald* 6 May 2007.
44. *Herald* 23 April 2007, *Sunday Mirror* 4 March 2007.
45. 12 April 2010.
46. *Herald* 22 September 2007.
47. Solidarity press release 6 May 2007.
48. Solidarity press release 4 May 2007.
49. Solidarity activist, John Dennis, made similar points (*Herald* 9 May 2007). If there was a political vendetta going on, it seemed the evidence for it was to be found in unlikely quarters: Alice and Lynn Sheridan stood against Keith Baldassara and Carolyn Leckie in the 2007 local and Scottish parliament elections respectively. Lynn polled twice that of Carolyn as heads of respective Solidarity and SSP lists in Central Scotland. Alice beat Keith by 39 votes in the Greater Pollok multi-member seat.
50. *Sunday Herald* 20 August 2006, 5 August 2007, *Sunday Times* 5 August 2007.
51. Ironically, Tommy referred to Solidarity 'as the only socialist party in Scotland with Credibility' (*Scottish Left Review* March/April 2007).
52. Solidarity press release 6 May 2007.
53. *Big Issue Scotland* 16–22 November 2009. Tommy did not stand in the Glasgow East by-election of 24 July 2008. In this contest, the SSP candidate, Frances Curran, beat the Solidarity candidate, Tricia McLeish by 43 votes but both lost their deposits, coming fourth and fifth respectively with 2.1% and 2% of the vote.
54. By contrast, the SSP polled 10,404 (0.94%) and the SLP 22,135 (2.0%) in the 2009 European election.
55. *Daily Record* 9 December 2008.
56. One leading Lothians' Solidarity activist believed that from the latter half of 2007 'the only thing keeping us [Solidarity] together is the defence campaign [for Tommy]'.
57. There was some disquiet inside Solidarity with members feeling Tommy bounced them into a position of Gail standing with George or for Solidarity before due process had occurred and putting them in a position which would leave Solidarity with egg on its face if it contradicted Tommy.
58. *Herald* 15 January 2011.
59. *Daily Record* 17 January 2011, *Herald* 17, 29 January 2011.
60. *Herald* 18 January 2011.
61. *Sunday Herald* 13 March 2011. This would have saddened Tommy given that he told *STV* (26 January 2011) Solidarity would stand everywhere. In order to sweeten the pill of a Solidarity candidate not heading the list, Galloway attacked the SSP leadership as 'flea-infested rats' (*Daily Record* 5 March 2011). The SWP and SPS alliance with Galloway was met by charges of unprincipled opportunism given the SWP break with Galloway over Respect (see *Socialist Worker* 27 October 2007), trenchant CWI criticism of Galloway as an apologist for various nefarious causes, and Galloway's refusal to adopt the worker's wage policy (where neither the SWP nor SPS (*Socialism Today*, 146, March 2011) raised the issue for his candidacy). Galloway was not elected to the Scottish Parliament.
62. Statement by the *Democratic Green Socialist* (*DGS*) network within Solidarity ('The Scottish general election was historic'), 9 May 2011.
63. In 2007, in only three regions (Highlands and Islands, Mid Scotland and Fife, and North east Scotland) was the Solidarity vote lower.

64. The original quote was 'The people of Scotland will decide whether it becomes an important part of the future of Scotland' (Sheridan, T. 'Solidarity forever' *Red Pepper*, October 2006, p. 28).

65. This was no doubt in part due to the Orwellian doublespeak of calling the organisation Solidarity when it and the SSP were engaged in a war of mutually assured destruction. Divisions repel voters and such acrimony led to voters to look at both Solidarity and the SSP as a 'plague on both your houses'.

66. 'Preparing to stand anti-cuts candidates in Scotland', SPS website, 24 October 2011.

67. Some went further, suggesting that there was a state and establishment vendetta against Tommy for his role in sinking the poll tax and Thatcher. If this was to be the case, it seemed a bit late in the day to have any credulity.

68. For example, campaigning against social injustice or imperialism.

69. *Daily Record* 24 December 2010.

70. *Sunday Herald* 16 March 2008.

71. For example, the *Daily Record*'s front page of 28 March 2011 was the exclusive story (with a page 9 continuation) of Tommy keeping fit in jail by playing football.

72. He said his need of money was his main motivation for entering (*Daily Record* 3 January 2009) showing that he could be 'bought' contrary to his mother's statement on 26 January 2011. Defending himself, he said it was a 'job' which involved crossing 'no picket line or breach[ing] no socialist principle' (*Big Issue Scotland* 5–11 February 2009). At the Solidarity National Steering Committee meeting beforehand, Tommy argued it was a personal decision as to whether he entered *CBB*, and then argued it also presented political opportunities to put across his political case. And, in an email circulated to Solidarity members (2 January 2009), he asked that 'as a private citizen … party members respect that … I have a right … to try to make some money honestly'.

73. Although Tommy said his first one would be his last (*Mirror* 26 February 2003), he fought others in 2007 and 2008.

74. His 2007 Edinburgh Fringe shows were not well received and were littered with swearing (*Sunday Herald* 12 August 2007, *Guardian* 15 August 2007, *Scotsman* 16 August 2007). For example, the *Guardian* (9 August 2007) suggested Tommy's 'next brush with the law may be for crimes against entertainment'. He cancelled his 2008 Glasgow comedy festival shows due to preparations for his perjury trial. Nevertheless, an element of defiance can be read into these shows, namely, using his court case victory to make money from and sticking up two fingers to those that believed he had perjured himself to win the case.

75. Paradoxically, Tommy did not attend the award ceremony dinners that he was invited to. Instead, Gail was accompanied by Hugh Kerr.

76. *Daily Record* 9 December 2006.

77. *Daily Record* 9 December 2006.

78. Tommy also explained that he turned down the *CBB* 2007 offer because 'Channel Four could not guarantee that I could talk about the political views of Solidarity without it being edited out' ('Tommy turns down £100,000 from Big Brother' Solidarity website 9 December 2006). This was not an issue for his 2009 entry.

79. See *Sunday Herald* 19 October 2008.

80. *Sunday Mail* 23 September 2007.

81. This was not before he represented a miner sacked for testing positive for drugs in which Tommy was admonished by the Employment Tribunal chair for unsubstantiated claims of a conspiracy by his client's employer (*Express* 6 February 2009).

82. Tommy was cognisant of this, saying 'I've become well-known and I've tried to use that notoriety for the cause as best I can. It's my belief that you've got to try to speak

up against injustice, against illegal wars, against poverty at every opportunity you've got' (*The Big Issue Scotland* 24–30 August 2006).

83. It was a spectacular *faux pas* after his astounding performance in front of the US Senate committee to wear a red leotard to act as a purring cat, licking milk from the saucer of actress, Rula Lenska.

84. By, for example, calling Coolio a 'rap superstar'.

85. *Sunday Herald* 4 January 2009.

86. He was not the only one to make such miscalculations. Paul McBride, Gail's QC, believed there would be no trial (*Sunday Herald* 1 February 2009) and Alastair Bonnington, legal commentator, believed that not only would there be no investigation but if there were to be one, it would concern the 11 SSP EC members (*Herald* 7 August 2006). Similarly, the *Daily Record* (5 August 2006) believed: 'One of the few people ... who will not come under the microscope [of a perjury investigation] is Sheridan himself'.

87. 2 October 2006, 4 April 2007.

88. *Observer* 25 March 2007.

89. *STV* 16 April 2007.

90. See, for example, *Scotland on Sunday* 24 February 2008, *Sunday Herald* 24 February 2008. It was believed the total costs, including the trial, were around £4m (*Herald* 24 December 2010, *Sunday Herald* 26 December 2010). What Tommy and his supporters refused to acknowledge was that Tommy had initiated this expense by his defamation action. However, Tommy's supporters saw no inconsistency in calling for equally large sums to be spent investigating the possibility of perjury by Andy Coulson, Bob Bird and Douglas Wight during his 2010 trial.

91. This made the case no ordinary perjury case which supporters of Tommy like Jim Monaghan, former Solidarity media coordinator, former Defend Tommy Sheridan Campaign secretary, and defence witness in the 2010 trial, failed to address (see his 'In whose interest?' *Scottish Left Review* March/April 2011 and with Stott, P. 'Police, politicians and the plutocrat' *Scottish Left Review* March/April 2008).

92. The cost of the police investigation was £1.1m by September 2008 (*Sunday Herald* 7 December 2008), rising to £1.8m (*The Firm* 11 February 2009) by its conclusion. Shortly afterwards, the Defend Tommy Sheridan Campaign was established. Notable by their absence of supporters on the campaign's website were the likes of Peter Mullan and Davy McKay. Mullan later distanced himself from Tommy (*DTTSS* p. 224). One of the campaign's most high profile supporters was John McManus, organiser of Miscarriages of Justice Organisation (MOJO) Scotland (*Sunday Herald* 7 September 2008). Until 23 December 2010 there could be no possibility of a miscarriage of justice. Interestingly, McManus said: 'Tommy supported our organisation from its inception. If somebody supported me in the past, I will support them when they need my help' (*Sunday Herald* 7 September 2008) and in relation to those MOJO Scotland supports in campaigning against miscarriages of justice: 'One lie and it's goodbye' (*Scotland on Sunday* 12 April 2009).

93. Solidarity press release 17 December 20-1807. This alleged motivation was criticised by the *DGS* in the summer of 2011 ('Editorial' summer supplement, August 2011).

94. This is more commonly known as conspiracy to commit, that is organise, perjury.

95. 27 January 2009.

96. 11 February 2009.

97. *The Firm* 12 February 2009.

98. *Times* 24 December 2010. In the summer before the perjury trial, a number of the leading independents within Solidarity met, reviewed the evidence against Tommy, and agree to make representation to him to accept the plea bargain. Needless to say, their advice went unheeded.

99. Tommy reported that he would have accepted the offer to save Gail but she insisted she would 'cut my f'ing tongue out' if he did (*STV* 11 January 2011). This is contradicted by some reports (e.g. *NoW* 26 January 2011). The statement by the *Guardian* (24 December 2010) that: 'Gail Sheridan had been under immense pressure before the trial to strike a deal, but she rejected the offers' did not explain the rationale for her rejection.

100. *Sunday Herald* 12 July 2009.

101. Tommy's solicitor, Aamer Anwar, frequently questioned why it was that so much of the pre-trial evidence was appearing in the media (*Daily Mail* 25 February 2008). After the trial, the *Scottish Review* (5, 6, 7, 11 January 2011) legitimately questioned the nature of media reporting of the trial and the BBC's obtaining of police video interview tapes. Neither had an impact on the trial's outcome though. The complaint to broadcasting regulator, Ofcom, by Tommy and Gail over the BBC obtaining and broadcasting these tapes (on *The Rise and Lies of Tommy Sheridan*) was dismissed. They had argued their privacy had been infringed and that Tommy had been treated unfairly given that the tape of him had not been shown in the 2010 court case (*Herald* 25 October 2011). The regulator ruled these considerations were outweighed by the BBC's freedom of expression and the public interest in the case. However, Gail gave notice that she felt 'compelled' to seek judicial review of the decision on her complaint (*The Firm* 25 October 2011). The argument that media reporting had prejudiced the perjury trial against Tommy was rejected by Lord Bracadale in a judgement of 18 November 2011. His reasons were that the jury being subject to a deep and sustained body of evidence well after the publication of prejudicial articles limited their impact so as not to be prejudicial (see also *The Firm* 21 November 2011, *Herald* 22 November 2011).

102. However, there were successful attempts by Tommy's lawyers to have reporting restrictions imposed on the later hearings in July and August 2010 (*DTTSS*, p. 287).

103. 4 October 2010. The *Herald*, BBC Scotland's website and 'The Sheridan Trial' (*TST*) blog were the best contemporaneous day-by-day accounts and their use is gratefully acknowledged (notwithstanding any criticisms of the media coverage of the trial – see Roy, K. 'The two trials of Tommy' *Scottish Review* 12 October 2010).

104. When the verdict came in on 23 December 2010, for the first and only time the early evening *STV* News was a news special, devoting its entire 30 minute bulletin to the matter.

105. From this point onwards, his solicitor, Aamer Anwar, worked for Tommy as 'amicus curiae' – 'friend of the court' – without being paid Legal Aid (*Herald* 3 January 2011). Tommy may have also been angered by Maggie Scott urging him the day before the trial started to accept the plea bargain that had been on the table for some time.

106. *TST* 14 October 2010.

107. *Herald* 21 December 2010.

108. It seems he did not always remember 'a wee saying from Lenin: he who loses his temper loses his head' (*Scotsman* 25 November 2000) as he said he did earlier.

109. Of course, it is up to the prosecution to prove the defendant is guilty rather than the defendant to prove he or she is innocent.

110. The same was true for Gail before all the charges against her were dropped.

111. In his lengthy summing up and mitigation speeches, Tommy also made his pleas for leniency partly based on tugging at the jurors' emotional heartstrings of being separated from Gail and daughter, Gabrielle.

112. Paul McBride QC believed that when defending oneself there is a loss of a sense of perspective and distance (*BBC Radio Scotland* 'Drivetime' 23 December 2010)

and: 'He chose to defend himself and that is his right. I suspect there are a number of things he will come to regret in relation to this particular trial and I think that will be one of them' (*BBC News online* 23 December 2010). However, Alice Sheridan proffered: 'I've absolutely no regrets about [Tommy representing himself because] numerous QCs have approached me since the trial to say they couldn't have conducted the defence as well as Tommy did. Most of them are experienced in dealing with everyday murder but, you see, no matter how good they might be, they're not well versed in conspiracy cases, and, as I keep stressing, this is a conspiracy' (*Herald* 27 January 2011). However, Tommy admitted to Lord Bracadale that legally he was 'out of [his] depth' (*Scotsman* 24 December 2010) and was instructed by him – at the behest of the jurors – not to shout in court.

113. *Sunday Mirror* 13 August 2006. Here Tommy wrote: 'I accused them of acting like an undeclared faction at the end of May. They squealed in protest. Then [they] formed the very faction I had spoken of'. Patterson, R. 'No more heroes' *Red Pepper* (October 2006) dated the United Left's existence from February 2006, when it was called the 'February 2006 network'. The 28 May 2006 NC turned this into the United Left (see Chapter 6).

114. *STV* 22 December 2010.

115. Of course, he could not dare explain it by virtue of the attempt by the SSP leadership to get him to deal with the *NoW* Cupids 'allegations' differently. In interviews (e.g. *Guardian* 15 August 2007), he cited that the hard-left had always been badly divided – even though the SSA/SSP were from 1996 to 2004 exemplars of left unity.

116. Neither did any of the interviews that Tommy did and for which he was paid (with the money invariably going to his political parties of the time).

117. *STV* 22 December 2010.

118. Interestingly, this tactic was not rebuked by Militant's successors, the Socialist Party and SPS.

119. *Herald* 6 November 2010.

120. *Herald* 6 November 2010.

121. *Herald* 20 December 2010. Cell site analysis of Tommy's mobile was tracked to Manchester (*Sunday Mail* 24 February 2008) but this evidence was not presented which appears to remain unexplained (even though it is not usual for not all evidence available to be put before the court because of legal sufficiency tests).

122. *DTTSS* p. 287.

123. Des Mclean had worked with Tommy on his various post-2006 comedy shows and, thus, could be taken to be a likely supporter of Tommy.

124. *Herald* 3 November 2010.

125. See Chapter 6.

126. *Herald* 6 October 2010.

127. *Herald* 7 November 2010.

128. Jock Penman was a prosecution witness but played the role of defence witness. He was called by the Crown in order to then call another prosecution witness who stated Penman had lied.

129. Interestingly, Tommy made no mention of the 'People' Party' cultural weekend in his *Scottish Socialist Voice* (20 September 2002, 27 September 2002, 4 October 2002) column given he claimed he attended the event on 27 September 2002. Normally, he would have mentioned prior to the event that the SSP was holding it and that he was going and/or that he had attended it in the column afterwards. He did, however, say he would not be able to attend the anti-war demonstration on 28 September 2002 (*Scottish Socialist Voice* 27 September 2002).

130. The accusation that the McNeilage tape was a fake was continued by the Defend the Tommy Sheridan Campaign in 2011 ('Continuing News Coroporation scandal – their use of actors for blagging ... and the McNeilage tape' 16 July 2011 and 'Questions submitted to Tom Watson MP, by the Defend Tommy Sheridan Campaign, for him to ask the Murdochs and Rebecca Brooks at the Select Committee Hearing on Tuesday 19th July 2011' Defend Tommy Sheridan website, 19 July 2011).

131. McFarlane also had his own personal interest in denying what he was alleged to have done as he was in a monogamous relationship.

132. However, there was no political, legal or public appetite, it seems, to pursue this (especially as the charges against the other five of the 'Sheridan 7' from the 2006 case were dropped on 23 December 2010).

133. *Herald* 18 November 2010. See also *Herald* 18 January, 27 March 2007, *Mirror* 24 March 2007.

134. *Herald* 24 December 2010 (see also *DTTSS* pp. 247–250). It was not known whether the claims by Tom Watson MP about surveillance conducted by News Corporation (*Guardian* 20 October 2011) involved the allegation concerning the bugging of Tommy's car. The revelations about a secret *NoW* mobile phone (*Independent* 26 October 2011) relate to the period 2004 to 2006, and not before.

135. The Crown chose not to present the *pro-forma* statements found in Tommy's house which were for use with Colin Fox, Richie Venton and Steven Nimmo.

136. This is because certain charges are used to allow certain pieces of evidence to be presented to the court, and having served this purpose, are often dispensed with.

137. Arising from the police search of their home in December 2007, accusations of theft of miniature bottles of alcohol from her work by her employer were also dropped (*Daily Record* 10 July 2008). This is likely to have been a ploy to cast doubt over the veracity of any testimony Gail might give in a perjury trial. Nonetheless, there were inconsistencies in how the miniatures were (not improperly) obtained (see *Daily Record* 12 March, 10 July 2008) and they did relate to one aspect of the police investigation (*DTTSS* pp. 264–265).

138. These were the same themes he used in a lengthy interview with Bernard Ponsonby before conviction on *STV* (but which was fully broadcast on 11 January 2011). The narrative of family was also heavily used in his last television interview before imprisonment (see *STV* 26 January 2011).

139. *Press Association* 22 December 2010.

140. The first involved one concerning an affair with Anvar Khan while married and the second an aspect of his sexual relationship with Katrine Trolle – having sex with her in his martial bed. It should be added that perjury pertains to the statements being competent evidence in the case in which they were made, and material to the subject of the case.

141. *Sunday Herald* 9 January 2011, see also *Herald* 10, 11 January 2011.

142. *STV* 26 January 2011

143. The rhetorical flourish of Tommy trying to have it both ways continued. While he argued in court he was 'fighting for his life', as soon as conviction and sentence were passed, he promised to be back, stronger than before, carrying on the fight. Clearly, his life was not at stake quite in the way he argued earlier. Tommy was granted bail between conviction and sentencing on 26 January 2011. It is worth recalling that when asked if he had any regrets over the 'Tommygate' affair, on *Newsnight Scotland* (26 April 2007) Tommy said he only regret was being naive in trusting others and expecting their support.

144. *Daily Mail* 24 December 2010.

145. However, according to the list of those suing News International over phone-hacking (*Guardian* 6 October 2011) and the list of these affected by hacking (*BBC News*

online 'Phone hacking: The main players' 28 September 2011), Tommy was not one of those, suggesting that his statement after his conviction may have been no more than bluster. Similarly, notice of taking action was given against Lothian and Borders police for the release of his interview video tapes to BBC Scotland. The reporting by the *Scotsman* and Daily *Record* (15 October 2011) concerned the Tommy Sheridan Defence Campaign attempting to raise money to help pay for legal fees for Tommy to try to recover the £200,000 in damages he was awarded from News International in 2006. However, as pointed out earlier, the appeal against the award is still potentially pending given that it has been lodged.

146. His prison blog (http://tommysheridan.wordpress.com/), which began on 27 September 2010 and had 14 posts in the time when Tommy was incarcerated, was not quite comparable to Gramsci's *Prison Notebooks*. Posts were full of invective and did not consider strategies as Gramsci did in terms of 'wars of position' and 'wars of manoeuvre'. But they were better than his earlier prison diaries in 2000. The last entry on his blog from Barlinnie was made on 7 May 2011. His entries were written out by hand and posted out to a political associate to type out and upload. His blog entries were ended after it became apparent that the Scottish Prison Service was becoming irked by them and this was likely to jeopardise Tommy's move to an open prison (*Sunday Mail* 19 June 2011). This shed ironic new light on the subtitle to Tommy's blog, namely, '100% unedited, 100% unflinching', suggesting he was willing to be censored. Tommy was moved to an open prison, Castle Huntly, near Dundee on 20 June 2011 (*Daily Record* 21 June 2011). Tommy was allowed his first home visit on 19 July 2011. Under the conditions of his home release, he was barred from speaking to the media (*Herald, Scotsman* 20 July 2011). However, Tommy claimed he was being victimised by having less leave than he was entitled to because of being categorised as a long-term prisoner or one that was a threat to the public or at risk of reoffending (*Scotsman* 20 July 2011).

147. 28 January 2011.

148. 4 February 2011.

149. 16 February 2011.

150. *Herald* 1 March 2011. He repeated this line of argument in his blog of 9 March 2011. After sentencing, he made similarly defiant statements on Facebook (*Sunday Mail* 26 December 2010).

151. Blog 14 April 2011.

152. 26 February 2011.

153. In his mitigation plea in particular, Tommy argued that no one had been murdered, there had been no physical violence and the like and that his perjury was a 'victimless crime'. While he may have had some legal foundation for this argument, politically the SSP had been destroyed and countless socialists had been defamed in the course of his actions.

154. *Daily Record, Scotsman* 27 January 2011

155. *Herald* 24 December 2010.

156. *Herald* 27 January 2011.

157. These emails were, subsequently reported not to have been lost. Nonetheless, they related to 2005 and 2006, and not 2004 or before (*Guardian* 29 March 2011). Thus, the importance of the emails to Tommy during the trial itself was not so much what they actually showed but that he may have been able to use them to sway the jury in terms of playing to their anti-*NoW* beliefs. See conclusion for further discussion of this aspect.

158. *Scotland on Sunday* 26 December 2010.

159. *Scotsman* 7 January 2011. Amongst the legal fraternity, there were some voices of dissent over the trial. For example, Ian Hamilton QC questioned the safety of the conviction by virtue of reliance upon paid witnesses – that is, those that were paid earlier by *NoW* (*BBC Radio Scotland* 24 December 2010, *The Firm* 3 January 2011). Hamilton is a well-known supporter of Tommy (*Scottish Review* 20 October 2011). See also the comments of Mike Dailly (*Scotsman* 27 January 2011).
160. *Herald* 8 January 2011.
161. *Herald* 6 April 2011.
162. *Press and Journal* 19 May 2011, *Herald* 20 May 2011.
163. *Herald* 23 June 2011.
164. *Scotland on Sunday* 10 June 2011, *BBC News online* 19 July 2011. The latter reported: 'Sheridan's appeal against his conviction is to be put on hold pending the completion of an inquiry by Strathclyde Police into allegations that witnesses at his trial may have lied under oath'.
165. *BBC News online*, *Herald* 5 August 2011.
166. Press release, Defend Tommy Sheridan Campaign, 4 August 2011.
167. *Herald* 5 August 2011.
168. 31 August-6 September 2006.
169. *Evening Times* 17 May 2001.
170. *Scotland on Sunday* 17 December 2000.
171. *Daily Mail* 4 July 2000.
172. By contrast, Tommy hoped: 'Solidarity does well in the other seven electoral regions we are standing in and maintain our position as the leading socialist party in Scotland ... [and] the rat-infested SSP get the electoral humiliation their coalition with the reactionary Murdoch press befits them' (blog 5 May 2011). After only gaining 2,837 votes across seven regions, it was a classic understatement to say – as Tommy did – that this was 'disappointing' (blog 6 May 2011). Any sense of a renewal for the SSP was tempered by its vote being in 2011 only two thirds of what it received in 2007 (which was a tenth of what it received in 2003) and that the SLP – as an almost non-existent and moribund organisation – gained twice the SSP's vote. Overall, on the regional list seats the three socialist parties gained a dismal 1.3% of the vote 'posing little challenge to the large parties' (*Herald* 7 May 2011).
173. McColl, P. ('Grassroots aren't green' *Scottish Left Review*, July/August 2011) suggested the 2011 result of 2 MSPs was a poor and disappointing result for the Greens, indicating this benchmark for the SSP was a low one.

8

Person, Persona and
Personality

Introduction

For many idealists across the political spectrum, it seems elemental that personalities should have no place in politics. Politics should be about issues and ideology – period. Yet, because we live in a society where the consciousness of citizens lags quite far behind those of politicians and political activists, this is not the case. Not only is room, thereby, created for the role of personality in politics but there often appears to be a need for it too, especially as the conduit of the very political matter that is being attempted to be conveyed. And, so it is that the person and personality of Tommy became vital to his ability to convey socialist messages and to lead resistance and opposition. He highlighted important aspects of politics that socialists seldom give much attention to. These are the relationships between the individual socialist leader and their socialist party, and between the person and their politics. It's an old adage that the personal is political, and by logical extension that the political is also personal. In the case of Tommy, this was true with a vengeance. For the socialist left especially, this might be an uncomfortable lesson because eternal faith is put in the message, and not the disciple or messenger. Where the role of the person is usually given any consideration on the far left, it is merely ventured that one leader was better than another simply because of their political understanding and perspective as if this was completely divorced from any personal characteristics or traits.

Because Tommy has been a high-profile politician and public figure of working class stock, there has been inevitable interest in his private life on the basis that he is a not just a celebrity of sorts, but a people's celebrity and one of the 'ordinary folk'. Many voters and citizens want to know what such people are like as individuals, as 'real' people, and what makes them 'tick'. There is nothing particularly untoward in this. Indeed, in an interview with the *Sunday Herald*,[1] Tommy said that he talked about his private life freely because he wanted it 'to be open and transparent'.[2] At other times, he stated he believed members of the public knowing about his personal life was essential to normalise him in their eyes. But the specific and manifest basis of this interest in Tommy's private life is four-fold. So in addition to his basic celebrity status which is based on – and in turn – generates a public fascination, first, the public has an interest in whether such an outspoken and unambiguous character lives his life as he says and suggests – whether 'he walks the talk'. More especially, in an age of widespread cynicism towards politicians as both individual self-servers and self-serving elite, Tommy became known as *the* politician of integrity and principle in Scotland and of the left. Consequently, many say they might not agree with his politics but they respect him as being selfless to his causes of fighting the rich and powerful, for socialism and against injustice, poverty and war. Second, on top of this, he has courted the media to deliberately build up his profile, to normalise himself, and to do so with a particular image of himself as an 'ordinary bloke' concerned with football and family.[3] This meant he was monogamous, married and heterosexual. While there were obvious advantages to doing so, choosing to conform to the dominant social norms in such a public way comes with the danger of being found out and pilloried for any transgressions. Thirdly, there is the sense in which the 'personal is political' and the 'political is personal' so that citizens have some right to information by which to try to judge and understand public figures in terms of what motivates and drives them forward, how they behave and so on without being wholly intrusive and denying them a private dimension to their lives. Again, there is a righteous need to know if politicians 'walk the talk'. Lastly, as a leading socialist, it behoves Tommy to have kept his 'nose clean' so as not to provide his political enemies with any opportunity to cast him and his politics down for reasons other than to do with his politics. Here, the analogy with the shop steward who makes sure he or she is a good time-keeper and conscientious worker is apt.

When it comes to politicians' sex lives, 'prudish' approaches should prevail over 'prurient' ones when sexual relations are between consenting adults and without harm to each other.[4] In terms of Tommy's sex life, there is no particular need or right for the public to know about it unless it somehow clashes with – and contradicts – his consciously constructed public persona, comments about his own private life, and the impressions he created of it. This clearly did happen in Tommy's case. It was not the case that he needed to have publicly lectured others on sexual morality[5] for this to be justified for what he did was very much at odds with the persona he constructed. But what also then gives the public a further right to know about his sex life is that he took a defamation case *against NoW* to disprove the Cupids 'allegations' that were true and in the process split asunder the SSP, a party then with six MSPs and of which he was leader. In order to judge the veracity of his claims and actions here as well as Tommy the socialist politician overall, the public is then entitled – and needs – to know what did happen in his sex life. Indeed, it was Tommy himself who brought about this situation. The possibility of Tommy being a liar and hypocrite demands this. The situation would have been altogether different if Tommy had, making this evident in public, a consensual open relationship with his partner and then wife, Gail, as well as pronounced frequently and very publicly that he did not believe in the hidebound norms of conventional bourgeois morality. Instead, by his words and actions, it is plausible to suggest that Tommy believed himself, and expected others to agree, that politicians should conform to these notions and that the public would think less of him and them if they knew what politicians did in their private lives. But also added to this was that he asked others to lie for him to provide him with cover and alibis over these very matters. Here one lie begat many more.[6] So there is the unfortunate sense that Tommy was hoisted by his own petards – the very ones he chose himself. However, there is another reason to examine the person and persona of Tommy. This is because the mainstream media – broadsheet and tabloid papers included – believed that Tommy had brought himself down through his own vanity, arrogance and delusion.[7] While there is evidence of vanity, as will be demonstrated, it was not this or his alleged arrogance or delusion which explains Tommy's actions.

People consciously and unconsciously project onto Tommy the bits they see, hear and experience of him and the bits they want to see, hear and experience of him. This can lead to varying interpretations of him, especially as their knowledge and experience of him are partial and context specific and can be direct and well as indirect. Thus, one facet can be made writ large to form a dominant personality. Tommy, of course, has played his part in this process. This socio-psychological process no doubt occurs with other figures which have emerged into some kind of notoriety in public life from popular campaigns and social movements but in the case of Tommy, it is of more significance because he became a consummate, combative, controversial and high-profile politician. So the case for knowing about Tommy, socialist politician, as person and personality is one that is not only overwhelming but also essential to judging him as a socialist politician. By the same token, it is also important to know about Gail Sheridan, for she played the role of 'best supporting actress' in many different ways throughout the stages of Tommy's career. With bombast worthy of Tommy, the most public and dramatic evidence of this was saying: 'I have and will always stand by Tommy' outside the court following his conviction and then: 'Tommy has dedicated his life to helping others. The real reason why he has been imprisoned today is because he has fought injustice and inequality with every beat of his heart. But it won't be long before Tommy is back – stronger and continuing the fight' following his sentencing.

This chapter, therefore, examines Tommy's traits and characteristics as a person, Tommy norms and standards of behaviour and his personal relationships with various key people in his life. As intimated elsewhere, Tommy is a proud and defiant, not paranoid and delusional, person. His unwillingness to ever say sorry and never admit defeat stems from this basic trait. Surrender is not in his vocabulary. And his battle-hardened character has been shaped by the extreme and intense environments of adoration and condemnation so he has a very definite sense of himself and his purpose in life. To summarise before moving on, his personality also comprises the following traits: boldness, brassneck, self-confidence and self-control, and tendencies towards hyperbole, bombast and risk taking.[8] His mother, as explained earlier, has had a role to play in creating and nurturing these traits. He cultivated the image of a settled relationship, then a settled marriage and then a traditional family in the media. Alan McCombes variously, thus, described Tommy as being 'the Daniel O'Donnell of Scottish politics'[9] and like 'John-Boy Walton'.[10] At the time, there was some disquiet in the SSP at the extensive use of his private life to promote himself and the SSP given that this was a step away from hardnosed socialist politics. However, some saw this as a good move, showing that a leading socialist figure could become normalised into the nation's public life, allowing a softer, more humane side to emerge to the party's leading member.

Going 'in Character'

Over time in the public and media spotlight, Tommy increasingly came to play the character of 'Tommy Sheridan' as was not only expected of him but which he wanted to and which was a winning formula.[11] The character was strong, fearless, angry, charming, in control and often self-deprecating (although he often also said there was no room for modesty in politics). There was no doubt about the first traits. For example, *Holyrood* commented that Tommy was 'like Rambo without guns ... regularly rag[ing] for Scotland'.[12] But it can be doubted whether the self-deprecation was genuine or more a case of politically correct false modesty.[13] One example was: 'I am just one individual. The movement is bigger than me, always has been, always will be'.[14] As the character, he gave consummate performances, combining 'man of the people' and 'socialist firebrand' (although some journalists questioned the ease by which he so quickly turned on these performances[15]. So in some circumstances he could 'do' humble with citizens and campaigners, and at other times 'self-assured – or 'blistering self-confidence' as the *Daily Mail*[16] put it – with political opponents and the media. With citizens, George McNeilage recalled he would ingratiate and flatter with his big smile, hand on shoulder and 'howzit going, pal?' line. But, according George McNeilage, 'Tommy's most used line to me was 'Who the fuck was that?' after meeting someone because he never took the time to get to know people and because he wasn't interested' even though it was his trademark to ask questioners, like journalists, their first name and then litter his answers with said names. Many of the ordinary folk who looked up to and admired Tommy would say to him, in Glasgow patois, 'oan youse go, big man' because he was the voice of the voiceless, the fighter for those who wanted to but could not or would not fight for themselves. In this, he was critically the same as them but also different. The character gave Tommy self-affirmation as he became what he always had wanted to be: a socialist tribune. This is not to argue that Tommy was an actor or was acting because the connection between himself and going 'in character' was too deep, organic and intimate.[17] Nonetheless, he was a performer who put on very strong performances.

Sometimes, as many journalists (including Joan McAlpine)[18] noted the sense of being 'in character' was evident when Tommy would come out with trite, pat and manufactured answers because he was not prepared to engage in self-reflection.[19] Sometimes, the earnestness to play the 'Tommy' role was a little too much and intense, betraying the sense of going into character. Joan McAlpine recalled:

> Sometimes he [tried] to show too much empathy with working class people [for example] he takes great pride in knowing nothing about culture except for football. He went so far as to say he was a Philistine by saying he was a Palestine just to show he's so authentically working class. ... Sometimes, he wants to play dumb and be unsophisticated ... be an ingénue and play up to that.[20]

Meantime, the *Daily Record* believed Tommy 'ha[d] a deep flaw – a surfeit of sincerity'.[21] The character had other flaws as Joan McAlpine saw it: 'He doesn't have the ability [to engage] in self reflection. If you ask him something difficult [about himself] or personal he comes out with a pat, stock answer ... Other politicians might be the same but because Tommy's reputation is built on being a real person, you expect something more [of him] ... [N]ow looking back on it, there was a certain sense that it was being rehearsed ... there's almost no spontaneity about Tommy.' Other journalists found that such answers to the question 'what makes Tommy tick?' were a little to hackneyed, formulaic and earnest: 'My whole lifeblood, every instinct in my body, is for unity of working-class people. I am striving to eradicate a repressive class system and create a more egalitarian society ... I'm married to revolution'.[22]

Nonetheless, this character was developed and road-tested in the heat of battle over many years from drafty halls, street corners, the council chamber and television studios to the parliament. It was a winning formula which made him feel he could take on all comers and win. Indeed, Alan McCombes recounted: 'During the poll tax, he learnt how to hone his skills and work an audience ... he'd be a brilliant actor and I don't say that in a derogatory manner ... some of the skills of an orator are those of an actor like timing, presentation'.[23] The character was not one-dimensional as Keith Baldassara observed: 'When he is with his male friends, he will brag about what he loves to do – sex, affairs. When he's with Gail, he the endearing partner, husband and now father – completely different. When he's with Gail's parents, he's the endearing son-in-law. He can do the different roles at the same event ... Tommy is a juggler, a spinner of plates, with different stories for different people in different places in his life'.

The later version of going 'in character' was centred round playing the victim. Tommy argued in his summing up on 21 and 22 December 2010 that he had been subject to a 'persecution not prosecution' and was the victim of a conspiracy and vendetta. The most obvious case of a similar but actual vendetta in recent times was Robert Maxwell's *Daily Mirror* campaign against Scargill in 1990 over allegedly taking strike support funds to pay off his mortgage. Scargill was exonerated after independent investigation by Gavin Lightman QC, and the newspaper's then editor, Roy Greenslade, disowned the story and admitted it was a groundless smear in 2002. Scargill was attacked not only because of what he had done – humbling the Tories in 1974 and leading a to the death battle with the Thatcher government in 1984–1985 which the NUM came close to winning – but because Scargill and the NUM would shortly face – in 1992 – their denouement with the massive pit closure programme. This smear was an attempt to finish Scargill off once and for all before this battle because he still commanded political authority.[24] By contrast, Tommy's situation was very different. The Cupids 'allegations' against him were more than just allegations, being based in fact, and the attack was to do with him being a public figure rather than a socialist politician. Scargill was not the author of his own fate while Tommy was. This whole turn of events led Joan McAlpine to wonder if Tommy was not what he said he was:

The key moment in the pantomime, for me, was when Sheridan emerged victorious into the sunshine outside the Court of Session [in 2006]. There he trembled with fury ... accus[ing] his former friends of being scabs and liars and employed a righteous anger I have heard before. It was the same anger with which he attacked the sheriff's officers, the Labour MPs, the boardroom fat cats, the Faslane nuclear submarine base. What if he didn't mean it, then or now? What if all this passionate intensity was a gift he could summon at will? This is the first time I have questioned his political integrity. Even private conversations with him can feel rehearsed. Might the whole working-class warrior persona be a careful construct?[25]

But, as explained below, the righteous 'scabs' anger was real, nonetheless, because Tommy genuinely felt hurt as he had, in his own words, been subject to 'deep, deep betrayal'[26] by close comrades and the effect of that betrayal was, he believed, to bring him to the brink of political destruction. The 'going in character' clearly calls into question whether Tommy was the 'real deal' who 'walks it' like he 'talks it'. This is not the same as saying he is a fake[27] but it does somewhat question his authenticity given that George Burns, the comedian, often opined: 'Acting is all about honesty. If you can fake that, you've got it made'.

From 2001 very close comrades and from 2004 close comrades believe they saw the veracity of his public persona unwind. For example, they saw coldness replace the warmth they noticed earlier and this led them to question whether the warmth was genuine. The sense of control and pre-determination were evident in one aspect of 'going into character' which was that Tommy did not really do humour,[28] and that which he did do was laboured and lame (as many of his Edinburgh Fringe reviewers commented). Thus, he often said: 'If you see a table and chairs on the street in Edinburgh, it's probably a bistro. In Glasgow, it's probably a warrant sale' and during Glasgow's City of Culture designation in 1992 'Never mind about the Pavarotti, what about the Poveratti?'.[29] During the perjury trial, he asked his brother-in-law: "Do I always beat you at Scrabble?', eliciting the response 'No'. Mr Sheridan stated that I would like to remind you that you are still under oath – but unfortunately you are right".[30]

Being and playing 'Tommy' had a couple of linguistic aspects. The first was that from 2004 onwards, Tommy increasingly talked of himself in the third person.[31] Upon resigning as SSP national convener, he said: [O]ur party is bigger than Tommy Sheridan'.[32] Third person usage is normally understood as a distancing technique, if not trying to hide from something.[33] The second was his tendency to talk in terms of 'we' and 'us', again from 2004 onwards, without making it clear whether he was talking about himself and Gail, himself and his supporters within the SSP or himself and Solidarity, or merely just using 'we' to suggest that he was bigger and stronger than himself as a single person and, thus, not an isolated individual.

Defiant Risk Taker

Tommy was an inveterate and defiant risk taker because he always played for high stakes in his battle for socialism. His means justified his ends.[34] He believed in 'will to power', 'needs must', 'who dares wins', 'chancing his luck'[35] and overall played not for compromises and concessions but for victories and advances pretty much no matter the objective conditions.[36] For him, nothing less than this was required in this battle which was his burning and abiding passion. Even if he aimed high and gained less, to him this was better than aiming low and securing an easy gain. George Galloway got something of the measure of him here when he said on 10 November 2009 in the Glasgow North East by-election that Tommy 'would charge the guns of the enemy without fearing the consequences'. Examples of Tommy's own expression of this were: 'I refuse to bend the knee to [NoW's] assault of me'[37] and NoW 'will never get me to bow my head ... [it] may hurt me but [it] will never destroy me politically'.[38] He told me at the 28 May 2006 NC that 'If I'm going to go down, I'm going to go down fighting' indicating that he thought it better to go down fighting no matter what, and even if this meant allowing the media to constantly re-air all the damaging allegations as a result of the 28 May 2006 SSP NC, the defamation case and perjury trial.

As outlined earlier, in many respects, Tommy was not risk averse – risk assessments were not part of his thinking. He was willing to take bold steps and was prepared to make personal sacrifices when required. He was something of a poker player in politics.[39] For example, prior to the 2006 libel case, he had defended himself in court on numerous occasions and often won – but when he did not win, he was prepared to serve the time. Indeed, he would rather go to jail than pay a fine as to him this was an admission of guilt, something he was not prepared to do because he did not recognise the legitimacy of the authority which meted out the punishment. The defiant risking was not without strategic calculation and became his guiding *modus operandi*. This was based on an assessment of his own ability and the forces behind him capable of winning over others and achieving desired goals. His ability to make good on such strategic calculation of risk and defiance in his political career dating back to the late 1980s explains why he thought he felt confident and able to continue to take risks and win when he did so.[40] But in the end, like Icarus, his equivalent of flying to close to the sun, was that he overreached himself by taking on too many opponents at the one time, trying to keep too many plates spinning at the one time and – for him – on a weak foundation of arguments that stretched the bounds of credulity just that bit too far. It seemed that 'bold and brave' turned into 'audacious and adventurous'.[41]

The willingness to take risk was not the result of self-delusion,[42] ego as vanity or arrogance.[43] Rather, it came from four sources. The first was the recognition he was in a David-and-Goliath situation against the massed forces of the *status quo* so courage, boldness and audacity, he believed, were not only required but were his only weapons when prosecuting socialism. His schooling in Militant played a role here for it gave him an exaggerated sense of what was possible (rather than probable). The second was that he was an impatient, often impulsive person as both his past[44] and present[45] close collaborators testified to. Some of this no doubt came from the influence of the force of the personality of his mother but some of it also came from being psychologically schooled in the heat of the successful battle against the poll tax where quick action was essential and paramount. Allan Green recalled: 'Tommy always wanted to push as far and as fast as possible'. This element of impatience chimed with Tommy's belief in political voluntarism, whereby sufficient subjective will was believed to be able to overcome many objective conditions. In other words, through a transformational style of leadership, inspiring and exhorting members and workers to put their shoulders to wheel longer and harder could achieve the desired political breakthroughs despite hostile environments.[46] The third was that he was a defiant person, again some of this coming from his mother. Defiance in the direct face of the enemy made him doubly unwilling to moderate himself, his views or his ambitions, even if he was facing defeat or the odds were so heavily stacked against him. The defiance could be seen in many aspects of his public persona such as smiling on the way in to court to be sentenced on 26 January 2011 or the refusal to show dismay immediately after being convicted on 23 December 2010. His persona of defiance seldom slipped. One occasion was a very momentary lapse upon being sentenced in 2011.[47] The defiance was reinforced by his sense of self-belief and self-confidence (see earlier). One aspect of this was a belief in his (own) omniscience. Ronnie Stevenson believed 'uncritical adulation' from Alice 'maybe led [Tommy] to believe that [he] ha[d] no need to be criticised ... that checks and balances [we]re not needed in [his] case'. Both Frances Curran and Richie Venton, in the former's words recounted: 'I've never known him to retrospectively admit he was wrong, made a mistake or take responsibility for a mistake'.[48] Fourth, Tommy had obvious communication skills of persuasion and charm so he was more able than most to make a fist of this defiance. Putting these all together made him a formidable operator even if, according to Peter Taaffe, he 'exaggerate[d] ... his own personal ability'.

Clear examples of being a risk taker are found in Tommy sacking his legal team in 2006 (after two weeks) and in 2010 (after a week). He won in 2006 and lost in 2010. Was this another spectacular misjudgement given the first trial was a civil one and the second was a criminal one whereby thresholds of legal expertise and repercussion were higher in 2010? There may seem to be something to this in regard of 2010 for it speaks to the old adage that 'a person who represents themselves has a fool for a client'. Given that his strategy was to concoct the fabrication that all the Crown witnesses 'had it in for him', selfrepresentation was not necessarily a mistake. No one knew the fabrication and conspiracy that Tommy was engaged in better than he did because he had invented and prosecuted it. He was able to engage in hard-hitting character assassination precisely because he had 'broken bread' with numerous of the witnesses. Tommy demonstrated beyond all reasonable doubt that he understood that the rights and wrongs of the case and the ins and outs of the law were nothing compared to persuading a jury by foul means or fair of the case he was putting to them. Comments by Gail suggest that Tommy being in control was also part of the psychology of these actions.[49] But clear examples of risking were also found in taking his position of total war within the SSP and then setting up a new political party a mere eight months before an election and in the circumstances where Tommy would always been dogged by the stories surrounding his sex life and Solidarity would always have been dogged by the split with – and from – the SSP. Personally, Tommy was in unchartered waters of leading a political formation with few credible confidants and advisors. In risk-taking, Tommy's moral code and compass increasingly came to be influenced by the dictums of 'the means justify the ends', 'win at all costs' and 'who dares wins' as a result of the combination of his Militant background and largerthan-life persona.

Part and parcel of this was that early on he became an inveterate practitioner of exaggeration, hyperbole and bombast.[50] Recalling especially his attitude to telling the truth in the 2006 defamation case, it may not have been such a big step with this foundation to do what he subsequently did from November 2004 onwards in terms of his grand conspiracy concoction and its various fabrications,[51] showing there were threads of continuity between the 'before' and 'after' of this critical juncture.[52] It was not arrogance that led him to deduce in his own terms that 'means justify ends' for he was, along with several others, critical to the success and existence of a renewed socialist force in Scotland. But the very strength of these features could also be a weakness for Tommy,[53] for in different situations and in different times, boldness and decisiveness became recklessness and irresponsibility. In showing defiance and taking risk, Tommy's single-mindedness to do so became, in the words of Richie Venton, an Achilles' heel: 'When it's right it's a brilliant asset, when it's wrong it's utterly destructive'. Whether it was one or the other depended on the intelligence gathering, analytical ability and so on. There was unanimity from both his SSP critics and Solidarity supporters that this trait needed to be reined in by others although some like Steve Arnott believed that 'for every [idea] he gets wrong he comes up with two or three [other] good ideas'.

Monstrous Egotist?

The media and political opponents were always quick to make the easy accusation that Tommy's 'problem' was that he had a massive ego and was egotistical. These accusations came particularly thick and fast after his conviction and sentencing for perjury – in other words, Tommy's downfall was due to his monstrous ego. For example, in the 2010 perjury trial Rosie Kane told Tommy: 'Your ego was on the rampage'.[54] She previously argued that Tommy's ego led to the split[55] while the SSP Executive Committee believed the split and the launching of Solidarity was 'a vehicle for the out of control ego of an individual'.[56] Alan McCombes believed Tommy was 'a rampaging egomaniac'.[57] Well beforehand, the *Scotsman Guide to Scottish Politics* reported: 'He is universally known as Tommy, and that is what he likes – being universally known'.[58] By contrast, Philip Stott believed: 'Tommy sees his personality and standing as an opportunity to advance the cause of socialism … it's not about him being in it for himself or that his primary focus is to make himself popular'. While it is far from the case that there is not some kernel of truth to the critics' accusation and statements, not only was the husk far more dominant but there was a fundamental misconception. If Tommy had no ego, he would not have been capable of doing what he did and achieving what he did, especially in regard of his drive, determination and brushing off criticism from opponents on the right. Ego as a conscious and sub-conscious sense of the self is critical if any person is to make an impact in politics or any other field. The issue is more what is done with the ego, and how and why. Thus, Peter Taaffe commented:

The role of the ego is very important to the socialist movement, and Tommy has an ego. That is indisputable .... When ego becomes bigger than the cause and the movement, you can become seduced by hostile class pressures. ... But without that drive no public leadership or figure [would exist or be achieved] without a consciousness of your own ability and power to influence individuals or course of events.[59]

Thus, the dispute was actually over the purpose or use of ego and the evidence of what it is used for, and not the existence of ego itself. This was not clear in the statement of his political opponents which collapsed what was a more complex argument into simplisms. For example, the United Left believed Tommy created 'a vain attempt to save his own vanity ...' while the SSP EC statement to the special 5 February 2011 SSP conference spoke of a 'rampant ego' and 'the dangers of allowing personal celebrity to displace political principles'.[60] Clearly, Tommy did believe – and not unreasonably – that he was important to the future of socialism in Scotland, notwithstanding the caveats concerning his self-deprecation and overall team effort. Given that the SSP was built, in large part, through and around Tommy by many of his subsequent critics, the issue can again be seen as what is done with the ego and for what purposes. It behoves serious criticism to point to these and not the use of ego *per se* if the arrow is to hit the target. What is not in dispute is that Tommy clearly found validation and affirmation from the various forms of media and public attention he received because he had secured his role as the leading spokesperson for socialism in Scotland. Thus, he recognised that he was making a major contribution to what he regarded as the most important activity he could ever engage in. He may also have needed some sense of adulation to continue that given to him by his mother when he was a child in order to satisfy his ego and to re-affirm himself. But whether Tommy's character was fundamentally changed by being in the limelight is something of an open question because it is normally the case that such exposure brings out and develops some traits more than others (rather than create them).

One aspect that people associate with Tommy's ego is his vanity, especially in regard of fake tans. He often admitted he was vain[61] and the roots of this may have come, in part, from childhood when he admitted to be a 'poseur'[62] and the sense of working class personal pride in one's appearance. Hating the 'peely-wally look',[63] and having used tanning machines since he was sixteen, he admitted that it was 'vanity'[64] and boosting his self-confidence that led him to do this.[65] With an interesting choice of words, his standard justification, despite admitting the health risks, was – in his own words – it was his one 'vice'[66] or 'sin'[67] as he stated he neither smoked, gambled nor drank.[68] Although he laughed off the derision this brought – like being called 'MSP for Fast Tan West' – he was sensitive to it because: 'One guy once accused me of being a legend in my own mirror. I'm very conscious about the vanity of the whole thing, and about what the working class think'.[69]

The fake tans relate to another aspect of his character, namely, the combination of seemingly simultaneous narcissism[70] and self-deprecation. In his *Mirror* columns which he more often wrote himself than his *Record* one, he promoted himself as a persona in regard of his looks, turning forty and so on.[71] There are several ways to read this. His harshest critics see it as shameless self-promotion of the individual celebrity. A more insightful view is to see it as a way of continuing the humanisation and normalisation of himself by showing that he had what he believed were the same concerns as normal people, whether this be family, male hair loss or being 'hen-pecked', and to do so in a self-deprecating manner while at the same time still talking about himself to maintain his personal profile. In this regard, Colin Fox commented: 'Publicity is like a suntan – you can't just go on the sunbed in January and expect to still have a tan by December – so you have to be in the limelight to keep it going. All the family stuff could be just because he [thought he] wasn't in the papers enough, nothing else was happening and he needed something to get his name in the pages again. He's desperate for publicity so he'd used anything'. On other occasions, he used personal circumstances to highlight political issues like mentioning his grans, Rose and Babs, in terms of the plight of pensioners. However, there did seem times when his praiseworthy mentions of Gail were gratuitous.[72] Alan McCombes recalled: 'After I stopped doing his *Mirror* column in 2003 ... the number of times Gail was mentioned was significant'. Some critics believed this was to counter the emergence of rumours on the grapevine about his infidelity. And, sometimes his namedropping of his celebrity friends was found to be tiresome and irritating. Tommy's justification for his pursuit and promotion of personal-based media coverage was that:

What I have to realise is that I am public property ... I've made myself public property ... If I want publicity when it comes to elections, then I need to take it when it comes to other things as well ... it humanises us ... it shows we are not full-time political animals ... on the left we are so marginalised and isolated because the media has constructed this barrier between the left, us and ordinary people by describing us as dangerous, fringe lunatics.

Stating he was happy to talk about his personal life,[73] he continued:

> What upsets my opponents is that it's enormously normalising ...
> I think it would be easier for them if I was monastic, because then
> you could get away with the idea that I was somehow weird. ...
> You may not know much about other politicians and their part-
> ners. That's fine; that's their decision, and I'm not going to knock
> that. But we get paid a lot for what we do and I want to be open
> and transparent.[74]

Yet, Tommy did more than merely answer questions put about his
personal life for he solicited coverage like that of a Karaoke night out.[75]
He also took part in events, like walking down the catwalk for charity at
the National Wedding Show exhibition in Glasgow in February 2000,
which went well beyond just answering questions on his personal life.
He and Gail became 'Scotland's answer to Posh and Becks'.[76] His
wedding became a society wedding, and there were over 20 lengthy
newspaper articles which focused upon both the person and the politics
before May 2003. With the exception of the sex scandal coverage, it
seemed Tommy subscribed to Oscar Wilde's dictum that there was no
such thing as bad publicity for he told the *Big Issue Scotland*: 'The only
thing worse than being talked about is not being talked about',[77] especially when he used his notoriety of the substance of his 2006 defamation case for the basis of his Edinburgh Fringe 'King of the Swingers'
shows.[78] When it came to being voted, or commented upon as, the
most handsome and sexiest councillor or MSP or some other such
appellation,[79] Tommy played it down with responses like 'politics is
Hollywood for ugly people' or saying this was the result of Thatcher's
abolition of free eye tests. Earlier, when in Saughton, he joked that his
greatest deprivation was not having pictures of himself in his cell.[80]
Only occasionally was he immodest – 'I've been told the camera loves
me but that's not my fault'[81] or 'I'm much more handsome than Derek
Hatton'.[82]

Psychopath?

Following from accusations of egotism were those of delusion and para-
noia.[83] Rosie Kane said of Tommy that he was paranoid[84] while Carolyn
Leckie believed Tommy had a personality disorder leading him to be a
psychopath with an inability for empathy and where 'socialist ideas are
a vehicle for him'. Alan McCombes reflected: 'I never accepted that
Tommy had a psychopathic personality ... I thought he was cowardly

and selfish ... I think I was wrong in retrospect ... [because] I couldn't recognise him as the person from before'. But an explanation which holds more water is that such appearances existed merely because they necessarily resulted from the knowing fabrication of a plot to provide cover for his sexual behaviour, and were not something more innate. It is in this light that the allegation of MI5 involvement in the McNeilage tape (where Tommy stated 'Just because you think everybody is out to get you, it doesn't mean you are paranoid'),[85] and in the SSP as well,[86] and reported comments like – to Anvar Khan of – 'don't talk about my business, MI5 are listening to me on the phone right now'[87] should be seen.[88] In other words, observers and critics confused the signs of Tommy doing what he believed was necessary at particular points in time after November 2004 with how and what Tommy was more generally. Ironically, there seemed little need of spooks inside the SSP when it proved capable of tearing itself apart of its own accord, unaided by third parties.

Friends and Friendship

To Tommy, friendship was a life affirming part of human relationships and humanity. Many of his friends were to use his own words – and regardless of how they looked – 'beautiful people' because of who and what they were.[89] His friends fell into two broad camps, the political and social, with occasional overlap and mixing. The political comprised SSP members, journalists and union activists. The social comprised family, old friends, footballers and some celebrities. Keith Baldassara and George McNeilage were examples of the overlap and of the 'beautiful people'. Tommy commented: 'Keith was like a brother to me', and in public he often referred to Keith as his 'comrade and treasured friend'[90] and his 'good friend and comrade'.[91] George came in for high praise from Tommy in *A Time to Rage* and afterwards[92] and chose Tommy as his best man for his wedding in 1997. But the construction of his fabrication from 2004 to 2010 necessitated character assassinating both Keith and George. So, for example, Keith became 'the mother of all backstabbers' and 'chief character assassin'.[93]

In a number of revealing admissions, Tommy indicated that loyalty was an aspect of friendship he expected, demanded and felt he had earned, especially where it had critical political implications for him. Although phrased in a doubtful manner given that one thing Tommy could not be accused of was being naive, he told the *Herald*: 'I didn't think some [other comrades] ha[d] different agendas, but over the years friends warned me that I was being naive, and I'd say that was my greatest crime,[94] the *Big*

Issue Scotland: 'The one thing I have been absolutely guilty of is naivety. I trust people and I see the best in everybody. I think that's a fault'[95] and *STV News*: 'I was naive in the way I thought the loyalty I showed to others would be reciprocated'.[96] On the McNeilage tape, he showed he was wounded by Keith – who he said he 'love[d] ... to bits' – for not having the loyalty to him to allow him to 'face it down' as he wanted as well as to not keep the information to himself. On the tape, Tommy said of Keith's contribution at the 9 November 2004 meeting: 'Fucking cut like a fucking [knife] right through my heart man ... a fucking poker right through my heart'.[97] Startlingly in terms of Gail, Tommy then said: 'The worst thing that's happened to me here isn't what going to happen in the future. Worst thing that's happened here is that I've lost two friends here. I've lost Alan McCombes and I've lost Keith Baldassara'. When Tommy met Frances Curran and Colin Fox on 10 November 2004, Frances asked 'Are you going to take the court action?' to which he said 'Yes'. Frances then said: 'Well, we want your resignation'. Tommy responded: 'For fuck's sake, Frances, I would have expected more loyalty from you'.[98] When Colin Fox refused to lie in court in 2006 for Tommy, Tommy felt betrayed having swung his supporters behind Colin for the national convenership election in 2005. Indeed, Tommy specifically singled out Colin Fox following his testimony against him, saying: 'I'm hurt beyond repair at what Colin ... has done'[99] and 'Colin has let me down'.[100] The intense and immense anger arose from his belief that he had been betrayed by those he thought should have supported and defended him and by those he thought he should have been able to trust, whether this be Anvar Khan and Katrine Trolle, or Keith Baldassara, George McNeilage, Alan McCombes or Colin Fox.

Given that Tommy 'works on the basis of loyalty' according to Colin Fox, it was this sense of betrayal, and not their supposed 'lies', which angered Tommy so much. Tommy believed their loyalty should have been to him as a person and as the embodiment of the SSP and not to the SSP itself.[101] But Tommy necessarily had to dress up what they said as 'lies' to square his circle.[102] The sense of betrayal was deepened by the fact that, in the words of Colin Fox: 'The split between Alan McCombes, Tommy, Keith Baldassara and George McNeilage was like the breaking up of a mafia family ... they all feel betrayal and vulnerability now because they know things about each other and what they did together'. Gordon Morgan was of the same view: 'Keith, Tommy and Alan were all different aspects of the same entity ... and what happened was the whole backup machinery was then withdrawn and you're cast out from the family ... this is a family divorce'.[103] For those on the receiving end of Tommy's venomous wrath, their sense of personal betrayal by Tommy was compounded by the political betrayal of throwing away all they had worked for over the years.

The basis of loyalty, unreciprocated loyalty and trust came under strain and contest from those who were close personal and political collaborators. They felt the relationship had been too much of a one-way street even though Tommy recounted: 'Keith and George are solid political allies as well as friends ... if I do anything politically questionable Keith and George are on to me straight away ... it's not a relationship of deference ... they are more than able to dissent'. The breaking point came over Tommy's actions over his sexual behaviour from 2004. For example, on the McNeilage tape Tommy recounts part of Keith's contribution at the 9 November 2004 meeting: 'I've been loyal to Tommy for the last few years – I've been obedient to Tommy and I'm not prepared to be obedient any more'. Keith recounted: 'Tommy loved me to bits because I was ultra-dependable ... I was a rock politically and socially'. Indeed, Keith was on the verge of resigning as Tommy's constituency worker because of Tommy's behaviour (see below). Peter Taaffe reflected: 'Tommy must have made some mistakes along the way to personally antagonise ... and alienate [people like Keith and George] and put them on such a collision course with him'. The issue was that when push came to shove, for Tommy, loyalty brooked no questions, doubts or criticism. It had to be total, unconditional and unreciprocated.

After the events of 2004 to 2010, many of his friends – those who thought they were friends with him – questioned whether they ever really knew him and began to feel they had been duped and used. George McNeilage said: 'Even after twenty years of thick and thin, he never opened up to me',[104] Alan McCombes reflected: 'It was difficult to get to know much about him, other than politics and football' and Colin Fox asked: 'Did any of us know the real Tommy Sheridan?' Thus, Alan McCombes expressed the indignation of many when he told Tommy that 'you were sticking the knife in the backs of other people who have stuck by you through thick and thin',[105] and both Keith and George began to wonder if Tommy had what they described as 'a conscience', social or otherwise, when they saw him denigrate and disparage others in the SSP and on the left. And, there were many that felt bitterly betrayed and let down by Tommy given that, in Colin Fox's words, former allies would have 'crawled over broken glass' for Tommy.[106]

Keith and Tommy

Keith Baldassara became one of Tommy's closest confidants and friends. He recalled they had an extremely good, close working relationship, where they could speak freely and openly to each other without taking offence although he sometimes found it difficult to get the time to speak properly and at length to him. Thus, 'Tommy was never a great socialiser, not a big pub person ... he did his own thing like football, running ... it was difficult to socialise with him because he was always the centre of attention so you couldn't really talk to him because everybody wanted to speak to him'.[107] Nonetheless, their relationship was a deep and long lasting one. Although Keith had crossed paths with Tommy in Militant and stayed briefly with him in 1986, this relationship began in earnest when Keith returned to Glasgow in mid-1988 to work on the anti-poll tax revolt (previously having been working at Militant HQ in London) and Tommy put him up in his flat at 265 Linthaugh Road, Pollok. Keith recalled: 'I had only been back for two nights ... when [of his own volition] he told me about his passion, his big desire for sex ... My attitude was fine – you're young and healthy ... All I said was don't use people. ... I think he was ... trying to get the measure of me [on this]'.[108] This was to begin a continual exchange on this terrain that led to the ending of their personal and political friendship.

In 1996, in the macho male environment of showers after a pre-season football training session, Keith recalled: 'Tommy was screaming and shouting about a closed doors session with a lap dancer where he was on stage with her ... He was bragging that he was the only one up for it, that he was the only one that kept a hard-on, and that the others weren't and couldn't'. In the car afterwards, Keith said: 'What was that about?' Tommy, he recollected, responded in an evasive way: 'Agh, it was just a wee night out ... nobody knows about it'. Clearly angered, Keith retorted: 'You were bragging about it in front of others who are politically not in tune with you. It only takes a phonecall ... and you're a councillor ... It's wrong. It's not right'. Dismissively, Tommy responded 'Aagh, nothing to worry about. It's a one off.' But such behaviour was becoming part of an established pattern. A couple of weeks later, George McNeilage had a stag night before getting married. A stripper had been arranged. Keith was convinced it was 'Tommy doing it in someone else's name'. Keith's view was: 'If it was a kiss-o-gram, I'd have just tried to ignore it but it wasn't. It was a hardcore erotic lapdancer [cum] stripper and I lasted five to ten minutes before I walked out ... Tommy was right at the front, completely entranced by it all ... when Alice heard about it and that only one person walked out, she was convinced it was Tommy ... but it wasn't'. A penny began to drop for Keith: 'After that, I started putting various things together like Tommy socialising with footballers who have a lot of money and go back to hotels for [paid] sex with women ... I raised it with him. He said: 'There's nothing to it''. Keith believed that confronting Tommy led Tommy to take a temporary step back but also to become more clandestine in his activities. It was, Keith believed, only then a result of loose tongues of the likes of Gary Clark – a friend of Tommy's from school and then professional footballer – and Tommy's brother-in-law, Andy McFarlane, also a professional footballer, that the stories of Cupids and the Moat House hotel emerged.[109] In all of this, Keith became 'convinced that he started this [type of behavior] when he made his connection with the East End brigade, with his connection with the people around TC Campbell and Joe Steele [over the miscarriage of justice campaign] and these kind of associates ... one of whom has a garage and a club above it ... where this all started and then expanded to Manchester'. Tommy, according to Keith, would 'frequently brag about who he was with ... but I wasn't part of this circle ... his closest political allies weren't part of this other circle'.

Tommy realised that the situation with Keith's concerns and leaks of information was getting serious. Keith believed: 'The problem he's got is that so many people know about it because people like Andy McFarlane have bragged about it so much ... showing people photographs of it'.[110] Consequently, instead of taking the organised bus to a vigil in Wishaw to protest against the racist murder of Surjit Singh Chokkar in late 2002, Tommy suggested that he and Keith go by car but follow the bus. Tommy wanted to talk to Keith in private because, as Keith recalled, Tommy told him: 'There's stuff that's circulating and may come out'. Keith recounted that Tommy said 'he'd been back to Manchester'. A big argument followed about what Tommy could and could not do as an individual and with his life. Tommy said he was sick of this: 'There are things I want to do and can't' Keith recalled. Keith responded, saying: 'You can do them but not as leader of a political party, and not when you promote your private and family life at every opportunity'. Keith took the opportunity to remind him the night before Gail's sister's wedding was the Moat House Hotel escapade and on the Sunday night after that he was on a religious chat show interview talking about his undying, unending love for Gail and about the perfect set up between the Catholic and the Marxist. According to Keith, the conversation to the Chokkar vigil finished with Tommy saying: 'It's only us two that know about this. ... don't break ranks ... don't acknowledge it if it comes out'. At this point, Tommy took legal advice from Paul Holleran of the NUJ and its solicitors in order to prepare the ground for a defamation case against the *Daily Record* if this story came out.

Around this time Keith came close to breaking point, drafting out a resignation letter as Tommy's parliamentary constituency caseworker but he was talked out of it by Tommy. He recalled Tommy did not deny that the Moat House hotel had happened but said that he did not participate. He also recalled Tommy said to him: 'What do you want me to do about it?', to which Keith retorted: 'Don't go on telly saying you have the perfect modern relationship'. To this Tommy shot back: 'I don't like doing that stuff … It's Alan McCombes and Hugh Kerr that encourage me to do it'. Keith said: 'I don't believe you'. Keith then decided to speak to Alan McCombes about the Manchester trips of 1996 and 2001[111] and the Moat House hotel. Fortuitously, Alan McCombes had just been notified about the 2001 visit to Manchester by Nicky McKerrell who had heard somebody was trying to sell the story. Alan went to see Tommy about this to which Tommy said: 'It was just gossip'. Keith then met Tommy in the City Chambers and told him he had told Alan. Tommy was angry, saying: 'You've betrayed my trust' to which Keith responded: 'You know what your trouble is? You think you're invincible and you're not'. After that Keith cut himself off from Tommy socially but relented when Tommy kept phoning him to come to his New Year party. Keith recalled: 'I went and remember sitting thinking when I was watching him and Gail: 'This guy is really capable of leading a double life' … singing love songs to Gail in front of the families' … I couldn't take it and had to get up and leave'. Alan McCombes corroborated some of these details outlined by Keith, saying:

> There were some incidents in the mid-1990s which would have been seriously damaging if they had come out publicly … being involved in live sex shows … on stage … I thought it had been dealt with and we'd moved on … After 2002, I didn't think there was a problem …I wasn't aware of anything [more] … I really thought he totally stopped ... I've heard since 2004 things that I didn't know about ... there is other stuff I've heard of that didn't come out in the court case that would make it appear minor … it would be more explosive … there is the potential for allegations to be made that are even more serious than anything that has come out so far.

Following this, Alan McCombes believed further allegations may come out about Tommy's sexual behaviour depending on the willingness of the concerned individuals to enter the public arena. NoW provided material on various infidelities (including arranging and taking part in group sex) which substantiated much of what Keith recounted and over which Tommy showed no sign of suing.[112] Ominously, NoW promised in 2011: '[W]e've even more to come about your lying, cheating ways'.[113]

A ~~Dialectical~~ Materialist

Some believe that socialists should wear sackclothes and sandals as a demonstration of their commitment to fight for the poor and the downtrodden. Some believe being poor is supposed to make this easier. But given that the poor are not necessarily their own best fighters, this makes no particular sense. And, Tommy never professed to believing in 'sackclothes and sandals'.[114] There was, nonetheless, some hoo-hah when Tommy moved into a semi-detached, three bedroom Victorian villa on Paisley Road West in Cardonald, Glasgow. The house was purchased for £96,000 in 2000.[115] Tommy had earned the right and the money (on the workers' wage) to buy it so it would be churlish of anyone to decry him for having a nice home. Moreover, Gail was earning more money than Tommy given his 'workers' wage' and also had the right and money to a nice home. But there were still problems in moving there. The first was that Tommy had made a name for himself as a son of Pollok, publicly announcing his deep and lasting love for Pollok by going as far to say: 'I could never live anywhere else' and 'If I ever have a family, I couldn't imagine bringing them up anywhere else' only seven years earlier.[116] If Tommy had changed his mind, he should have said so and publicly. Tommy had already rubbed some people up the wrong way in Pollok when he dropped them in favour of others (see below). The second was that he made out that buying the Cardonald house was all Gail's doing, and he went along with it out of matrimonial duty and obligation. According to Keith Baldassara: 'Tommy always put the emphasis on Gail wanting the house but a couple of years ago Gail alluded to how hard Tommy had worked to secure the house because she never wanted the house ... she said he was desperate to get it. I thought so why make out it was Gail?'[117] This, for Keith, tied into a wider realisation: 'It made me question things he said like 'Gail has got the £30,000 from the *Daily Record*' ... Every time Tommy wants something, he says Gail wants it. ... He uses Gail as camouflage when he doesn't need to because we [close comrades] have always been dead relaxed about things like the houses'.[118]

The move to the Cardonald villa also touched another raw nerve. Tommy had lived with Gail in her Cardonald end terrace house since 1994 although he kept on his flat in Pollok for a year after. But over time, George McNeilage detected that Tommy was not putting in the time to Pollok and its community that he should given that he was the councillor and it was his powerbase. For example, in 2001 George asked Tommy to compere the community summer Gala Day. Tommy said he could not as he was playing a celebrity charity football match in Castlemilk with the likes of Ally McCoist, Tam Cowan, Chic Young and Tony Roper (even though George had notified him of this gala in February).[119] Before then, and after the community meeting that led to a gun being put to George's head, Tommy was infrequently in Pollok, George believed, because of the family Tommy 'shopped' and only there at certain times and in the company of others. This unwillingness to go into Pollok extended into the 2000s according to George. Tommy did not go to see Rose Gentle, mother of shot soldier Gordon Gentle and who he both knew well, because her house was just behind that of the 'shopped' family. Indeed, when Tommy heard about Gordon's death after coming back from holiday, he asked Keith to go to see Rose (which contrasts with his portrayal of these events in the media – like his newspaper columns). Matters came to something of a head when Rose asked George to deal with the funeral arrangements, and then when George began thinking about a campaign for justice for Gordon. According to George:

> Tommy tried to muscle in by offering to chair the [first] press conference ... and called a demo [on the issue] after speaking to Rose [though no one else] but he was nowhere to be seen in organising it in the next eleven days up to the demo. I had to organise it all. ... He'd tried to squeeze his way into the front of the demo. Then he offered to compere the event [the rally after the demo]. I told him to be happy with speaking at the event.[120]

The sense that Tommy had let his Pollok roots wither and had moved onto new ground was expressed by Keith Baldassara: 'Tommy loves being an MSP ... loves being in the Parliament ... loves playing in the institution and its processes ... he enjoys the kudos of the profile ... he loves the sense of theatre, he thrives on it ... his community centre was Parliament or Cuba Norte [the restaurant]'. The sense of Tommy using Gail as camouflage for fear of the charge of hypocrisy – for things he wanted or they both wanted – testified to Tommy's view of how he should be seen as a socialist leader and the importance of how he would be perceived by the public.

Energy and Drive

Alan McCombes was more than happy to 'admire [Tommy's] dynamism, energy and enthusiasm ... [his] sheer mental and physical energy, [his] indefatigability'. Tommy showed tremendous reserves of determination and energy in pursuing his political and personal interests. This was no more so evident than in his two court cases when he represented himself during the day and spending most of the hours in between preparing for the next day's representation. Although he seldom had any health problems, even his physical and mental energy was sapped, with court observers, Raymond Buchanan noting: 'By the end of week five Sheridan's energetic performances were waning ... By week six he was off with exhaustion and facing hospital tests due to increased blood pressure'[121] and James Doleman reporting there were quite a few days when Tommy 'did not perform that well',[122] one of these being 26 November 2010 when: 'During [an] exchange, Mr Sheridan mistakenly addressed Mr Wight as 'Mr Bird' for the third time over the course of the day'.[123]

Plagiariser and User?

Few ideas in politics are genuinely fresh and new.[124] What makes old ideas stand out and seem new is how and when they are applied. For example, key ideas that Tommy and SML/SSP used were from the Communist Party (APTUs and the Scottish Service Tax) or anti-poverty campaigners (free school meals). Tommy openly acknowledged Alan McCombes' contribution to the ideas and strategies he championed and popularised, with Alan feeling: 'What Tommy is good at doing is taking an idea, widening its appeal and getting wide support for it'. Tommy was also adept at using the skills and help of others in researching his arguments like that of the lawyer, Gordon Dangerfield, in the anti-poll tax campaign. This meant Tommy could not be said to not have done his homework. Yet others felt Tommy was less than full in his acknowledgement of others' contributions and ideas because, according to Keith, Tommy 'has the capacity to suck information out of people, hold it and then express it verbally and in written form. You think he's discovered this information himself ... He's involved in scores of dialogues to get this information – but he never let's on where he gets it from ... He wouldn't deliberately say it was his idea and he wouldn't deliberately not either'. Similarly, Carolyn Leckie and Richie Venton compared him to a magpie, being good at borrowing ideas from others and presenting them as his own. Whilst the dictum there is 'no room for modesty in politics' – as Tommy often said – might explain the surreptitious adoption of ideas and the like, there are two other important aspects here. First, within organisations, there is a need to give people their due in order to maintain cohesion and unity. Colin Fox believed that Tommy had 'the ability to reward, respect and give loyalty' while Philip Stott thought Tommy praised others and acknowledged their contribution of others but others did not. Some thought Tommy used people without acknowledgement and some thought he had a poor way of giving compliments and show gratitude. Of the latter, Richie Venton commented: 'He knows to say thank you but he overdoes it – 'you're a diamond, a star, an amazing human being' – so you never get an absolute, genuine one. He'll thank you or praise you but never on a one-to-one: he has to do it in front of people … [it's] patronising and giving out a patronage'. Second, Keith pointed to a darker side to Tommy's information gathering:

> When he's out, after a meal, and the people have split up into groups of men and women, he loves to play games. He'll say let's go round the table and ask everyone about their biggest regrets. … He'll say: 'My biggest regret is the amount of women I've shagged in my house when my wife has been at work' … What's he's trying to do is find out about people's weak spots and get under your skin.

Like Rosie Kane and Frances Curran,[125] Carolyn Leckie also believed: 'He gathers intelligence and information on people, about their vulnerabilities, he stores up dirt on people, he stores up favours from people … he holds people close to him … he makes it difficult for them to walk away from him … very early on he attempted to manipulate me … trying to get personal information from me directly … to get me to openly express my opinions about things when you thought you could trust him … he was trying to work out what buttons to press … [so that he could] wind individuals up against each other'. Richie Venton was of a similar view: 'He's masterly at finding somebody's strengths, weaknesses or vulnerabilities and trying to play on them with flattery and mind games to pull you closer to him ... he's a past master in using flattery, charm and apparent warmth to get what he wants from people [but] there's a coldness there and a very calculative and manipulative person … he's a user of people … [a] user and abuser of people and their trust'. Colin Fox had a slightly different take: 'I wouldn't say he is manipulative … he has the skills and abilities to get round someone without making an enemy of them ... Is he devious, sly, cunning? Absolutely. No question. Does he need to be like that? On occasion, yes. Alan [McCombes] and Keith [Baldassara] also have that skill'.

Misogynist?

There are plenty of men and women – former Militant as well as former and current SSP members – who believe Tommy has been sexist in attitude and behaviour towards many women in his personal and political lives. Yet whether he was also a misogynist – hating women because they are women – or believes women are either 'whores' or Madonnas' with nothing else in between – as some do believe[126] – is difficult to ascertain. Certainly, there was disdain, belittling and character assassination of women (especially Carolyn Leckie, Frances Curran, Catriona Grant and Rosie Kane) as a result of the faction fight and legal battles. But whether this reflected or constituted a deeply held belief about all women, just some women or was merely part of his fabrication is open to question. There seems more evidence to suggest he used politically backward arguments (about 'covens of witches' and a 'gender obsessed discussion group') as a cover to try to a) deal with a number of strong, independent minded women who opposed him; b) to avoid the unpleasant reality that it was two men in particular – Keith Baldassara and Alan McCombes – who stood up to Tommy, and c) to build support for himself in the faction fight by appealing to those that opposed the adoption of the 50:50 policy on women's representation at the SSP 2002 conference (which was passed by 10 votes with the SWP supporting and the CWI opposing). Before the faction fight, Tommy argued: 'Sexual exploitation of women and children is part of male violence. It is important for children, women and men that they see positive images of women rather than passive, sexual pictures and stories denying women their sexuality and showing them as something for men to take and possess'[127] and he took a stand against pornography when in Saughton.[128] He then supported the '50:50' proposal on the SSP EC and at the 2002 SSP conference policy vote (which crucially led to an equal number of women as men heading the regional lists for the Scottish Parliament).[129] Some pointed out Tommy was less than forthright in his support, with the insinuation being his support was based on wanting to be on the side that would win. Moreover, Tommy's hostility to Carolyn Leckie in particular could be explained, in part, by her reputation for abrasiveness and frostiness.[130] And, Tommy also surrounded himself with some women whom he feted while attacking others. Meantime, that those women were attacked and believed the attacks to be grounded in misogyny was not in itself *prima facie* evidence of misogyny.[131]

However, what is not open to doubt is well before the 2006 and 2010 court cases, allegations of what were regarded as Tommy's unacceptable past standards of sexual behaviour and conduct in the 1980s and 1990s had long circulated.[132] Tommy referred on the McNeilage tape to political disagreements with Catriona Grant and Frances Curran – and these concerned sexual politics and sexual behaviour from the 1980s onwards. Indeed, in Barbara Scott's handwritten minute of the 9 November 2004 SSP EC, she recorded a contribution from Frances Curran as: 'In the

Militant I [was] asked to cover up stuff [-] left all that behind. Not going back there'. Referring to the substance of this, Frances recalled:

I had cause to talk to him ... [about] his attitude to young women ... on a number of occasions ... in the mid to late 1980s ... he can't relate to women [unless on] a level of sexual banter ... I didn't see it as a problem ... I saw it as a personality trait ... of stunted growth of [not] being able to deal with women in an adult way [and] work with them in an equal and level way ... [he had] a very demeaning attitude to [certain] types of women that he categorised ... Tommy was a sexual predator. I wouldn't have put those words to his behaviour then ... but I would now.

He was doing one night stands all over the place with young women [when he was travelling around Britain speaking at meetings] ... [I was asked to intervene after] Young Socialist women members raised with me that a young women ... [was] very upset about the way she'd been treated by Tommy ... and a number of older Labour Party members in the Militant also raised [his behaviour] with me [because] it wasn't acceptable because these women were young, vulnerable and thinking that they were going into a relationship with Tommy- [that] it wasn't just casual sex.

It was the power imbalance [and] and what they expected [that bothered me] ... [when I confronted him] he said: 'One, it's none of your business; two, it takes two to tango – you can't have sex with someone unless it's consensual'. I was trying to say: 'Yeh, it may be consensual but what are the expectations here? And you must ... use the powerful position that you're in responsibly, especially in a movement that is striving for women's equality'. He wouldn't have it. He absolutely wouldn't have it.

Richie Venton recounted Tommy 'was not a passive victim of groupies but one who readily searched out [women] ... he was absolutely notorious in the Militant for that ... he was not just disloyal in the traditional sense but pretty obnoxious in his sexual behaviour when he was living with one women ... being blatantly disloyal and blatantly hurtful'. He continued:

Tommy had a certain predilection for vulnerable women, drunken included ... and an almost conscious appetite for married women [because] this was a greater prize and victory ... he's definitely a sex addict ... [for him] it's not about love or physical or sexual pleasure ... it goes deeper and darker than that ... it's about [the consequences of] his [political] power and personal public profile

... about self-loathing involve[ing] humiliation in sex clubs as an antidote that he required ... and about risk taking ... the risks he took and got away with, then the more [his] appetite grew and the risks had to be bigger because [the risks] weren't sufficient for him any more ... in more recent years some of the alleged incidents – which I do not have any direct evidence of other than that which he confessed to us – ... fit into place ... in his psychological make-up that he has an addiction to danger and risk as well as being a sex addict and those patterns of self-loathing and self-abuse go with it.

In the light of this, Richie Venton believed that in the mid- and late 1990s Tommy had 'a pattern of behaviour [of a] calculated predator'.[133] However, Ronnie Stevenson believed that while Tommy was 'flirtatious ... there was no evidence of Tommy being abusive to women [at this time] ... the idea of Tommy ... seducing women against their will ... is a distorted, perverse feminism'.

Other reports from former female Militant members from these days chime with these accounts, noting that their allegations were not dealt with seriously or adequately.[134] These include being persistent in his pursuit of some for no other reason that his desire to have sex with them, and completing blanking or ignoring these women the next time he was in their presence (or them in his) as he moved on to other women targets. The point raised by many of these critics was that it was either incumbent upon Tommy given his standing and his leadership role to be sufficiently open and unambiguous about his intentions or not to behave like this at all. Some of these women Militant members believed that when alerted to these allegations, the leadership in Scotland and London refused to act sufficiently firmly because of some ingrained sexism on its part and its unwillingness to take to task a rising star in their organisation who had the much desired mass appeal amongst the public at large.

In various media interviews, Tommy appeared to give some ground to these kinds of allegations by admitting that he was 'not proud of my younger days in terms of being footloose with my favours. I would argue that I was quite irresponsible sexually and emotionally as well',[135] that 'I have never made it a secret ... that I was very sexually active and I slept with lots of women ... I am very open about having been sexually active and I enjoy sex. I had a lot of sex when I was younger when I wasn't in any kind of long-term relationship. I enjoyed sex then as it was carefree'[136] and that 'I used to have a series of causal sexual relationships'.[137] Wanting to carry on by not settling down, he said: 'I was Davy Crocket at the Alamo in that respect'.[138] Later, he said: 'I probably led the best of bachelor lives – that's a polite way to put it'[139] and 'I was footloose and fancy-free with other people's emotions'.[140] In interesting turns of phrase, he said: 'I was probably a bit of a male whore. Sex was a form of recreation'[141] and described himself as 'male ho ... I used to have targets – how many girls I could sleep with in one day'.[142] Even Gail proffered: 'Tommy was never a one-woman man. He liked to spread his wings'.[143] Pretty soon after returning to Glasgow, Keith Baldassara picked up that Tommy's 'nickname was 'Tiptoe' ... because he was always tiptoeing out of places [on his way to a liaison]'. And in testament to what would be shown on the front page of *NoW* in 2011,[144] Keith recounted that Tommy was 'involved in a threesome when he was 25 years old and in a relationship, with two young women ... there were photos of him dressed up in suspenders'.[145] Finally, at his wedding, one of his best men, George McNeilage made heavy allusions in his speech to Tommy's past sexual activity which created a certain frisson amongst the guests.

So, Tommy had no problem divulging he had an 'adventurous' past sexual history to the media, whether this be because it showed him to be a bit of a 'lad' with some normalising effect then set in train[146] or because it could not be denied as it was common knowledge in Glasgow. But in making these public statements he also sought to draw a line under these activities by stating that he had changed since he started a relationship with Gail in 1993.[147] Thus: 'When I met Gail things changed ... she's the person who got a grip of me [here]'[148] and she 'taught him the difference between love and sex'.[149] But the significance of these previous statements is that they chime with the later sexual behaviour that was aired in the defamation and perjury cases concerning the post-1993 period, suggesting his behaviour had not changed since his younger days and despite his protestations to the contrary. In the McNeilage tape, Tommy recounted his sisters had told him: 'You better not be doing this all again'. In a conversion with Frances Curran in a car during the 1997 Paisley by-election, Tommy indicated he had, according to Frances, curbed his sexual activity as he was aware that people knew who he was and what damage it would do if publicly exposed. Interestingly, Alan McCombes recalled that before 2004, Steve Arnott, one of Tommy's staunchest supporters in the post-2004 period 'had the raised the issue amongst a number of people that we'd be damaged by association with Tommy's sexual behaviour ... he argued for disassociation'.

Time Management

Tommy did not normally run on Greenwich Mean Time. His lateness was notorious. At the infamous 'unity' press conference of 16 November 2004 in parliament, not only was Tommy the last of the SSP

MSPs to arrive but all the press were already seated and waiting for him, prompting Colin Fox to try to break the tension with a play on the accusation of Tommy's political death: 'It's the late Tommy Sheridan'. At his 2010 trial, his sister, Lynn, commented that for him lateness was 'not an unusual occurrence'.[150] And, Tony Benn recorded in his diary that he invited Tommy to lunch on 19 January 2004 at 12.30pm, only for him to turn up at 1.50pm (after addressing the launch of the Respect party, led by George Galloway).[151] Kenneth Roy recalled: 'He didn't show up [to a conference he was due to speak at], failed to let us know that he wasn't showing up and, when we complained about his non-attendance, failed to respond'.[152] Tommy was a poor time keeper. This was a result of either being waylaid by other people through no fault of his own or speaking for too long at meetings or to those that wanted to speak to him afterwards. It suggests that he very much got caught up in the importance of the moment and was a little less respectful to his next appointments than he might otherwise have been. It was probably the case that he calculated that he could get away with this because of his charm, charisma and political stature. In countless interviews with journalists (and as reported by them), he ran late for their appointments and then made them late by engaging with them for many hours. This made him not only late home but much later than he told Gail he would be. Gail made this clear on STV's *In Confidence* programme.[153] Indeed, the *Herald* reported:

He's embroiled in a bit of a Dinnergate scandal. Again. After promising he'd be in at eight it's now nearer ten. And, much to my amusement, I'm getting the blame. Tommy brings me back to his house to call a taxi, despite the fact that I've got a perfectly good mobile phone, just to prove to Gail I'm the reason he's late. To be fair we were at a local tenants and residents meeting in Pollok for an hour until we headed back to Keith's for a chat. The trouble with Tommy is that he loves talking politics. He loses all track of time.[154]

In the light of his sexual dalliances, some may conclude that the cover of the journalist here indicated that he was skating on thin ice on other occasions to explain his lateness.

Alan and Tommy

It would be easy to categorise the relationship between Alan McCombes and Tommy as one respectively of thinker and doer or of writer and speaker.[155] However, Tommy was also a thinker and writer but of a different nature to Alan. Alan was a thinker in terms of big ideas in regard of creating SML/SSA/SSP and the pursuit of independence. According to Allan Green, the division of labour embodied in *Imagine* 'was [also] true of policy and campaigning ideas. Tommy championed them and motivated the party ... He championed them ... but did not devise them'. Tommy was also able to judge the merits of these strata-gems because, as Alan recounted, Tommy 'more than anyone else has attended more public meetings and met more people so is able to sniff the wind' with his skills lying in being a 'good tactician ... he's ... got a very opportunistic element to his political conduct and always has done ... this isn't a negative thing if it's about taking advantage of, and exploiting, opportunities'. Alan McCombes believed: 'Tommy was always quite happy with skills he had developed – he didn't show a desire to develop others ... because he knew he could rely on others for those'. In terms of the internal battles to establish the SML/SSA/SSP, Alan and Frances Curran played by far the greatest roles. Alan believed that this was reflective of Tommy's desire within the SSA/SSP to remain as 'popular with everybody ... because he seeks popularity ... by taking the line of least resistance' and avoiding bitter internal battles. As such, Alan believed that what Tommy did in the post-November 2004 period was not his 'natural way'. Prior to November 2004, Alan's one lingering disagreement with Tommy was over Tommy's reliance upon Hugh Kerr given allegations of Kerr's inappropriate behaviour towards women and his arrogance.[156] An area where Tommy did have a weakness, notwithstanding the necessary division of labour with the likes of Alan on writing perspectives and analysing developments, was that he seldom wrote any pieces longer than newspaper articles. This, especially after the split of August-September 2006, meant that not only did Tommy deny himself a wider audience but that he did not try to develop his understanding further in this arena now that he was operating without Alan McCombes. Outsiders to the relationship like Colin Fox observed that both Alan and Tommy had the charac-teristic of being bold while mutually complementing each in terms of Tommy's 'sniffing the wind'[157] and Alan's aloofness from this which allowed him to engage in strategic thinking. In this, Colin Fox con-firmed Tommy was more than capable of saying to Alan: 'Nah, that won't work'.

Alan's firsthand, personal account of his unfolding battle against Tommy from 2004 onwards was published on 10 June 2011.[158] Despite believing otherwise,[159] the tone of his account came over as that of a somewhat jilted or spurned lover. And, whilst there was some limited self-reflection on his culpability for aiding and abetting the production of the figure of Tommy Sheridan,[160] there was little self-critique. *Downfall* was an opportunity to reflect upon whether the management of the information about Tommy's sexual behaviour was correct and whether Alan and Tommy reinforced a number of tendencies in each other (like boldness and bombast). The explanation proffered by Alan in *Downfall* was that very similar to that offered by journalists, namely, that Tommy has a personality disorder, being variously deceitful, conceited, cowardly, selfish, deranged, a fraud and so on.[161] This was a particularly non-materialist analysis.

Cultural Choices

When former Liverpool manager, Bill Shankly – to paraphrase him – commented: 'Football isn't a matter of life or death, it's much more important than that', he could have been talking specifically about Glasgow. Tommy claimed to be a Celtic supporter on many occasions[162] and that he was physically attacked for being so.[163] The controversy here was not that he sided with one particular half of the 'old firm' or the other but that he changed his allegiances on more than one occasion between the two,[164] and then also supported Motherwell because his long-time friend, Billy Davies, was the manager there for a time. Richie Venton recalled: 'I used to joke to him and others [saying] you couldn't trust someone to be reliable in their loyalties when they could change their football teams so easily'. Alan McCombes believed this was a hamfisted attempt by Tommy to win the support of those that were not ordinarily supportive of the SSP (i.e., Rangers fans) because Celtic fans already were so. In the end, McCombes believed, Tommy alienated both sides far more than he gained their support.

Although lambasted by fellow Militant comrades for poor political-cum-cultural choice like liking Carly Simon, Billy Joel, the Eagles, Elton John, Rod Stewart and the Beatles, Tommy's taste in music did not changed much over the years.[165] In 2006, he cited John Lennon's *Imagine*, Deacon Blue's *Dignity*, the tale of a council worker saving up to buy a boat, and Labi Siffre's anti-apartheid anthem, *So Strong*, as his three favourite songs.[166] He also for a time used 'Lifted' by Lighthouse Family on his answering machine. For someone of his age and generation, it was surprising there was no place for The Clash,[167] Billy Bragg, Woody Guthrie, Bruce Springsteen, Johnny Cash, Bob Marley or Bob Dylan. Such honesty when others might have chosen those songs they thought they should choose or be seen to choose was refreshing even if it hints at a lack of impassioned and youthful rebellion.

Tommy continued to talk in the working class Glasgow vernacular – like being 'scunnered' – and this provided the basis of one part of his persona, the Glasgow or west of Scotland man. This comprised part 'hardman' (where, for example, his blog begun in September 2010 was subtitled '100% unedited, 100% unflinching') and his love of playing football was well known. As noted elsewhere, he also portrayed himself as a red blooded male. But none of this was entirely one sided because he complained of being 'soft' as he felt the cold in prison[168] and he confessed to being, in his words, 'a boring bastard most of the time',[169] with Gail doing her supporting confirmation role of 'Tommy is really Mr Boring. Sweet ... but boring'.[170] Of course, being a teetotaller also did not fit the Glasgow or west of Scotland mould. Tommy's childhood experience of getting drunk himself and seeing the impact of alcohol and alcoholism on others – including his father[171] – put him off it for a lifetime but there was more to it than this. While there was the political worldview that alcohol is opium for the masses and a legalised drug,[172] the influence of his mother's anti-drinking culture and respect for his body in terms of fitness[173] and well-being, the critical point would seem to be that Tommy, in his own words, 'always wanted to be in control of my faculties',[174] portraying his driven and determined nature.

Cult of the Personality?

In the parties he was a member of, Tommy was certainly a big enough personality to have spawned a personality cult as his Labour and latter internal SSP critics alleged.[175] Whether or how much Tommy did to consciously create such a phenomenon is open to doubt. But the effect of deploying Tommy in such a concentrated and consistent way was that the public, inactive party members and political sympathisers, in particular, got an exaggerated sense of Tommy's importance and centrality, with the effect that there seemed to be a personality cult in operation. This was to some extent a bargain with the 'devil', for the price of the need to have media coverage of policies and activities was that the media chose who and what it thought was most interesting and newsworthy and presented them accordingly. Nonetheless, as Jim McVicar reflected: '[T]hrough the Militant, SML, the SSA and the SSP, we need to carry part of the blame too because we helped create him despite being aware of the lessons of Derek Hatton and despite thinking we had checks and balances in place'. In a similar vein Catriona Grant believed: 'Tommy became a spoilt man and he's taken advantage of that. In Frankenstein, [at least] the monster knows what he is ... Tommy doesn't'. The problem was that developing Tommy worked as an impediment to developing other 'Tommies' if that was possible. When asked how to avoid the fate of a George Galloway or Derek Hatton, Tommy believed:

> Ideology and politics are the essential bedrocks that we rely on ... if you don't have that ideological compass then I think you can lose your way ... I'm not sure that Derek had both the ideological compass and the party association that is necessary to keep you on the right track ... for George the same problem is as a socialist in a non-socialist party ... I've had the advantage of the compass and the grounding through a group of political comrades that I've worked with through thick and thin in various political parties and this is what ensures that I don't get beyond my station ... I'm morally and politically accountable to these people.

Gail Healy

Gail is an essential part of the public figure of Tommy Sheridan. A strong and feisty character in her own right, it was said of her that she was 'the only Scottish party leaders' wife who is a political asset to her husband ... [and] can match him in looks, charm, confidence and overall tan'.[176] Her turn of phrase as the loyal but no doormat partner was evident well before the 2006 court case – she told the *Sunday Times*: '[H]e's going away for a stag weekend to Spain with the lads. I've told him if he appears in some newspaper with a blonde claiming to have bonked him all night – mind you I'll know that's no true – I'll kill him'.[177] She is the foil to his seriousness, telling him 'to lighten up'.[178] Joan McAlpine believed Gail 'knocked him into shape by making him more normal and educating him culturally and socially'.[179] Keith Baldassara thought Gail 'sanitised his style' while Gillian Bowditch argued Gail brought Tommy 'credibility' by 'softening' his image.[180] Just as importantly, Gail was also a 'performer'[181] with a big 'in character' public persona too. Rosie Kane was of the view that while Gail was an accessory to Tommy, she was not unwilling to play that role because she liked the limelight.

Early Years

Gail (then Gail Healy) has known Tommy since they were both 13 or 14 years old but did not particularly like him when she first came across him at Lourdes secondary school: 'He didn't stand out, he was the same as everybody else, being into football, and not that opinionated'. They first hooked up together when he was seventeen, but with Tommy going off to Stirling and Gail staying at home and going to Paisley College of Technology, their romance fizzled out.[182] Tommy phoned a few times for Gail when he was at university but Gail, in her own words 'was always not in' as she was seeing another guy. Some years later, when they were both twenty three years old, they got together again when at a play that Gary Stevenson (later an accomplished actor) featured in. However, with Gail already working for British Airways, they still did not really 'take-off' then either. Yet the political hand of fate was more kind to them. Tommy was lined up to speak at both the Glasgow and London anti-poll tax demonstrations on 31 March 1990. To get between the two, he flew from Glasgow to London and saw Gail, who was flirtatious with him.[183] They arranged to meet that night when he got back from London. But Tommy felt unable to come back that night as he and Steve Nally, the secretary of the All-Britain APT Federation, had to respond to the media about the riot that happened that day on the London demonstration. Gail went to meet him off the plane but was stood up without an explanation and felt best to leave him alone. But again the political hand of fate intervened again two years later. When Tommy was jailed in Saughton in 1992, Gail felt sorry for him so wrote to him. She felt impressed by his courage and compassion, feeling a 'surge of respect for him ... he's got bottle' which endeared and attracted her to him.[184] So, in her own words, she 'sent postcards from Paris, Miami and Barbados – not so much wish you were here as how are you, I'm having a good time'.

Political Conviction and Support

Gail has had political and personal sympathy with Tommy because of her family background – being from Govan, working in the shipyards and being union members. Although her family were not members, they were staunch Labour voters (although Gail voted for Jim Sillars in the 1988 Govan by-election). However, Gail has a considerable degree of her own political conviction, having been a union activist and rep in her twenty five-odd years as a British Airways cabin crew member and standing as an SSP candidate in 1999 and 2003. Although she was not a regular activist, she did have something of a political standing in own her right, making her more than just 'Tommy's wife' or a 'trophy wife' as many people saw her or as 'glamourous Gail, first Scottish lady of socialism'.[185] Some of her political outlook also comes from being a practising and ardent Catholic. Nonetheless, for her politics does not come before family.[186]

Like Alice Sheridan, she gave assessment and feedback on Tommy's performances as both critic and fan. She was outspoken on how he looked and dressed, and said she wanted 'nothing to detract from the message'. This meant she bought Tommy clothes, told him to get his hair cut or that he was getting 'too orange'.[187] Tommy put it that: 'In terms of dress code and personal hygiene, Gail advises me' and 'Gail made the point to me that ... I should think of a suit as my work uniform'.[188] But just as importantly she saw her role as being a 'different voice ... a more ordinary voice' as she thought too many people around Tommy agreed with him, did not disagree with him or told him what they thought he wanted to hear so that he needed another perspective which she was prepared to give. Often she said to Tommy: 'Tell me what it means because if I don't get it, others won't' in order to get him to present some idea or proposal differently and more usefully. She also saw her role to 'keep him grounded'. Thus, Tommy was happy to acknowledge: 'Gail makes the point that I'm not always in touch with people, not so much because of the people and circles that I move in, but more that people won't tell me exactly what they think because they think I'll argue back or because they might sound embittered doing so'. Tommy admitted he found this useful although he was quick to point out that his friends who were not politically involved also told him what they thought. Alan McCombes recounted: 'I always felt he was influenced by Gail ... [she] would say something and he would latch on to it ... like Gail was some kind of political oracle because he said she was clued in and talking to more people'.

However, and despite the personal and political sympathy and involvement, Gail had an embittered attitude towards the SSP and Solidarity for – to her – the more time Tommy spent on political activity, the less time was spent with her (and from 2005, Gabrielle, their daughter). She recounted: 'The party is his mistress. It takes money, time and him away from me, and I work shifts. I'd like quality time with him. Sometimes, the only time I get with him is in bed sleeping because he's up early back late and then answers calls, watches the politics programmes and has to write a [newspaper] column'.[189] She said the biggest, most regular fights they had were over time. On a number of occasions Gail expressed being 'pissed off' by him being late and put after politics.[190] After 2003, with the election of five other SSP MSPs, she pointed out Tommy should be not be working any harder or longer than he was when he was the SSP's sole MSP. For Tommy, the opposite was true – with more MSPs to do the work, the higher the ambitions could be. Going out with Tommy, Gail said, was no great joy as people wanted to talk to him, meaning he can take ages to walk anywhere: 'Going shopping is like him holding a surgery as he's stopped so often'. Quality time to her was mostly at home or on holiday when she could see the private individual, not the public figure, who likes playing scrabble and doing crosswords, singing karaoke (unaided by alcohol) and can be a 'wee daft boy'.[191] Whether on the street or because of his media presence, she said 'used to get big kicks out of publicity but that then wore off'. After the 2006 trial, Gail made clear her desire to see Tommy leave full-time politics and look for a career in law, education or the media.[192]

As alluded to above, Gail's attitude to money was different to Tommy's. He said: 'The one thing we argue about most is money'.[193] Gail believed she financially subsidised Tommy and the SML/SSA/SSP/ Solidarity because she brought in a full wage while Tommy brought home half a wage as well as donating any earnings from journalism and media appearances to various good causes: 'Half of the money he gives to the party, half of that I think is mine ... but he doesn't see it'. She also believed he spent money in a way he thought he should be seen to be spending money – by this, she meant giving money to charities that he did not actually have, leaving big tips out of both genuine empathy and being worried about being seen as tight-fisted, and for a while paying for taxis to get to media interviews rather than accepting provided taxis because he did not want to be seen to be getting above his station.[194] All in all, she firmly believed that not only did he earn less that he should because of the workers' wage policy but he worked such long hours that he earnt very little per hour (and much less than the average worker). Tommy's response was to be critical of her 'materialist' impulse because she is a staunch Catholic – he argued she was contradictory here because as a Christian she should not be materialistic. Like Alice, Gail also believed Tommy was 'too generous' with his time and did not take his due: 'He needs to be more confident about being up there at the front ... representing the working class and not feel that he doesn't deserve to be there'. This she believed came from modesty and lack of confidence.

Marriage and Kids

Clearly, their relationship would not work if Gail was not sympathetic but Tommy argued Gail knew what to expect by having a relationship with him for eight years and then getting married in 2000: 'I don't feel guilty about it as she knew what she was getting into'. Gail has had to put up with some stick from her friends who asked and told her before Tommy became an MSP (which was seen as a career): 'What are you doing with him? You could do better'. For the first years of their relationship, Tommy reported that the subject of marriage did not arise and was not a problem, with Gail not showing any sustained interest until 1998. He told the *Sunday Herald*: 'Gail wanted to get married. For Gail it was important to get married. For me it wasn't ... a piece of paper is not essential to declare your love for another human being ... We had lived together – contrary to her religious beliefs if she was really honest with herself – for a number of years before getting married. We had lived my way of life'.[195] Being an atheist would present many others with problems in being in a relationship with a practising Catholic and then marrying this Catholic in a Catholic church. Getting married in a Catholic church was not an issue for Tommy for once he'd agreed to marry, it became an issue that he was content to let Gail decide upon:

A lot of women want their day of glory, and I thought it was unfair of me [to deny her that] given that I loved Gail and I wanted to spend the rest of my life with her ... [so] then the idea that we shouldn't get married because it was a bourgeois institution became less and less important ... after that where we got married was irrelevant ... it was Gail's marriage so she chose where it should be.

Elsewhere, upon being asked why he was getting married and in a Catholic church, he proffered 'because I love her'.[196] However, Laura Smith recalled: 'Tommy told me he had to get married to Gail – it was the right time. It was for his career. He didn't want to, but it looked good'.[197] It may have also been the case that marriage was easier, as Tommy commented, 'because of the class basis of Militant, it was more easy for these issues [of marriage] to be addressed ... it was normal for members to be married'. Tommy also recalled: 'I could have done it semi-secretly but what I have to realise is that I am public property'[198] but whether Gail wanted the coverage of the wedding is less clear even though she was no shrinking violet when it came to media attention.

As he often portrayed himself, Tommy was married to the revolution, telling the *Sunday Mail*: 'Right now, I don't have the time for the commitment a wee Tommy would need'[199] and Gail commented: 'If it happens, it happens but we're 36 so we'll see'.[200] But Gabrielle was born on 30 May 2005. When Rosie Kane congratulated Gail at the Calton Hill declaration on her pregnancy, Gail revealed it was unplanned and unexpected, responding, according to Rosie: 'Fuck off, I'll cut that bastard's balls off ... it wasn't planned ... I'll fucking kill him: he was meant to get off before Govan'.[201] Both the pregnancy and birth were public events in line with Tommy's obligation and desire.[202] Upon arrival, Tommy became a gushing father: 'As a human being, I feel more complete now than at any time in my life ... I am going to bed at night and waking up in the morning with a wee baby that has filled my life with so much joy it's unbelievable'[203] and 'The most important thing that has happened to me in recent years is the birth of my daughter ... It has changed my priorities and she is number one'.[204] While in prison, Tommy said: 'Wee Gabrielle has the voice of an angel. Each time we talk I turn to mush. She asks me to come home immediately and I feel so sad as I just want to hold, hug and smother her with kisses again'.[205]

Domestic Arrangements

For many years, Tommy confessed to having an aversion to gardening[206] and DIY so it was not quite a case of 'socialism in one household' but he, nevertheless, did see himself as approximating to a 'new man' when it came to contributing to the general running of the household.[207] Thus, he commented: 'Gail tends to cook and I do the dishes but that's because she's a better cook that me ... She does most of the cleaning up but I do most of the hoovering ... I do most of the ironing'. Overall, he believed: 'I try my hardest to approach our life as a partnership of equals and not a relationship of domination ... I don't think there are wide areas of my life where someone could say: 'Some fucking socialist he is!''. But Gail's take on this was a little less charitable. Leaving instructions on how to clean and cook while she was in hospital giving birth to Gabrielle, she said: 'New man? It's all talk'[208] and a bone of contention was that Gail had higher expectations and standards of cleanliness.[209] After the birth and losing his seat and until 26 January 2011, Tommy had more need and time to do his fair share. However, when it came to shopping: '[To] Gail [it's] a drama ... and a pleasure, it's about getting dressed up, talking to everyone ... to me it's making a list, going to get it and coming straight back'.[210]

The Court Cases

There are different, and often opposing, views about Gail and her relationship to Tommy in terms of the post-November 2004 events. Some see Gail as an abused victim of circumstance who has been kept in the dark by Tommy, and is nothing more than a loyal partner.

Some see her as knowing the truth and colluding with Tommy because she sinks or swims according to Tommy's fate.[211] Others see her as duty bound to believe Tommy is innocent – otherwise she has to admit she has been wronged and living a lie – which is a difficult cross to bear given her devout Catholicism.[212] Indeed, Gail told the *Daily Mail*: 'Nothing will change between Tommy and me, whatever the outcome'.[213] But all views stress that she became to be defined as Gail Sheridan and not Gail Healy. These views are expressed in various statements of former close friends and leading SSP members. For example, Keith Baldassara commented: 'I'm saddened to see what she been dragged through out of loyalty to somebody she loves ... I think she's let herself down coming this far with him' while George McNeilage believed Tommy's fabrication came down to not being able to come clean to Gail.[214] Carolyn Leckie, Rosie Kane and George McNeilage all believed Gail had been used as a human shield by Tommy without being aware of the fabrication.[215] Rosie Kane went so far as to say: 'It truly sickens me that he used his wife as a human shield throughout this entire process, despite the fact that he was covering up his betrayal of her'[216] and Tommy 'manipulated' her.[217] Tommy professed her support was because of their deep love for each other that could not be broken,[218] that 'we have had to dig deep in resources of love for one another and our trust for one another ... we have become an absolute rock'[219] and 'I could never love anyone like I love her and she couldn't love anyone like she loves me. More than ever, we are cemented in rock. We will live and die together'.[220] However, some other comments from Tommy and Gail suggest there may be more to this than first meets the eye. Thus, Tommy alluded to the impact of Gail's Catholicism, saying: 'I think she would have lost faith in me, been disappointed even, but I think she would want her daughter to have her father and she would have stood by me'[221] and '[I]f I had been unfaithful to her I think she would have forgiven me although she would have been deeply, deeply disappointed in me. She's a very pragmatic person and she wouldn't have ordered me to leave the house because she wouldn't want Gabs to grow up without a father. But she would never have trusted me again'.[222] Meantime, despite saying she never 'doubted my man, not even for a heartbeat', Gail made it clear that she checked her diaries and thought the 2006 case might be lost[223] even though she later emphatically said she did not doubt Tommy for 'one solidarity second'.[224] There were also reports of blazing rows between Tommy and Gail just before and during the perjury trail and these seemed to mostly relate to Tommy's refusal to take the plea bargain which, if accepted, would have avoided putting Gail through the trial as an accused.[225]

Conclusion

There is little doubt that in Tommy's case the 'personal' was 'political' and vice-versa because of choices he made about how to present and portray himself. In the public mind, Tommy became a distinctive political brand of socialism whose appeal far outstretched the political parties he was a member and leader of. This was based as much upon his persona as it was his politics.[226] In constructing this persona, an important part of this was that which, he believed, normalised himself. Until troubled waters were encountered, others were either ignorant of this or happy to go along with it as it was paying considerable dividends for the socialist cause.[227] Opinion remains sharply divided between his supporters and critics over the balance between personal promotion and political promotion, and the bridge between the two, in his case. Tommy has been shown to be a consummate politician in his private life – but not one without significant flaws. For better and ill, the socialist project to the left of Labour was constructed around his persona as socialist leader. Basing it upon him so much meant that the project became hitched to boldness as well as to risk.[228] But more significant than any other component of his personality for this project were his conceptions of loyalty and betrayal. Indeed, and as a consequence of this, Tommy played the character of Tommy in trying to save himself and that very selfsame character from political decapitation and defenestration.

Notes

1. 23 February 2003.
2. Of course, there is an obvious irony here, suggesting this was only a partial truth because it was when it suited him.
3. Prior to the loving partner and family man persona, Tommy had a tendency to portray himself as a 'bit of a Jack the lad'. Some observed that the former became more pronounced after 2001 when rumours of his private life started circulating on the journalistic grapevine.
4. It was an irony of the argument that was used in Tommy's defence that no one had the right to inquire into Tommy's sex life when, through his own actions (especially the two court cases), he allowed as many as possible to know of this by virtue of creating the conditions for the media to report on it.
5. See, for example, *Mirror* 12 November 2004 where he discussed his sex life. After his 2006 trial, Tommy stated: 'I honestly don't think there is anything wrong with people who want to be swingers, as long as they are consenting adults ... T[he rejection of] an accusation that I was a swinger ... was never a moral judgement on my part' (*Daily Record* 5 August 2006). However, saying: 'I won't preach monogamy because I think it's women who get short-changed by it. ... The idea of being faithful is a matter between two people. It's not something society or the state should interfere in. It's

up to the individuals in the relationship to practise what they preach' (*Scotland on Sunday* 16 January 1994) was his only recorded public statement on such matters.

6. Author and poet, Mike Rosen, tellingly commented: 'People lie about sex. Then they lie about lying. Then they recruit people to help the lie about lying seem like it was true. But why do people lie about sex? What unwritten rules and social constraints make this part of how people conduct their lives? Presumably people like TS [Tommy Sheridan] think that others will think the worse of them if what they do is known. And so the whole miserable Puritan cycle of shame and blame goes on' (*Socialist Unity* blog 24 December 2010).

7. See the press coverage after his conviction and sentencing. This was also the view of registered psychologist, Dr Dorothy Rowe (*Herald* 24 December 2010). Moreover, Professor of Criminology, David Wilson, believed Tommy 'convinced himself he was innocent' (*Sun* 24 December 2010).

8. Seldom was Tommy not surefooted on television with cases like STV's *Politics Scotland* (31 August 2006) being few and far between. However, in his television interviews of December 2010 and January 2011 he came across as wooden and less than convincing.

9. *Herald* 2 November 2010.

10. BBC Scotland *The Rise and Lies of Tommy Sheridan* 23 December 2010.

11. Rosie Kane, Steve Arnott and Richie Venton, amongst others, also noted the playing of 'Tommy' (*cf. Herald* 2 November 2002).

12. 29 April 2003.

13. For example, commenting on those who believed he was under stress and strain in the run up to his perjury trial, Tommy said somewhat too earnestly that people should 'retain a sense of proportion and perspective. Unlike millions across our planet whose challenges are incomparably more serious, we face ours surrounded by the love and support of our families and friends. We are never alone. That is not always the case for others' (*Big Issue Scotland* 5–11 February 2009). He made the same point when his contract at Talk107 was terminated (*BBC News online* 31 March 2008). Tommy also told the *Evening Times* (28 April 2007): 'For many years, the Sheridan name has been carried by me, but the truth is that there are more talented Sheridans than me'. In this connection, the *Sunday Herald* (19 November 2000) commented he 'doesn't do vulnerability very convincingly' and *Holyrood* (29 April 2003) that he 'doesn't harbour doubt'. John Aberdein believed Tommy was 'as modest as he is brave' (*Herald* 5 November 2002).

14. *The Big Issue Scotland* 24–30 August 2006.

15. See *Scotland on Sunday* 22 April 2007.

16. 8 December 2003.

17. In this connection, Joan McAlpine recounted that when asked Tommy said he'd like to be an actor if he was not a politician.

18. These comprise those that conducted full-length interviews with him in the *Scotsman/ Scotland on Sunday* and *Herald/Sunday Herald* on the relationship between the personal and political between 1999 and 2004.

19. This seemed to apply to matters of the moment and not in regard to matters of many, many years before (see Chapter 2).

20. The *Daily Mail* (18 August 1999), commenting on a BBC interview with Tommy about the Edinburgh festival, said he 'profess[es] to be a complete Philistine'. Tommy is, however, known on occasion to mangle the English language. One example was that he referred in the 2006 trial to his accusers as being 'allegators' (*Sunday Times* 6 August 2006). Nonetheless, the linguistic distance between Philistine and Palestine is sufficient that Joan McAlpine's point stands.

21. 11 December 1998.

22. *Herald* 13 March 1995, see also *Scotsman* 25 November 2000.

23. Despite insinuating Rosie Kane and George McNeilage were aspiring wannabe actors who were acting out the truth but not telling the truth in the 2010 perjury case, Tommy had his own thespian credentials. His acting debuts were as Tom Johnston, a socialist janitor, in the *Fallen Women* play, by the single parents group, The Lone Rangers, in September 2000 and in April 2001. This was followed by a small part in play, *Bright Colours Only*, in 2002 at the Edinburgh Festival and one in a comedy sketch on *BBC Radio Scotland* in July 2008. He also did a talking part in Jasmine Mink's 2001 single, 'Daddy Dog'. Although not himself singing on the track, it was a measure of Tommy's impact that on James Kirk's, formerly of Orange Juice, 2003 'Get on board' song (from the album 'You Can Make It If You Boogie'), Kirk sang repeatedly the line 'Mr Sheridan, he's alright'.

24. See Milne, S. *The Enemy within: Thatcher's secret war against the miners* (Verso, 2004).

25. *Sunday Times* 8 October 2006.

26. *Guardian* 11 December 2006. Tommy also stated he had been 'betrayed' on other occasions (see *Evening News* 29 November 2006, *Sunday Express* 5 August 2007, *Guardian* 15 August 2007).

27. A number of activists like Carolyn Leckie and George McNeilage did believe Tommy was a 'fake'.

28. According to *Holyrood* (29 April 2003), Tommy 'appears to be left on the waiting list for a sense of humour'.

29. This saying was taken from someone else (see *ATTR* p. 111, *DTTSS* p. 22). For some of his others see Gall, G. *Revolutionary Witticisms of Colin Fox, Carolyn Leckie and Rosie Kane MSPs* (Wordpower, 2004), pp. 9–10. Tommy could not be given the billing of the other three MSPs here or in the subsequent *More Revolutionary Witticisms of Colin Fox, Carolyn Leckie and Rosie Kane MSPs* (Flying Pickets Press, 2006) and *Yet More Revolutionary Witticisms of Colin Fox, Carolyn Leckie and Rosie Kane MSPs* (Flying Pickets Press, 2007) because he did not use humour enough. This was to Gail's annoyance, telling me at the 2005 SSP conference that he justified inclusion. However, he did publicise the first volume of witticisms in his *Mirror* page (8 December 2004).

30. *TST* 16 December 2010.

31. See, for example, *Sunday Herald* 20 August 2006, *Daily Mail* 6 September 2006, *BBC Scotland News* 4 May 2007, *Evening News* 29 November 2006, *Herald* 12 November 2004, 18 January 2007, 19 December 2007, *Sunday Herald* 12 August 2007. A crop of examples was also found in his response to the McNeilage tape (see, for example, *Mirror* 4 October 2006). Other examples are to found in this biography. The *Observer* (30 July 2006) also commented upon this tendency.

32. *BBC Scotland News* 11 November 2004.

33. A less kind interpretation would be to recall that socialist comedian, Mark Steel, used to wonder whether Arthur Scargill was beginning to 'lose the plot' when he kept referring to himself as 'Arthur Scargill'. Derek Hatton also spoke of himself in the third person (see Hatton, D. *Inside Left – the story so far* (Bloomsbury, 1988)).

34. This runs contrary to Trotsky's perspective, where he argued that those means that are 'permissible and obligatory are those and only those means' which further the cause of social revolution and human liberation so that 'not all means are permissible' (Trotsky, L. *Their Morals and Ours* (Pathfinder Press, 1973), p. 49).

35. These are phrases and not quote, direct or indirect, from Tommy.

36. Thus, the *Sunday Herald's* (11 April 1999) observation of pragmatism is interesting but seems more likely to emanate from his willingness to bargain with opponents to win what could not be won with outright opposition.

37. Sheridan, T. 'Open letter to SSP members – 28 May 2006: From Tommy Sheridan', 28 May 2006.
38. *Herald* 22 July 2006.
39. As he was in his leisure time along with passions for Scrabble and chess.
40. Contrary to much other writing in the *Herald* on Tommy's personality, its editorial (27 January 2011) was perceptive enough to comment that his approach to his perjury trial 'was the foundation of a calculated strategy of self-preservation'.
41. In this connection, Gordon Morgan reflected that this tendency may have come from '[a] confidence [that] sometimes you don't realise when you're walking into something, you're taking on more than you realise and underestimate the opposition … it's a weakness of the [far] left in general'.
42. If there is a case for delusion – in terms of genuinely believing in Tommy's innocence – the strongest candidate is likely to be Alice for she alleged: 'Tommy is the victim of the biggest, most insidious conspiracy since the Dreyfus affair [of the 1890s]' (*Herald* 27 January 2011). She might well have cited the Zinoviev letter of 1924 as well. Interestingly, George Galloway (*Daily Record* 25 February 2008) also proffered: 'The Procurator Fiscal would be well advised to ponder his chances of finding a jury willing to send the fragrant Mrs Sheridan to prison … And if he tries and fails he will be open to the charge that this whole thing is a repugnant witch-hunt, Scotland's own Dreyfus Affair'. The sense of Alice being delusional about Tommy is also to be found in her statement at the 22 October 2011 anti-cuts candidate meeting in Glasgow (see later) where she proffered that the only person that could unite the left in Scotland was Tommy Sheridan. The response from many at the meeting was to burst out laughing or to experience palpable embarrassment given that Tommy was widely recognised to be the least likely person to unite the left in Scotland.
43. See, for example, *Herald* 24 December 2010.
44. Like Allan Green, Ronnie Stevenson and Richie Venton.
45. Like Steve Arnott, Gordon Morgan, Jock Penman and Philip Stott.
46. The tension between subjective will and objective conditions speaks to the perennial problem that socialists face in appropriately aligning their ambitions with the difficult conditions for trying to achieve these in. Specifically, the Trotskyist left – and those with a heritage from it – has a debilitating tendency to 'talk things up' in the belief that by being optimistic of the possibilities for socialist or working class advancement, it will be able to convince and inspire its followers that their efforts can be effective or will be more effective. This becomes a case of 'will to power' (or 'political voluntarism') with the evident downside that burnout, disillusionment and demoralisation of activists ensue when palpably false promises of success and advance are not realised. In this mindset, few questions are ever asked about why certain prior perspectives were not realised and why certain activists dropped out because the organisation is always necessarily looking forward to the 'next big thing' and is, thus, onto the next set of perspectives and looking to recruit fresh blood. Of course, the flipside is that the appeal of ideas and the appeal of gaining success for these ideas are patently important in motivating individuals to give up large amounts of their time, money and emotions to the cause of socialism.
47. *Express* 27 January 2011.
48. This view of Tommy's inability to engage in self-reflection was not shared by all. Close collaborator of recent times, Gordon Morgan, commented: '[H]aving spent a lot of time with him personally over the last couple of years, I do believe that he has got the ability to be self-reflective … indeed at times he has been very unsure of himself … but in public he doesn't show it. You're an actor [in this public arena] … You wouldn't be human if you didn't have some degree of self-reflection and self-

doubt and he does have these. ... Showing weakness in any form in politics isn't sensible'.

49. *Scotland on Sunday* 25 February 2007.

50. Alan McCombes recalled Tommy had a 'penchant for harmless little lies that made him look good' (*DTTSS* p. 136). This suggested that Alan and others in Militant/ SML/SSA/SSP could be viewed as agreeing with the tactic of hyperbole and bombast, indicating that he and Tommy were cut from the same cloth on this issue.

51. One appears to be his recounting in his perjury trail of the 'terrifying' police 'raid' on his house when he was arrested on 17 December 2007. That no complaint was made about this seemed odd.

52. In this connection, psychologist, Dr Dorothy Rowe (*Herald* 24 December 2010), proffered: 'He started to perhaps just tell little lies, just omit certain things. It is that basic need to protect other people's image of us and our image of ourselves and to protect ourselves from being shamed'.

53. As there were for others on the far left like the SWP. This double-edged trait has to be held in two regards. Firstly, other rising stars in Militant at the same time were not immune to this influence either. But, secondly, even with that influence either none took the trait as far as Tommy did or were in a position, as Tommy was, to take it that far.

54. *Herald* 19 October 2010.

55. *Sunday Herald* 6 May 2007.

56. SSP press releases 20 August 2006.

57. *DTTSS* p.153.

58. 2004 edition, p. 216.

59. There are strong parallels here with another son of Militant, Derek Hatton in terms of his ego and Militant's use of him as their 'front man' (see Hatton, D. *Inside Left – the story so far*, Bloomsbury, 1988).

60. 'Statement in Response to Tommy's Sheridan's Defamation Case', 4 August 2006. This was also the form of words in the SSP's statement (26 January 2011) on Tommy's sentencing.

61. For example, *Scotsman* (25 November 2000), *Sunday Times* (26 November 2000).

62. *ATTR* p. 7.

63. *Herald* 2 November 2002, blog 17 March 2011.

64. *Mirror* 1 June 1999, *Herald* 2 November 2002, *Times* 30 July 2007.

65. *Sunday Herald* 2 August 2009.

66. *Scotland on Sunday* 16 January 2000, *Herald* 2 November 2002.

67. *Sunday Herald* 23 February 2002.

68. *Mirror* 1 June 1999, *Sunday Herald* 1 August 1999, *Scotland on Sunday* 16 January 2000. Tommy did admit to smoking a Cuban cigar (*Mirror* 13 August 2003), smoking cannabis once as a student (*Sunday Herald* 10 October 1999), and eating dope cake in 2001 (*Press Association* 29 January 2004).

69. *Herald* 13 March 1995.

70. Tommy was nicknamed 'Narcissus' by a Militant full-timer worker in 1989 because of his vanity (*DTTSS* p. 13).

71. For example, 31 December 2003, 10 March 2004, 21 April 2004. Nonetheless, Tommy was still less pompously self-referential in his columns than George Galloway was in his.

72. For example, how 'beautiful' she is and they were 'so in love' (*Mirror* 3 October 2003, 14 January 2004).

73. *Independent* 24 April 1999.

74. *Sunday Herald* 23 February 2003. However, it should be noted such normalisation is not *de rigueur* for successful and respected politicians like Alex Salmond and John

McDonnell have kept a closed door on their personal lives and maintained their reputations for honesty and integrity.
75. *Evening News* 22 September 1999.
76. *Sunday Mail* 20 February 2000. Or 'Dosh and Specs' as Rosie Kane labelled them.
77. 27 December 2007–2 January 2008.
78. *Daily Record* 1 August 2007. It would, therefore, probably have been disappointing that Channel 4's intention to turn the 2006 defamation case into a docu-drama (*Sunday Mail* 12 August 2006) was shelved in 2007 by its director of regions and nations, Stuart Cosgrove, because Tommy was not sufficiently well-known south of the border (*Express* 8 March 2007). The idea to make a stage show out of the 2006 trial also came to nothing but did reveal that Tommy had been receptive to acting in a proposed show called 'Aye Cooncillor' ('Yes Councillor') as an Glasgow adaptation of 'Yes Minster' (*Daily Record* 4 August 2006). In this connection, Peter Taaffe observed: 'Tommy can sometimes make the mistake of thinking all publicity is good publicity and not all publicity is good publicity'.
79. See, for example, *Daily Record* 7 July 1999, *Sunday Herald* 26 September 1999, *Scotland on Sunday* 10 October 1999, *Scotsman* 16 June 2000, *Evening Times* 2 October 2001, *Mirror* 26 January 2004.
80. *ATTR* p. 210.
81. *Scotsman* 18 March 2000.
82. *Press Association* 28 January 1992.
83. *Herald* 24 December 2010. Alan McCombes also believed this (*DTTSS* p. 223). In this example, Tommy was not being paranoid about 'a group of female SSP witnesses laughing as they entered the Coury of Session [in 2006]'. Rather, he sought to use this as a clever means of attempting to convince the jury that the witnesses relished the task of giving evidence and thus were part of a conspiracy against him.
84. *Herald* 19 October 2010. Earlier, Rosie Kane, Carolyn Leckie and Frances Curran had issued a statement after the 2006 court case saying Tommy had a 'paranoid imagination' (*Scotsman* 5 August 2006).
85. *Daily Mail* 4 October 2006.
86. *Sunday Herald* 25 March 2007
87. *Herald* 29 Octoer 2010.
88. However, Tommy did believe his phone was tapped during the poll tax revolt (*ATTR* p. 165).
89. Alice also appears to the source of Tommy talking of people being 'beautiful' (see *Evening Times* 8 April 2006).
90. *Evening Times* 14 March 2001.
91. *Mirror* 4 June 2003.
92. *Evening Times* 19 November 2002.
93. 19 August 2006.
94. 24–30 August 2006.
95. *SSP All-members Bulletin* 'Crisis in the party: the fight for the truth', August 2006, p. 11.
96. 26 January 2011. See also *Daily Record* (7 August 2006) and *Newsnight Scotland* (26 April 2007) on his self-confessed 'naivety'.
97. After the 2006 court case, Tommy repeated this with testimony of Keith and Alan McCombes 'hurt[ing] like a hot poker inserted into my heart' (*Sunday Mail* 6 August 2006).
98. *Herald* 28 October 2010.
99. *Daily Record* 7 August 2006.
100. *Herald* 9 August 2006.

101. In this connection, Steve Arnott commented: 'Tommy is very loyal to people who he sees as being loyal to him ... he felt a deep sense of hurt and betrayal'.
102. Defiantly, he still constructed it to be a blessing in disguise: 'The court case showed me who my real friends are, and what value can you put on that? It was like an exorcism' (*Sunday Herald* 12 August 2007).
103. Alan McCombes also talk of them being a 'close knit family' (*DTTSS* p. 17) and him and Tommy being 'like brothers' (*DTTSS* p. 156).
104. Former longstanding colleagues and comrades like David Archibald, Rosie Kane, Richie Venton, Colin Fox, Catriona Grant and Frances Curran also recounted that Tommy 'never opened up' to them in a personal way about himself and his feelings. When they sought to engage in any personal matters, they recalled 'the shutters came down' in the words of Richie Venton.
105. *Herald* 2 November 2010.
106. *Express* 24 December 2010.
107. Others like Richie Venton and Colin Fox also attested to the difficulty in socialising with Tommy.
108. Alan McCombes recounted that one of Tommy's sexual partners told him that Tommy 'confessed to her that he was obsessed with sex and thought about it all the time' (*Scotsman* 10 June 2011).
109. Keith's testimony here is substantiated by that from Alan McCombes and Richie Venton.
110. Keith testimony here is substantiated by that from Alan McCombes, Colin Fox and Richie Venton.
111. Tommy never admitted to attending Cupids in 2001, only in 1996 and 2002.
112. 26 December 2010, 2 January 2011, 30 January 2011, 6 February 2011. This also included material on the Moat House party and the alibis Gail gave Tommy. The *Sun* (28 January 2011) also reported further details of the Cupids' visit.
113. 6 February 2011. This may relate to events surrounding Kirsten Walker, one of Tommy's first serious relationships (see *ATTR*, p. 97). With the closure of the *NoW* in July 2011, such stories may now be published in a future *Sun on Sunday*.
114. *Scotsman* 1 June 2001, *Herald* 2 November 2002.
115. *Herald* 4 October 2000.
116. *ATTR* p. 2.
117. Tommy's description of the motivation for buying the house supports this (*Scotland on Sunday* 12 April 2007). Keith was in a good position to see and judge these issues given he also had a close relationship with Gail because she respected Keith as a decent guy who was able to challenge Tommy on things that she also challenged Tommy on. Rosie Kane was also of the view that Tommy used Gail as cover in this regard of the house and lifestyle.
118. Alan McCombes put the figure of the *Daily Record* deal at £20,000 (*DTTSS* p. 210). Others, like *Herald* (11 August 2006), suggested the fee was £30,000 – this may have included the hotel accommodation and the like which – when rounded up – came to £30,000.
119. It was this rebuke that probably led Tommy to say in his newspaper column that because he had chosen the Pollok gala day over two celebratory charity football matches 'it better be as good as previous years' (*Mirror* 6 August 2003) and to congratulate 'Big George' for organising it (*Mirror* 12 August 2003).
120. George surmised: 'He did this because he knew of all the shit that was coming. And it [the *NoW* 31 October 2004 story] happened the day after the demo'.
121. *BBC News online* 23 December 2010.
122. 'The Trials of Tommy' *BBC Radio Scotland* 26 January 2011.

123. *TST* 27 November 2010.
124. Tommy referred to many instances of this in *A Time to Rage*.
125. See Chapter 5.
126. See *Guardian* 28 January 2011. This was also the view of Frances Curran and Carolyn Leckie. See also Kevin Williamson's letter of resignation from the SSP (21 August 2006) where he believed Tommy 'suffers from the classic Catholic psychological dichotomy that treats the women close to him as saintly Madonnas whilst those he engages with in meaningless sexual encounters are Magdalene-ish whores to be used and then discarded'.
127. *Scotsman* 30 November 2000.
128. *ATTR* pp. 210–211.
129. The roots of a sizable feminist milieu in the SSP predate 2002 and implicit consequent criticism of Tommy for not taking on board the full feminist agenda can also be levelled at others in the SSP leadership.
130. It should also be noted that Tommy supported, and championed to some degree, Carolyn Leckie's candidature as the lead list candidate in the Central Scotland region for the 2003 elections.
131. See the comments of Rosie Kane – 'Tommy only has two ways to deal with women. If he can't fuck us, he will fuck us over' and Catriona Grant – 'Whatever their views of Tommy Sheridan, folk need to realise that this case was a fight between men and women. This was not about class, but gender' – in the *Guardian* (28 January 2011, 8 August 2006 respectively) and a letter in the *Herald* (10 August 2006). Carolyn Leckie on Twitter called Tommy 'a serial abuser of women' (8 July 2011) while former SSP national secretary (2006-2010), Pam Currie, believed Tommy 'was a product of society that facilitates men's abuse of power' (*Scottish Socialist Voice* 8 July 2011).
132. It was presumably for reasons of this biography dealing with the issues of his sexual behaviour and its political consequences that Tommy attempted to smear it by terming it as 'salacious' (*Scotland on Sunday* 20 March 2011).
133. Writer, activist and former Militant/SML member, Kevin Williamson, termed the process one of the 'manufacture of sexual consent' in his letter of resignation from the SSP (21 August 2006). There is no suggestion, however, that this behaviour was anything on a par with that which occurred with Gerry Healy in the WRP. It is alleged that Tommy used very disparaging language of some women like one being a 'bike' which was to be ridden and that 'Every hole is a goal' (see also *Herald* 2 February 2011). Such alleged use of language is compatible with Tommy calling golf 'a game for pussies' with 'eighteen holes and not a hair on any of them' (recounted from *Celebrity Big Brother* in *DTTSS* p. 277)
134. There was no sense that any of the allegations came from women with political axes to grind against Tommy.
135. *Evening Times* 17 May 2001. In this connection, Colin Fox recalled: 'I was aware that his relationships didn't seem to end well' (*Times* 24 December 2010).
136. *Mirror* 12 November 2004.
137. *Daily Record* 5 August 2006.
138. *Sunday Herald* 23 February 2003.
139. *Times* 30 July 2007.
140. *Sunday Herald* 29 January 2006. There are a host of other statements from Tommy which appear compatible with the aforementioned ones and indicate a longstanding strain in his behaviour. Of his teenage years he says: 'I was never a fighter. All I was really interested in ... was earning a wage, playing football and chasing women ... My mum would have skelped me if she knew how I was behaving towards girls. She never brought me up to be like that – but peer group influences are very strong'

(*ATTR* p. 8) where he also admitted to being sexually active in his schools years (*ATTR* p. 9). Elsewhere, he highlighted his 'chasing [of] young ladies' (*Scotland on Sunday* 2 April 2000) and 'pursuit of the opposite sex' (*Herald* 12 June 2001) as among his favourite activities at school as well as 'flirting with girls' (*Scotsman* 11 August 1999) when working at Burtons. Later, when in Saughton, he joked when asked what he missed most: 'As most of you have family readerships and audiences, I can't answer that properly' (*Independent* 24 March 1992).

141. *Scotsman* 25 November 2000.

142. *Daily Record* 16 January 2009.

143. *Sunday Times* 28 May 2000.

144. 30 January 2011. If Tommy were to stand for election after being released from jail, it would not be surprising if some political opponents attended any of his press conferences or public meetings for this with these pictures blown up and attached to placards in order to embarrass him.

145. Tommy's seeming penchant for group sex may be related to the culture of foot-ballers. There is an added element of risk to such activities in regard of maintaining confidentiality about them when more people are involved in them.

146. In another example, he recounted of his university days a woman told him: 'If you fuck the way you dance you must be a lousy lay!' My confidence was torpedoed and I never returned to the dancefloor. The rest of her analysis wasn't far out either!' (*Big Issue Scotland* 23–29 September 2004).

147. There is little point detailing the various sexual liaisons and practices that were the subject of the 2006 and 2010 court cases, and which came out after these cases, for this information is not only already in the public domain but easily accessible through the internet.

148. *Mirror* 12 November 2004.

149. Close, A. 'I'm not unusual – Tommy Sheridan' *Scotsman* 25 November 2000 (which was a 3,000 word piece on Tommy). See also *Times* 30 July 2007. The sense that Gail 'tamed' Tommy was played up elsewhere – for example, *Daily Record* 15 June 2000.

150. *TST* 17 December 2010.

151. Benn, T. *More Time for Politics: Diaries 2001–2007* (2007, Hutchinson), p. 162.

152. *Scottish Review* 8 February 2011.

153. 11 November 2001.

154. 2 November 2002.

155. Another version of this was: 'McCombes had the strategic insight, Sheridan the oratory and charisma' (Davies, L. 'A Scottish tragedy' *Red Pepper*, August/September 2011).

156. From interviews with Felicity Garvie and Carolyn Leckie. In this connection, it is interesting to note Steve Arnott commented: '[Tommy] doesn't always identify the right people for the task ... if someone comes along and is keen he encourages them but they're not always the best person for the job ... but sometimes you need to think harder about whether they're the right person for the task or to be taking advice from. ... Historically, Tommy hasn't always picked his friends wisely'.

157. Some like Richie Venton believed the skill of 'sniffing the wind' was sometimes overrated as detecting a mood did not preclude this mood being a passing one.

158. My review of *DTTSS* and the reception to it can be found on the Wordpower book shop website (29 June 2011) and on *Socialist Unity* (30 June 2011). For reasons outlined there, such as shallowness of analysis, Alan McCombes' account cannot be treated as the 'definitive' one of Tommy's demise as the *Scotsman* (9 June 2011) and *Herald* (18 June 2011) believed. For example, Alan told the *Scotsman* (9 June 2011) that the narrative of the book wrote itself, indicating that the foundation

of underlying analysis and explanation was sparse. Similarly, writer Alan Bissett (*Sunday Herald* 27 November 2011) was, thus, mistaken to believe that *DTTSS* was the 'definitive account of the Tommy Sheridan trials'.

159. *Scottish Socialist Voice* 10 June 2011.

160. See *DTTSS* pp. 55–57. Alan appeared unaware of the similarities between himself and Tommy, especially in regard to bombast and boldness. He did not also address the ramifications and responsibilities of keeping his knowledge of Tommy's sexual behaviour under wraps (see Chapter 6). See also the reviews of *DTTSS* by Ian Bell and Stephen Low (See Chapter 10 notes).

161. *DTTSS* p. viii, 56, 97, 151, 224, 258, 313, 314, 317.

162. For example, his blog (28 March 2011).

163. *Herald* 2 November 2002, *Daily Record* 14 January 2009.

164. See *Scotland on Sunday* 10 October 1999, *Herald* 2 November 2002.

165. See also *Scotland on Sunday* 15 December 1996.

166. When Tommy compiled a tape for the car journeys to the 2006 court case, a number of these featured in it (*Sunday Mail* 6 August 2006).

167. This would have been ironic given its reworking of The Bobby Fuller Four's 'I Fought the Law (and the law won)'. Equally ironic would have been its other songs of 'Stay Free' or 'Jail Guitar Doors'.

168. *Evening Times* 22 December 2000.

169. *Scotland on Sunday* 16 January 2000.

170. *Daily Record* 15 June 2000.

171. *Times* 24 December 2010 (and which Colin Fox confirmed).

172. *ATTR* pp. 212–213.

173. Tommy told the *Daily Record* (8 August 2006) he 'take[s] great pride in my fitness ... The fitter I am the harder I can fight those who tried to destroy me ... If you keep your body healthy, your mind will stay sharp ... I'll need every ounce of strength to defeat my enemies ...'.

174. *ATTR* p. 212.

175. *Scotland on Sunday* 16 January 2000, *Newsnight Scotland* 8 August 2006. After 2004, he did have the 'Sheridanistas' around him.

176. *Sunday Times* 28 May 2000.

177. 28 May 2000.

178. *Sunday Times* 28 May 2000.

179. This was also the view of *Scotland on Sunday* 6 August 2006.

180. *Sunday Times* 30 January 2011.

181. *Scotland on Sunday* 25 February 2007.

182. This story was recounted on a number of times such as in the *Daily Record* (18 May 1999), where Gail took the opportunity to tell readers: 'Tommy says I'm the only person he knows that can go on holiday and get a tan on my tongue''. This set a pattern for their presentation of themselves in the media as full of fun and good natured rivalry.

183. Tommy often publicly recounted this event (e.g., *Herald* 20 April 1999).

184. Later she said: 'He has no fear of anything and therefore I always feel dead protected that way' (*Scotsman* 25 November 2000).

185. *Sunday Mirror* 23 May 1999.

186. *Scotland on Sunday* 25 February 2007.

187. See also *Sunday Mirror* 23 May 1999.

188. *Scotsman* 1 June 2001.

189. See also *Sunday Mirror* 23 May 1999, *Sunday Times* 28 May 2000, *Herald* 2 December 2002.

190. *Daily Star* 10 November 2001, *Herald* 2 November 2002.

191. Elsewhere, she talked of him as the 'wee boy of mine' (*Daily Record* 15 June 2000, *Express* 2 August 2006).
192. See, for example, *Mirror* 11 August 2006, *Herald* 19 August 2006, *Evening Times* 2 September 2006. The possibility of this after May 2007 was stymied by preparing for the perjury trial.
193. *Sunday Express* 5 August 2007.
194. Another example concerned his consistent refusal to take his pass, which he was entitled to as an elected councillor and which allowed free access to Glasgow City Council's sunbed, sauna and jacuzzi facilities. He did so as such access was not available to council staff (*Sunday Herald* 1 August 1999).
195. 29 January 2006. See also *Scotland on Sunday* 16 January 2000.
196. *Scotland on Sunday* 17 December 2000.
197. *NoW* 26 December 2010. This raises questions about whether Tommy genuinely believed in marriage. If he did not, it might explain his unwillingness to abide by its conventions like faithfulness.
198. Here, and in other previous instances, the line between becoming 'public property' as a result of outside imposition by others or direct solicitation by Tommy became somewhat blurred.
199. 12 July 1998.
200. *Daily Record* 15 June 2000.
201. Rosie Kane explained that the term 'getting off before Govan' was a Glaswegian colloquialism for the *coitus interruptus* method of contraception (although other versions exist like 'getting off at Paisley' i.e. before getting to the terminus at Glasgow).
202. In this connection, Rosie Kane believed: 'It was extremely timely that Tommy, the man who espouses family values, suddenly had a wee baby on the way when it all started to go horribly wrong'.
203. *Sunday Herald* 29 January 2006.
204. *Sunday Herald* 12 August 2007. He used private medicine for his daughter to get single doses of MMR vaccines (*Sunday Herald* 29 April 2007).
205. Blog 17 March 2011. Tommy's gushing over Gabrielle can be read as not just a further attempt at normalisation but also one of playing the victim of being unjustly separated from his daughter.
206. Gail tells the story of how it took her to physically stop him leaving the house to get three bags of bark laid down after sitting there for nine months (*Scotland on Sunday* 16 January 2000). However by 2007, Tommy admitted he now 'enjoyed' gardening (*Scotland on Sunday* 12 August 2007).
207. Earlier, Gail recounted when he moved into her house, Tommy told her he was a 'new man' who was into doing his share of the chores to which she said: 'Aye, but do you do the lavatory and the bath?' (*Daily Record* 15 June 2000). The fact that Gail cleans most of the house came out in the 2006 court case when Katrine Trolle remarked upon the smell of bleach when she was there and the *Daily Record* (15 June 2000) reported: 'Tommy has been known to complain about the smell of bleach'.
208. *Herald* 31 May 2005.
209. *Scotland on Sunday* 16 January 2000.
210. See also *Daily Record* 5 January 2000.
211. See *Sunday Mail* 26 December 2010. Some like Frances Curran and Richie Venton believed Tommy could not bring himself to tell Gail of his sexual activities and so engaged in a denial strategy involving the defamation case. This is supported by Tommy's comment on the McNeilage tape of 'I can't go to Gail'. However, Tommy told Colin Fox that he had 'come clean' to Gail and his mother, Alice. In all of this

Gail's comment on Colin Fox, Rosie Kane, Frances Curran and Carolyn Leckie is intriguing: 'I thought that was a prerequisite for politicians – that you can stand up, be convincing and lie. That is what you've got to be able to do ... Politicians stabbing each other in the back? Commonplace in that game' (*Scotland on Sunday* 25 February 2007) for there is no reason why this could not equally apply to Tommy (or Rosemary Byrne).

212. See *Daily Record* 24 December 2010.
213. 5 August 2006.
214. *Herald* 6 November 2010.
215. *Herald* 9, 19 October 2010.
216. *Guardian* 28 January 2011.
217. *Sunday Mail* 26 December 2010.
218. For example, BBC Scotland *Sex, Lies and Socialism* 7 August 2006, *Mirror* 4 October 2006, *Herald* 18 November 2010.
219. *STV* 11 January 2011.
220. *Daily Record* 5 August 2006.
221. *Daily Record* 5 August 2006.
222. *Herald* 19 August 2006.
223. *Sunday Mail* 6 August 2006, *Daily Record* 5 August 2006.
224. *Scotland on Sunday* 25 February 2007. Tommy also made it clear that Gail had quizzed him (*Mail on Sunday* 6 August 2006).
225. *Herald* 24 December 2010, *NoW* 26 December 2010, *Sunday Times* 30 January 2011.
226. For example, Ian Hamilton QC nearly joined the SSP (*Scottish Review* 20 October 2011).
227. This meant that 'The Tommy Sheridan story stands as a screaming warning to those who value personalities over principles [and thus politics]' (*DTTSS* p. 317) is far too blunt and ham fisted an assessment.
228. In this regard, Mike Jones, QC for *NoW*, argued in his summing up that Tommy was an example of '[h]istory [being] littered with the political corpses of great men who have been brought down by their own recklessness' (*Herald* 3 August 2006).

9

Political Perspectives

Introduction

Tommy made clear early on that 'politics for me is about practical realities ... [but] what I won't apologise for, however, is having a vision for tomorrow'.[1] This summed up his approach to fighting in the here-and-now to defend and advance workers' interests with the goal of longer-term, deep-seated social change running in tandem. So, in promoting the SSP in election campaigns, he had a raft of immediate aims on the social wage and other issues that were more aspirational as well as lofty ambitions of a socialist society based on need and not profit and independence for Scotland. His long standing advocacy of a maximum wage, where he sought to level up – not level down as some critics alleged – workers' incomes, was an example of combining short-term and long-terms goals. Critically, coming from a Militant background, Tommy understood the economic and material basis of popular grievance. In his role of advocate general for the SSP especially, he showed that the SSP's success was not just down to the situation where 'new' Labour had vacated the left ground but that he and the SSP could also fill it (in Scotland). He offered, to use the mainstream parlance of the time, not just 'Scottish solutions' to 'Scottish problems' but credible Scottish socialist solutions. This was not to everyone's taste within the SSP for the CWI and SWP frequently argued that Tommy needed to raise the pitch of his ambition so that he appealed not only to more advanced consciousness but also pushed forward those of a lesser consciousness. But it was on the more attuned perspective created with the likes of Alan McCombes and others that for the radical and socialist left, Tommy played a major part in taking socialism out of the ghetto without befalling for the dangers of nationalism and electoralism. This chapter takes the opportunity to do credit to Tommy's full political palate by examining his overall political perspective as well as particular issues and subjects in a way that was not possible in the preceding chronological account of his life.

Transitional Method

Although Tommy very seldom articulated the transitional method or approach in public – or even behind closed doors – it did lie at the core of his thinking and actions, and resulted from his political apprenticeship in Militant. Taken from Trotsky's writings in particular, the approach is one that seeks to raise both working class oppositional consciousness and capacity to struggle against, and ultimately, overthrow capitalism. The grist is that in getting workers to fight for what are called 'transitional' demands, workers will come to realise that capitalism cannot meet their needs, and they will then deduce that capitalism must be overthrown and can be overthrown as a result of the development of their organisational capacity. Transitional demands differ from calls for reform in and of itself (or minimum demands) because they constitute demands that governments are unwilling or unable to offer, and therefore, progress towards obtaining them will likely weaken capitalism and strengthen the working class. Yet transitional demands also differ from calls for revolution (or a maximum demand) because they constitute primarily economic demands that could be achieved under capitalism and do not constitute demands for socialism *per se*. Examples of transitional demands are jobs or housing 'for all', and which sound reasonable but are practically impossible for capitalism to deliver upon. To quote Trotsky:

> It is necessary to help the masses in the process of the daily struggle to find the bridge between present demand and the socialist program of the revolution. This bridge should include a system of transitional demands, stemming from today's conditions and from today's consciousness of wide layers of the working class and unalterably leading to one final conclusion: the conquest of power by the proletariat.[2]

In this conception, to paraphrase Trotsky, revolutionaries are the best reformers (rather than reformists). Thus, Tommy argued: '[Y]ou really can go from wanting to change the street lighting to wanting to change the world'.[3] The utility of this approach can be verified to some extent by the growth and implantation of SML and later the SSP.

Socialists of a non-Trotskyist heritage have also commonly, if implicitly, worked on the same notion of a transitional approach of workers being changed through the experience of collective struggle and, like Tommy, they have not articulated this strategy publicly either. While a public figure like Tommy may have consequently been decried and ridiculed for explicitly using what could be described by some as an underhand, covert method of operating, something was also lost as a result of not doing so. Whether more was lost or gained is an open question because the consequent strength of not doing so was that an appeal to a certain milieu disillusioned by 'new' Labour and a market-friendly SNP was strengthened. In other words, the non-articulation made Tommy (and the SSP) look more 'old Labour', reformist and social democrat than revolutionary or radical socialist. Alongside this, not discussing the transitional approach openly prevented Tommy and the SSP from being accused of engaging in arcane and introverted discussion on questions that could be characterised as 'how many angels can dance on the head of a pin?'. Thus, the charge of ultra-leftism here was avoided because the SSP could be said to be looking at the wood and not the trees of the immediate issues facing workers in Scotland. Not openly articulating the transitional method was not a conscious decision for Tommy believed that 'it's a bit like being trained at football ... after a while it becomes inbuilt ... it becomes second nature'. But not articulating and discussing the transitional approach did have a downside for within the SSP it added to a loss of sense of direction after the 2003 breakthrough although this was far from Tommy's responsibility alone.[4] Specifically, it was not clear from the SSP leadership how the election of six MSPs fitted into their 'roadmap' to socialism and independence. Was it a slow war of attrition to accrue more MSPs and then legislate for socialism within parliament once a majority was achieved (notwithstanding 'reserved' business and the like)? Or were the MSPs to merely be tribunes of the extra-parliamentary struggle which would lead to an insurrection? Or was there to be a mix of the two? For those voters within the orbit of the SSP, these were not necessarily pressing questions but this was not so for SSP members and activists. Moreover, and again with the same paradox of strength and weakness, Tommy often thus appeared as not much more than a 'Mr Angry' which fitted well by articulating what was wrong with Scotland and capitalism. But he was light on what the alternative was by dint of explaining what the strategy was to get there – which for the credibility of this alternative was crucial. This was all the more so for him as a lone MSP between 1999 and 2003 and for the relatively small band of radical and revolutionary socialists of SML/SSA/SSP.[5]

Conception of Socialism

For Tommy, there was a very practical nature to (his) socialism (see Chapters 2 and 3). It was not one based on workers' councils (soviets) and permanent revolution of the Trotskyist tradition. Rather, it was one of expressing common humanity, decency and solidarity through teamwork at whatever level of society, which was not dissimilar to Scottish footballer and then Liverpool manager Bill Shankly's idea of football as a form of socialism when he said: 'The socialism I believe in is everyone working for each other, everyone having a share of the rewards. It's the way I see football, the way I see life'. Indeed, in his first *Daily Record* column Tommy wrote: 'The late, great Bill Shankly once likened the co-operation and teamwork of a football side in action as a form of socialism'.[6] Tommy's orientation on this conception was founded on a belief that workers and citizens needed to find within their own lives the basis of understanding what a future socialist society would look like through close-at-hand examples and direct experience. While this could comprise strikes and demonstrations such as those of the miners' between 1984–1985 or the anti-poll tax revolt, it could just as easily comprise community activity such as voluntary work and the community's own provision of facilities for itself. In this sense, it formed part of his transitional approach whereby certain parts of the present showed, in a pre-figurative way, how the future could be. For example, in explaining that his fee for his *Daily Record* column would go to support a community hall in Pollok (see Chapter 4), he wrote: 'I believe the Jack Jardine Memorial Hall, as it is to be called, is also a form of local socialism in action – and provides a glimpse of the type of society we could build in Scotland by harnessing the skills, talents and energy of millions of ordinary people'.[7] For Tommy, the choice of this language and these examples were more than merely the means of expressing and presenting a vision of socialism that could be more widely understood. In keeping with the characteristics of his transitional approach, the strength of this conception was that it fitted with the situation when merely raising the banner of socialism was the fundamental task of the day. Yet, Tommy (along with others in the SML/SSA/SSP leadership) did not theorise this conception to deepen their understanding of its strengths and weaknesses.

Following from this conception, and in tandem with it, Tommy reported that Tony Benn was one of his 'political heroes'[8] and, according to Benn, both agreed on the necessarily practical and short-term reforming bent to leftwing politics.[9] In other words, it was all very well talking about the big ideas of socialism and revolution but not if you could neither relate to workers' and citizens' existing concerns and grievances nor deliver improvements in their living standards in the here-and-now.[10] Thus, Tommy argued with a very down-to-earth perspective: 'Undoubtedly the biggest single problem is poverty. From poverty emanate poor diet, unhealthy living environment, ignorance, inability to access leisure and fitness facilities and severe lack of motivation and self-esteem. The eradication of poverty through fundamental wealth redistribution will not only lead to a more equal and productive society, it will also lead to a much healthier society'[11] and 'lack of education is at the root of all society's ills. Ignorance breeds intolerance, racism and sectarianism. And education is one of our best weapons in the fight against poverty. When people are educated they know when they are being exploited or denied opportunities. They know what options are available to them and how to go about fighting injustice'.[12] The latter statement, in particular, would have struck his former CWI comrades as decidedly un-Marxist (see below) as it placed neither the exploitation of workers for the benefit of capitalists nor workers being the only social class with the interest and ability to abolish capitalism at the heart of its analysis. Yet, it reflected the influence of the common argument – made by his mother amongst others – that working class people need to 'get an education' if they are make something of themselves as people and to change society. However, for Tommy, this was not necessarily to go as far as believing 'knowledge is power' in and of itself.

Consequently, Tommy's conception of socialism in Scotland was that of a socialised mixed economy where the 'private sector will have a role in the independent Scotland, just not the dominant one'[13] and where he advocated supporting small businesses against big business, sometimes in alliances with unions.[14] (Nonetheless, there is still some ambiguity as to whether this conception of socialism was for the present time and situation or whether it was for all time and any situation – see later.) For allegedly showing capitalist tendencies, he was heavily criticised by his former CWI comrades in its own press[15] and by going as far as press releasing a statement where they attacked Tommy as a 'neo-Stalinist capitalist'.[16] Key to this accusation was alleged political backsliding from Marxism and Trotskyism towards reformism and the right. With this, and the repudiation of the need for a revolutionary party or vanguard organisation, Peter Taaffe categorised Tommy as 'a socialist but not a revolutionary socialist' while Ronnie Stevenson believed that Tommy was 'kidding' himself if he thought he was still a Marxist.[17] While this may not have been problematic for all, that Tommy seldom explained and justified, openly or otherwise, his moving on from long-held and previously cherished political positions did cause consternation.

This conception of socialism also explained why Tommy was so enamoured with Cuba and Venezuela.[18] In so doing, he was able to show that his political outlook extended beyond mere protest and resistance (even if the questions of how to get to these nirvanas were left unaddressed). Thus, in line with this focus upon the practical, Tommy was a plaudit for what he regarded as the actual, progressive social experiments of Cuba and Venezuela, lauding their achievements despite the many obstacles they faced.[19] Indeed, he declared his 'love of the Socialist Republic of Cuba',[20] promoted it[21] and welcomed in the New Year with a toast to Cuba: 'The Cuban Revolution has been an inspiration to socialists across the world. They have shown what is possible, despite blockades by the USA and a hostile capitalist world, Cuba has improved the lives of working class people year after year. It is a testament to the revolution that such a small country sends more medical staff to assist in third world countries than the USA'.[22] Tommy also put his money where his mouth was and visited both countries with Gail on holiday, thus fusing the personal and political. Earlier, he had been drawn to the 1979 Nicaraguan Sandinista revolution even though it was not socialist because it represented an example of the mass of citizens exerting control over their own destiny. This contrasted to Militant's fundamentalist approach which critics characterised as 'if it's not socialist then it's not worth bothering about'. For Tommy, the link between Cuba and Scotland was thus:

Scotland should be proud of its contribution to knowledge, science, technology, education and humanity but all of these things are becoming tiny anecdotes and footnotes when they could be central to our identity ... they could become our identity ... Cuba is synonymous with health and education ...Why couldn't we be and why are we not synonymous with these things any more? We are a potentially rich and resourceful small country and we could become a player on the world stage and punch well above our weight.

Parliamentary Cretinism

The 'sin' of parliamentary cretinism in the lexicon of revolutionary socialists was referred to before. To quote Tommy from earlier, that revolution was a process, not an event (like a 'big bang' insurrection a la October 1917 in Russia), suggested the notion of creeping and encroaching control through parliamentary means had a significant place in his worldview. Again this indicates the continuing influence of the Militant mode of thought. So does Tommy stand accused by some of parliamentary cretinism? This question cannot be easily answered because the matter was again seldom articulated. But when viewing Tommy's actions, parliament was a very important arena but not to the exclusion of all others. Neither were all other *modus operandi* in other arenas shoehorned into that of the parliamentary one. Tommy took parliament seriously and was a supremely effective parliamentarian as shown earlier. He was also a party builder, especially between 1999 and 2003. Yet because this matter was seldom articulated, it would be wrong to draw a definite conclusion on what his perspective was because his attitude and actions between 1999 and 2007 were largely conjunctural – they were the application of his perspective to a certain situation and period and did not necessarily constitute the overall perspective itself.

Scotland and Scottishness

Tommy was open and proud of being Scottish[23] but this meant a certain version of Scottishness and a radical one at that. Thus:

I consider myself a socialist, a Marxist and an internationalist. I am also committed to Scottish independence. There is no contradiction. Internationalism is an inter-nation association. I associate with other countries across the world as a Scot, not a Brit. My sense of national identity is not chauvinistic but rooted in social justice and tolerance of others. The real 21st century Bravehearts don't want 'freedom' in an abstract sense. We want freedom from poverty, nuclear weapons, war, racism and ignorant intolerance. ... Scotland as a free, democratic republic is not an idea of the past, it is an idea whose time is coming. Just as Venezuela is building a socialist nation rooted in a democratically agreed constitution and public ownership of its wealth and raw materials, so Scotland could be a voice of peace, co-operation and social justice in future.[24]

The problem is, I don't want to be British, I don't feel British and I don't identify myself with Britain. On holiday abroad I get angry when people think you are British or English because you talk English. I am Scottish. Not in a chauvinistic or superior way, but by dint of my whole life experience. I consider Britain to be a bloodthirsty monster which spread its influence across the globe at the end of a bayonet and a cannon ... The British role across the world was mainly to conquer markets through brute force and plunder the natural resources and raw materials of emerging nations in the name of "civilisation". I reject, therefore, any semblance of British identity. ... My Scotland would be a nation of liberty and social justice enshrined in a written constitution. An independent socialist republic which banished poverty, obscene inequality and nuclear weapons from our shores would secure my allegiance.[25]

To encapsulate all this, he stated: 'I love Scotland. It's my country. It's where I want to live and die'.[26] Tommy even admitted there was an emotional and psychological aspect to his love here: 'It's hard to be coldly logical for me when I think of Scotland ... it's more to do with emotional attachment ... for me it's about community, warmth, home ... a small country with a relatively big heart because communitarianism is rich within the fabric of society in Scotland'. But he was not an uncritical admirer for he was clear in his belief that society in Scotland 'needs radical surgery to address the serious ailments dragging it down'.[27] So, in what seemed an adaptation of the transitional method when applied to Scotland:

[Tommy was] able to speak to wider milieus of people than had hitherto been possible by using the conception of Scottish society to convey radical and socialist ideas. Sheridan argued for 'another Scotland' and a distinctive version of the 'new Scotland' that included a vision of Scotland of peace (no nuclear weapons, no part in imperialist ventures), democracy (republicanism, independence), social compassion (redistribution of wealth, full employment, better public services) and a socialised economy (reduction in the role of the free market through state intervention) ... 'Another Scotland' combined the politics of the SSP with the progressive and class-based aspirations embodied in the dominant version of Scottish national identity.[28]

In a powerful exposition of this, at the 9 October 2004 Calton Hill declaration for an independent Scottish republic, Tommy spoke in terms of the kind of Scotland he wanted his child to grow up in. Here, he was skilful in adopting and fusing the language of several discourses.[29] But, for some, this was described with disdain as 'left nationalism' or just plain 'nationalism' which breaks up the unity of the working class in Britain.[30] Later, he told *Newsnight Scotland* that independence was just a 'means to an end to a better and fairer Scotland.[31]

In a relatively unusual critical foray, Tommy argued the unwillingness to appropriate national identity in England for progressive ends was remiss. So, on various speaking engagements south of the border, he would variously point out:

There is a failure of the left in England to define nationality from an English point of view which has left a huge gap to be filled by the right ... why should England not be defined as William Morris, Watt Tyler and the Tolpuddle matyrs and so on? There is a radical tradition there ... by trying to avoid being contaminated by English nationalism they end up being contaminated by British nationalism which is a nationalism of wars and imperialism ... they moved away from what could be a progressive tradition to tacitly backing up a reactionary one ... the left has a lot to do to get to grips with this. There are millions of people who are passionate about supporting the England football team are not all racists or fascists ... but they have a belief in being English.

The problem is that the British left has never grappled with the issue of English nationalism and they are going to have to ... waving a St George Flag or an England top doesn't making some a fascist or reactionary but the British left's attitude is that it does ... the only English tradition that is brought up [here] is the empire not the struggles of the Chartists and the like ... having an English identity doesn't mean you can't be a socialist.

Tommy also made the argument that many Scots' antagonism towards England is most attributable to the legacy of Thatcher and Thatcherism, and so the best way to remove this friction was to have an independent Scotland whereby both countries existed on an equal inter-nation footing.

Internationalism

Tommy was firm in his belief of internationalism as a foundation of his conception of socialism – but it was not an orthodox definition for one coming from a Trotskyist background. Thus, he argued:

I would challenge anyone on the left to define internationalism as anything other than *inter-nation-alism* ... internationalism stands for respect for humanity and your brothers and sisters as part of the same race ... we relate to each other on a nation-by-nation, nation-to-nation basis ... I do not want to assume a British identity as those that reject a Scottish identity do ... that's not the way I want to relate internationally to brothers and sisters elsewhere ... [Differences of national identity are] a reality of life that should be celebrated not condemned [and] that there will be diversity [in terms of] colour, religion ... the view that there will be or should be no national identity is a utopia worth holding onto but, let's be honest, that it's not going to happen for several generations after socialism is created

In this sense, and given his views of socialism and his favoured form of Scottishness, Tommy could be said to be a Scottish internationalist. Again, for the far left, this was some form of nationalism because its understanding of internationalism was essentially transnationalism, where socialism would exist without nation states and only with class-less states as the key form of social organisation. For Tommy, there was another contemporary dimension to his internationalism – the decline of socialist forces meant that other forms of progressive resistance to neo-liberalism and imperialism had to necessarily be seen in a more positive light:

In this modern era of imperialism, what the left has to get grips with is that the nation state is now often an impediment to, a block on imperialism ... that's why many national self-determination move-ments are now radical, left-wing which they do not necessarily endeavour to be that at their beginning ... for example Chavez has enlisted national pride with a socially progressive set of politics and now that national independence becomes a barrier to global impe-rialism and neo-liberalism ... The Chilean, Cuban and Nicaraguan revolutions all had a national content ... and in the 1990s with the anti-globalisation movement you can see that national identity is a revolutionary strand now in it ... you can see it with the Chavez-led Bolivian revolution in Venezuela which is a mass movement ... [capitalist neo-liberal] globalisation by its very nature tries to remove national boundaries so the question becomes what kind of nationalism ... narrow, reactionary chauvinism of Eastern Europe or that of Latin American, Caribbean and South American nation-alism which is of a more progressive, socially liberating form.

He continued:

People [on the left] often in a simplistic way counter-pose nation-alism to internationalism ... so that if you support Scottish inde-pendence then you're not an internationalist and [they] forget that the very term international means between two nations ... and by implication if you don't believe in Scottish independence then you are a British nationalist ... because your international-ism is of the British nation linking up to other nations ... that's not my idea of internationalism because British nationalism is a bastardised product and an imperialist weapon ... any socialist worth their salt has to want to see the break-up of Britain ... of course, not all those that want to see the break-up of Britain are socialists because they are nationalists ... but for socialists the route to socialism now is to have national movements intermingling with industrial struggles that will take on an increasingly national character as well

For a lot of the left in Britain, they would support the right of self-determination but not for Scotland or an independent Scotland because they don't think Scotland is a country ... they think Britain is a country ... that denies history and reality. They say 'I'm an internationalist, not a nationalist' ... what does it actually mean? ... It's so weak and pathetic.

John Maclean and the National Question

The sense of fusing together Tommy's conceptions of socialism and Scottishness came from his appreciation of Scottish revolutionary, John Maclean. Thus: 'I am asked the same question consistently: 'Who is my inspiration?' Politically the answer is always the same, the great John Maclean ... [whose] life and experiences educate and inspire ... [because] he was often on the wrong side of the law but always on the right side of the people'.[32] Maclean was the single most frequent topic that Tommy wrote at length on.[33] In a show of political bonding, Tommy wore the Maclean tartan at his wedding. He also argued that a film of Maclean's live should be made so that a 'real Braveheart' was immortalised.[34] For Tommy, Maclean's key contribution was to bring forth the idea of the Scottish socialist republic because it laid the basis for the adoption by SML/SSA/SSP of a socialist approach to the national question in Scotland which resulted in socialists being in favour of independence. Tommy recounted:

This was fresh thinking in one sense for the left but it was also a revisiting of Maclean ... Maclean's only problem was that he was ahead of his time because the British union was still developing and there was still a material benefit to the working class [in Scotland in terms of shipbuilding and engineering] of being in the empire so he was running against the stream at that time ... compared to today where there is almost nothing left to those industries and much of what is left is owned by multi-nationals corporations where Britain plc is redundant because they own it ... [today] there is now more of a material benefit to be had in being independent in terms of natural resources.

But Tommy was also quick to point out that 'independence of itself would be meaningless. Changing the Union Jack for the St Andrew's flag isn't going to improve wages, homes and job prospects. Only the flag of justice, equality and socialism will do that'.[35] The 'fresh thinking' Tommy referred to was that 'Alan [McCombes] has to take great credit for his hard work to develop a theoretical justification for our political turn ... and emboldened those of us who argue for a socialist world on the one hand and an independent Scotland on the other'. But in this connection, Peter Taaffe maintained:'[While] Alan McCombes was the theoretician, Tommy had a very simple position: 'Let's go for independence', a left nationalist position, not a rounded Marxist position that favoured autonomy within a federation and that was sensitive to how the issue of independence waxed and waned'.

Militant's Legacy

For the making of Tommy, there were many positive features of Militant's political perspective and practice. These concerned the sense in which they influenced him to be bold and decisive, and to necessarily be an eternal optimist with attention given to workers' economic and material grievances. But Militant also gave him a large measure of self-confidence and self-belief through its politics of certainty and the certainty of being right and correct.[36] At its height in the mid-to late 1980s, and when Tommy began to become an important player within it in Scotland, Militant had around 8,000 members with around 1,000 of these in the west of Scotland. This strength cemented the influence of Militant upon him. Notwithstanding, its crisis which began in 1987 and accelerated following the fall of the Berlin Wall and 'actually existing socialism', these aforementioned influences were on Tommy not undone. The headway made by Tommy and SML protected and extended these influences. Nonetheless, because of the development of SML and the transmogrification of its majority part into the more heterodox and freer thinking ISM within the SSP, Tommy – along with others in it – was able to break free intellectually and psychologically[37] from the narrow confines of political practice and perspective associated with the CWI.[38] However, it is apparent from one aspect of Tommy's conduct in the post-2004 period in relation to the SSP and left that he practiced rather more of the centralist than the democratic part of the democratic centralism method that Militant operated under. Indeed, some of his United Left critics went as far as to label Tommy's methods in his faction fight as 'Stalinist' because of the way he sought to close down debate and discussion on some issues.[39]

Unions

Although Tommy had been a shop steward and was a high-profile supporter of workers in a number of industrial disputes like Timex, Glacier
and the nursery nurses, he did not play a particularly significant role in
the SML/SSA/SSP's union work. Typically, he was used – and with
good effect – to speak at union and strike meetings to help build the
SML/SSA/SSP but was not part of policy or strategy formulation or
their implementation in this area. This role was led by Richie Venton,
and indicated that with a division of labour and expertise Tommy was
occupied elsewhere. Nonetheless, on occasions, when he did advance
the previously decided course of action to union members and strikers, Richie Venton recalled he was a 'brilliant advocate'. In 1993, for
example, Tommy was as instrumental in gaining the breakthrough of a
£250 donation from NUPE Edinburgh District Council branch to SML,
following attacks on its members' wages by the Labour-run council, as
he was later in the 1990s in gaining donations from the Glacier worker
(who occupied their plant) and two joint-shop steward committees at
the Victoria and Southern General hospitals in Glasgow. Taking his cue
from others, Tommy advocated occupations and the calling of 24-hour
general strikes/days of action, for example, in the 2003–2004 nursery
nurses' strike. His own analysis of unions as organisations stressed the
social distance between members and leaders with the consequence of
the latter's conservatism and timidity.[40] However, Tommy did cause
something of a stir with Richie Venton over attempts to persuade him to
downgrade Richie's union function and upgrade his Glasgow organiser
function in regard of securing his re-election to parliament after standing down as the national convener and over what Richie saw as making 'unnecessary concessions' to Labour in putting the case to win the
affiliation of RMT branches to the SSP.

Political Development and Perspective

Some of the explanation for the underdevelopment in Tommy's political
thought can be attributed to pressures of time because of being on the
frontline inside and outside parliament as well as a division of labour,
especially with Alan McCombes. But to attribute this all to these would
be unconvincing. Alan McCombes believed Tommy was not a 'deep
thinker' and showed no inclination to develop his talents and skills
beyond those which he already had. An obvious aspect of this was that
Tommy's writings were of such an abridged nature that they did not

help him develop a deeper political understanding of big issues. Over and above his short journalistic pieces, when Tommy infrequently wrote at greater length, he wrote to around a 1,000 words[41] and occasionally to just over 2,000 words.[42] Like many leading former SML members, once the break with the CWI took place in 1998, he did not participate in the ISM platform which further emphasised his isolation from deeper political discussion, particularly as that provided by the SSP was not of a cadre type.[43] Overall, this chimes with a view from some on the far left that Tommy, with his Militant heritage, was good at articulating the basic injustices of capitalism but far less skilled in going much beyond this. Ironically then, Peter Taaffe commented that while 'some would love what Tommy said, others would say that he'd not go far enough' and put this down to 'his weakness [which was] that he has adapted and lowered to the level of the prevailing mood in 1990s because he did not have the sufficient theoretical grounding or it was blunted because of his position in the public arena'. The irony here is that when Tommy's star was in the ascendancy, it was because of a combination of organising resistance and relating socialism to the new found difficulties it faced, namely, the rise of 'new Labour', the implosion of 'actually existing socialism' and triumph of western capitalism. Nonetheless, and for a period when the organised radical left had failed to make a breakthrough during the extended crisis of neo-liberalism, this underdevelopment of understanding became a problem. Yet, the paradox was that such a move away from orthodox Trotskyism and a form of class reductionism – as presented by the CWI/Militant – did allow Tommy to become more heterodox and appropriately applied in his thinking even if this remained underdeveloped. Thus, as a result of rejecting having only 'one set of spectacles [to look through] for every issue'[44] from his Militant training, he was able to engage in contemporary thinking on issues of the national question, and socialism and revolution and at least ask questions like 'there is a need for the left to address the issue of what we mean by freedom ... we know what we want freedom from but what also do we want freedom for and freedom to do?' In so doing, he rejected the 'definitive determinism' of hard left which doubted all things except the pronouncements of its leaderships. Tommy believed this type of questioning of old certainties was required because of the fall of the Soviet Union and the triumph of neo-liberalism.

Conclusion

Tommy's overall political perspective provided him with the basis of popular appeal because he was able to relate to the concerns and aspirations of a mass of citizens. He did not distance himself from them with a politics of lofty and far away ideals. He raised the banner of socialism in a practical and pragmatic way. He was a sufficiently intelligent and wily operator that if the level of popular resistance to neo-liberalism had been greater, he would have changed his pitch accordingly. Yet, it remained the case that some of his critics believed he had only one pitch – to those of a lower consciousness. Whether this also meant not developing those activists into a social force that might have been capable of helping to deliver the higher and greater level of popular resistance to neo-liberalism must remain an open question.

Notes

1. *Holyrood* 22 November 1999.
2. Trotsky, L. *The Death Agony of Capitalism and the Tasks of the Fourth International* (Pathfinder, 1983) p. 114. Originally published in 1938.
3. *ATTR* p. 237.
4. The issue of overall SSP strategy was, effectively, left in the hands of Alan McCombes. An attempt to raise explicit discussion of the transitional approach by myself at a NC in late 2003 resulted in the accompanying motion being remitted to the EC. This then lead to the suggestion from Allan Green, then SSP National Secretary, that a pamphlet should be written on the issue which was a nice, neat way of sidelining the issue.
5. The non-articulation of the transitional method and, nonetheless, Tommy's advance on this basis spoke volumes about the shrunken state of contemporary working class and oppositional consciousness. In other words, because they had become retarded, Tommy as a seemingly predominant 'old Labour' warrior fitted well with their shrunken states.
6. 26 May 1999. See also *ATTR* p. 6 on amateur football as a form, in Tommy's view, of collective community action.
7. *Daily Record* 26 May 1999.
8. *Scottish Socialist Voice* 15 January 2001. On his blog of 28 September 2010, Tommy called Benn 'an inspiration and a socialist legend'.
9. Benn, T. *More Time for Politics: Diaries 2001–2007* (Hutchinson 2007), p. 163. Peter Taaffe believed: 'If Tommy has a fault, it is to exaggerate the role of individuals. For example, he doesn't see the political deficiencies of Tony Benn'.
10. It was for this reason that the campaign for free schools meals was so critical.
11. *Sunday Herald* 1 August 1999.
12. *Scotsman* 3 March 1999.
13. *Mirror* 9 June 2001.
14. *Daily Record* 14 July 1999, 20 September 2000.
15. Taaffe, P. *A socialist world is possible: the history of the CWI* (Socialist Books, 2005) and Stott, P. 'Socialist success in Scotland' *International Socialist Voice* 18 May 2003.
16. *Daily Record* 17 January 2001, see also Chapter 6.
17. Judged by ornaments like busts and pictures in his home, Tommy's heroes moved from Trotsky and Lenin to Maclean and Guevara.
18. Consequently, other political heroes were Fidel Castro, Che Guevara and Hugo Chavez. Tommy characterised Guevara an incorruptible fighter against oppression. Evo Morales in Bolivia also became a hero of Tommy's.
19. See *Scottish Socialist Voice* 15 March 2002 and 17, 31 October 2003 respectively.

20. *Mirror* 22 December 2004.
21. *Daily Record* 28 June 2000.
22. 'Tommy Sheridan brings in new year with a toast to Cuba', Solidarity website 30 December 2006. The deficiency in punctuation is from the original text.
23. In his Foreword to my *The Political Economy of Scotland: Red Scotland? Radical Scotland?*, Tommy made it clear the extent to which he saw Scotland as being distinctive and different from the rest of other parts of Britain by being a nation. He took exception to the comparison of statistical data on Scotland with that for regions of England that were comparable in population size because he saw this downgrading Scotland to being 'another 'region' of Britain'. Despite this, he gave it a puff in his *Mirror* (6 October 2005) page.
24. *Mirror* 25 August 2005.
25. *Mirror* 11 August 2005.
26. *Mirror* 21 July 2005.
27. *Mirror* 21 July 2005
28. Gall, G. 'In search of a Scottish outside left' in Perryman, M. (ed.) *Breaking up Britain: four nations after a union* (Lawrence and Wishart, 2009), pp. 164–165. See also Gall, G. 'Debating Radical Scotland' *Frontline* 2/1:28–32, 2006.
29. This would seem to have parallels with the importance of language for the UCS struggle – see Foster, J. and Woolfson, C. 'How workers on the Clyde gained the capacity for class struggle: the Upper Clyde Shipbuilders work-in, 1971–72' in McIlroy, J., Campbell, A. and Fishman, N. (eds.) *British Trade Unions and Industrial Politics, Volume 2: The High Tide Unionism, 1964–1979* (Merlin Press, 2007 (second edition)).
30. For a critique of this argument, see Gall, G. 'In search of a Scottish outside left' in Perryman, M. (ed.) *Breaking up Britain: four nations after a union* (Lawrence and Wishart, 2009).
31. 26 April 2007.
32. Sheridan, T. 'New edition foreword' in Milton, N. *John Maclean* (Clydeside Press, 2002), p. i and p. iv.
33. See 'John MacLean – Scotland's Socialist Champion' *International Socialist*, 1998, 1, winter, the 'New edition foreword' in Milton, N. *John Maclean* (Clydeside Press, 2002), *Morning Star* 30 November 2006 and *Scottish Socialist Voice* 6 June 1997, 4 December 1998.
34. *Herald* 5 June 1997.
35. *Daily Record* 11 December 1998.
36. This was not the only source of this toughness. Another was the male culture of Glasgow and the west of Scotland – see Hassan, G. 'The End of the Revolutionary Line: the demise of Tommy Sheridan' *Open Democracy*, 24 December 2010.
37. It can be doubted that the force of the attribute given by Tommy to Peter Taaffe – '[You need] a sense of perspective, a sense of proportion and most importantly a sense of humour to be a socialist' has remained with Tommy.
38. See Tourish, D. 'Ideological intransigence, democratic centralism and cultism: a case study' *What Next?* 27, 2003. This paper was a version of one published in the *Cultic Studies Journal* (1998, 15/1) and served as the basis of a chapter in Tourish, D. and Wohlforth, T. *On the Edge – political cults right and left* (ME Sharpe, 2000). The paper and chapter were based on a case study of the CWI. Tourish was a member of the CWI in Ireland from 1974 to 1985, being a CWI full-timer for six of those years. The book was reviewed in Pitt, B. 'Cults, sects and the far left' *What Next?* (17, 2000).

39. See, for example, 'SSP is split by Sheridan' Socialist Resistance statement, 27 August 2006.
40. See *ATTR* pp. 248–252, *Sunday Times* 6 May 1994, *Herald* 3 March 1995.
41. For example, Sheridan, T. 'Anatomy of a movement' *Scottish Left Review*, November/December 2003, pp. 6–7.
42. For example, Sheridan, T. 'John MacLean – Scotland's Socialist Champion' *International Socialist*, 1998, 1, winter.
43. Indeed, like others of these leading members, Tommy did not see a need for the ISM or for platforms in the SSP.
44. *Sunday Herald* 23 February 2003.

10

The Final Chapter?

Introduction

Ten years before Tommy was born, Marlon Brando as Terry Malloy in the 1954 film, *On the Waterfront* about the longshoremen's union, proclaimed: 'I could have been a contender. I could have been somebody'. He was referring to his ill-fated decision to throw a boxing fight in order help an associate win a bet. Tommy *was* a contender and *was* somebody in the fight for socialism and social justice. But he threw this away on his own ill-judged bet.[1] In 2004, he used Mark Twain's famous phrase to say: 'Rumours of my [political] death are greatly exaggerated'.[2] But by his own hand, he had come very close to this by 2011. That makes his story all the more galling. He helped create and lead the biggest, most popular and credible socialist force in Scotland for a generation. And this was achieved at a time before neo-liberal capitalism went into economic and political crisis. Thus, the 'what if' questions asked at the outset still ring loudly. So, what if Tommy had still been the leader of a healthy and vibrant SSP which had parliamentary representation when this crisis hit and then turned into the age of austerity with its swingeing cuts in public services?[3] Could this have been another situation in which he would not only have said 'this will be bigger than the revolt against the poll tax?' but been proven right? And, how much further along the road to resistance, reform and revolution would the situation in Scotland then have been? Given that Scottish socialism was at the core of Tommy's thinking, these questions were all the more sharply posed by the election of the SNP to office as a majority government in 2011 and its plan to hold a referendum on independence towards the end of that parliament (i.e., in 2015). In other words, the Tommy of 2011 was much less able to influence the referendum result and the kind of Scottish independence that may emerge from it than the Tommy of 1999 or 2003 would have been.

This biography has sought to provide a full account of Tommy's ideas, activity and impact as well as his life. In this task, new material has been brought to bear and much existing material has been brought together to shed new light on Tommy. In painting a portrait, the purpose has also been to assess, explain and analyse. The biography has not been mesmerised by events since 2004 but neither has it ignored or downplayed them. In doing so, it has been necessary to study and scrutinise Tommy as a public figure, the media representation of him, the public persona he cultivated as well as to unearth and illuminate the Tommy the general public does not see and does not have access to or knowledge of. This has meant delving into the Tommy that is active behind the scenes, behind the cameras, radio programmes, newspaper coverage and public meetings. It has been to examine how and why such a public figure has emerged as well as how and why that public figure worked and operated. It has also been to make and understand the connection between the public figure and the private figure. Here, private does not necessarily or only mean 'private life' but the behind the scenes processes and events that have led to public – and publicly-observed – outcomes. In this sense, the purpose has been to get underneath the skin of the public figure and to understand what makes that figure tick. It has been not about revealing the unknown Tommy in the manner of a 'crash and burn' or 'kiss and tell' expose. Unlike newspaper comment and reportage which necessarily reacts to the previous day's or week's events, this study has been able to stand back from the immediacy of these to assess their longer-term significance in order to see the wood from the trees.

The broad approach taken has been to bring nuance and sensitivity to the subject matter which has traditionally been dealt with in journalistic simplitudes or tribal political loyalties. By this, I mean recognising that Tommy was *both* talented and flawed and understanding the importance of *both* the person and the period in history. So 'great men' are not seen as the prime movers in history yet nor are they reduced to mere automatons of impersonal macro-social forces. Likewise, for certain individuals to play important roles in history, the context in which they operate in needs full cognisance. All others things being equal, a socialist with a brilliant theoretical mind or great powers of oratory is likely to made a bigger, positive impact if that figure is active or applies him or herself in a period of rising and successful social struggles. By contrast, the same socialist is unlikely to make as big a positive impact in the absence of significant levels of social struggle in which to engage and anchor. Nor is such a socialist likely to make as big a positive impact if significant social struggles are defeated. The same types of point can be made about a socialist being the head of a growing social movement or political force. Cognisance of this is what is meant by the subtitle of 'a political biography' but where the political is also accompanied by the study of sociological and psychological aspects. This has been very much required in Tommy's case for the media's perspective has given the impression to the untrained eye that, as the SSP's public face, Tommy 'did it all'.

In studying Tommy, it became apparent that not only are there different views and perceptions of him, particularly after the events of late 2004 onwards, but that people have had different experiences of him and in different contexts. However, it would be to slip into a postmodernist form of relativism to say that there can be no definite characterisation of him or that one perception or view is as valid as any other. Yet, it is important, nonetheless, to understand that these different views and experiences exist, that some are more or less partial, and that they reflect certain types of close or distant interaction with Tommy for different purposes and for different periods of time and in different contexts. And, into this not uncomplex picture must also be inserted the personae that Tommy has actively created, cultivated and promoted.

Finally, this biography represents a combination of academic rigour, involving robust analysis based upon substantiation and triangulation using varied fieldwork and sources as well as participant observation. Participant observation when conducted responsibly and sensitively allows insights that would not be available to the non-sensitised, non-participant observer. Tommy has been revealed not to be an extremely complex character but neither has he been revealed as one-dimensional either. This will not satisfy everybody. Some would want any biography of Tommy to necessarily conclude he is a monster (to the socialist cause) while others would want it to necessarily conclude he is a martyr (for the socialist cause). Such views of him speak to the reality that he remains a public figure – rather than some historical figure from the distant past – and one whose contribution and standing are now so highly contested and divisive. He is a figure who has not only polarised opinion between the right and the left but now has polarised opinion within the left as well.[4] There is a strong sense on the left that 'you' *have* to be either 'for' or 'against' Tommy. But this biography has pursued a middle way – not because splitting the difference is somehow fair and easy to do but because seldom are things in life quite so black and white. The middle, if not third, way has sought to identify and explain Tommy's strengths and his weaknesses as well as understand the relationship between the two. Sometimes strengths can also be weaknesses depending on the situation, and this has been plainly evident in Tommy's case. None of this means that Tommy should be erased and forgotten from the 'history books'. But it does mean that his pre-2004 achievement should be recognised at the same time as not letting post-2004 events solely determine his historical significance.

Hero to Zero?

The biography's subtitle posed the question. With breaking though into the public consciousness in 1992 as a result of being jailed over opposition to a poll tax warrant sale to being jailed for perjury in 2011, it is now time to present an answer. The fundamental options are: still hero, now zero, hero *and* zero. It would be easy, as the mainstream press, has done to simply plump for the 'zero' option, where the irony of Tommy being a 'conviction politician' is evident – the conviction to go jail because of his principles in 1992 to being convicted in 2010 because of his lies in court in 2006. Rather, this biography's argument has been that Tommy was a 'hero' to use the term as shorthand for all that he achieved as a socialist in the fight for socialism and social justice. But he is now simultaneously and dialectically *also* both 'hero' and 'zero'. From different sides of the split in the SSP, Richie Venton and Steve Arnott both believed that Tommy was a figure, in the latter's words, in which 'people could place their hopes and aspirations'. But, to take from Christopher Harvie's title of his history of twentieth century Scotland, Tommy's demise all the more means we live in an era of 'no gods and precious few heroes'.[5] Clearly, just being and remaining a 'hero' does not fit into the assessment presented in this biography. Similarly, the analysis put forward here contrasts with the view amongst many centre left commentators and socialists that Tommy has become (only) a 'zero' for he had, this argument runs, undone any good that he had previously done for the socialist cause. The SSP put it this way: 'History will now record that he did more harm to the socialist cause in Scotland than any good he ever did it'.[6] Alan McCombes went further and believed that Tommy had done more damage to the left in Scotland than Thatcher and Murdoch combined.[7] These assessments seem unconvincing, neither because an overall assessment cannot be made nor because one cannot use the present vista to do so. Rather, it is because to remember the 'harm' is necessarily to remember the 'good' because one cannot stand without the other. They are dialectically and inextricably linked and will forever remain so. And, given the stark cusp that the 9 November 2004 represents, differentiation of 'before' and 'after' by people and 'history' is more than possible, aided and abetted by iconic images and memories of Tommy as poll tax rebel and socialist parliamentarian. Moreover, the unfolding of events will always beg the question of whether 'good' could not have continued but for certain actions. There is also the danger of what can be termed 'retrospective analysis' – either to wipe out the 'the good' completely because of what happened afterwards or to take 'disagreeable' features of the post-2004 Tommy and read them back into the pre-2004 Tommy so as to reverse the analysis that did hold of Tommy until 2004. In this context, the simultaneous sense of both 'hero to zero' and 'hero and zero' can now be set out.

Tommy has taken the forces of socialism (outside Labour) in Scotland back to the pre-1996 or 1998 position in terms of their unity, numbers and social weight. And at the launch of the Jimmy Reid Foundation by the *Scottish Left Review* magazine in August 2011, a number of the foundation's patrons made the point that the left in Scotland had spent more time fighting itself than the right, with Tommygate being the prime example.[8] But none of this can be said without recognising that he could not have created this regression had he not helped get these forces there in the first place. In other words, he (and they) had so far to fall because they had risen so much already. He was the figure around which all three – SML, SSA and SSP – organisations united to project themselves and grow. The SSP was not robbed of its message but rather its messenger to carry this message where the messenger helped make the message credible.[9] This analysis is not incompatible with the point Alan McCombes made regarding the outcome of the 2006 defamation – 'It could set back the cause of socialism by years if not decades'[10] (even if that equated socialism *per se* with the SSP). One of the major components of this was that as a socialist, Tommy lost – or gave up – his credibility to 'speak truth to power' as well as his mantle of honesty, sincerity and integrity. To recall, in the *Sunday Herald's* 'Greatest Scot' poll, 'the words 'honesty', 'integrity' and 'passion' ... were repeatedly attached to him [by voters]'[11] and *Scotland on Sunday* commented 'few question his sincerity'.[12] Indeed, Tommy extolled honesty and principles in politics (including his own) in his *Daily Record* column,[13] was critical of liars and cheats like ex-MP Neil Hamilton[14] and said: 'I would hope people, whether they agree with me or not, would say at least I was honest'.[15] Instead, he joined the ranks of former disgraced Tory MPs and perjurers, Jonathon Aitken and Jeffrey Archer.[16] No longer could he credibly tell the joke (as he often used to): 'How do you know when a politician is lying? Because their lips are moving!' because he became one of those politicians that told lies. He critically gave up the most precious of commodities, namely, credibility, trust, respect and integrity with a large swathe of citizens in Scotland and, simultaneously, became pretty much like all other politicians. His antithesis to their thesis became his synthesis with them. And, questions began to be asked apropos of this: if he lied over his sex life, what else might he have lied over? For all this to be true on the basis of the way he chose to deal with allegations about his personal life is not just plain disappointing but also ridiculous. This raises the question of whether Tommy was not just 'one of the last in the line of the Red Clydeside tradition of articulate, passionate working class radicals'[17] but the last one.

Found guilty of perjury despite his elaborate fabrication, he became a fake and a fraud to many as a person and politician. Content analysis of posts left on the comments pages of *Daily Record* stories on Tommy on its website after his conviction and sentencing confirms this.[18] Long-time acquaintance, Mandy Rhodes for example, wrote: '[T]he squalid reality is that he was not sent to prison for attempting to throw a spanner in the inner gubbings of the evil capitalist machine, [rather] he was convicted for lying about his grubby little ways'.[19] For many like her, he became a 'zero'. No longer was he the 'real deal' because he did not 'walk it like he talked it'. No longer was he a rebel with cause and without pause. And while not everyone shares this view, it is evident, nonetheless, that it is a numerically significant view which now undermines what Tommy once was. After losing his seat in the Scottish Parliament, he did not come last or attract zero votes but he did plumb hitherto unknown depths by being beaten by the BNP in the Glasgow north east by-election. But to compound his tragedy, Tommy also politically lived by the sword of truth and politically died by it too. Not only was he convicted of being a liar but he was also, thus, exposed as a hypocrite too. Yet, despite all this, a great part of this biography has been given over to Tommy's achievements and the historical record must not be erased. In summary, from the period of the retreat of 'actually existing socialism' and huge defeats for organised labour in the 1980s to the rise of the global justice movement, Tommy played a major role in not only raising the banner of socialism but also took the idea of socialism to wider numbers and to a higher level. For that reason, Tommy will be remembered as 'hero' as well.

How the Mighty are Fallen

Some have wondered whether Tommy's fall from grace was because somewhere along the way from street corner to the Scottish Parliament, he was changed by what he did and what he had publicly become. The subtext was often that he was somehow corrupted not by money but by the flattery of media attention and/or by moving in the circles of celebrities (and no longer those of grassroots activists, the impoverished of the schemes and ordinary wage workers).[20] In a nutshell: ego, delusion, arrogance, and losing his roots. Thus, Rosie Kane twittered on 26 January 2011: 'Sheridan you put celebrity before integrity. No plot no conspiracy. You lied. You got caught, your fault. You hurt and destroyed good people for an out of control ego. You destroyed everything for your ego. We did all we could but you would not listen or stop lying. If you had listened to your friends in 2004 you would not be facing prison'. It would be naive to think Tommy had not changed, not least because he was older and because people are influenced by their surroundings. However, as this biography has argued, this was not the cause of his downfall. His faulty political calculation about his political goals led to political mistakes, and his self-righteous sense of being wronged came from his belief he had been betrayed. If he was so concerned with ego, it is much less easy to understand why he would have set out on a course of action that could – and did – ultimately lead to jail and worse. If Tommy could be accused of making his destiny synonymous with that of socialism in Scotland, that may be immodest to say the least but it would not have been totally without foundation.

Phone-Hacking and Missing Emails

When Tommy's mobile phone details were found, alongside those of many others, in the possession of a private investigator hired by *NoW*, it became clear he could have been the subject of phone-hacking. However, whether he did have his phone-hacked was not *prima facie* evidence of a plot by *NoW* to target him as a leading socialist fighter as he and his supporters alleged. The vast majority of those whose phones were hacked by the paper were celebrities of one sort or another. Of the small handful of politicians targeted, John Prescott, Chris Bryant and Tessa Jowell could hardly be said to be leftwing and subversive, belying Tommy's notion that what *NoW* was doing was part of a political vendetta against socialists and socialism. If that was the case or intention, the likes of John McDonnell and Jeremy Corbyn would have been put in a similar situation. Rather, Tommy's inclusion along with George Galloway was likely to have been because both were public names as well as celebrities of sorts for whom the *NoW* thought that carrying stories about their personal lives would sell (more) papers. But more importantly, there is no evidence that *NoW* – if it did then hack Tommy's phone – used any material it may have gained to construct its stories of late 2004, defend itself from Tommy's defamation action or proffer evidence for Tommy's perjury trial.[21] Indeed, James Doleman – of *TST* blog – argued 'the phone-hacking allegations are slightly peripheral'.[22] Fundamentally, the phone-hacking did not relate to whether Tommy had or had not been at Cupids in 1996 and 2002, whether he had or had not admitted this and whether he had or had not denied having a sexual relationship with Katrine Trolle. In other words, the alleged phone-hacking had no material bearing on the critical issues at hand. So, Tommy's case in regard of phone-hacking allegations was not just a smokescreen to divert attention away from what he did do but it was also to press the buttons of the jurors (and wider public during and after the trial) who did not like *NoW* in order to generate sympathy and support for him. The question of the missing emails provided only slightly stronger grounds for Tommy. The reported lost *NoW* emails – during transfer storage to India – were then found in a warehouse in London in early 2011.[23] However, they related to the years 2005 and 2006 with the same insignificance to many years earlier regarding Tommy visiting Cupids, denying visiting Cupids and so on – even if they may show *NoW* to have acted in a reprehensible, dubious or unethical manner.[24] If the subsequently found emails were to have been any use to Tommy in his 2010 trial, this is likely to be because they showed reprehensible, dubious or unethical practice which Tommy could have used in a tangential way to politically – rather than legally – sway the jury but with a not intangible outcome. It was for such reasons that Paul McBride QC – who had intimate knowledge of Tommy's case from defending Gail Sheridan – believed that the phone hacking scandal and related matters had no material bearing on outcome of Tommy's trial.[25] In this he was supported by other legal experts.[26]

Only Labour MP Tom Watson went so far as to suggest the missing emails meant Tommy's trial and conviction were unfounded, unsafe and unsound[27] although he was joined in doing so by fellow Labour MP, Jim Sheridan, albeit in less certain terms.[28] Interestingly, Tommy's lawyer, Aamer Anwar, was relatively more circumspect on the issue, suggesting the missing emails '*could* [emphasis added] form part of a key part of an appeal',[29] that the jury had been misled intentionally or otherwise by absence of sight of the emails[30] and then later claiming he was 'sick to the back teeth' at a public meeting of those who claimed that the *NoW* phone-hacking scandal had no bearing on Tommy's conviction.[31] Indeed, Solidarity did not explicitly suggest the phone-hacking or allegedly lost emails made Tommy's conviction unsafe or unsound.[32] However, the Defend the Tommy Sheridan Campaign often claimed or suggested that perjured evidence from *NoW* and its personnel facilitated the jury delivering a guilty verdict which was, thus, unsafe and unsound.[33] Yet, James Doleman pointedly did not suggest either the phone-hacking or missing emails cast much conclusive doubt on the reliability of Tommy's conviction.[34] Only the CWI/Socialist Party of Scotland was unambiguous in its view that the perjury conviction was clearly the result of perjury and the like by *NoW*,[35] with the *DGS* network within Solidarity declaring the existence of 'key e-mails', *inter alia*, demanded 'in the interests both of common sense and natural justice that Tommy Sheridan should be freed'.[36] Nonetheless, the *Herald* reported that Aamer Anwar was expected to launch a new appeal based on the emails.[37]

Rather than suggesting that Tommy's supporters and sympathisers were suffering from 'mass delusion' (again), it appears his supporters and sympathisers were adept at directly and indirectly using the downfall of *NoW* as a result of the phone-hacking scandal to cast as much doubt as possible on Tommy's conviction albeit through tangential means.[38] Thus, much was made of the Crown Office's decision to ask Strathclyde police to make a 'preliminary assessment' of the implications of and issues surrounding the *NoW* phone-hacking allegations for the Procurator Fiscal[39], and then the decision to mount a full investigation ('Operation Rubicon') of possible perjury at Tommy's 2010 trial, particularly concerning the testimony of Andy Coulson, former Scottish *NoW* editor, Bob Bird and former Scottish *NoW* news editor, Douglas Wight, as well as phone-hacking and unlawful accessing of other data.[40] And, Lynn Sheridan subsequently took the opportunity to restate the victimisation case: 'We [the Sheridan family] have said all along that the *News of the World* were out to get Tommy and that they used all means available to them, including phone-hacking. It now appears they were also prepared to lie in court to achieve their aims'.[41] Such emotive statements allowed attention to be diverted away from, for example, Andy Coulson, being a *defence* witness who may have told lies in court but his testimony did not relate to the veracity of the Cupids visits and sexual relations with Katrine Trolle.[42] Indeed, Tommy called Coulson (and tried to call Glen Mulcaire) not because they would help his case, but by putting Andy Coulson in the witness box he was able to hold him to 'account'.[43] Moreover, the focus of Tommy's supporters upon Coulson as the former *NoW* editor and media chief for David Cameron (rather than Bird or Wight who edited and wrote the stories of 2004) demonstrated they were mounting a political campaign within the arena of public perception to overturn Tommy's conviction. It, thus, appears the evidence from a number of key prosecution witnesses like Katrine Trolle and Gary Clark and the George McNeilage video tape held sway with the jury and not any tangential testimony from Coulson. Therefore, if Coulson or any other *NoW* employee or associate were to be convicted of perjury or even conspiracy to commit perjury as a result of their testimony in the 2010 trial, this would again not change the facts of Cupids and Katrine Trolle and, thus, overturn Tommy's conviction. Indeed, the logic of the use of the *NoW* phone-hacking scandal was that the next best thing to trying to overturn the conviction in a court of law was to try to overturn it in the court of public opinion. Winning in the court of public opinion over the allegations about his sexual behaviour had always been a major consideration for Tommy, for after his 2006 court case he commented: 'whatever the verdict, I had won in the minds of the public'.[44] If this victory was to be achieved after conviction in 2010, Tommy would be in a relatively better position to try to politically pick up from where he left off notwithstanding the many difficulties of doing so (see below). But if anyone could have opined to have 'brought down' Rupert Murdoch, the likes of actress, Sienna Miller, Mark Lewis, the solicitor of the family of Milly Dowler, *Guardian* journalist, Nick Davies, and Labour MP, Tom Watson, would have reasonable claims. Thus, Tommy had no role to play here.[45]

Mistakes of Tommygate

'Tommygate' was the fabrication of a conspiracy and one which ultimately failed, and failed badly for its progenitor landed up in jail. Tommy played and lost. In doing this, he made a number of fatal mistakes which in terms of his own logic were the equivalent of a 'Watergate' where, no matter that the inconvenient truth could always at some time in the future rear its head, the crime – as with Nixon – was being found out. Tommy committed some cardinal sins here by his 'tower of lies' being ill-constructed. For example, believing that Karine Trolle[46] was 'solid' and a 'diamond' showed how little Tommy really knew of her. Some of his mistakes compounded others, some consequentially followed on from others. First, there were a serious of admissions to Keith Baldassara, Alan McCombes, George McNeilage and then to others like Nicky McKerrell and Liam Kane as well as that of the 9 November 2004 SSP EC meeting. Second, there was the strength of his reputation of integrity and honesty which ironically then became his Achilles' heel. Third, there was the coming true of what George Galloway warned of, namely, even if there was no truth to the Fiona McGuire allegations, all manner of other evidence would be brought into the case. Fourth, if there was no truth to any of the allegations, then standing down as national convener only gave the media the real reason to search for – and this was not becoming a father. Then there was visiting Cupids with a *NoW* journalist, and stepping down as SSP leader for family reasons, which Tommy admitted on the McNeilage tape: 'I've done it too well … it was farfetched'. This was followed by his initial strategy being based upon *NoW* settling before going to court by either printing a retraction, thus, stymieing the action or by paying damages. But it did come to court necessitating the committing of perjury in 2006 and which would then result in the 2010 trial and conviction. Within this Tommy was inconsistent, denying the 9 November 2004 minute existed and then calling it dodgy (as a 'United Left factional account'[47]), or calling the McNeilage tape concocted with splices of his voice and then saying he was played by an actor. Another mistake was refusing a plea bargain offered before the trial of a two-year sentence with the charges being dropped against Gail. This would have staved off the prospect of a longer sentence – especially when he pleaded not guilty – and kept a lid on the media's opportunity to report for the umpteenth time on his sex life. If taken early enough like in September 2009 when he dispensed with the services of Donald Finlay QC for urging him to take the plea bargain, it could have resulted in a sentence that was low enough to then be commuted to such a point that he could have stood in the May 2011 Scottish Parliament elections.

To compound these, there were a series of other mistakes. These included the inconsistency of contesting the 9 November 2004 minute in 2006 when it had not been contested before and denying it existed even though Tommy had asked for it not to be distributed and to remain confidential at the 27 November 2004 NC as well as asking for it to be destroyed, and the relying upon a fake minute (which was also in the wrong style and format and had some attendees missing) and sending the motion to destroy the minute from his parliamentary email account. Along the way, and because of the strategy he pursued, Tommy made enemies of those like Colin Fox, Richie Venton and Steven Nimmo who were initially sympathetic to the plight he found himself in. In the end, the fake minute was of no obvious help as Lord Turnbull ruled it inadmissible while the actual minute was admitted as court evidence. There was also signing in at Cupids as himself.[48] These more minor mistakes were so many as to provide a firmer foundation for the major ones, indicating that while Tommy was conscious and strategic in his actions, even his abilities were over-stretched by the course of action he engaged in because he set off a course of events that he lost control over. No longer was politics, to quote Bismarck again, 'the art of the possible'. Politically, too many people knew the truthful veracity of the Cupids 'allegations' so that it became harder to advance his fight. Others would have no doubt concluded there is no smoke without fire and that further stories may have emerged over time in a backlash against him. So even if he had won twice, his reputation would still have been seriously besmirched. The mistake of 'Tommygate,' committed by his supporters, was not to recognise that the point at which they were asked to engage in his fabrication was a Rubicon – not so much about lying but about a step-change in what Tommy was as a politician and in his moral economy. Consequently, his supporters thought they were defending the Tommy of old, not the Tommy of new.

The Mother and Family of all Errors of Judgement

Tommy brought himself down not over *NoW's* allegations about his personal life but over the way he chose to deal with these. He was, thus, convicted of perjury about telling lies in court about visiting Cupids and having a sexual relationship with Katrine Trolle, and not about visiting Cupids itself or having a sexual relationship with Katrine Trolle, which he was both free to do so even if they were – especially the former – extremely foolhardy. Previous chapters outlined that Tommy was unwilling to admit or recognise that he made mistakes. On the McNeilage tape, he uncharacteristically admitted that confessing to 20 people at the 9 November 2004 SSP EC about his 1996 and 2002 Cupids visits was 'a big mistake. A fucking huge mistake. Humungous fucking mistake ... the biggest mistake of my life'. It was a mistake precisely because it was so risky as to expect that he could win the majority of the SSP EC to his chosen strategy of denial and defiance. The consequence was that he, thereby, let 'the cat out of the bag'.[49] Here, it was not so much that Tommy had made a plethora of serious political mistakes over his lifetime but more that he was unwilling to show any personal or political fallibility. His internal self-belief system and outward persona was of omnipotence and omniscience so he very seldom admitted to mistakes and errors of judgement.[50] But greater than any of these errors of judgement was that Tommy failed to comprehend, despite his political adroitness, that as an influential radical socialist with a counter-hegemonic ideology and counter-establishment strategy, he had to keep his nose clean in his fight for socialism. This may not have been fair or right but it was an attested reality of the class war because he could help bring himself down by doing otherwise. Then trying to right what he saw as the wrong against himself, namely betrayal by others, merely compounded this error. Perjuring himself in court in 2006 was such an example, as lies to cover up a lie were others. But even when he told *STV News*: 'Show me someone who has no regrets and I'll show you someone who has never lived. Of course, there are regrets', he then went on to say his 'biggest regret [was] I have ... be[en] naive. I was naive in the way I trusted some people, I was naive in the way I thought the loyalty I showed to others would be reciprocated, I was naive to believe certain people'.[51] So he gave himself some succour that it was far from his fault. He then went on to add 'Was I naive to take on the *News of the World*? I don't think so'. This indicated he was not genuinely prepared to admit to mistakes or see the wood for the trees.

In all of this, Tommy's style of leadership and political *modus operandi* maintained much of its transformational content (see Chapter 2). Yet, increasingly, he came also to deploy a more transactional style of leadership as well. So, on the one hand, Tommy laboured the political and ideological dimensions of his fabrication in order to create his political and legal strategy and its attendant supporters. However, on the other hand, he began to trade on, and recall the investment of, the aspects of his past profile, his public role as a socialist leader and so on in a more transactional manner, where a strong link was made between his political survival and the survival of the SSP and radical socialism in Scotland. His combined evident charisma and personal forcefulness was a common feature, if not also bridge, between the two styles. The weakness of his post-2004 political (rather than legal) fight was that the balance between the two styles tipped too heavily towards the transactional, with it being a less strong source of political authority and legitimacy. Engulfed in a battle to save himself, it became increasingly tenuous to argue that he was the salvation of socialism in Scotland because he relegated the very activities that had earlier supported this claim as he spent more and more of his time and energies fighting not for socialism but for his own personal and political survival. Consequently, without renewing and replenishing the foundations of his political authority as a result of his previous concentration on a transformational style of leadership and its use in campaigns and mobilisations, Tommy necessarily had to rely on the more transactional style of leadership and *modus operandi*. This was a less inspiring and altogether less inspirational tool. The irony was that particularly after 2007, when Tommy lost his seat in the Scottish parliament, he then had less of a firm and sound basis upon which to even operate in a transactional manner.

Trapped by His Own Fabrication

Some, like John Aberdein[52], Colin Fox[53] and Alan McCombes,[54] variously believed that if Tommy had made an apology and shown some humility or magnanimity after the 2006 court case, this would have made some amends. But Tommy was incapable of doing so and for some very good reasons. First, there was the no small matter of Tommy's belief that he had been betrayed in the most heinous manner by his closest of collaborators, Alan and Keith, and then a cast of others. With this river having been crossed, the logic of Tommy's personality and plight was that they had to be cast out of the family without compassion or compulsion. Second, and more importantly, politically and legally, Tommy could not apologise because to do so would be to admit he had perjured himself in court and lied consistently since 9 November 2004 in order to construct his conspiracy. It was not so much that Tommy was in 'too deep' to recall his phrase, more that he was locked in so there was no way back for retracing his steps once he had carried out such acts. The same cruel logic applied to any *mea culpa* after the 2010 trial (see below).

Lessons for The Left

There is no doubt that the radical and socialist left in Scotland is that much poorer for the breakup of the relationship between Tommy and Alan McCombes. But for all that it delivered, it also says a lot about the state of the left in Scotland that this statement can be true. In other words, that their relationship was so important and that when it broke up there has been nothing comparable to replace it. This outcome resulted from the over conflation of Tommy with the SSP[55] and the SSP with socialism. And to judge Tommy is also at the same time to necessarily judge Alan McCombes – even if their respective circles in the Venn diagram of their political relationship never completely overlapped prior to November 2004.[56] For example, Ronnie Stevenson detected impatience, a cavalier attitude and lack of accountability in both. The SSP, knowingly or not, played with fire for it rode the rollercoaster in good times – and bad. It bore a heavy responsibility in creating 'Tommy', and in so doing retarded the development of other publicly recognised leaders.[57] This was one of the reasons why it was not only so hard hit by what happened but also was unable to recover – in other words, it had no other leaders of a similar standing. But the reliance of the SSP on Tommy was also the stuff of a 'rock' and a 'hard place' given the asymmetry of political power in capitalist society.[58] Yet, there is more to the situation than this. It was not as if the SSP as a political party was oblivious to what was happening for there were occasions when criticism of the particular method of Tommy's promotion as the very human embodiment of the party was brooked but it was to no effect. This was because others saw it as sufficiently unproblematic at the time or *per se* and because Tommy was not amenable to change. He had the power to continue his will here as he was in a position of power relative to other party members and because he maintained personal contact and relations with journalists (rather than through a press officer acting as a gatekeeper and conduit). Thus, the sense of forewarned is forearmed did not come into play.[59] Underneath all this, some of the SSP's weaknesses were cruelly exposed, primary amongst these being poor and stunted cadre and activist development. The flipside of this was a party very much dominated by the troika and associated wider leadership. The effect was to exacerbate the aforementioned problems.

One of the main media focuses since November 2004 has been upon internal SSP workings, with the accusation of jealously of who Tommy was, what he achieved and what he could do. This was a very easy and superficial accusation to make – as the media did – at his SSP critics who had not scaled the same political heights that Tommy had and neither not made the very public contribution to socialism that Tommy had. However, the complexity here is seldom recognised. As Tommy was so heavily lauded by political friends and foes prior to late 2004 and promoted by the SSP, this had created such a doubly lopsided situation. On the one hand, Tommy's vast contribution was overestimated by the media because they seldom peered beneath the surface to see the milieu of party activists. A good example of this was the *Scotsman's* assessment: '[Tommy] managed what many thought impossible: he united disparate and disputatious factions of the far left, forging them into a winning force which threatened to destabilise the old Scottish political order'.[60] On the other hand, it appears that when any criticism of Tommy was mooted, this looked like disloyalty and irrationality to the socialist cause and to a socialist icon. To point out that a leading socialist had flaws and weaknesses was by no means new and should not necessarily have been seen as news. People in politics should be viewed as multifaceted and sometimes complex characters which are not entirely reducible to their professed or public positions on various issues. But when that leading socialist helps fuel such media accusations of jealousy, when the media use such criticisms to undermine other leading socialists and when activists get locked into protecting their leading figure, the political analysis on which any criticism is based is lost or ignored. Sure, activists should be wary of making reckless sorties which can be used by others to undermine one of their own but this should not preclude evaluation, accountability and criticism of a leader, no matter how good or how high profile.

The radical and socialist left has most often been built around individual high-profile leaders (like Scargill and the SLP, George Galloway and Respect, Tony Benn/Ken Livingstone/John McDonnell and the Labour left, Joe Higgins and the Socialist Party of Ireland, Derek Hatton and Militant).[61] Quite apart from the inherent fragility of operating in this way, in that any one leader could be run over by the proverbial bus, it thus behoves such leaders of these projects to act in a way that understands that their 'personal' is 'political' in a very public way.[62] This is because personal acts that could become political hostages to fortune need to be avoided because of not only the disproportionate impact they can have only these small, fragile projects but because hegemonic forces of the *status quo* will gladly see them used to impair those projects. The additional responsibility is to recognise precisely that if such projects can be built to a considerable extent around the public persona of one individual, then they can also fall by it too. Thus, building radical and socialist left projects heavily through the persona of an individual leader can be a strength as well as a weakness in the context that the promotion of such individuals is often necessary to deal with the challenges of low levels of worker, class and political consciousness as well as the control of communication, culture and education by forces of the *status quo*.[63] Within such projects, it also then needs to be appreciated that not only structures of accountability but also cultures and political ideologies of accountability (and democracy) are needed.[64] Structures comprising such components as rules and regulations are barren without the cultural norms and the political will to ensure their effective application and operation.[65] This task requires recognition of the sources of power and authority within political parties. Sociologist Max Weber identified the sources of political authority as rational-legal (rules and regulation), traditional (inter-generational customs and habits of social deference) and charisma. Tommy's political authority stemmed neither from his position as national convener nor from bureaucracy, tradition or patronage[66] but from charisma, oratorical skills, appropriate ideology and battle worthiness producing what can be termed political authority and stature. Using Stephen Lukes' radical theory of power[67] helps explain Tommy's authority by virtue of his ability to shape desires and beliefs through the mobilisation of bias within and without the SSP. But the task of building socialist forces through or around an individual as the fairly singular public face of their leadership also has to be cognisant that different types of persona and personalities have different political and practical implications. The figures of Olivier Besancenot, Tony Benn, Joe Higgins and John McDonnell indicate that not all must necessarily be of the Tommy Sheridan, Derek Hatton, Arthur Scargill or George Galloway type. It, therefore, behoves socialists to consider the specific ramifications of particular types of leadership personas and personalities for their socialist organisations (in addition to different types of leadership).

Socialist leaders and socialist parties need to be bold and courageous given both the scale of their political aspirations and ambitions and the asymmetry in power and influence in capitalist society. Boldness and courage are needed to inspire and to mobilise as well as to provide confidence. But boldness, in particular, can easily shade into exaggeration, hyperbole and bombast as the case of Tommy easily demonstrates. Such a trait was not his alone in the leadership of Militant, SML/SSA/SSP and Solidarity for it is common and prevalent amongst the far left, and the Trotskyist left especially.[68] It exaggerates both the weakness of opponents and the strength of (one's own) socialist forces. But in

Tommy's hands, the trait reached new heights, and ones that not only were more reported upon than any others but also had more impact than any others. And in doing so, lines were crossed whereby extremely generous self-conducted appraisals and interpretations of situations were stretched so as to become not just untenable and incredible but often constitute untruths as well.[69] Consequently, the balance between ideas, aspirations and objective assessments of situations was very much out of kilter.

Despite hitherto comments from Tommy like 'no matter what differences socialists have among themselves – they're totally inconsequential compared to our differences with the boss class and their mouthpieces in the other political parties'[70] and overtures like those of late 2008,[71] there is no prospect of re-fusing the SSP and Solidarity. Since the split, strategic political differences between constituents of both have widened but that aside, the divisions over Tommy are so deep as to be beyond a truth and reconciliation commission. While the SSP position over Tommy has been largely vindicated, this is not the same as the vindication or exoneration of the SSP itself.[72] Either the SSP or Solidarity will triumph over the other or the two will fight a war of attrition to 'the last socialist standing'. Either way, revival of radical socialist fortunes in Scotland is not conceivable any time soon.[73] Indeed, putting the socialist Humpty Dumpty back together again in 2011 or afterwards would only be to put together two shrivelled and atrophied groups. Contrary to what he argued in 2006 about socialism in Scotland being set back by decades by Tommy, Alan McCombes then believed after the wipe out of May 2007 that 'two or three years down the road, the events of the past year will have begun to fade into the mists of history. With the removal of Tommy Sheridan from Holyrood, the Solidarity bubble will burst. That will be a massive step forward for the left, allowing Scottish socialism to be rebuilt under the clean banner of the Scottish Socialist Party'.[74] The elections results of May 2011 showed how ill-judged this prediction was. Even if Frances Curran's belief was correct – '[Tommy] has made a positive contribution in the sense that the experience of Tommy as a charismatic leader of a left party has been so extreme that it has taught us all a lesson … if this hadn't happened maybe in ten years' time we'd still be buying into that model … the rupture has forced us to look at things much more critically' – this was scant comfort given the May 2011 result for the SSP. It continued to barely simmer, to borrow a phrase from Alan McCombes, as 'smoking ruins'.[75]

But before there is any prospect of 'throwing the baby out with the bathwater', it should be recalled that Tommy's abiding positive (strategic) contribution to socialism was to recognise that the mainstream media was a beast that could not be simply treated as a hostile force and, thus, mistakenly ignored[76]. It was not just the force of Tommy's personality and his skills of oratory and networking (or social capital) that helped take socialism out of its self-imposed ghetto. It was also this – his – key realisation that socialists had to engage with the media in order to temper its natural tendencies for selling socialist newspapers and the like was never capable of matching the resources and reach of the mainstream media in an age of reduced working class and oppositional consciousness. Tommy broke the mould here and developed the personality and traits to be able to do so successfully. Ironically in doing so, he made the SSP look much bigger than it actually was and in, thus, concentrating on essentially the activity of making propaganda, he helped inhibit the development of the capacity to campaign at a grassroots level in communities and workplaces. But there was also another downside to this. The manner in which Tommy solicited favourable media coverage for the socialist cause may seem rather more tarnished now when looking back on the glory years of 1999 to 2004. This is because it is perfectly possible the Machiavellian methods he used in the post-2004 period could have been used in the pre-2004, indicating that the coverage was gained in a less than honest and scrupulous manner, and that he had back then an aptitude and willingness to stretch the truth to breaking point albeit in regard of his political rather than personal interests. For many attracted to the socialist cause, any dubiety about ethics and morals undermines their support for socialism.

The SSP

The (red) star of the SSP burned brightly and loudly for a short number of years. Under Tommy's leadership, the promise of what the SSP could become was at least as important as what it was able to achieve in its short period of ascendancy. Come the 2007 election, the SSP could have hoped to maintain its representation in Glasgow, West of Scotland and Central Scotland, giving its three or four MSPs, but for 'Tommygate'. That is not then to say it could have entirely resisted the SNP momentum nor exactly maintained or increased its representation for the SSP rowed with the tide of the anti-war movement and the support for the firefighters' strikes of 2002–2003. Come 2007, the anti-war movement had subsided – especially after its failure to stop the Iraq invasion – and there were no other comparable industrial disputes like that of the firefighters which were in proximity to the election. Come the 2011 election, the same tendency of maintaining a significant toehold may have been possible notwithstanding the surge to the SNP (again but for 'Tommygate'). Under these conditions, a further realignment of the radical left towards the SSP may have been possible as well as the SSP organising and leading extra-parliamentary resistance to the crisis of neo-liberalism and the cuts in public spending and public services. In particular, the SSP could have played a significant role in stopping the terms of the public debate changing from 'who is responsible for the crisis?' to 'how should the crisis be managed?' for this was the key achievement of the forces of the *status quo* and allowed them to impose the sacrifices of paying for the crisis upon those who were not responsible for the crisis. None of this is to ignore the problems the SSP had or was encountering in terms of activist and cadre building, internal education, balancing the tension of party and parliament, and wider implantation in society as Chapter 5 alluded to. Yet, the SSP demonstrated in its short ascendancy that it was reasonable to suggest that more could have been achieved in the following years but for 'Tommygate'.

Redemption and Return?

What of the probability of Tommy's Lazarus-like return to the political stage? Kevin McKenna proclaimed 'Tommy will return stronger and wiser,'[77] Iain Macwhirter raised the possibility of him returning as an MSP in 2015,[78] Ian Hamilton QC argued: '[d]o not think for a moment that one who has contributed so much to our dream of a fair Scotland is finished. Tommy ... has been silenced by the monopoly capitalists whose greed has brought our means of exchange to destruction. He will speak again soon. Tommy ... is silenced. He will not long be silent',[79] and the *Scotsman* ventured 'an elder statesman's role similar to that of Tony Benn'[80] while, contrastingly, *Newsnight Scotland* asked 'Will anyone be listening?' to his message when he is released from prison.[81] For some, such a return as leading figure or MSP cannot happen at all or in any meaningful way even with apology, atonement and penance for the lies perpetuated and the wreckage wrought.[82] Tommy's only admission was on the McNeilage tape: 'I've made a mistake and I need to pay for that mistake ... I'm going to pay for it'. For many, a point of no return has been passed.[83] For others, whether genuinely believed or not, he has become in their eyes a socialist martyr, with jailing only further enhancing his integrity and standing as a socialist fighter because there was, they believe, a political conspiracy to undermine him and put him in jail.

Tommy's problems of making a comeback are several-fold despite keeping his name in the frame when in jail through his blog and solicited media coverage.[84] He is duty bound to maintain his innocence lest he undoes all his work of November 2004 onwards and opens himself and others (like his court witnesses) to possible further charges of perjury.[85] He will be defiant to the end, no doubt seeing himself forced into a similar situation to that of John Maclean who defended himself in court but was jailed for sedition. But after the perjury trial those in need of an apology were in the ascendancy.[86] But even if the balance between the different schools of thought about Tommy was not of this order, it is difficult to see him redeeming himself in such a way as to be able to rescale the heights he previously had. Although he is still young enough for a comeback, Tommy is now, in most eyes, damaged or soiled goods. Admittance, apology and atonement would not rid him of this. The left he is part of is also, in most eyes, damaged goods. Tommy would have to pull off a remarkable feat to not only regain the trust and credibility he threw away but also then be in a position to use this in the way he did before. Just because he retains some supporters does not alter this. The attempt to use the implosion of *NoW* as a result of phone-hacking to cast doubt on his conviction in the public's mind does not dramatically change this.

But there are some further hard objective factors that probably preclude a comeback. The radical and socialist left in Scotland is now not only split but much smaller than it was once. Opposition to neo-liberalism is now longer so monopolised by radical Scottish identity as it was under its Thatcherite incarnation.[87] The figure of Tommy Sheridan of 2011 is not the figure he had been in 1999 or 2003 because since 2007 he had no longer been an MSP and between 2004 and 2010 he spent more time fighting the left than he did the right. He ceased to be the draw he once was. The last lifeblood in Solidarity was just about crushed by the outcome of the 5 May 2011 Scottish elections so there was no fertile party to come back to once released from jail.[88] So even if he could untaint himself, he would not be able to avail himself of the similar launch pads of before. That would apply to Holyrood in 2015 or to the local council elections in 2012. Indeed, the longer he has been away from frontline politics, the harder it is to come back – to make any sort of comeback. And, to boot, Tommy was not part of leading the resistance to the Conservative-Liberal Democrat coalition government's spending cuts programme. He was not the leader of either the (actual) Scottish Anti-Cuts Alliance or the 'All-Britain Anti-Cuts Campaign' and for both the union organised demonstration of 26 March 2011, the biggest since those in support of the miners in 1984 and 1992, and the 30 June 2011 and 30 November 2011 coordinated public sector strikes, he was in jail.[89] Just as he put himself in the right place at the right time before, he was in the wrong place at the wrong time this time around. The battles he signalled he intended to fight at the point of being jailed were with the justice system over an allegedly prejudiced trial and with *NoW*. Such battles were not likely to broaden

or regain his appeal as a (class) fighter for workers. Into this equation
must be placed the media. The feeling amongst journalists seems to
be that Tommy took them for a ride and they will not let this happen
again. Contrasting the coverage of the outcomes of his 2006 and 2010
trials makes this evident.[90] His appellations have gone from 'socialist
firebrand' to 'former MSP' to now 'disgraced' and 'shamed politician'.[91] Without similar support in the 'press pack', Tommy would
not be able to politically rise again in the same way as he did before.[92]
Being covered in the media for being a jailed celebrity figure does not
alter this equation.

Despite defiant proclamations from himself and Gail after conviction
and sentencing that he would 'come back stronger' and 'keep fighting',
and that because socialism was an eternal cause, there would always
be a need for a Tommy Sheridan, in a moment of candour Tommy
reflected: 'It may be that the public are tired and fed up and are looking
for new champions. That happens, we've all got shelf lives, and it may
be my shelf life has expired. Time will tell on that'.[93] In so doing, he
suggested that maybe he was but a product of his time – and that the
defiance was for show and not much else. Put bluntly, could Tommy
have emerged – or been who he was – without Pollok, Glasgow and
Scotland with their receptiveness to a radical socialist message *and* at
the time of the poll tax or Thatcherism?[94] The fight against the poll tax
as a plank of Thatcherism helped sharpen the appeal of Scottish socialism. Similarly, could Tommy have emerged without being in Militant?
Militant had the distinct advantage over its far left rivals of being inside
Labour at a time before 'new' Labour so that it could swim in a bigger
sea where socialism was not yet a dirty word but where it could also
pitch itself as 'real' Labour.

But being a product of his time was not just of being against the
poll tax, Thatcherism and 'new' Labour. It was also about the fight for
socialism as an idea, rather, than as a mass practical activity. Tommy
frequently talked about the historic need in his lifetime to raise the banner of socialism given the defeat of 'actually existing socialism' after
the fall of the Berlin Wall and the Soviet Union's collapse (and the
triumph of western capitalism epitomised in Francis Fukuyama's 'end
of history' thesis[95]). This perspective of socialism being in retreat –
alongside the defeats of organised workers and notwithstanding the
poll tax revolt and the rise of the global justice movement – meant
for Tommy that the ideological dimension of the struggle was foremost. This fitted well with his skills as an orator, propagandist, and
populariser as well as being the voice for the voiceless. Indeed, given
this was his perspective, he developed these necessary skills accordingly. That did not mean that agitation and action for reforms had

no place but there was an overall framework to work to and within. In 2012 and beyond, there is still a need for ideological warfare but it must remain an open question as to whether, with the survival of neo-liberalism despite its massive crisis, the situation is any more opportune than before, or whether the stage is now set for ideas to be operationalised into action with the age of austerity. Alongside the above, the answer to the redemption and return question must influence any assessment of whether, how and when Tommy could make a comeback given his 'skills set'. But making a comeback could also include becoming a minor celebrity as Derek Hatton did with his local radio show on Merseyside.[96] The ability of Tommy to command the *Daily Record's* front page while in jail[97] suggests this may be the more distinct possibility after his experience at Talk107.

Point of Departure

In a world of grey politics, where all the mainstream parties were dominated by neo-liberalism, Tommy brought the colour red to the table. But by 2011, Tommy's personal frailties had far outstripped his political virtues and talents. In what seemed like a sign of another nail in his political coffin, Scots crime writer, Denise Mina, announced her forthcoming novel was based on Tommy's fateful fabrication.[98] Yet Tommy will always be somebody because he was something. He will always be notorious, for reasons good and bad.[99] But he cannot merely trade on past glories in the future. This is the challenge he faces when he leaves jail. He faces an uphill challenge to re-establish himself as a socialist fighter, leading or otherwise, for he will either be tagged 'disgraced' Tommy Sheridan – which he will compound if he makes his life's work protesting his innocence – or a low grade celebrity. Gaining in 2011 only 13% of the vote it gained in 2007, Solidarity will not be a credible launch pad for a comeback.[100] It was not just the SSP without Tommy that was facing 'virtual oblivion'[101] – to use his own words – but also Tommy and Solidarity. In time, this biography will either need the update of a substantial additional chapter or just a further footnote.

Notes

1. This analogy is all the more pertinent giving Tommy's love of boxing and poker.
2. *Mirror* 17 November 2004.
3. George Kerevan (*Scotsman* 28 January 2011) also raised this point: 'Imagine if today there were an untainted Tommy Sheridan and a united ... SSP going into the Scottish

elections on an anti-cuts platform. Given the political climate, Sheridan and some of his comrades would be returned to Holyrood in triumph this May. ... Instead, Tommy has split the anti-capitalist movement down the middle and effectively neutered it during the worst recession since the Thirties'. Ignoring this, Tommy's own slant was a personalised one: 'It is so frustrating on the political front to be incarcerated whilst the anger against the ConDem cuts agenda grows' and 'Being locked up in here and unable to play an active role in the resistance is frustrating' (Blog 5 March 2011 and 16 February 2011 respectively).

4. For the activists of the SSP and Solidarity, the acrimony has been such that it appears similar in nature, if not in scale, to the divisions between working and striking miners in the 1984–1985 miners' strike. An indication of this can be seen in the reaction to Alan McCombes' *DTTSS*. For example, a threat was made in late June 2011 to the Wordpower radical book shop in Edinburgh that unless my review of Alan McCombes' book was taken down from its website then there would be 'trouble'. This threat was from a critic – not a supporter – of Tommy.

5. The title comes from a song by Brian McNeill which was popularised by Dick Gaughan. Harvie's book has gone through five revised and updated editions since first being published in 1981.

6. SSP statement 23 December 2010.

7. *DTTSS* p. 314.

8. *Sunday Herald* 7 August 2011, *Herald* 11 August 2011.

9. By contrast the *Scottish Socialist Voice* (10 December 2004) claimed 'the vast majority of people who back the SSP are voting not for the messenger but the message'.

10. *SSP All-members Bulletin* 'Crisis in the party: the fight for the truth', August 2006, p. 2. At the first SSP NC after the split, Alan McCombes was more definitive in his view – the setback would be of the order of 10 or 20 years.

11. 25 January 2004.

12. 17 December 2000.

13. 6 October 1999.

14. *Daily Record* 24 December 1999.

15. *Scotsman* 1 June 2001.

16. Gall, G. 'The tragedy of Tommy Sheridan' *Guardian Comment is Free* 23 December 2010.

17. Hassan, G. and Lynch, P. *The Almanac of Scottish Politics* (2001, Politicos), p. 280.

18. Dominant public reaction judged by *BBC Radio Scotland* phone-in programmes also suggests this.

19. *Holyrood* 28 January 2011.

20. It is certainly the case that he counted the likes of Ally McCoist, Peter Mullen, Elaine C. Smith and Bernard Ponsonby, for example, amongst his friends.

21. This is even though the noting of Tommy's PIN numbers etc in Glenn Mulcaire's notebook is most likely to relate to 2004 (*Guardian* 24 December 2010).

22. *Scotland on Sunday* 10 July 2010. *Cf.* Monaghan, J. 'Why has Tommy Sheridan not been granted an appeal?' *Scottish Review* 11 August 2011.

23. *Independent* 31 January 2011. Many of these emails may have been deleted under instruction from News International to its server and email management provider (*Guardian* 2 August 2011).

24. See *Guardian* 2 November 2011 on the extent of the cover-up and denial at the senior echelons of News International over phone-hacking and unlawful accessing of information in 2008 concerning Professional Footballers' Association chief executive, Gordon Taylor. The deletion of some emails by a senior News International executive (*Guardian* 9 July 2011) may have been to attempt to erase evidence, for example, of paying

police officers for information. Such evidence may, for example, also concern the possibility of the phone-hacking of Fiona McGuire (see *Record* 17 August 2011).

25. BBC Scotland *Politics Show* 10 July 2011.
26. *Scotland on Sunday* 10 July 2011, *Sunday Mail* 10 July 2011.
27. *Press Association* 5 July 2011, *Scotsman* 5, 7, 9 July 2011.
28. *Scotsman* 7 July 2011.
29. *Scotsman* 5 July 2011.
30. *The Firm* 7 July 2011.
31. *Herald 14* July 2011. See James Doleman's *lefthooked* blog (14 July 2011) for a fuller report on the meeting.
32. 'Statement regarding developments with the NOTW' 7 July 2011.
33. *Cf.* 'The Defend Tommy Sheridan campaign condemns the News of the World over further phone hacking allegations and calls for Tommy Sheridan's conviction for perjury to be quashed' press release 5 July 2011 and others press releases on 8 July 2011, 18 July 2011 and 22 July 2011. See also Monaghan, J. 'Why has Tommy Sheridan not been granted an appeal?' *Scottish Review* 11 August 2011.
34. His *lefthooked* blog 6 July 2011, *Scotland on Sunday* 10 July 2011, *Socialist Worker* 16 July 2011.
35. Articles on SPS website (8 July 2011) and the SPEW website (6 July 2011) both by Philip Stott and *The Socialist* 13 July 2011 (see also 20 July 2011 edition claiming Tommy was 'wrongfully imprisoned'). Former Liverpool councillor and Militant/ SPEW member, Tony Mulhearn, called for the 'for the immediate release of Scottish socialist Tommy Sheridan' (*Liverpool Daily Echo* 16 July 2011).
36. 'Editorial' summer supplement, August 2011 to *Democratic Green Socialist*, No. 15, summer 2011.
37. *Herald* 16 August 2011. This was still be awaited. Furthermore, although the Metropolitan Police was then given access to the allegedly lost emails (*Independent* 29 September 2011), Tommy was not reported to be suing News International despite his statement on 23 December 2010.
38. Good examples of this phenomenon were Aamer Anwar using the occasion of Clive Goodman's revelation of the extent of knowledge of, and consent by, senior managers at *NoW* over phone-hacking to say that it revealed 'a serious contradiction of the evidence given by Andy Coulson' leading to arrests and imprisonment if lying took place (*The Firm* 16 August 2011, *Herald* 17 August 2011) and 'Private Lives, Public Morality' (*Scottish Review* 26 July 2011) where Kenneth Roy commented on 'the curious decision to prosecute, the suggestion that the Murdoch empire influenced that decision, the extent to which the jury was swayed by the prejudicial media coverage of the trial, the dubious character of the media empire hounding the accused, the quality of some of the evidence which is now being re-examined for possible perjury'. Indeed, Roy went further and on spurious grounds – because such sympathisers were not prepared to comprehend that one act of perjury (i.e., Coulson's) does not undo another act of perjury (i.e., Tommy's) - called for the release of Tommy by 26 October 2011 (see Roy, K. 'Tommy Sheridan should be released a week tomorrow' *Scottish Review* 18 October 2011). A rejoinder was made the following day to Roy by Norrie MacQueen (*Scottish Review* 19 October 2011). Interestingly, *The Firm* (19 October 2011) approvingly covered Roy's piece and set up a poll on the issue on its website which asked the question 'Should Tommy Sheridan be released next week when he becomes eligible for tagged parole?' Five days later, the result of the poll was 62% 'no' and 38% 'yes'. The number who voted is not known. It seemed that most journalists in their rush to condemn the malign influence of News International and Rupert Murdoch, whether for genuine reasons or those of stable

rivalry, forgot that Tommy had been convicted of lying in court for they did not subject the claims made by his supporters over possible perjury by *NoW* personnel and the like to anything approaching the level which they subjected various issues around the phone-hacking scandal to. For Rosie Kane's take on these issues, see 'Shut up Tommy! You're bad news' (her blog, The Wee Round Box, 7 July 2011).

39. *Scotsman* 8 July 2011.

40. *Sunday Herald* 24 July 2011.

41. 'The Defend Tommy Sheridan campaign calls on Strathclyde Police to investigate complaints against News of the World witnesses at Sheridan perjury trial' press release 7 July 2011. In a campaign press release of 18 July 2011, Lynn Sheridan stated unequivocally: 'Tommy's car was bugged and his phone was hacked ...'

42. *Cf.* George Galloway in *Morning Star* 9 July 2011.

43. *TST* 22 December 2010.

44. *Daily Record* 5 August 2006.

45. *Cf.* James Doleman in *Scotland on Sunday* 10 July 2011 and John Wight ('Solidarity with Tommy Sheridan' *Socialist Unity* 20 July 2011).

46. The attempt by Duncan Rowan, SSP organiser for north east Scotland, to divert *NoW* attention from Fiona McGuire by highlighting Katrine Trolle allowed the latter's name to come into the frame. More than any other single witness in 2010, her testimony was seen to hole Tommy below the waterline.

47. *Herald* 3 November 2010.

48. *Herald* 4 November 2010.

49. But even if he had not admitted this to the SSP EC (with this being recorded in the minute) or denied this, he still would not have been out of the woods for he had already admitted his visits to Cupids to others (see Chapter 6) and this would have reared its head at one time or another.

50. Colin Fox commented that Tommy told him: 'there is no place for modesty in politics. You can't suggest you are anything other than a superman, because otherwise your enemies will pick away at you. The other side of the coin is that [such] people are unable to apologise, to be humble, to retreat. And that's Tommy' (*Times* 24 December 2010).

51. 26 January 2011.

52. *Sunday Herald* 6 August 2006. The piece reported: 'Aberdein believes that Sheridan will be magnanimous to his accusers within the party and not seek revenge against them in the form of pushing for them to face perjury charges'.

53. *Herald* 7 August 2006.

54. *Scotsman* 8 August 2006, *Sunday Mail* 12 June 2011.

55. See Patterson, R. ('No more heroes' *Red Pepper*, October 2006): 'When you campaigned on the streets, or canvassed at elections, you said, 'The SSP, you know, Tommy Sheridan's party.' That was lazy and dangerous; and, boy, did we pay the price. ... Tommy wasn't really a single leader, in that he had no more say in party policy than anyone else. But he was seen to be, and ultimately that was our undoing'. Carolyn Leckie also believed that too many of the SSP's eggs were but in Tommy's basket: 'We were lazy in relying so much politically on Tommy'.

56. Ian Bell's review of *DTTSS* ('What's left?' *Scottish Review of Books,* Vol.17, No.3, 13 August 2011) made this point in a rather different way: '...You wouldn't touch that sort of creep with a barge-pole. So who was the working class hero promoted so assiduously, once upon a time, by the Scottish Socialist Party (SSP), with McCombes – his 'closest political associate' – in the van? The men knew each other for decades. So in all those years our author failed to notice that the comrade was even slightly dubious? See also Low, S. 'Review of *Downfall' The Citizen,*

Autumn 2011 (magazine of the Campaign for Socialism within the Scottish Labour Party) for a number of similarly made points. Mary McGregor's review of *DTTSS* in *Emancipation and Liberation* (RCN website, 23 October 2011) also raises some issues concerning the SSP leadership's culpability in developing the Tommy persona. And, Alex Miller makes an interesting observation of *DTTSS*'s analysis of the genesis of this persona: '... the comment made by Isaac Deutscher about Trotsky's biography of Stalin could also be applied to Downfall: 'Trotsky's Stalin is implausible to the extent to which he presents the character as being essentially the same in 1936-8 as in 1924, and even in 1904. The monster does not form, grow, and emerge – he is there almost fully fledged from the outset' (*Socialist Resistance* website, 25 July 2011).

57. In the *Socialist Socialist Voice*, Tommy's column/page included the same things as his *Record* and *Mirror* columns/pages, namely, personal items like personal reminisces, playing football, going on holiday and so on (and which included mentions of Gail). This suggested the SSP leadership was – at the very least – not unwilling to countenance such introversion, with Tommy's photo adorning the papers' top left front page corner between 2001 and 2003.

58. This relates to playing the media by providing it with a recognisable leadership figure and one that had 'money in the bank' from Tommy's previous track record of campaigning.

59. A full examination of the SSP will come with Gall, G. *The Scottish Socialist Party – the rise and fall of a new political force* (Welsh Academic Press, forthcoming).

60. 5 August 2006.

61. This is also true in the terms of the centrality of Gerry Healy (Socialist Labour League/WRP), Tony Cliff (International Socialists/SWP) and Tariq Ali (International Marxist Group).

62. Although it was not the only reason for the WRP's implosion in 1985–1986, Gerry Healy's sexual and associated behaviour contributed to it (see Pitt, B. *The Rise and Fall of Gerry Healy*, What Next? Publications (n.d.), Chapter 11).

63. *Cf.* Harman, C. 'The personality is political' *Socialist Worker* 2 September 2006. Here Harman ventured: 'Once such personalities begin to have a prominent role there is, of course, the danger that they will later use their prestige to mislead the movement ... But socialists cannot, out of fear of what might eventually happen, simply turn our back on their capacity to stimulate the growth of a movement'.

64. Thus, even with very little internal political support, Tommy as an individual could have still taken his defamation action (although to win it would required more internal support in terms of manufactured corroboration).

65. The wider lesson for the radical and socialist left, contrary to some conclusions drawn, is not that leaders are always corrupted and corruptible, whether by money or flattery. Nor is it that they inevitably get too big for their boots. Leaders – at all levels – are needed and demanded this side, at least, of a revolutionary transformation of society.

66. All positions within the SSP like its EC and spokespersons were elected at annual conference, and not in the gift of any one individual. Similarly, ballots were held to decide upon the order of candidates standing in list elections.

67. See his *Power: a radical view* (Macmillan, 1974).

68. This includes Alan McCombes.

69. Referring to providing the affidavit to the *Sunday Herald* in 2004, Alan McCombes stated in the perjury trial: 'By that stage I had concluded you were a pathological liar who was capable not just of telling a few lies to protect yourself but rewriting a history of events, a whole fantastical series of events'(*Herald* 2 November 2010).

70. *Mirror* 10 February 2005.

71. See Chapter seven and *Daily Record* 9 December 2008.

72. Indeed, even after conviction and sentencing, Tommy was still continually referred to as 'former SSP leader' by the media so the connection – and with it all the associations – had not been broken. This suggests that the SSP will forever be associated with Tommy in the public's and media's mind. Compare the argument that Tommy was not a problem for SSP anymore since he left (Curran, F. 'Party rises from the rubble' *Socialist Resistance*, December 2006, p. 10). Conversely, Tommy was seldom ever referred to by the media as leader (or co-convener) of Solidarity, emphasising – and helping maintain – the marginality of Solidarity as a political organisation.

73. See Gall, G. 'What future for a united left in Scotland?' *Frontline*, 2/13, 2010, and 'Will the activist stand up and be counted?' *Morning Star* 14 October 2011. After the implosion of Respect, this is true for England as well following the faction fight between Galloway and the SWP.

74. *Scottish Socialist Voice* 11 May 2007. A SSP EC/Anniesland branch motion to SSP conference on 20 October 2006) made a similar mistake.

75. *Sunday Mail* 12 June 2011. The full quote was that the SSP was reduced 'almost to smoking ruins'

76. It should also be noted that Pat Edlin, Militant press officer, understood the need to construct a favourable relationship with the media for Militant (see Crick M. *The March of Militant* (Faber and Faber, 1986), pp. 205–208).

77. *Observer* 26 December 2010.

78. *Herald* 27 January 2011. Contrary to some media comment at the time, a jail term of more than a year for a criminal offence did not bar Tommy from ever standing again for elected public office. The bar only applies to standing at a time of still serving sentence. However, bankruptcy may do depending on whether it is discharged or not. If George Galloway had been elected as a Glasgow list MSP in 2011, this would have queered the pitch for Galloway may have sought re-election in 2015 and there may not have been enough support to elect both him and Tommy. There remained uncertainty over whether the next Scottish Parliament elections would be held in 2015 or 2016. The latter date was supported by the SNP to avoid the election and the general election in Britain being held on the same day. It then became clear that 5 May 2016 would be the chosen date.

79. *Scottish Review* 20 October 2011.

80. 22 July 2011.

81. 26 January 2011. Tommy was shortlisted for the Scotscare poll for 'Scot of the year' in late 2010. When the result was announced in 2011, he obtained just 3% (*Daily Record* 25 January 2011). And, unlike Jimmy Reid and Mick McGahey, Tommy did not make it into the twenty-fifth anniversary poll of those in 'Who's Who in Scotland' on the twenty-five greatest Scots of the last twenty-five years (*Scottish Review* 29 June 2011). This was not because figures had to be deceased to be eligible. However, Tommy did make it into the collection of *Greatest Scottish Speeches* (Torrance, D. (ed.) Luath, 2011) with his speech in the Scottish Parliament proposing the abolition of warrant sales in 2000 (as did Jimmy Reid with his University of Glasgow rectorial address in 1971). In the fuller list of sixty speeches (see *Scotland on Sunday* website 24 October 2011), Tommy's speech on warrant sales and his victory speech in 2006 after his defamation victory against *NoW* were included. It should also be noted that, however, Mick McGahey had three entries while Jimmy Reid had two in this longer list. Meantime, Tommy's solicitor, Aamer Anwar, believed Tommy 'has a lot still to contribute [to the people of Scotland]' (*Scotland on Sunday* 26 June 2011).

82. So, *Take That*-like, there can be no return for 'Robbie' to the SSP in order to make a comeback.

83. Just after the defamation case in 2006, some of Tommy's staunchest opponents suggested a public apology could repair the situation. For them, that opportunity passed

with the splitting of the SSP and the character assassination strategy in the perjury trial of 2010.

84. A fair proportion of this coverage was directly related to his blog which he wrote out by hand and had uploaded by a friend outside prison.

85. In regard of the 2010 trial, this would also open up Tommy to the more serious charge of conspiracy to commit perjury in regard of his many witnesses.

86. In his mitigation plea, Tommy made some recognition of this by arguing the conviction was sentence enough. One example was Campbell Martin, former SNP and then independent MSP. In a reference to 'Tommygate' upon joining the SSP in August 2011, he commented on the SSP '... having survived an experience that would have killed-off lesser bodies ... [on] issues far removed from politics'. This was a particularly scathing criticism given that Campbell had been close politically to Tommy.

87. The other side of the coin is that the figure of Tommy Sheridan – as a Scottish socialist – was unlikely to have emerged without the existence of a deep strain of social democratic thought intermingled with a radical notion of Scottish national identity (see Gall, G. *The Political Economy of Scotland: Red Scotland? Radical Scotland?* University of Wales Press, 2005). There was discussion within Solidarity of winding itself up after the 2011 elections but following a request from Tommy this was deferred (see before).

88. The only organised part of Solidarity which appeared to openly and vociferously maintain its support of Tommy was the CWI-section, the Socialist Party of Scotland. Examples of this were Philip Stott's review of Alan McCombes's *DTTSS* (see 'Whose downfall?' *Socialism Today*, July/August 2011) and his pamphlet, *The Rise and Fall of the Scottish Socialist Party: a reply to Downfall – the Tommy Sheridan story* (SPS, 2011). By contrast, Gary Fraser ('The Trials of Oscar Wilde' *Democratic Green Socialist*, No. 15, 2011) cleverly but implicitly used the case of Wilde's libel action and criminal trials to raise questions about the ethics and deftness of Tommy's strategy of lying in his 2006 and 2010 trials. John Wight's review of *DTTSS* in the same issue of *Democratic Green Socialist* had previously been published on *Socialist Unity* (14 June 2011) and *Scottish Review* (21 June 2011) but was the act of an individual as was James Doleman's review in the *Scotsman* (18 June 2011). Former SSP national secretary (2006-2010), Pam Currie's review of *DTTSS* was entitled 'Setting the record straight' (*Scottish Socialist* Voice 8 July 2011). Meantime, previously loyal lieutenant, Hugh Kerr, joined the SNP in late 2011, the decision finding sympathy with Tommy (*Scotsman* 15 November 2011) (although he was reported to be a regular visitor to Tommy in jail, bringing him books to read).

89. This was also true of the 'Occupy' movement against neo-liberalism of late 2011.

90. For example, the *Sunday Express* (6 August 2006) opined: 'Scottish politics needs individuals like Tommy Sheridan ... with fire in their bellies and passion in their policies' while Tim Luckhurst proffered Tommy 'add[ed] desperately needed spice to Scottish politics' (*Mail on Sunday* 6 August 2006). But then many felt angered and let down. For example, Tommy opened the Park GP surgery in Baker Street in Shawlands, Glasgow in the early 2000s. A plaque was put on the surgery's outside wall to mark this. However, following his conviction for perjury, patients lobbied the GPs to remove the plaque, which they did.

91. These appellations continued despite the attempt by his supporters to rehabilitate him as a result of the *NoW* phone-hacking scandal (*cf.* James Doleman's comments in *Scotland on Sunday* 10 June 2011).

92. The manner in which the media covered Tommy previously was to often merely report what he said and did rather than to analyse and evaluate these. Consequently,

the media relinquished its ability to critically analyse and evaluate what he said and did. It was this sense of a benign and sympathetic disposition that Tommy undid.

93. *STV News* 26 January 2011. This contrasted sharply with his 'I will come back stronger line' in *The Rise and Lies of Tommy Sheridan* (BBC Scotland 23 December 2010).

94. There are strong parallels with the rise of Derek Hatton in terms of the specific hegemonies of the Labour Party, Militant and leftwing oppositional culture on Merseyside at the time of deindustrialisation, rising poverty and the political stimulus-cum-challenge of Thatcher and Thatcherism. Ratecapping was the poll tax in this regard. Hatton also defended himself, unlike Mulhearn, without the aid of lawyers when cross-examined by the Labour Party NEC (Crick, M. *The March of Militant* (Faber and Faber, 1986) p. 291).

95. Fukuyama, F. *The End of History and the Last Man* (Free Press, 1992).

96. Hatton appeared to repudiate his strategy of defying government spending cuts when he stated Liverpool's current Labour-led council would commit 'political suicide' if it set an illegal, needs budget (*Liverpool Echo* 14 May 2011). His subsequent home visit was only covered, and in a very minor way, by the *Sun* (22 September 2011). This suggested that the solicited media coverage of his first home visit had irked the prison authorities and that he was told to desist from doing so again lest his home visits were put in doubt. Again, this highlighted the limits to his willingness to be 'unflinching'.

97. See, for example, 30 January, 28 March and 11 April 2011. His first visit from open prison was covered by the *Daily Record, Express, Herald, Mail, Scotsman, Star* and *Sun* on 20 July 2011. Despite, Rupert and James Murdoch testifying before Parliament on the same day, the coverage of Tommy comprised almost full-page spreads at the front of the newspapers. The next day many papers in Scotland covered his participation in a football match and visiting his lawyer. His subsequent home visit did not receive any publicity after Tommy was told by the prison authorities that they did not appreciate the publicity he generated through associates for his first visit. Both the *Scotsman* and *Daily Record* (15 October 2011) reported the Defend Tommy Sheridan Campaign fund raising event that both Tommy and Gail attended.

98. *Scotland on Sunday* 17 April 2011. In the 2011 (Edinburgh) Festival Fringe *King of Scotland*, Jonathan Watson played the character called Tommy McMillan. This character could easily be read as a scathing indictment of a deluded Tommy Sheridan. Playwright Pamela Carter's 'Equality' was staged in 2011 and presented 'a fictionalised version of the moment when any hopes invested in the Scottish Socialist Party were destroyed by revelations about the leader's private life. In a teashop near the parliament, the Tommy Sheridan character and his chief adviser confront one another, staring into the abyss of political oblivion' (Joyce McMillan, Scotsman 16 September 2011).

99. There is unlikely ever to be an end to the controversy surrounding Tommy's activities just as there is still debate decades on about whether John Maclean was right or wrong not to have joined the newly founded Communist Party in 1920.

100. Comparing the seven like-for-like regions, Solidarity polled 22,522 votes in 2007 but only 2,837 in 2011. In Glasgow, the Solidarity vote was that which helped give George Galloway 6,972 votes in 2011. Not only was this just 80% of what Solidarity (with Tommy its lead candidate) won in 2007 but it was drawn from a wider constituency of voters, suggesting that if Tommy had stood in 2011 his vote may have been more on a par with that of the Solidarity vote of 2011.

101. *Daily Record* 7 August 2006.

Appendix 1

Methodology

The research materials and methods[1] for the biography comprised the fairly standard means of fieldwork interviews as well as using an array of primary and secondary sources[2] and personal observations. In regard of the latter, the writing of the biography has been immeasurably assisted by the willingness of the media to cover Tommy and Tommy's willingness to be covered by it, both in detailed and frequent ways. Since the late 1980s, tens of thousands of newspaper articles have been written on – or in some way covered – Tommy[3] and these were all accessed through a combination of maintaining a press cuttings file from 2003 and using the Lexis-Nexis database.[4] *A Time to Rage* was also extremely useful (even if, Tommy admitted, some of the details were 'jazzed up' a little for dramatic impact). Alan McCombes' *Downfall – the Tommy Sheridan story* was also useful in supplementing the final draft of the biography.[5] The interviews with Tommy consisted of taking him on a chronological journey through his past political activity and then examining a number of themes in his personal and political value system. The interviews with others consisted of a basic structured schedule which allowed tailoring to the individual interviewee depending on the capacity in which the interviewee knew of, or worked with, Tommy. This schedule was structured around an outline of the points at which the interviewee became aware of Tommy either publicly or personally and then an assessment of his personal and political strengths and weaknesses, culminating in an evaluation of his contribution to the left in Scotland. The two exceptions to this structure were those interviews with Tommy's mother, Alice, and his wife, Gail.[6] These involved more biographical investigations. The interviews, amounting to over 80 hours, were then transcribed before being analysed and employed in the writing of this biography. However behind this bare detail, lies a more complex situation that requires both elaboration and explanation.

The idea of writing a biography on Tommy was suggested to me by Ashley Drake of Welsh Academic Press after I had gained a contract with this publisher for *The Political Economy of Scotland: Red Scotland? Radical Scotland?* in May 2003.[7] I agreed in recognition of Tommy's standing and contribution as a socialist politician, whereby the significance of no longer being a 'one-man band' but the leader of a parliamentary group after the May 2003 election was balanced by recognition of his immense contribution and achievement as a lone MSP. Therefore, I approached Tommy and Alan McCombes, his then close political collaborator, meeting them together on 18 November 2003 at the old Scottish Parliament building to ask whether both would cooperate in being extensively interviewed for the project of writing a biography of Tommy. My reason for requesting such cooperation was that in order to be able to write an authentic biography as well as one which would be able to get beneath the surface or one-dimensional aspect of the public personae of Tommy, I wished to avail myself of access to information, explanation, reflection and recollection of the key insider figures (Tommy included). However as an independent academic, I also made it clear the biography would go ahead regardless of a decision not to cooperate because of my belief in the importance of there being a robust, rigorous and independent assessment of Tommy as a leading socialist and significant politician. After this meeting, at which Tommy indicated a little unease about being the living subject of a biography and one who was still relatively young, both their cooperation was secured, leading to the laying out of the detailed specification of the research project by letter of 1 March 2004 to Tommy and the beginning of the interviews with Tommy.[8] As laid out in Appendix 2, these interviews began shortly after. Despite being a member of the SSP (see below), I made it clear to both Tommy and Alan that I was not prepared to write a hagiography but rather an independent, critical and serious evaluation and analysis of a major socialist political figure. Consequently, their cooperation did not mean that the biography was in anyway an official or authorised biography. At the same time, they indicated no wish to exercise any editorial control over the biography (and I would have objected and not accepted if they had). The significance of being an SSP member was that access to Tommy and Alan as well as a host of other leading SSP members was almost inconceivable – certainly to the degree of access and frankness given – without being a SSP member who was held in some measure of trust and respect.

   The interviews with Tommy proceeded to cover his political activity on first a chronological and then a thematic basis. By the time of late October 2004, the chronological aspects had been covered up to that point in time. One further interview, on 3 December 2004, was conducted after Tommy resigned as SSP national convener. This unfortunately did not entirely finish off the thematic concerns. He agreed at this interview to do some more in the new year. Before and after these interviews, I observed Tommy in meetings with others, chatted to him casually and on one occasion spent a day with him while he visited two secondary schools (Govan High and Crookston Castle) in Glasgow following invitations to speak to the students about politics. Had Tommy not resigned, had not the ensuing crisis so gravely destabilised the SSP and had not a defamation action been raised, the biography would have been published in late 2005 after others had been interviewed. However, the ensuing faction fight and civil war within the SSP and Tommy's intended defamation action and the possible detrimental impact of these on Tommy's prospect of re-election to the Scottish Parliament in May 2007 meant that it would have been unwise to publish a biography which could not take account of, and analyse, these momentous events. This need to wait also allowed the splitting of the SSP with the formation of Solidarity to be taken into account.

Given that momentous events were unfolding and that it was unclear what their outcomes and ramifications would be, no interviews were conducted with either Tommy or any other potential interviewees during the period from the end of December 2004 to September 2006. Moreover, in order to be able to appraise such developments in a clear headed, dispassionate manner, it was felt to be unwise to engage potential interviewees in this period because their then current concerns would likely weigh too heavily on their minds, thus, possibly distorting their assessments, and that much of the surface detail and minutiae of the various factional twists and turns would obscure the underlying dynamics and in time be of less consequence. After the 2006 court case, I approached Tommy on 3 September 2006 at the Solidarity national launch rally in Glasgow to ask for a meeting to discuss his further and continued cooperation for being interviewed for the biography. This meeting took place on 28 September. At the meeting, I asked him for his continued cooperation in order to be able to gain from him *his* account of events since November 2004, concentrating particularly on his motivation, rationale and strategy in the internal SSP battle, the court case and the launching of Solidarity. In essence, I wished to give Tommy the opportunity to present his case in his way in a situation which had become highly charged and contentious. He agreed at this meeting to continue to cooperate, given two factors. The first was because as he said 'trust was important to me [him] given what has happened ... and that so far you [I] have not stabbed me [him] in the back ... and ... I [he] could trust you [me]'. The second was that the biography's publication date would not interfere with the intended publication of an autobiography by his wife, Gail (which subsequently did not materialise). He concluded by saying, he 'was prepared for some hard questions'. The interviews were to resume after his return from the Lebanon in late October 2006.

At the founding conference of Solidarity in Glasgow on 4 November 2006, I approached Tommy to agree on dates for interviews. In this very brief discussion of a couple of minutes, Tommy indicated that he was no longer prepared to cooperate because of the McNeilage video tape and the publication of its content on 1 October 2006. He stated 'there's broad and there's broad', meaning that some parts of the left (i.e., the SSP) were, to him, no longer part of the left and gave his specific reason that he could not cooperate with a member of an organisation, namely, the SSP, which had not disciplined George McNeilage for making the tape and selling it to the *NoW*. I responded by stating that I believed I bore no personal responsibility for the tape and that I did not condone its selling.[9] In another brief discussion at this Solidarity conference of just a few minutes (and subsequent to speaking to Tommy), this time with Hugh Kerr, close collaborator with Tommy and Solidarity's parliamentary press officer, I asked Hugh if I could interview him for the biography, to which he replied 'I'd have to ask Tommy Sheridan for permission' and that the reason Tommy was no longer prepared to continue cooperation was because I had already interviewed George McNeilage. This was untrue (see Appendix 2) and so possibly casts some light on what might have been the actual underlying reason for the decision to not continue cooperation.

Given that Tommy's continued cooperation on the more recent issues at hand would be an important component of the overall biography, I asked for a meeting in order to gain a fuller understanding of his reason(s) for refusing to continue cooperation. This meeting took place on 30 November 2006 in the Scottish Parliament canteen. He expressed his anger and dismay at the betrayal displayed by the making and selling of the videotape as well as its sale to the *NoW* in particular, again stating his criticism of the 'failure' of the SSP to discipline George McNeilage and my part in this alleged 'failure'. Specifically, he cited my alleged 'failure', alongside that of the new SSP national convener, Colin Fox, to raise a motion within the SSP to discipline George McNeilage. This seemed a strange condition of cooperation given that Tommy was no longer a member of the SSP and that no motion to discipline him over his behaviour (for example, over his open letter of 28 May 2006, undermining the new SSP National Convener, his character assassination of court witnesses, his characterisation of SSP as 'political scabs' and the like) had ever been raised. However at this meeting, Tommy stated that he still believed that I was a fair, honest and balanced person so that the decision not to continue cooperation was not a personal matter with regard to myself. I asked him hypothetically if there was anything which I could do which would change his mind on the issue of cooperation. The response was in the negative. His refusal to continue cooperation could be viewed in at least two ways, namely, personal and political hurt at the general situation he found himself in (and which was not specifically related to myself) and/or an unwillingness to be subject to exacting and demanding questions over his activity and behaviour. The latter is maybe more probable in that a central line of investigation of my questioning would have concerned his rationale for taking the case against the *NoW* and the lengths he was prepared to go to politically to support this action as well as how these matters of more recent sexual behaviour related to previous sexual behaviour. Indeed, the McNeilage tape may have been a convenient foil for this. But whatever the reason, Tommy's refusal to continue cooperation meant that he did not take the opportunity to explain his court case strategy or to disavow the possibility of continuity in his sexual behaviour.

Another downside of Tommy's decision to desist from continuing cooperation was that I was then not able to interview him about salient material and issues that were unearthed, or which new or additional light was shed upon, as a result of the interviewing of others and subsequent events after late 2004. The added twist to this was that the personal and political split of late 2004 onwards, and especially after the spring of 2006, opened up a frankness and candidness amongst interviewees that was probably not available when there was a high degree of personal and political unity around a common project and figurehead (although the disintegration of the ISM, the former majority breakaway from the CWI in Scotland would have helped in any case). But what this also meant was that full triangulation (as opposed to forensic corroboration and substantiation) and response with regard to some aspects of some issues by putting them to Tommy Sheridan could not always be achieved. Nonetheless, three points should be noted here. First, it would be unwise for a social scientist to take the subject's word, final or otherwise, as definite confirmation or denial on any issue. Second, triangulation need not solely rely upon the subject's ultimate pronouncement. Third, the conviction for perjury – that is, knowingly lying in court – will also query the sense in which Tommy could be said to have provided completely full and honest answers to questions (see also below). There are several other aspects of the methodology that are pertinent here. Given the tumultuous events of late 2004 onwards, it was important that I was aware that other interviewees may have a tendency to recast their views about Tommy in a way which was more or less favourable given which side of the political fence they fell on during the faction fight, court case, and split.[10] Finally, it appears to me that Tommy situated his extant cooperation for the biography in being interviewed as part of a strategy of projecting a certain image of himself and of limiting his degree of self-reflection and self-appraisal. In essence, I often got the impression when interviewing him that he was trying to 'play' me (see also interview in *Sunday Herald* for another instance of this[11]). Consequently, these aspects were taken in appraising his interview data.

Despite the ending of interviews with Tommy in late 2004 and his subsequent withdrawal of cooperation for interviewing, this biography is fortunate in that so much of what Tommy did and said was voluminously covered by the media in the subsequent period. Indeed, gaining such coverage was necessarily part and parcel of Tommy's legal and political strategy. As outlined earlier, this was as a result of his solicitation and that of the media's. The extent of this public coverage through either means was magnified by the events of the 28 May 2006 SSP NC, the defamation case and the perjury trial. Consequently, it is believed that the effect of no further interviews with Tommy has been heavily ameliorated and mitigated (notwithstanding what those may have delivered in terms of useful and veracious content).

During the course of the interviews and meetings with Tommy, he suggested in October 2004 that I interview Keith Baldassara, Felicity Garvie and George McNeilage because he had a close working relationship with them. In September 2006, he suggested I interview Philip Stott and Ronnie Stevenson of the CWI and agreed that Steve Arnott (former SSP and then Solidarity Highlands Organiser) would be another person to approach. For details on these interviews and other interviews, see Appendix 2 below. Given the relative albeit temporary closure represented by the events of early September 2006, from early October of that year, I made contact with a host of other potential interviewees, informing them of the purpose and outline of the proposed interviews, and the (changing) attitude of Tommy to his continued cooperation. From some of these interviewees, further suggestions were made of other people that might be worth interviewing. Furthermore, and with Tommy's decision to desist from cooperating, I widened the scope of potential interviewees in order to demonstrate an actual and obvious case of interviewing different shades of opinion on him. Specifically, this meant interviewing those leading figures that had left the SSP to form Solidarity and become leading figures within it. Whilst this was achieved in many cases (see Appendix 2), Rosemary Byrne MSP, co-convener of Solidarity, declined the invitation to be interviewed because she was 'not interested' (email, 5 December 2006), Hugh Kerr failed to respond to several emails and then when I had the chance to ask him face-to-face as to why he had not responded he replied: 'There was no point. If Tommy's not speaking to you, I'm not speaking to you' (12 January 2007). Meanwhile, Iain Ferguson of the SWP declined and Mike Gonzalez of the SWP ignored my emails. Whilst Iain Ferguson and Mike Gonzalez were chosen as longstanding and leading SWP members in Glasgow who have had close political dealings with Tommy, two longstanding and leading SWP members in the east of Scotland, Neil Davidson and Pat Smith, did agree to be interviewed. Pat Smith, was a member of the SSP EC in 2004 and testified in court in favour of Tommy and left the SSP to join Solidarity. Neil Davidson was interviewed while after initially agreeing to be interviewed on 11 December 2006, and confirming this on 21 December, Pat Smith then declined on 27 December 2006 because neither 'Tommy nor Rosemary were cooperating'. Unfortunately, a period of prolonged illness leading to his death in September 2007 meant that I was unable to interview Chic Stevenson, a longstanding and leading member of Militant who served as a Glasgow councillor for Labour and then SML for ten years, and who was thus a fellow councillor with Tommy. Another obvious gap was Bob Wylie who was a mentor of and role model for Tommy up until the mid- to late 1980s. In an email of 8 January 2007, he responded to the request for an interview by saying: 'Sorry for not getting back to you sooner on this but I have had to take soundings at my new job with Strathclyde Partnership for Transport. Unfortunately, they are not keen that I should give comment on your project with Tommy Sheridan as it may get a lot of media coverage and that would conflict with my current responsibilities'. Unfortunately, he did not then not respond to my suggestion of being interviewed and the material being used on the anonymous basis of an unnamed senior and close working colleague of Tommy's. Since leaving that job in mid-2010, time constraints on my part have not allowed further attempts to secure an interview with Bob Wylie.

In addition to the data derived from the interviews, a wealth of secondary sources and materials were deployed. These include Tommy's own writings and broadcasting in the leftwing and mainstream press and media as well as press and media interviews of him. On top of these has been the reporting of and about Tommy in these presses and media, namely his words and deeds, particularly amongst the Scottish and Glasgow press (for example, *Daily Record*, (Glasgow) *Herald*, *Evening Times*, *Scottish Mirror*, *Scotsman*) and amongst the leftwing press including *Scottish Militant Labour* and *Scottish Socialist Voice*. Further sources of materials consulted consisted of the speeches of Tommy, documentation from the political groupings and tendencies that Tommy has been a member of and leading light in. Finally, Joan McAlpine's *A Time to Rage*, which documented Tommy's rise to prominence and was conducted with his active involvement, has been a useful source of information, again as has Alan McCombes's *Downfall – the Tommy Sheridan story*.[12] Putting together the voluminous interviews, the personal observation and the various secondary sources means that this biography comes as close as it possible in terms of source material to being a definitive and authoritative biography as possible.

Lastly, and as already alluded to in terms of the methodology, there is my own involvement in the SSP and leftwing politics in Scotland, and the study of these,[13] to consider. This has two salient aspects, namely, participant and proximate observation and a sympathetic but objective and critical perspective on the subject of the biography. My approach has been to write this biography as an academic who is a socialist and member of the SSP, and not as a socialist and SSP member who happens to also be an academic. Essentially, I have sought to fuse the tools of rigorous academic inquiry with knowledge of socialist politics derived from involvement and observation so that not only does one complement the other but the whole is greater than the sum of its parts. In other words, being proximate to the events is a virtue and not a flaw because while I have not been detached I have been objective as a result of using the principles of social science to gather and then analyse evidence. In the faction fight and ensuing battles, I was an observer not a participant.

My own history of political activity dates from membership of the Labour Party (where I was not a member of any internal grouping) from 1985–1988, membership of the SWP from 1990–2004 and membership of the SSP from 2000 onwards. Although never a member of Militant or any of those groupings which it spawned, in the salient period of time, and in the broadest sense, I have been a fellow traveller of the wider far or hard left political tradition represented by Tommy. I lapsed my membership of Labour as a result of the choice of its leadership not to organise a non-payment campaign against the poll tax. I lapsed my membership of the SWP because of my belief that it is an ultra-left and, often sectarian, organisation.[14] My criticisms of, and disagreements with, the SWP existed for over a decade before finally leaving and led to my joining of the SSP in 2000 (and in advance of the SWP in Scotland joining en masse in May 2001) and to myself adopting a specific position on the relationship between the projects of socialism and independence.[15] I have also made clear that I believe the Militant project in Scotland, in comparison to that of the SWP, has been a far more productive one overall.[16] Within the SSP, I was a branch activist from 2000 to 2008, as well as branch delegate to national conference and NC in most of those years. And, from 2006 to 2008, I was chair of the SSP Lothian region and for a year between 2007 and 2008, a member of the SSP EC. Other than the EC, which met every month, the NC, which met bimonthly, is the key internal body within the SSP and the scene of some of the key events in recent SSP history. With the creation of Solidarity in late 2006, I attended its national launch rally in Glasgow (3 September 2006), the regional launch rally in Edinburgh on 26 September 2006, and its founding conference (4 November 2006) as well as its first annual conference in February 2007. (Additionally, I have monitored and reviewed the content of Solidarity's website, publications and documents.) This aspect is thus concerned with my activity here as being in effect – that is, for the purposes of this biography – participant observation. It would have been impossible to be a non-participant observer in what were closed meetings to non-SSP members. In the course of these meetings and afterwards, I made contemporaneous notes.

The relevance of this introspection is also that I have been a keen observer of Tommy and his activities since the late 1980s, whether through public meetings and campaigns or internal SSP meetings, forums and discussions. Although I knew of Tommy in the manner of a distant acquaintance since 2003, my (only) close personal involvement with him has been through interviewing him for this biography. Thus, I have been able to call upon a wealth of knowledge and understanding gained through such political activity that a writer and researcher from outwith such a political tradition would not have been able to call upon and benefit from. Anyone could be a Tommy 'watcher' given his high public profile and coverage but such a watcher would be unable to also avail themselves of 'behind-the-scenes' knowledge and deeper understanding. Put bluntly, without such a background and involvement, an outsider would be unable to either know about or understand the salient intentions, dynamics, processes and outcomes. More specifically, this involvement has given me access to interviewees, debates and documentation as well as a credibility and seriousness by which to gain the cooperation of individuals for the purpose of conducting interviews and collecting data.

In all of this, I have been partisan – that is, 'for' and 'of' the radical left – but also a dispassionate and hard-headed close observer and participant, with no personal axes to grind. Through my fortnightly column in the *Morning Star* since 2005 and my membership of the editorial boards of the *Scottish Left Review*, *Frontline* and *Solidarity* as well as writing for them, I have shown, by common acclaim,[17] the trait of being of politically committed while having a non-sectarian and balanced, open and fair perspective and analysis (even where this has incurred wrath for allegedly being a critic of, and dissident in, the SSP from some within the SSP).[18] Being an academic means that I have also been able to bring to bear both a critical faculty and a critical inquiry to the subject matter that are independent minded, rigorous and robust. This means while the biography is sympathetic, it is by no means unconditionally uncritical either as will have become clear. By the same token, the biography is not the property of any party, tendency or internal grouping. During the declared and undeclared faction fight within the SSP since late 2004, I was quite consciously neither a supporter nor member of the United Left (a broadly anti-Sheridan grouping) nor the SSP Majority (a broadly pro-Sheridan grouping), nor Tommy's personal support base, termed the 'Sheridanistas', or his subsequent political allies, the SWP or the CWI.

To some readers, such as non-academics, those unconcerned with the intimate detail of the SSP or those outside Scotland, this section on methods may seem slightly irrelevant and far too introspective. However, to academics, those concerned with the intimate detail of the SSP and those within Scotland, any biography of Tommy is likely to be something of a political 'hot potato' because he has been such a controversial figure. And, this state of affairs is only likely to continue. Consequently, an open and elaborate setting out of the nature of the research methods and approach, and its attendant issues, has been deemed highly necessary. It would have been naïve and remiss not to have done so, for it would have raised questions as to why I was not open or honest about the nature of the methods and methodology employed, and that would have done the biography no favours.

Notes

1. For the resources of the time to research and write, I am grateful to my previous and present universities (Stirling and Hertfordshire respectively).
2. Primary sources refer to writings by Tommy and documents of the SSP and Solidarity. Secondary sources refer to newspapers, magazine and web material. On salient matters of Scots law, I am grateful for being able to cross-check my understanding of the issues by virtue of calling upon the resources of Paul McConville's *Random Thoughts Re Scots (and Other) Law blog* and that called *Lallands Peat Worrier*. I am particularly indebted to Paul for entering into personal correspondence with me in late 2011 in order to explain the likely scenarios regarding the appeal of News International against the 2006 court award damages. The most likely of these would be that a new trial by jury would be required to be held but the issues would be complicated by the tarnished reputations of both Tommy and News International. The factor of costs to pursue the action would also weigh heavily. .
3. For example, it took five full days to read all the 2006 coverage of which Tommy was mentioned in and a further two days to make notes on this. Mentions of Tommy to 5 April 2011 in the *Herald* – the main Scottish and Glasgow broadsheet – were 4,671 and in the *Daily Record* – the main Scottish and Glasgow tabloid – were 2,501. Moreover, it took two full days to read all the postings (but not comments) on the *TST* blog.
4. A key principle employed in using press reports was not only to specify the publication and the date of publication but to quote verbatim from the journalists or those interviewed by the journalists so that ambiguity or dissonance were avoided.

5. For the avoidance of any doubt, Surhone, L., Tennoe, M. and Henssonow, S. (eds.) *Tommy Sheridan – socialist, politician, solidarity* (Betascript Publishing, 2010) is the publication in a book form of Wikipedia articles on Tommy and associated subjects like Militant.

6. I am grateful to Tommy for arranging to make both Gail and Alice available for interview (see Appendix 2).

7. The book was subsequently published by the University of Wales Press.

8. In all interviews, the ethics of social science research were adhered to (particularly concerning that of gaining informed consent from interviewees). Essentially, and where no minors or vulnerable adults are involved, this comprises explaining the research purpose, the nature of the interview and how material derived from it may be used according to the research purpose whereupon agreement is obtained from the potential interviewee to be interviewed. In a seemingly bizarre turn-of-events, on 29 March 2011 Tommy's solicitor, Aamer Anwar, wrote to my university alleging that Tommy had not been asked to give, nor had given, informed consent to be interviewed for the biography. This formed part of a dishonest and disingenuous action to smear the biography as defamatory and politically motivated as well as to try to stop its publication (see also *Scotland on Sunday* 20 March 2011). A subsequent investigation by my university dismissed all the allegations of research misconduct made by Aamer as being without merit, substance or foundation because the research was conducted in line with university and national and international guidelines for social science research to ensure integrity, quality and transparency of process and outcome (Letter to author from Vice Chancellor, University of Hertfordshire, 10 August 2011 see also *Herald* 16 August 2011).

9. Therefore, this seems a strange turn of events given that Tommy had in September 2004 asked me to be the editor of a collection of his newspaper columns in the manner of Paul Foot's *Words as Weapons*. This project came to nothing, despite myself working on it until spring 2006, as Tommy chose to concentrate on his faction fight. Similarly, in early 2005, I helped Tommy put down on paper his own somewhat controversial thoughts about knife crime for the collection *Whose Justice? The Law and the Left* (Scottish Left Review Press, 2005) for which I was the lead editor.

10. Although not an interviewee, former SSP national secretary (2006-2010), Pam Currie, in reviewing *DTTSS* showed this tendency by arguing: 'Tommy was never the central figure ... [because Alan McCombes was] the brains of the operation' (*Scottish Socialist Voice* 8 July 2011).

11. 29 January 2006.

12. Other prospective books like those forthcoming from James Doleman and Jim Monghan were not published (sic) by the time this biography was published and so were not available to be used.

13. See, for example, various refereed articles in *Scottish Labour History* (1998, 2001, 2003, 2006, 2010) and my *The Political Economy of Scotland: Red Scotland? Radical Scotland?* (University of Wales Press, Cardiff, 2005), for which Tommy kindly wrote a foreword, albeit it a critical one.

14. See *What Next?* (30, 2005) and *Socialist Unity* interview (June 2005).

15. *Socialism, 'the national question' and the Independence Convention in Scotland* (Flying Pickets' Press, 2003).

16. *Socialist Unity* interview (June 2005). That I was not a member of Militant/SML means that I have been freer and more able to engage in a wide-ranging critique of a leading member from that tradition. The pitfalls of not being so are highlighted in longstanding SWP member, Ian Birchall's, biography of SWP founder and leader, Tony Cliff (*Tony Cliff – a Marxist for His Time*, Bookmarks, 2011), for although Birchall is critical of Cliff, the overall sense given in the biography is that even where

Cliff did 'wrong' or was 'bad', he was still nonetheless 'right' and did 'good' because of the purpose he strove to achieve. This results from an over close political and psychological commitment to Cliff and the Trotskyist tradition he established.

17. A further indication of this is that various members of Solidarity were willing to be interviewed for the biography and that I have maintained an on-going and regular dialogue with a number of Solidarity members since 2006.

18. For example, my analysis of the state of the SSP stimulated official and lengthy responses from the SSP (see *What Next?* 31 2007 and *Frontline* 2/4, 2007).

Appendix 2

List of Interviewees

The following list gives details of the interviewees and the dates and lengths of interviews. All interviews were tape recorded and transcribed by myself in order to maintain confidentiality, with the interviewees given an assurance of the confidentiality of the information they gave (prior to publication), whereby this would not be discussed with other interviewees or non-interviewees. All interviewees were also given, prior to publication, sight of the quotes from them that were used in the biography (but without any negotiation entered into on this).The purpose of documenting the details of the interviewees is several-fold. First, to establish that they have had either or both intimate, close or important working relationships with Tommy for a considerable length of time or at certain key points in time. A major point here has been to use these sources to examine Tommy as a political figure and operator in the behind-the-scenes activities that are not covered by media or under the public spotlight. Second, and particularly with regard to the acrimony and fratricide since 9 November 2004, to show that an array of views and opinions have been canvassed and used in researching and writing this biography. Third, to indicate that a considerable number of the interviewees are from Tommy's political past – here the point is that Tommy should not solely be viewed through the lens of the events of 2004 to 2010 or judged on the basis of these years. I would like to take this opportunity to record my thanks to Tommy and all the other interviewees for making their own personal or work time available in order to be interviewed. All details of affiliations and post are correct as at the time of interview. (* denotes a witness for either one or other or both the court cases of 2006 and 2010; ^ denotes mentioned in *A Time to Rage*). The interviews varied considerably in length. At their most basic, they consisted of questions concerning Tommy's contribution to the left and an assessment of his personal and political strengths and weaknesses. Depending of the nature and length of the working relationship with Tommy, the length of each interview varied considerably (see below). This meant each interview comprised a standard structured set of questions, whereupon it then became tailored to the individual interviewee. Where some interviewees were not quoted from or at length, or where no material is attributed to them, the material from their interviews was still, nonetheless, extremely helpful in building up an overall picture of Tommy from which subsequent analysis and assessment could be constructed.

^*Davie Archibald:* Former Militant full-time organiser (Chair Young Socialists in Scotland and Militant Youth Organiser) 1985–1994, active branch member of SML, SSA and SSP thereafter, 21 December 2006 (2.5 hours).

**Steven Arnott:* Militant and SML member 1983–2001, Highlands and Islands SSP organiser 2000–2006, Solidarity full-time worker and member of Solidarity national steering group 2006–, 6 April 2007 (2.5 hours).

^***Councillor Keith Baldassara:* Militant and SML organiser, SSP councillor for Pollok, Glasgow, 2003–2007; Tommy Sheridan's Parliamentary case worker 1999–2006; National Executive member of SML, SSA and SSP, 24 October 2006 (4.5 hours).

**Frances Curran MSP:* former Labour Party National Executive Committee member, former Militant and SML full-time organiser, SSP MSP (2003–2007), 13 December 2006 (2 hours).

Neil Davidson: Scottish Committee of the Socialist Workers' Party/ *Socialist Worker* Platform in SSP and Solidarity, and author and writer on Scottish history and affairs, 14 November 2006 (1.5 hours).

^***Colin Fox MSP:* SSP National Convener 2005–, SML/SSA/SSP East of Scotland Organiser, 1995–2003, SSP EC member 1998–, SSP MSP (2003–2007), 10, 20, November, 1 December 2006 (7.5 hours).

**Felicity Garvie:* parliamentary office manager for Tommy Sheridan, 1999–2006, minute secretary for SSP EC and then full member thereafter, 27 November 2006 (3 hours).

**Catriona Grant:* SML/SSA/SSP member, co-chair of SSP 2003–2004, EC member 2000–2005, 17 January, 20 March 2007 (3 hours).

**Allan Green:* SSA and SSP National Secretary 1996–2006, 19 October 2006 (3 hours).

**Rosie Kane MSP:* SSP MSP (2003–2007), SSA/SSP EC member (various years including 2004–2005), environmental activist, 25 May 2007 (3 hours).

**Carolyn Leckie MSP:* SSP MSP (2003–2007), former NALGO and Unison (lay) office holder, SSP EC member, 2002–2007, 30 November 2006 (3 hours).

Joan McAlpine: formerly deputy editor *Herald*, assistant editor (features) *Sunday Times* (Scotland) and author of *A Time to Rage*, 30 January 2007 (2 hours).

^**Alan McCombes:* SSP Policy Director and previously editor of *Scottish Socialist Voice* and *Scottish Militant Labour*, and Militant full-timer, 31 October 2006 (4.5 hours).

**Graeme McIver:* SSP south of Scotland organiser, SSP EC member, and then Solidarity National Secretary and member of Solidarity national steering group 2006–, 14 December 2006 (1.5 hours).

^**George McNeilage:* longstanding community and leftwing (e.g. SML) political activist in Pollok, Glasgow, 13 December 2006 (3 hours).

^**Jim McVicar:* longstanding Militant, SML and SSP member, Glasgow councillor 1984–1996, 29 January 2007 (2 hours).

**Gordon Morgan:* former secretary, Glasgow Pollok Constituency Labour Party, senior activist and executive member in the Socialist Movement in Scotland, SSP deputy treasurer, and Solidarity National Treasurer and Solidarity national steering group member 2006–, 12 January (1.5 hours).

**Jock Penman:* former Militant member and SSP Mid Scotland and Fife Organiser, now Solidarity full-time worker and member of Solidarity national steering group 2006–, 11 January 2007 (2 hours).

^*Alice Sheridan:* mother of Tommy Sheridan and political activist in her own right, 3 August 2004 (2.5 hours).

^**Gail Sheridan (with Tommy Sheridan):* partner and wife, 8 July 2004 (3 hours).

Tommy Sheridan MSP: SSP MSP (1999–2006), Solidarity MSP (2006–2007), Glasgow City councillor (1992–2003), 8 July (with Gail Sheridan), 3, 10, August, 17 September, 13, 29 October, 3 December 2004 (14.5 hours).

^*Ronnie Stevenson:* Former Militant full–timer in Glasgow 1984–1994, Unison social work convener and CWI member 1974–, 10 January 2007 (2 hours).

**Philip Stott:* SML executive, SSA/SSP regional organizer, Scottish Secretary of the International Socialists, the Scottish section of the CWI, 8 December (2 hours).

^*Peter Taaffe:* General Secretary, Militant Labour/Socialist Party (of England and Wales) 1992–, sister organisation of CWI Scotland (Internationalist Socialists) and SPS and main driver of CWI, previously, editor *Militant* newspaper, 1964–1992, 2 February 2007 (2 hours).

^**Richie Venton:* SSP Glasgow organiser and SSP national trade union organiser, previously Militant, SML and SSA fulltime organiser, SML/SSA/SSP EC member, 1 November 2006 (3 hours).

Index